A No 1or

OWEN MATTHEWS read modern history at Oxford before becoming a journalist. He covered conflicts in Bosnia, Lebanon, Chechnya, Afghanistan and Iraq, and was Moscow Bureau Chief for *Newsweek* magazine.

His first book, *Stalin's Children*, was published to critical acclaim in 2008, shortlisted for the Guardian First Book Award and the Orwell Prize for political writing, and selected as one of the Books of the Year by the *Sunday Times*, *Sunday Telegraph* and the *Spectator*. It has been translated into twenty-eight languages and the French version was shortlisted for the Prix Medicis 2009.

Owen Matthews lives in Istanbul and Moscow.

GLORIOUS MISADVENTURES

Nikolai Rezanov and the Dream of a Russian America

Owen Matthews

BLOOMSBURY

LONDON · NEW DELHI · NEW YORK · SYDNEY

First published in Great Britain 2013
This paperback edition published in 2014

Copyright © 2013 by Owen Matthews
Maps by John Gilkes

The moral right of the author has been asserted

No part of this book may be used or reproduced in any manner
whatsoever without written permission from the Publisher except in the
case of brief quotations embodied in critical articles or reviews

Images are from the author's personal collection except where credited otherwise

Every reasonable effort has been made to trace copyright holders of
material reproduced in this book, but if any have been inadvertently
overlooked the publishers would be glad to hear from them

Bloomsbury Publishing Plc
50 Bedford Square
London
WC1B 3DP

www.bloomsbury.com

Bloomsbury is a trademark of Bloomsbury Publishing Plc

Bloomsbury Publishing, London, New Delhi, New York and Sydney

A CIP catalogue record for this book is available from the British Library

ISBN 978 1 4088 3399 5

10 9 8 7 6 5 4 3 2 1

Typeset by Hewer Text UK Ltd, Edinburgh
Printed and bound in Great Britain by CPI Group (UK) Ltd, Croydon CR0 4YY

To Xenia, Nikita and Teddy

Like all of us sinners, General B. was endowed with many virtues and many defects. Both the one and the other were scattered through him in a sort of picturesque disorder. Self-sacrifice, magnanimity in decisive moments, courage, intelligence—and with all that, a generous mixture of self-love, ambition, vanity, petty personal ticklishness, and a good many of those things which a man simply cannot do without.

—Nikolai Gogol, 'Dead Souls'

Contents

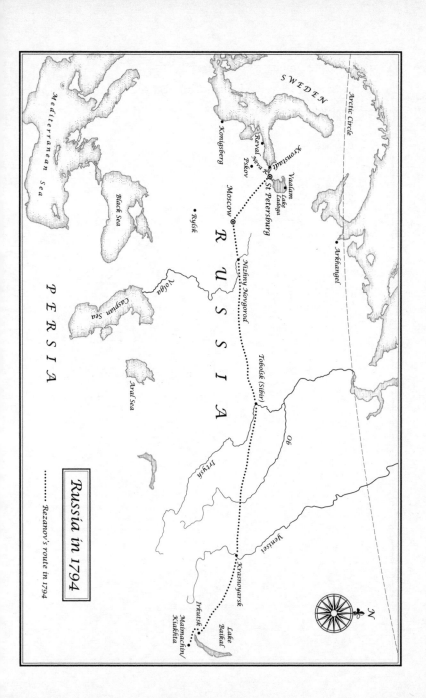

Russia in 1794

.... Rezanov's route in 1794

N

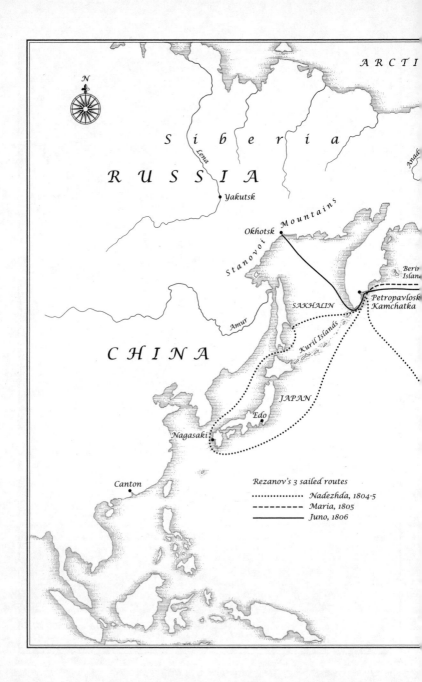

N

ARCTI

S i b e r i a

RUSSIA

Lena

Anad

•Yakutsk

Stanovoi Mountains

Okhotsk•

Berin
Islan

Petropavlosk
Kamchatka

SAKHALIN

Amur

CHINA

Kuril Islands

JAPAN

•Edo

Nagasaki

Canton

Rezanov's 3 sailed routes

.... Nadezhda, 1804-5
- - - - - - - Maria, 1805
——————— Juno, 1806

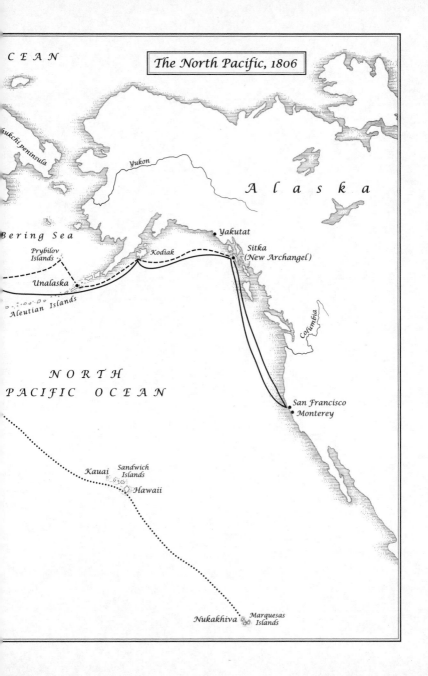

The North Pacific, 1806

Prologue

O, Russian Columbuses, scorning a grim Fate;
Between the mounts of Ida will open a new path to the East;
And we will plant our State on America's shores . . .

                    Mikhail Lomonosov, *Russian Columbuses*, 1747[1]

This Mister Rezanov was a dynamic fellow, hot tempered, a dedicated scribbler, a talker, with a head more inclined to making castles in the air in his study than to making great deeds come true in the world.

                    Captain Vasily Golovnin[2]

On a warm spring evening in May 1806, a betrothal was celebrated in the tiny fort of San Francisco, the northernmost outpost of Spain's American empire. The single-storey adobe governor's house, with its sweeping views over the bay, was decorated with wildflowers.[3] Fresh straw had been strewn on the floor and honey cakes and sweet yellow wine set out for the guests. Tacked to the wall of the small reception room was a pair of flags. One was the newly designed red and yellow ensign of the empire of New Spain. The other, somewhat weather-beaten, was the red, white and blue civil flag of the Russian Empire.[4]

The bride-to-be was the governor's fifteen-year-old daughter, Doña María de Concepción Marcella de Arguello, a 'bright-eyed angel'[5] known to her family as Conchita. She wore a robe of white homespun cotton.[6] The groom was a tall Russian with a severe face and cropped

hair, prematurely grey for his forty-two years.[7] His name was Nikolai
Petrovich Rezanov, widower, a nobleman of the Russian Empire and
master of a fur trading empire that extended from the Urals to Alaska.
He wore the dark green uniform of a chamberlain to Tsar Alexander I.
At his throat was the white cross of a commander of the Order of
Malta, worn by the favourites of Alexander's recently murdered father,
Tsar Paul. On his chest was the diamond-encrusted star of the Order of
St Anne first class, a sign of the Russian emperor's high favour.

Rezanov was a wealthy man, with powerful friends at court. But here
in California he was also a desperate man, with madness hatching within
him. Three years at sea had battered him. He had failed utterly in the
primary task with which his emperor had entrusted him: an embassy to
Japan to open trade with the hermit nation. He had become morbidly
conscious of his own status and dignity, and donned his decorations like
armour. Rezanov had also become volatile, a bully and a martinet. He
wept when making patriotic toasts in honour of the emperor and played
lyrical pieces on his violin, yet he did not hesitate to tell his fellow officers
to go screw their mothers. He had spent much of the voyage furiously
bickering, scheming and denouncing his colleagues, and his shipmates
returned the favour by devoting pages of their diaries to castigating him.
They called him an 'ignoramus,' an 'arch rascal'[8] and 'the biggest scoundrel whom the D[evil] ever put into the world',[9] but some of them would
and did follow him to the end of the earth.

Rezanov was also a charmer, a skilled diplomat and a gambler.
California was the ultimate point in his long journey from the Russian
imperial court, where he had spent much of his career, to the remotest
wildernesses in the world. And it was here, on the barely explored
north-east coast of North America, that he hoped to find redemption
in the form of a great imperial coup that would restore him to the
favour of the Tsar. And perhaps personal redemption too, in the form
of a new life with Conchita, the 'beauty of the Californias'.

The bride's father, Don José Dario Arguello, commander of the San
Francisco garrison, was a man from a very different world from
Rezanov's. He had been born a peasant in the pueblo of Santiago de
Querétaro in modern-day Mexico. He was tall but dark-skinned, and

through intelligence and determination he had risen through the ranks of the Spanish dragoons. As a twenty-eight-year-old sergeant he showed his mettle by taking command of a party of colonists after the murder of their officer and leading them to found a new settlement named for Nuestra Señora la Reina de los Ángeles.[10] It was a humble little place, one of the poorest missions in California, but Don José Dario doubtless hoped that his settlement of Los Angeles might amount to something one day. Arguello was now fifty-three years old, a trusted servant of the empire of New Spain, a pious man deeply attached to his wife and thirteen surviving children.

Arguello clearly had mixed feelings about the proposed marriage. Rezanov had burst in upon his family's quiet lives less than a month before in a battered American-built brig, his breath foul from scurvy and starving in his finery. In the intervening weeks he proceeded to turn Arguello's carefully ordered world on its head. First the Russian busied himself with making friends with the local Franciscan friars and encouraging them to break the Spanish empire's ban on trade with the outside world.[11] He flirted with Arguello's eldest daughter – perfectly respectably, always with a duenna present. Then, scorning all objections of rank, faith and politics, he proposed marriage to Conchita and the girl had immediately accepted. Though they had no common language other than Rezanov's Frenchified, improvised Spanish, the Russian had clearly made an impression.

Of course he had. Rezanov was a professional courtier: he knew how to dazzle, and to charm, and to make himself indispensable. He had spent much of his life in St Petersburg, Europe's most glittering court now that the French one at Versailles has been so rudely decapitated. He was by far the most impressive and worldly man that Conchita had ever met. Small wonder that she enthusiastically agreed to the Russian's offer, even though it meant she would be taken to St Petersburg, half a world away. But to Arguello the betrothal meant that he would most probably lose his daughter for ever. Nor was Conchita's suitor even a Roman Catholic.

Perplexed he might be by his fast-taking future son-in-law, but Comandante Arguello was determined to put on a good show for an event as momentous as his eldest daughter's engagement. Dancing was arranged in the modest hall of his residence. A band of soldiers was assembled from among the fort's forty-strong garrison, and they played the *barrego*, a courtly Spanish minuet, on violins and guitars. The Russians took their turn by playing English country dances. Rezanov performed on his fiddle and danced with his dark-eyed Conchita.

'She was lively and animated, had sparkling love-inspiring eyes, beautiful teeth, pleasing and expressive features, a fine form, and a thousand other charms, yet her manners were perfectly simple and artless,' wrote Rezanov's German doctor and the expedition's natural historian, Georg von Langsdorff. For dinner the party was treated to 'an excellent soup of pulse and vegetables, with roasted fowls, a leg of mutton, different vegetables dressed in various ways, salad, pastry, preserved fruits and many very nice sorts of food, the produce of the dairy . . . the wine, which was the production of the country, was but of an ordinary quality, but was succeeded by super-excellent hot chocolate'.[12]

Bullfights had been arranged for the next day, and bear-baiting. Arguello dispatched eight soldiers at dawn to find the required wild animal, and they returned at dusk dragging a large brown bear, its limbs bound and carried on a bier of stretched ox hide. Langsdorff observed the bear 'splash about in the water to cool himself . . . No-one dared venture near him for he growled, gnashed his teeth and seemed very indignant at the treatment he received.'[13] None of the Russians was tactless enough to comment that their hosts were proposing to bait their national animal to death the following day. The connection certainly did not occur to Arguello, as artless in his manners as his daughter. But in any case the poor bear died in the night, so in the end the company had to make do with traditional Spanish bulls instead.

Little did the Arguellos suspect as they drank and danced into the chilly evening that their courteous and impressive guest was viewing the rich lands of California with the envious eye of empire. Or that within a decade the southernmost outpost of Russia would be planted in modern-day Sonoma County, just seventy miles to the north of where they toasted Conchita's future happiness.

Introduction

I shall never see you –
I shall never forget you.
                    Andrei Voznesensky, *Junona i Avos*[1]

Those of depraved minds go nowadays to America solely with the aim of
growing rich and then upon their return journey fritter it away in a few
days, scattering like dust the riches obtained by many years of other peoples'
tears. Can such desperate people respect their fellow beings? The poor
[native] Americans are, to Russia's shame, sacrificed to their debauchery.
                    Nikolai Rezanov, quoted by Hieromonk Gideon[2]

I first heard of Nikolai Rezanov in the summer of 1986. I was fifteen
years old and visiting my mother's sister Lenina in her cluttered apartment on Frunzenskaya Embankment in Moscow. I had no inkling that
I was living through the old Soviet Union's last summer, the final
months of calm before the winds of change that were to scatter the old
order began to blow. Mikhail Gorbachev had come to power the previous year, and was just about to open the twin Pandora's boxes of *glasnost*
and *perestroika*. But that summer the certainties of the Soviet empire
and the Communist Party had not yet been shaken by the ghosts of
exhumed history, nor by unvarnished news of the unfolding Soviet
defeat in Afghanistan. Orderly queues still formed outside Lenin's
mausoleum; Western cars were unknown on the traffic-free streets of

Moscow, and buildings were still decorated with huge heroic posters celebrating socialist labour.

Various chaperones had been assigned by my aunt to guide me around the capital during those dusty summer holiday weeks. One of them – Victor Elpidiforovich, a war veteran who wore a pinstriped jacket with an impressive collection of medals – announced the dramatic news that tickets had been procured to Moscow's number-one hit show, the rock opera *Junona i Avos*. The title is incomprehensible, even in Russian, if you don't know that it refers to the names of two ships. But everybody in the Soviet Union did know. The show had premièred five years before, at the Theatre of Lenin's Communist Youth League – colloquially known as LenKom – just off Pushkin Square. It had been an immediate sensation, and remained so for years: in the spring of 2013 *Junona i Avos* is still playing to packed houses. In the mid-1980s fans would queue for days for tickets for the performances, which occurred, with characteristic Soviet indifference to the laws of supply and demand, only once a fortnight. In those innocent days it was still considered deeply shameful to purchase a ticket at an inflated price from free-market 'speculators'.

The show was indeed an overwhelming and moving spectacle. The story, based on historical fact but heavily embellished by librettist Andrei Voznesensky, begins with Nikolai Rezanov, a handsome Russian aristocrat and intimate of the Tsar, arriving in Spanish California with the two eponymous ships of the title. Russia's American empire – the first time I had ever heard of such a thing – is expanding southwards, and Rezanov eyes the rich lands of California with a view to conquering them. The Spanish are depicted as religious, effete and decadent. The Russians, in their smart tsarist naval uniforms, are bluff, energetic and down to earth.

This being an opera, it is a love story. Being Russian, it's also of course a tragedy. Rezanov and Conchita, daughter of the Spanish governor, fall in love. Her father and the Catholic priests who surround him are horrified. In the fictionalized version Conchita's fiery Spanish fiancé – invented by the librettist – even fights a duel with the upstart Russian suitor. Rezanov's own officers warn him that the Tsar will have to give permission for him to marry a foreigner and a Catholic. Our hero brushes aside all objections: on wings of love, he will rush to St Petersburg, petition the Tsar and return to marry Conchita. She does not dare believe it. 'I will never see you: I will never forget you' is the couple's last duet, still as famous in Russia as the theme from *Jesus Christ Superstar* is in the West. On the road home Rezanov falls from his horse and dies. But Conchita, disbelieving rumours of his demise, continues to wait for her lover for thirty-five years. She ends her days a nun, faithful to his memory.

It's hard to imagine today quite how extraordinary it was to see a Russian aristocrat and tsarist officers cast as heroes on a Soviet stage. The production also featured a vast icon of the Virgin looming over the actors, and haunting Orthodox liturgy. There were references to the 'Lord Emperor', and the tsarist flag was raised in triumph at the finale. The director, Mark Zakharov, was amazed when the censors passed the opera uncut. But *Junona i Avos* caught the mood of the moment. As Russians awoke to the disintegration of the Soviet empire, here was a nostalgic story of a lost empire in America. And as Gorbachev pressed for détente with the West, the romance of Rezanov and Conchita reminded us that love could cross national boundaries. *Junona i Avos* conjured up a romantic vision of pre-Soviet Russia even as audiences began to contemplate the reality of a post-Soviet Russia.

What impressed me most was that the story of *Junona i Avos* was largely true. Russia really did once have an American empire. By 1812 the border of the Tsar's dominions was on what is today called the Russian River, an hour's drive north of San Francisco along California's Highway 1. Russia also – briefly – had a colony on Hawaii. Rezanov spent much of his life passionately advocating the idea that America's west coast could be a province of Russia, and the Pacific a Russian sea. This was no mad pipe dream but a very real possibility.

———

As Rezanov set off from St Petersburg bound for the Pacific on a July morning in 1803, he was sailing into a world changing faster than ever in history. France, the greatest power in continental Europe, had recently been convulsed by revolution, but was now ruled by an upstart Corsican busy redrawing the map of the world. Napoleon had conquered – and then lost – Egypt, defeated Prussia and Spain and overrun Italy and much of Germany. He had even plotted with Russia's Tsar Paul to seize India from Britain.

The newly-founded British empire had been created by a couple of decisive battles and could, Napoleon wrote to Paul, be undone just as quickly. The memory of England's two great colonial coups was still only a generation old: in 1757 the British East India Company's General Robert Clive had broken the Mogul empire at the Battle of Plassey. Two years after that, Major General James Wolfe's daring attack on the fortress of Quebec ensured that the vast territory of New France, stretching across much of modern Canada, had come under the British crown.

It was an age of prodigies of conquest, navigation and empire-building. Napoleon had shown the way, but his alliance with Russia had collapsed with Tsar Paul's murder in 1801. Nonetheless, the time had come, Rezanov believed, for Russia to make her own move on the world stage. But her bold imperial gambit would be in the New rather than the Old World. Russia would colonize America from the west.

Rezanov's instrument was to be, like Clive of India's, a powerful private company. The Russian American Company, founded by Rezanov in 1799 with an exalted list of shareholders headed by the Tsar himself, was closely modelled on Britain's East India Company. It had a royal charter, the right to raise armies and dispense justice, and a trade monopoly designed to bring both dominion and profit.

Since the 1780s Russian merchant-adventurers had established a hold – albeit a precarious one – on the Pacific shore of America. A string of lonely stockades and forts manned by a motley array of convicts, fur trappers and foreign desperadoes spanned 4,000 miles of the northern Pacific rim from the Kamchatka peninsula through the Aleutian archipelago to the newly founded capital of Russian America at New Archangel – modern Sitka – at the southern end of the present-day US state of Alaska. Nonetheless Rezanov was convinced that the unclaimed 1,500 miles of territory that separated New Archangel from

San Francisco was ripe for the taking – as was the sparsely populated and barely defended empire of New Spain that lay beyond.[3]

'Your Excellency perhaps may laugh at my far-reaching plans, but I am certain that they will prove exceedingly profitable ventures. If we had men and means even without any great sacrifice on the part of the treasury all this country could be made a corporeal part of the Russian Empire,' Rezanov wrote to his patron the minister of commerce after his return from California in 1806. 'Not through petty enterprise but by great undertakings have mighty commercial bodies achieved rank and power.'

The betrothal of Rezanov and Conchita Arguello on the shores of the Pacific marked the closing of a circle. The Spanish and the Russian empires had been working their way towards each other since the late fifteenth century. Spain had sent its conquistadors west to the New World of the Americas; Russia had dispatched Cossack adventurers east into the wildernesses of north Asia. The Spaniard Vasco Núñez de Balboa was the first Westerner to set eyes on the Pacific Ocean, crossing the Isthmus of Panama in 1513. One hundred and twenty years later the Russian fur trapper Ivan Moskvitin crested the ridge of the Okhotsk Mountains and gazed eastwards at the same ocean. American gold fuelled a century of Spain's European wars and the glory of the court of Madrid, while Siberia's 'soft gold' – fur – paid for campaigns against the Swedes, Turks and Tatars as the Russians carved themselves an empire and a place on the European stage. And now the two empires had finally met, with the hungry Russians regarding the fat and ill-defended Spanish lands of California with greedy eyes.

Of the two fledgling European colonies on America's northern Pacific coast at the dawn of the nineteenth century, it was New Archangel, not San Francisco, which was the more populous and better defended. Ships were built on New Archangel's slipways and Boston traders regularly stopped in for news and supplies.[4] Spanish San Francisco, in comparison, had a garrison of just forty soldiers and no docks when Rezanov visited in 1806. The Spanish governor of Nueva California told Rezanov that 'the Spanish Court feared Russia above all the other powers'.[5]

For Rezanov, not to seize the territory would be a crime against posterity. 'If we allow it to slip through our fingers, what will succeeding generations say?' he wrote. 'I, at least, shall not be arraigned before them in judgement.'[6]

———

Any historian who sets out to search for a hero will almost inevitably uncover something of the scoundrel. Heroism, it seems, is visible only through a long lens. And so it was with Rezanov. I followed the man's shade from the boulevards and palaces of St Petersburg to the squat rain-dripping counting houses of Pskov, where he passed a dreary provincial apprenticeship. Travelling by train, coal truck and bouncing Lada, I tracked him from the Siberian city of Irkutsk, once the capital of Russia's wild east, into the land of the Buryats and to the borders of China. I crunched along the black sand beaches of Petropavlovsk in Kamchatka and the black sand beaches of Kodiak Island, Alaska, at opposite ends of the Pacific. I stood in the remains of the *presidio* where Rezanov had danced with Conchita and shivered in the rain on the windy outcrop known as Castle Rock in Sitka, once the citadel of New Archangel, where he had spent the cold, hungry winter of 1805–6. And I spent hours – many hours, since Rezanov was a bureaucrat, a courtier and an ambassador who wrote something almost every day of his life – in the company of the reports, diaries and letters in which Rezanov described his ideas and circumstances voluminously, but his feelings only barely. It is only in the last three years of his life, far from home and viciously bullied by the officers of the round-the-world voyage he believed he was commanding, that the man himself begins to emerge from the officialese, indignant and in pain.

The far side of the world was where Rezanov found both humiliation and, perhaps, love. Either – or both – seem to have liberated his spirit. But the privations he suffered and the power he wielded in those remote provinces of the Russian Empire also drove him a little mad. Rezanov was a great imperial visionary, but he could also be a liar and a schemer. He had moments of great bravery and sacrifice, but he was capable of shameless acts of buck-passing cowardice. Rezanov was a courtier and politician of genius, but he also dispensed summary justice and launched a private war against Japan for reasons of personal revenge. He probably loved Conchita, but in his official reports did everything to portray the relationship with the poor girl as a cynical political game. He was morbidly conscious of his own status to a degree that seems absurd to us today, yet during his embassy to Japan and his visit to California front and bluster were really all he had to offer, and they took him remarkably far.

So Rezanov was perhaps not a hero. But certainly he was a man whose life spanned worlds. The two worlds in which he moved – the court and the wilderness – were separated by a social and geographical distance almost too vast to be grasped by a modern mind. Rezanov spoke to tsars and numbered the Russian Empire's greatest men as his friends and enemies. His plans for Russian America were the subject of lively correspondence between Napoleon and Tsar Paul as they laid their plans for world domination. Yet Rezanov spent much of the last years of his life scrabbling for food and squabbling with illiterate mutinous frontiersmen.

Nikolai Rezanov wanted to make his country a match for the upstart France with only a gang of Cossacks, criminals and the renegades of the frontier at his command. He wanted to plant a new, better Russia in the New World just as old England had created a vigorous new version of herself in the Thirteen Colonies which had recently formed themselves into the United States. Russian America would not be a republic, of course, but a well ordered company-run empire under the Tsar's protection. That was his imperial vision – a dream of which almost nothing remains today. And yet in his lifetime it seemed, for a few tantalizing years, that Russia could successfully colonize America, with incalculable consequences for both.

Man and Nature

There, by the billows desolate,
He stood, with mighty thoughts elate,
And gazed . . .'
Alexander Pushkin, *The Bronze Horseman*, 1833

Our Russian land can bring forth her own Platos,
And her own quick-witted Newtons . . .
Mikhail Lomonosov, *The Delight of Earthly Kings and Kingdoms*, 1741

No childhood could be more calculated to instil in a growing boy a sense of the supremacy of man over nature than growing up in St Petersburg as that great city rose from the marshes. In 1703 Peter the Great had ordered the construction of the first building on a sandy island on the northern bank of the Neva River, among mosquito-infested bogs criss-crossed by sluggish streams. A yearly levy of between thirty and forty thousand serfs – one conscript for every nine house-holds in the empire – was brought on foot and under military escort to dig embankments and haul stone for the new palaces. Within two decades this slave army had transformed Peter's plan into a great city of elegant houses and paved streets.

By the time Nikolai Petrovich Rezanov was born on 28 March 1763 in the modest Rezanov family house near the Admiralty, St Petersburg was already a European metropolis. 'The city could be called a wonder of the world,' wrote the awestruck Hanoverian ambassador, 'was it only in consideration for the few years that have been employed in the raising of it.'[1] St Petersburg boasted an academy of sciences, a university, an academic gymnasium and a fine neoclassical cathedral, and its grid of streets had been laid out according to the latest principles of town planning by the finest architects of Europe.

The city was defined by its artificiality. Its genesis and continued existence were wholly dependent on the person of the Tsar. St Petersburg was the ultimate *Residenzstadt* – a city built around an imperial court and financed by the state and, less willingly, the nobility. 'St Petersburg is just a court, a confused mass of palaces and hovels, of *grands seigneurs* surrounded by peasants and purveyors,' wrote the French encyclopedist Denis Diderot in 1774 after visiting at the Empress Catherine the Great's invitation.[2] As Rezanov was growing up in the 1770s only three of the city's grand streets – Millionaya, Lugovaya and the English Line, later known as the English Embankment – had been fully completed. Behind these streets were rows of 'wooden barracks as unpleasant as it is possible to imagine', as the Empress herself noted,[3] interspersed with the wooden houses of the lesser nobility, forced by decree to maintain residences in the capital.

Sophia Fridericke von Anhalt-Zerbst, called Ekaterina Alexeyevna by her adopted countrymen, had taken the Russian throne as the Empress Catherine II six months before Rezanov's birth in a coup against her sad little husband, Tsar Peter III. Catherine, with her characteristic energy, saw the half-built city as a challenge. 'I found St Petersburg almost entirely of wood and will leave it covered with marble,' she wrote to a friend in July 1770.[4] In the meantime the city was a strange mixture of the grand and the ramshackle. 'The [palaces'] walls are all cracked, quite out of perpendicular, and ready to fall,' wrote Francesco Algarotti, a Venetian visitor, who attributed the poor quality of the buildings to the fact that they were constructed 'of obedience rather than choice'. In Italy 'ruins generally form themselves', quipped the Italian, 'but in St Petersburg they are built from scratch'.[5]

Thus the Petersburg of Rezanov's childhood was a vast building site. As a boy he would doubtless have joined the crowds of gentlemen in

English-cut coats and the blinking Finnish fishermen who watched the great four- and five-ton blocks of granite manhandled from barges to create the new embankments along the Neva, an effort that began in 1763 and continued sporadically well into the next century. In 1781 Elizabeth, wife of Thomas Dimsdale, the English doctor who had been invited to inoculate Catherine and her children against smallpox, wondered if the titanic embankments would ever be finished. 'The Russians are with great truth remarked to begin things with great spirit,' Mrs Dimsdale observed. 'And for a little time to go on very rapidly – then leave for some other object.'[6]

As a young gentleman Rezanov would have attended plays in French at Russia's First State Artistic Theatre near the Admiralty. We know he learned German and French – most probably from foreign tutors, members of the thriving colony of Western European dancing masters, tailors, teachers, soldiers, sea captains and adventurers who had flocked to the new Russian capital following the powerful scent of money.

One of them was the French sculptor Étienne Maurice Falconet, who arrived in St Petersburg in 1766 at the Empress's invitation. He spent twelve years creating his masterpiece, the equestrian statue of Peter the Great known as the *Bronze Horseman* (in Russian the *Copper Horseman*), a monument not only to Peter the Great but also to Catherine's claim to be heir to Peter's greatness. The pedestal on which the statue stands is a 1,200-ton piece of Karelian granite known as the Thunder Stone, which was dragged bodily by 400 workers across four miles of forest before being placed on a barge stabilized by two warships before being hauled again by hand to its current position on Senate Square.[7] The progress of the awesome stone and the repeated unsuccessful attempts to cast the statue itself at the state foundries on Liteiny Prospekt were an ongoing drama in the life of the city, the subject of gossip and incredulity throughout the young Rezanov's boyhood.

The final ensemble was finally unveiled in 1782, and it is likely that the eighteen-year-old Rezanov was among the thousands of citizens and soldiers who turned out to witness the event. It was the kind of elaborate pyrotechnic ceremony Catherine loved. A giant pine box decorated with bunting, which had hidden the statue from public view, was collapsed with charges of gunpowder, accompanied by fireworks and massed drum rolls.[8] In this Age of Enlightenment there could be no more dramatic proof that the vast powers of the Russian empress could bend land and sea to her will, and remake rude nature in the image of reason and order.

Half finished as it was, the St Petersburg in which Rezanov grew up was already very distant from the rest of Russia. 'A capital at the edge of an empire is like an animal with its heart in the tip of its finger,' observed Catherine's confidant Lev Naryshkin.[9] But that was the point: Peter wanted a Russia as it could be, not as it was. St Petersburg was a maritime city in a largely landlocked country. It was a European capital for a nation which just a century before had resembled a Tatar khanate more than any European principality.

The fortunes of the Rezanov family had closely mirrored those of Muscovy itself. Like many within the Russian nobility, the Rezanovs were not in fact Russians at all but descendants of Tatar nobles who had pledged allegiance to Russian princes. 'Scratch a Russian and you find a Tatar,' Joseph de Maistre, Savoy's ambassador to St Petersburg, quipped to Napoleon.[10] But for up to a quarter of the Russian aristocracy, it was literally true.

The principalities of Kiev, Muscovy, Tver, Novgorod and Pskov had been under Mongol-Tatar suzerainty from 1237 until 1480, when the Muscovite Prince Ivan III finally defied the Golden Horde and ended the payment of tribute. His grandson Ivan IV *Grozny* – the Terrible, or more accurately the Stern – took the Tatar capital of Kazan in 1552. Ivan's musketeers annexed Astrakhan, the capital of the Tatars of the lower Volga, in 1556. That year a Tatar *beg* or lord, Murat Demir Reza – later Russified to Rezanov[11] – swore fealty to the Muscovite tsar and was rewarded with noble status.

Unlike the feudal nobility of Western Europe, who held land in their own right, Russian noblemen were first and foremost personal servants of the tsar. They were called *namestniki*, literally 'placed men' and given lands and vassals to support them and their families, but their lands remained the property of the tsar. In this, as well as in its court dress, arms and armour and diplomatic customs,[12] the Muscovite court closely resembled the khanates it had deposed. Murat Demir Reza's switch from Tatar lord to Muscovite nobleman was an easy one. The Rezanovs, Russianized and baptized into Orthodoxy within a generation, became loyal and energetic servants of the tsars.

In 1697 Tsar Peter I – later known as the Great – embarked on an eighteen-month incognito expedition to Holland and England during which he personally learned many useful skills, including tooth-pulling, shipbuilding and woodturning. The twenty-five-year-old tsar also discovered many wonders of Western technology. One was the wheelbarrow, in which, when drunk, Peter and his companions used to push each other into the prize holly hedges of Sayes Court, the Deptford house they rented from the diarist John Evelyn. (After the royal party had left the King's Surveyor Sir Christopher Wren was called in to repair the damage to the gardens, while Charles II picked up the £350 bill for his Russian guests' rampages.[13]) More importantly, Peter's new interest in all things modern, from fire hoses and lepidoptery to city planning and astrology, inspired him to unleash a cultural revolution on his backward homeland.

On his return Peter began his reforms with the nobility, banning arranged marriages, Tatar-style kaftans and tall hats and imposing a tax on those boyars who refused to shave their beards in the Western manner. Peter's modern ideas, however, did not extend to political reform. He saw the nobility as servants of the state and agents of his royal will. In the final years of his reign Peter codified the strata of the Russian bureaucracy, army and court in a unified table of ranks. The idea was to create an educated class of noble bureaucrats, with each of the fourteen ranks corresponding to an order of nobility. Thus up-and-coming men – not to mention flocks of ambitious foreigners – could join the nobility by virtue of their service to the state. Some of the hereditary nobility, primarily from old Muscovite families allied with Peter's estranged first wife, attempted to resist and were soon marginalized. Newer, more opportunistic families like the Rezanovs quickly saw that they had much to gain from Peter's revolution, and remade themselves in the image of the new age.

Gavriil Andreyevich Rezanov, grandfather to Nikolai, was born in 1699 and brought up as the ideal Petrine man. War, engineering and shipping were the growth industries of Peter's Russia, and the young Gavriil mastered geometry, mathematics, engineering and shipbuilding and was one of the early residents of Peter's new city on the Neva. By 1723 Gavriil Rezanov was working as an engineer on one of the Tsar's pet projects, a seventy-two-mile canal intended to ease navigation between the Volga to the Baltic by bypassing the stormy Lake Ladoga.

The Ladoga Canal was a classic Petrine project: faddishly scientific and technically ambitious, with its double locks and reinforced banks. But despite its Western and progressive conception the plan was executed by the slave labour of thousands of conscript soldiers and state-owned peasants. The canal was also – not unlike St Petersburg itself – more about vanity than utility, since its one-metre depth allowed only shallow-draught barges to pass along it. Within a generation it was abandoned in favour of a deeper parallel canal, and today the old water-way survives only as a picturesque weed-filled ditch cutting through the dacha-lands on the lake's southern shore.

Gavriil Rezanov's superior on the Ladoga project was Burkhard Christoph von Münnich, a Danish-born soldier and engineer. Like many of the foreign military adventurers who came to Peter's court, Münnich spent Russian lives freely in pursuit of his own ambitions. Nonetheless, Gavriil Rezanov thrived under this martinet, and by the time the canal was finally completed in 1730 Rezanov was Münnich's deputy in charge of construction. The Dane was to be a useful patron. On Peter the Great's death in 1725, his widow – crowned Empress Catherine I – appointed Münnich *général en chef*, the highest rank in the Russian army. The Dane went on to open Russia's first engineering school and formally founded the Izmailovsky Life Guard Regiment. When the Empress Anna – Peter the Great's niece and the second of the four empresses who ruled Russia in the eighteenth century – came to the throne in 1730, it was General Münnich who was instrumental in fulfilling her ambition to push Russian power deep into Europe.[14]

Münnich's campaigns were a rehearsal in miniature for the Russian Empire's even greater conquests under Catherine the Great. He besieged the East Prussian port of Danzig, allowing Russia to install the first of several puppet kings of Poland in 1736. Then he took his new Izmailovsky Guards south for the first of a series of campaigns against the Tatar Khanate of Crimea, the final outpost of the Golden Horde. Major Gavriil Rezanov was one of many aristocratic officers of Tatar origin to march with him against his former kinsmen. A fellow officer was Baron Hieronymus von Münchhausen, whose tall tales of the siege of the Turkish fortress of Özi and other 'Marvellous Travels and Campaigns in Russia' became a comedy classic when written up by an anonymous parodist and published in 1781 as *The Surprising Adventures of Baron Münchhausen*.

But Russia's fortunes – and Rezanov's – really took off with the outbreak of the Seven Years' War in 1757. Sparked by a colonial skirmish between British and French forces in Pennsylvania, this conflict was in many senses the true first world war. It was fought by at least fifteen European powers and principalities, with hostilities extending from Canada to India to the Philippines. Up to 1,400,000 people are believed to have been killed across the globe as a result of the prolonged hostilities, which destroyed many fledgling colonies and beggared swathes of Central Europe.[15]

Russia managed to escape becoming deeply embroiled in the upheavals, but even its peripheral involvement in the Seven Years' War was to have a profound impact on its standing as a European empire and naval power. Empress Elizabeth I – Peter's feisty daughter, who had seized power in 1741* – began with an opportunistic land grab, ordering her armies to seize the Baltic provinces of East Prussia while Prussia's king, Frederick the Great, was busy attacking Bohemia. In 1760 Elizabeth's troops seized Berlin.† Russia soon retreated from Berlin but retained Königsberg, capital of East Prussia and ancient coronation place of Prussia's kings. The loss of Königsberg to the Russians marked the

---

* From the Empress Anna's infant nephew Ivan VI, who was kept a secret state prisoner until his death in captivity twenty years later.

† It was to be the first of three Russian invasions of Germany: 'Iwan' would be back in Berlin in 1814 and, in rather greater numbers, in 1945.

definitive arrival of a powerful and unpredictable new player in the politics of central Europe. And Gavriil Rezanov, now a lieutenant general and decorated war hero, was appointed Königsberg's first Russian commandant.

Gavriil Rezanov probably first met Gavriil Okunev at the Admiralty in St Petersburg, a 400-yard-long complex of offices, rope-walks, dry docks and sawpits on the southern bank of the Neva next to the newly built Winter Palace. Major General Okunev, a nobleman from Pskov and a talented shipwright, had in 1746 been appointed head of Russia's shipbuilding on the Baltic, which after the seizure of Königsburg became centred in the old Prussian port of Pillau. So Okunev and Rezanov had much business to transact together.

Besides a professional interest in Baltic shipping, the two Gavriils had much else in common. They were both born in 1699; they were military men who owed their position to the Seven Years' War, and their families had both been ennobled by Ivan the Terrible – the Okunevs nine years before the Rezanovs.[16] They were also close neighbours in St Petersburg. Okunev lived at 2 Dvoryanskaya Street, on the Admiralty Canal, around the corner from the Rezanovs on the Neva Embankment. In terms of status Rezanov was the senior man, third in Peter the Great's table of ranks; Okunev was, however, richer, thanks to extensive family estates around Pskov. All in all the men were well matched, financially and socially, and it was entirely natural that the two generals should eventually arrange a marriage between their children, Rezanov's son Pyotr, a young guardsman of the Izmailovsky Regiment, and Okunev's daughter Alexandra. In 1763 the couple's first son, Nikolai Petrovich Rezanov, was born in St Petersburg.

Sadly for Alexandra – and one suspects to the disapproval of both his father and father-in-law – Pyotr Rezanov's military career proved a disappointment. A few years too young to profit from the frenzy of promotion, plunder and glory of the Seven Years' War, Pyotr soon came to see that the outbreak of peace between Russia and Prussia made a career in the army a dead end – at least until the start of the next war. He was, however, freer than his ancestors to choose a career path outside the army. Tsar Peter III, architect of the alliance with

Prussia that caused the untimely (for Rezanov at least) cessation of hostilities, reigned for just 186 days before being deposed by his energetic German wife Catherine in July 1762. But one of the few laws to survive from his mayfly reign was the liberation of the nobility from compulsory state service imposed by his illustrious grandfather and namesake, Peter the Great. Unfortunately, Peter III neglected to lift the other half of the original law on nobility, which barred members of the aristocracy from engaging in commerce. This meant that aristocrats now indeed had a career choice of sorts, but it was a narrow one between state service or idleness.

For noblemen of modest means like Pyotr Rezanov, however, unemployment was not an option. Within civilian state service there were three pathways. The more ambitious and well connected of the nobility could attempt a career at the imperial court, the fickle *fons et origo* of all power, wealth and favour. For the less socially elevated, there was the civil government, consisting of the governing Senate, which supervised the bureaucracy, and ten ministries. This was the option energetically pursued by Pyotr's younger brother Ivan, who had joined the College – Peter's term for his embryo ministries – of Foreign Affairs and by the 1770s had risen to deputy head of its chancellery. But there was a third option: a career in Russia's wild and distant colonies. This was risky, dangerous and not wholly respectable, but could lead to great wealth. Like many young and indigent noblemen across Europe, Pyotr Rezanov chose to leave his birthplace and seek his fortune in distant lands. For a young Russian aristocrat this meant the vast half-tamed land of Siberia.

2

The Final Frontier

In Europe we are hangers-on and slaves, but in Asia we are masters. In Europe we were Tatars, but in Asia we too are Europeans.

Fyodor Dostoevsky, 1881[1]

The boiling ferment and the frantic, aimless activity which distinguishes young nations.

Alexander Pushkin

Spain and Russia were medieval Europe's marcher kingdoms. Spain held the North African Moors at bay in the west, while in the east Russia battled the Mongols and their successors, the Muslim Tatars.[2] Both Spain and Russia, as a result of the demands of centuries of military effort, remained more autocratic, more religious and more deeply feudal than their less-threatened continental neighbours. But both Madrid and Muscovy were richly rewarded for their struggles against the infidel in the form of vast unexplored lands full of worldly riches. Divine providence gave Spain the New World – or so Spain's Most Catholic monarchs believed. Likewise Russia's most Orthodox Tsars were convinced that their divine reward was Siberia, whose boundless natural resources funded the emergence of Muscovy as a European power, and forms the foundation of Russia's oil wealth today.

The grand princes of Muscovy had had dreams of empire since 1472, when Ivan III married Zoë Paleologina, the niece of the last Byzantine emperor, Constantine XII. Zoë brought not only her double-headed eagle coat of arms to Muscovy but also the idea that Moscow could be the successor to her fallen Byzantine homeland – a third Rome. Russia's expansion to the west was blocked by the powerful kingdom of Poland-Lithuania and the Baltic trading cities of the Hanseatic League. But to the east the power of the Mongol-Tatars was weakening.

It was Zoë's grandson Ivan the Terrible who decisively turned the balance of power on Christendom's eastern flank when he took the Tatar capital of Kazan in 1553. Ivan crowned himself caesar – in Russian, tsar – in recognition of his conquest. In 1556 he pushed his armies south along the Volga and annihilated the southern Tatars in their stronghold at Astrakhan. At a stroke Ivan had made the Volga, the great southern artery of European Russia, into a Muscovite river, opening trade to the Caspian and beyond to Persia.

The capture of Kazan had also given Muscovy easy access to the Kama River, the Urals and the riches of Siberia itself. At the same time Europeans in search of furs and a north-east passage to China began arriving at the Arctic village of Kholmogory – later known as Arkhangelsk – at the mouth of the Northern Dvina River. The first was Richard Chancellor, head of the English Muscovy Company, London's first chartered company of merchant adventurers, who visited in 1553.

Meanwhile Spain's conquests in distant America were transforming the economy of Europe with a huge influx of gold. Northern Europe was also undergoing a boom in trade and manufacture centered on wool-cloth. With this new prosperity came a burgeoning demand for luxury goods from the East, particularly for the sixteenth century's two greatest luxuries – spices and furs. Portuguese and English seafarers were driven to prodigies of navigation and discovery by the search for high-value spices – particularly peppercorns, nutmeg and allspice – to flavour the foods of the wealthy. In the same way Russian adventurers drove ever deeper into Siberia in search of the fox, sable and marten with which the rising merchant classes of Europe trimmed their clothes.

Fur, in a cold and poorly heated world, was not only a symbol of wealth but also a bringer of comfort and, in the case of Russia, literally a lifesaver. Fine furs were staggeringly valuable. In 1623 one Siberian official reported the theft of 'two black fox pelts, one worth 30 rubles the other 80'.[3] The thief could have bought himself fifty Siberian acres, a cabin, five good horses, ten cows and twenty sheep on the proceeds, and still have had some of his ill-gotten money left over. No wonder painters of the new bourgeoisie, from Jan van Eyck in the Netherlands to Sebastiano del Piombo in Rome, painted their subjects' sable collars in such loving detail. They were often worth more than the artist could hope to make in years.

Siberian fur transformed Muscovy from a minor principality on the fringes of Europe into a great power.[4] In 1595 Tsar Boris Godunov had so much of it that he sent Holy Roman Emperor Rudolf II fur in lieu of military assistance against the Turks. Boris's tribute was a dazzling show of Russia's new wealth. The 337,235 squirrel skins and 40,360 sables, as well as marten, beaver and wolf skins Boris sent took up twenty rooms of Prague Castle. At the beginning of the seventeenth century 'soft gold' accounted for up to a third of Muscovy's revenues. Without the Siberian fur rush, the wealth it brought and the vertiginous territorial expansion that it drove, the Russia of Peter the Great would have been unimaginable.

Like the Spanish captains of the New World or the seafarers of Queen Elizabeth I of England, the conquistadors of Siberia were essentially pirates licensed by the Russian crown. The Stroganovs, a trading dynasty from the Hanseatic city-state of Novgorod, which had been incorporated into Muscovy in 1478, financed the first fur-trapping expeditions into the uplands of the Urals and pioneered the use of licensed privateers. In April 1558 Ivan the Terrible gave Anikei Stroganov rights over five million acres of Urals forest, effectively making him viceroy of the unexplored territory responsible for its development and security.[5] Beyond the Urals, however, lay the Tatar khanate of Sibir, an obstacle both to obtaining furs and to the expansion of the Tsar's dominion.

In 1577 the Stroganovs recruited a young buccaneer named Yermak Timofeyevich. Yermak was a scion of a family of notorious river pirates who had plied the middle Volga but had found themselves out of business with the fall of Kazan and the establishment of Muscovite control over the great river. With his band of professional – and temporarily jobless – marauders Yermak headed eastwards, pushed deep into Tatar territory and in 1580 took Sibir. To placate the Tsar for taking such a step without royal permission, Yermak sent a vast haul of 2,500 sables to Moscow. Ivan was suitably impressed. In return for his gift, he made Yermak Muscovy's viceroy in Siberia – just as Yermak's former employer Stroganov had become lord of the Urals. Yermak also received a handsome suit of armour from the Tsar, which was to prove his undoing five years later as he attempted to swim away from a Tatar ambush but was drowned by his heavy breastplate.

Yermak was a Cossack, one of a growing community of men who had fled serfdom in Poland, Livonia and Muscovy and sought freedom in the no-man's-land of the mid-Volga and the south-east steppes of European Russia. Cossacks were a social caste, not a racial or national group. Their freedom was a precarious one because of the regular Tatar slaving expeditions which filled the markets of Constantinople with hundreds of thousands of new Slavic captives every year. Moscow itself had been raided and burned by Khan Devlet Giray of Crimea as recently as 1571, and the Crimean Khanate would not be finally subdued until the reign of Catherine the Great in 1783.[6] Ivan the Terrible, borrowing the Stroganovs' methods, was the first tsar to harness these outlaws to the service of the state. In the absence of any natural boundaries to his fledging empire, Ivan offered the Cossacks freedom from serfdom and a licence to exploit native peoples in exchange for their service as guardians of Russia's eastern and southern borderlands.

The Tsar organized the Cossacks into 'hosts', a military and administrative term for a tribe of armed colonists who could be instantly turned into a military force. The names of the successive hosts is a chronicle of Russia's growing empire – Don, Kuban, Terek, Asktakhan, Ural, Orenburg, Siberian, Turkestan, Transbaikal, Amur, Ussuri. The Cossack *sotni*, or hundreds, elected leaders known as *atamany*, and when the host was not in state service it was free to explore – and maraud – on its own account.[7]

These Cossacks were tough men. 'I believe such men for hard living are not under the Sunne, for no cold will hurt them,' wrote Richard

Chancellor of the men he saw on the northern Dvina in 1553. 'Yea and though they lye in the field two monthes at such times as it shal freeze more than a yard thicke the common soldier hath neither tent nor anything else over his head.'[8] Of the three drivers of Russia's eastward expansion – the quest for security against the Tatars, a consciousness of its imperial destiny as the inheritor of Byzantium and the adventurous avarice of Cossacks – it was the last which was by far the most potent.

The Cossacks went east not as farmers or traders but as masters and conquerors. Muscovy was in many ways a kind of Christian khanate, and as they expanded eastwards the Russians behaved towards the natives exactly as the Tatars had behaved towards them. The peasantry was considered the personal property of the Tsar, tied to the land, and the nobility his servants. 'When a poore Mousick meeteth with any of them [nobility or the emperor] upon the high way he must turn himself about, as not daring to look him on the face, and fall down . . . as he doth unto his Idol,' wrote Giles Fletcher, another English visitor to the court of Ivan the Terrible.[9]

The Cossacks therefore saw themselves as a kind of eastbound horde. From the native peoples they encountered they demanded hostages and tribute – tellingly known by the Tatar term *yasak*. In many cases Cossacks also considered the 'provision of women' an obligation.[10] In exchange, the natives would be brought under the protection of the Tsar – a dubious privilege, since it was mostly the Russians from whom the natives most needed protection – and spared massacre.[11] Over in the New World the fledgling fur trade on Canada's St Lawrence River and Hudson Bay was based on trapping and barter with the natives. On the east coast of North America the English colonies of Virginia and Charleston were made up of property-owning agriculturalists. In Russia, however, the colonization of Siberia began and remained an economy of confiscation – just as it was in the Spanish empire in Central and South America.

For those indigenous Siberian communities who refused to pay *yasak* the Cossack hosts held a crown licence, as one seventeenth-century charter put it, 'to wage war and capture [native] children'.[12] In 1642 the Buryat chief Bului was made to swear to his new Cossack overlords that his people would pay tribute in sables and foxes, or else 'the sun will not shine on me, I will not walk the earth, I will not eat bread; the Russian sword will cut me down, the gun will kill me, fire will destroy all our villages'.[13] Initially any native converts to Orthodoxy were spared the payment of *yasak*.* But by the mid-seventeenth century priests were accompanying Cossack raiders with orders to 'burn all idols and toys', herd natives into rivers for mass baptism and force them to choose just one wife.[14] In 1706 all natives, regardless of religion, were made subject to the Russian *yasak*.[15]

The Cossacks were excellent at the application of violence, but not so good at grasping the principles of sustainability. The gathering of fur-tribute was more like mining than farming – when a particular area was exhausted of its population of fur-bearing animals, usually within two decades, they would move on to new lands.

On a modern map Siberia appears as a vast block of land stretching 170 degrees of longitude across almost half the earth. Cossack explorers, however, would have seen it as three separate, huge river systems: the Ob-Irtysh, the Yenisei and the Lena. Each river runs south to north and drains into the Arctic Sea an area bigger than the Nile basin.[16] To the south of these great river systems lie the steppes of Eurasia, the historic highway of grassland which stretches from Manchuria to Hungary. But though more easily passable, the steppes were inhabited by civilized and warlike peoples such as the Bashkirs, Kazakhs and Kyrgyz, who were subdued by the Russian Empire only in the late nineteenth century. Moreover, they yielded no furs.

So the Cossacks became river farers and forest dwellers, making their zigzag way across Siberia up and down the great rivers and their tributaries in flat-bottomed boats, which they carried across the low hills between. Where they stopped, usually at the confluences of rivers, which were also often traditional native trading places, they built forts they called *ostrogs*. These rectangular timber compounds were around a hundred yards square with stockades ten to twenty feet high, with bastions mounting artillery in the corners and a parapet around the top. Inside, typically,

---

* A similar rule regarding converts to Islam applied in the contemporary Ottoman empire, which was at the time powering through the Balkans.

were the house of the *voevoda*, or chief, a granary, barracks and a church.[17] Groups of Cossacks caught by winter too far from the nearest *ostrog* would build *zimoviye*, so called from the Russian for winter. These fortified blockhouses would house as many as fifty men as they sat out the impassably deep snows and lethal frosts of the Siberian winter. In 1639, 120 years after the Spanish explorer Vasco Núñez de Balboa stood on a peak in Darien and became the first European to see the Pacific,* a Cossack party of trappers under Ivan Moskvitin crossed the Okhotsk Mountains and reached the ocean from the other side. Just fifty-eight years after Yermak had taken Sibir, Russians had crossed Siberia.

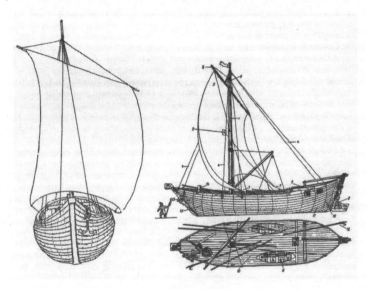

A Cossack sea-going *koch*.

Other Cossacks, travelling in the same manner in similar boats, traversed the Arctic Ocean by hugging the northern coast of Siberia and reached the Pacific by sea in 1648. Semyon Dezhnev, a Cossack from Veliky Ustug, had assembled seven snub-nosed square-sailed riverboats known as *kochi*, each crewed by up to nineteen men. Sailing east in search of

* *Pace* John Keats; not 'stout Cortez'.

sable his expedition rounded what is today known as the Bering Strait, passed between Little and Big Diomede Islands – the modern-day border between Russia and the USA – and founded an *ostrog* at Anadyr on the Chukchi peninsula. Four of his boats were lost, along with sixty-four out of his eighty-nine men. Undaunted, Dezhnev returned later with a new expedition, discovered a portage through the tributaries of the Kolyma River to the Sea of Okhotsk, from where he sailed as far as the border of the Chinese empire on the Amur River in 1650.[18]

News of the explorations of Russian travellers was greeted with keen interest in Western Europe. The Dutch trader Nicolaas Witsen, one of the first Europeans to travel in Siberia and thirteen times mayor of Amsterdam, incorporated Dezhnev's observations into the groundbreaking world map he produced in 1690 alongside his encyclopedic study of the Russian Empire, *Noord en Oost Tartarye*. Unfortunately for Russian navigators, however, Dezhnev's discoveries remained virtually unknown in his home country. The only extant copy of his official report[19] was buried in an archive in Yakutsk until discovered in the 1730s.[20]

Peter the Great may not have been aware that his countrymen had already succeeded in rounding Russia's eastern extremity, but his twin enthusiasms were seafaring and the expansion of the Russian Empire, and the exploration of Eurasia was a lifelong interest. In Siberia, and what lay beyond, Peter met a challenge vast enough for his ambition. In 1681, when Peter was nine, one of his father's final acts was to order a royal fort built at the Cossack *ostrog* of Okhotsk, the first Russian settlement on the Pacific.[21] In 1711 Peter ordered a naval wharf built at Okhotsk – an optimistic move, for there were as yet no Russian naval ships on the Pacific to use it.[22] Peter fantasized about trade missions to China, Japan and India and of extending Russian sovereignty over the North American coast from the Bering Strait to the Spanish empire. But it was not until 1724, when Peter was already dying, that he finally commissioned Vitus Bering, a Dane with twenty years' service in his navy, to explore the 'Eastern Ocean', Russia's final frontier.

There being no Russian ships sturdy or fast enough to make the round-the-world journey, Bering and thirty-four officers, shipbuilders and workmen set off across Siberia to build their own craft when they arrived at

the Pacific. It took the party over two years to drag their tools and equipment such as anchors and cordage across eleven modern-day time zones to
the Kamchatka peninsula. There, with the help of workmen and sailors they
had picked up on their way, they built the three-masted barque *Arkhangel
Gavriil*. Bering set off across the Pacific in 1728. He mapped parts of the
Bering Strait and the north-eastern corner of Russia in some detail, but, to
the frustration of St Petersburg, failed to find the 'great land' beyond, which
had been appearing on Cossack seafarers' primitive maps since 1710.

Bering was sent off again in 1733 on a more ambitious two-ship
expedition along the same gruelling route. His men, who now included
naturalists and scientists, built the barques *Svyatoi Pyotr* and *Svyatoi Pavel*
on the shores of one of the world's greatest natural harbours, Avacha Bay
on Kamchatka, which they named Petro-Pavlovsk after their vessels. Stepan
Krasheninnikov, a young botanist who became the expedition's chronicler,
found the natives of Kamchatka unusually degenerate and disgusting even
by Siberian standards. They 'eat their own lice and wash in urine . . . share
their food with their dogs and smell of fish', Krashennenikov reported.
They also 'cannot count beyond three without using their fingers'.[23]

View of Avacha Bay and the settlement of Petropavlovsk of Kamchatka, 1740.

This time the expedition made landfall in America. Bering's first officer, Alexei Chirikov, aboard the *Sv. Pavel*, almost certainly hove to just south of Jakobi Island, near the modern-day Alaska–Canada border. Chirikov dispatched a longboat to explore the shore, but it never returned. Nor did a smaller jolly boat sent to search for it. Both were probably lost in the tidal undertow that even today makes the Jakobi Channel extremely treacherous.[24] Fires were seen ashore and a native canoe briefly emerged and signalled to Chirikov, but he had no boats left to follow it.* After several days' fruitless waiting he had no choice but to abandon any possible survivors to their fate and turn for home.[25] More serious even than the disappearance of fifteen men was the loss of both the *Sv. Pavel*'s boats. Without them the ship could take on neither supplies nor water. During his return journey Chirikov had to exchange valuable knives for bladders full of fresh water brought out to the ship in canoes by Aleut islanders.

Bering was even less lucky. Separated from Chirikov's ship early in the voyage, Bering's brig the *Sv. Pyotr* cruised along the American coast, spotting Mount St Elias near modern Yakutat. But he was unable to make it back to Kamchatka before the end of the sailing season and was forced by contrary winds to winter on the island which today bears his name. The ship dragged its too-small anchor in a storm and was wrecked. That winter the sixty-year-old Bering died, probably of heart failure,[26] along with thirty-one of his seventy-five men, who mostly perished of scurvy.[27] The survivors, including the German naturalist Georg Steller, lived on the meat of the giant slow-moving sea mammals Steller named sea cows. A full-grown specimen weighed nearly 7,000 pounds and could feed the entire crew for a month.[28] In the spring of 1742, nine years after they had set out from St Petersburg, the remaining members of the expedition built a smaller boat from the salvaged wreckage of the *Sv. Pyotr* and limped back across the short distance remaining to Petropavlovsk. Bering's party had spent the winter just four days' sail away from salvation.

---

* The natives commemorated the disaster in petroglyphs found nearby, which appear to show a sailing ship and boats.

Despite its high death toll, the second Bering expedition marked a breakthrough for Russian expansion to the New World – not least because in Russian eyes Chirikov had made the land Russian by right of first discovery. Chirikov was not the first European to explore the northern Pacific coast of America – that honour goes to the Elizabethan privateer Sir Francis Drake, who sailed up the coast as far as San Francisco in his ship the *Golden Hind* during his 1577–80 round-the-world voyage. But Chirikov was the first navigator of modern times to record a landing on the coast, albeit a disastrous one, and had thereby staked a claim to the New World in Russian blood.

But like the conquest of Siberia, it was not state ambition but private enterprise that drove Russians forward towards America. Word of Steller's descriptions of islands full of fur seals spread quickly across Siberia. Over the next decade over thirty groups of Cossack explorer-adventurers visited the Aleutian Islands, sailing in forty-foot *shtitik* boats – single-masted square-sailed vessels of archaic design – out of Okhotsk and Petropavlovsk. For the crews who returned from these two- or three-year fur expeditions the profits were vast. One merchant returned from the Aleutians in 1754 with the pelts of 1,662 sea otters, 840 fur seals and 720 foxes. For the natives, however, the consequences of Russian violence, disease and the depletion of their fragile fishing grounds were devastating. Vladimir Atlasov, an early Cossack explorer of Kamchatka, reported a population of two to three thousand adult males on the peninsula in the 1730s. By the first official census in 1773 only 706 souls remained.[29]

The Bering–Chirikov expedition also fired imaginations in St Petersburg with dreams of adding America to the Russian Empire. 'O, Russian Columbuses, scorning a grim Fate;/ Between the mounts of Ida will open a new path to the East;/ And we will plant our State on America's shores,' wrote Mikhail Lomonosov, the autodidact scientist who founded Moscow University, in his 1747 ode 'Peter the Great'. Lomonosov, as well as being Russia's first secular public intellectual, was also part-Pomor, a northern Russian people who had been the first explorers of the north Siberian coast. He therefore had an inherited, as well as an academic, interest in Arctic navigation. In 1755 Lomonosov penned an influential essay, 'Letter on the Northern Route to East India via the Siberian Ocean'. He also drew the first map of the world as seen from the top, with the North Pole at its centre, showing Alaska as a natural adjunct of Siberia.[30] Lomonosov suggested that a navigable north-east passage along the Arctic would open all Asia to Russian shipping.[*] Russia, he wrote, was now 'an Empire on three Continents: Europe, Asia and America'.

The reality of imposing the Tsar's laws on these vast new territories was, however, trickier than the armchair strategists of Moscow University imagined. Authority died over Siberia's vast distances. If detached from European Russia, Siberia would still be the largest country in the world – it is bigger than the United States and Europe combined. Feudal Russia's institutions – serfdom, aristocracy and the authority of the Church – all dissolved in the rough egalitarianism of the frontier. The self-reliant Cossacks were followed by equally independent-minded ideological exiles. First came the Old Believers, adherents of a traditional Orthodox liturgy who had been vigorously persecuted by Peter the Great's father. They were followed by restless and ambitious peasants attracted by the freehold land they were able to own in Siberia, as well as by fugitives from justice. Like frontier America, the empty land filled with a mismatched population of God-fearing schismatics and violent criminals.[31]

But Siberia was not just a place of escape and new beginnings. Almost as soon as it was colonized, it also became a place of banishment and punishment. As early as the 1690s the state began to use Siberia as a dumping ground for its criminals, as though its vastness could quarantine evil.[32] *Katorga* – from the Greek word for galley – was the judicial term for a penal settlement where inmates performed hard labour in the service of the state. The sentence was commonly imposed in place of death from the reign of Peter the Great onwards.

Under the Empress Elizabeth, who swelled the ranks of convicts by abolishing the death penalty for most offences in 1753, the crimes for which a man could be exiled included fortune-telling, vagrancy,

---

[*] Thanks to global warming, the north-east passage has since 2008 become navigable (with the help of icebreakers) for enough of the year to make it a commercially viable shipping lane.

'begging with false distress', prizefighting, wife-beating, illicit tree-fell-ing, 'recklessly driving a cart without use of reins' and for a brief puritanical period in the 1750s, even taking snuff.³³ Until the mid-eighteenth century these exiles were always branded, usually on the face or right hand, to prevent them ever making their way back to the world. The convicts would spend up to two years shuffling in columns to their exile along the great Siberian trunk road known as the *Trakt*. The jingle of their chains and the ritual cries of 'Fathers, have pity on us!' as the condemned men held out their caps for food was, for all the travellers who passed them in their high-wheeled carriages, the sound of Siberia. By tradition at Tobolsk, 1,100 miles from Moscow, the prisoners' leg irons were removed – a mercy, but also a sign that they had gone too far into the wilderness for escape to be survivable.

Irkutsk, founded as a Cosssack *ostrog* in 1652 where the Anadyr River flows into Lake Baikal, straddled the trade route between Russia and China. It soon became the entrepôt and then official capital of eastern Siberia. By 1754 there was a government school there for navigators, geodesists, mining engineers and – a sign of where the strategists of the capital were focusing their hopes for trade – translators of Japanese, taught by Japanese sailors shipwrecked on the Pacific coast of Siberia.

The combination of a vigorous outlaw culture and a thriving merchant class made Irkutsk vital and dangerous in equal measure, a place filled with turbulence and opportunity. Fur traders came from thousands of miles around after months or years in the wilderness to turn their pelts into gold and their gold into swinish pleasures. The drinking dens and gaming tables of Irkutsk were as notorious in eighteenth-century Russia as those of Deadwood would become in nineteenth-century America. The archives of the Irkutsk criminal court record at least one murder every day. The French monk and astronomer Abbé Jean Chappe d'Auteroche, sent to Siberia by Catherine the Great to observe the passage of the moons of Jupiter in 1770, reported that the clergy were so drunk and libidinous that priests were 'often found in the streets unable to walk home'.³⁴

Cut off from European Russia like the French of Quebec or the British of Bermuda, the merchants of Irkutsk preserved a language and dress considered antiquated even by the late eighteenth century. The

Mongol belted kaftan, abandoned in the capital under Peter, was worn in Irkutsk into the twentieth century. Merchant money built grand mansions along boulevards lined with pine-plank boardwalks against the mud, but the backstreets stank, reported Auteroche, with pigs feeding in the open sewers.[35]

Government postings in Siberia attracted the desperately ambitious or the desperately disgraced. The tone was set by Matvei Gagarin, Peter the Great's appointee as governor of Tobolsk, in western Siberia. Early in his nine-year reign the wilderness called to something greedy and vicious in Gagarin. He began minting his own coinage and made such a fortune from smuggling that he shod his horse with silver and dispensed his own justice, ordering arsonists burned alive. Peter had his wayward lieutenant brought back to the capital in chains and hanged. The Tsar ordered that Gagarin's body remain on the gibbet as an example to others. When the rope around the corpse's neck rotted Peter had it replaced by a chain.

Yet even such drastic punishments did little to improve Siberia's notoriously corrupt, rapacious and brutal government officials. 'Written laws should not be treated like playing cards,' stormed Peter in a decree of 1723. 'This *ukaz* seals all orders and regulation like a stamp so that nobody can act according to their own whims or in breach of instructions.' But repeated laws to protect natives against extortion, abuse, sex slavery and being deprived of their hunting grounds are clear evidence that previous laws to that effect had been ignored.

———

Pyotr Rezanov must have viewed the prospect of a job in this barely-civilized outpost of the empire with trepidation. But he knew that if he was lucky and clever the post promised lucrative possibilities for patronage and self-enrichment. As an aristocrat he required no legal qualifications to become a judge, and this was the post he sought and received. In spring 1769 Rezanov left his wife and young children in St Petersburg and set off to dispense justice in the wilderness. The foundations of a long and lucrative – for his son, if not for him – family connection to Russia's wild east had been laid.

3

The Court

I am a Tsar – I am a slave,
I am a worm – I am a God . . .

Gavriil Derzhavin, 'Ode to God', 1784

For the Russian aristocracy the court was the centre of the world: it was the source of all power and patronage, gossip and scandal, disgrace and ruin. The sovereign's favour could raise ambitious men like Catherine the Great's lovers Grigory Orlov and Grigory Potemkin to the heights of wealth and power. Catherine may have corresponded with François-Marie d'Arouet Voltaire and Denis Diderot about enlightened ideas for ruling Russia, but in reality her court was as unpredictable, Asiatic and dependent on the caprice of the monarch as Ivan the Terrible's had been two centuries before. The glittering reception halls of the Winter Palace were a giant casino of fortune, and the two thousand wax candles that burned every interminable St Petersburg night on the palace's chandeliers illuminated an elegant game of risk which the milling men and women below were playing for their lives.

From a tender age the young Nikolai Rezanov was put to work cultivating powerful patrons. The Russians, like the eighteenth-century English, called it 'interest' – the network of connections without which no job could be lobbied or career made. Noble rank alone was no guarantee of advancement. The Russian monarchy may have been the most absolute in Europe – peasants were expected to prostrate themselves flat on the ground as the imperial carriage passed by – yet Russian society was surprisingly upwardly mobile.[1] This was partly the legacy of Peter the Great, who had gone out of his way to break the power of the Moscow boyars by promoting both foreigners and humble men such as his favourite Prince Alexander Menshikov, a former pie vendor, to greatness. Tsar Peter himself married a buxom peasant girl from Livonia who succeeded him as the Empress Catherine I.

The prevalence of self-made men – or rather, tsar-made men – in the upper ranks of Russian society was a sign not of any democratic instinct but rather the desire of the tsars to surround themselves with their own protégés. Aristocrats with inherited wealth and connections could have complex and shifting loyalties. Foreigners or Russian men of no rank owed their advancement solely to the favour of their monarch. They were therefore their sovereign's creatures, and his or her most obedient lieutenants. As a result the court history of eighteenth-century Russia is full of talented parvenus and pampered lover-favourites. Gavriil Derzhavin, a poor nobleman who rose to the highest posts in the state, was the archetypal brilliant upstart and was to play a vital role in the life of young Nikolai Rezanov. Derzhavin was from an impoverished gentry family from Kazan who were, like the Rezanovs, of Tatar origin. Derzhavin had made his way to the capital as a teenager and joined the Preobrazhensky Guards as a private, not being able to afford to buy an officer's commission. He quickly rose through the ranks. The young Derzhavin was befriended by Nikolai Rezanov's uncle Ivan, who was himself busy hustling his way upwards through the Foreign Ministry.

Derzhavin's breakthrough came in 1773 when a peasant named Emiliyan Pugachev raised the standard of revolt on the eastern borderlands of the empire. Claiming to be Catherine's murdered husband Peter III, Pugachev and his army of Cossacks and outlaws moved west, burning noble estates and hanging all army officers they captured. In 1774, when the rebels took Kazan, Catherine grew seriously alarmed and sent the full might of her forces against the rebels. Derzhavin, serving under General Alexander Bibikov, was one of the young officers to emerge with glory. He also showed the poetic prowess which was to make him remembered as one of the greatest poets of pre-Pushkin Russia, penning his 'Ode on the Death of General Bibikov' after his chief died of typhus while pursuing the rebels across the Orenburg steppes.

Certainly by 1775, after Pugachev had been brought to Moscow in a cage and publicly executed, it was clear that Major General Derzhavin was a coming man. That year the eleven-year-old Nikolai Rezanov wrote to Derzhavin in a neat copperplate hand, addressing his uncle Ivan's influential friend in his best schoolboy German. '*Mein Herr!* That you condescend to take an interest in my fate I am most humbly grateful,' wrote the boy. 'I have heard from my mother that you wish to take me from the Izmailovsky Guards to the Preobrazhensky Guards under your patronage, for which consideration I am most delighted.'[2] Rezanov had been put down for his grandfather's regiment – the Izmailovsky – as an infant. Whether this mention of a transfer to Derzhavin's Preobrazhensky Guards was a tactful request or thanks for an offer already made isn't clear. In any case, though Derzhavin remained Rezanov's patron and friend for life, the change of regiment never happened. In the late summer of 1778, at the age of fourteen and a half, Officer Cadet Rezanov joined the Izmailovsky Guards after all.

The guards regiments of the Russian army were modelled, socially as well as militarily, on their Western European prototypes. Most socially prestigious were the three Life Guard regiments created by Peter the Great, who named them after the 'toy armies' of boys he had recruited as a teenager from villages around his father's palace outside Moscow – Izmailovo, Preobrazhenskoye and Semyonovskoye. Guards officers were drawn largely, but not exclusively, from the nobility. In any case, thanks to Peter's table of ranks, all officers above the rank of captain became hereditary nobles ex officio. When Rezanov joined the Izmailovsky Guards his regiment was officered by the empire's top people. The commanding officer was General Prince Nikolai Repnin, while its recently formed cadet corps was commanded by Major Prince Golitsyn. Among his fellow cadets was Alexander Alexandrovich Bibikov, son of the regiment's former commander who had died putting down Pugachev's revolt. Rezanov's generation of cadets would go on to command the Russian army during the war against Napoleon in 1812.*

Unfortunately, young Rezanov soon found that he had been born at exactly the wrong moment for a glittering military career – just like his father before him. Early in her reign the Empress Catherine had set to projecting Russian naval power across the Mediterranean. A brilliant victory over the Ottoman navy by a newly built Russian fleet in the Turkish port of Cesme in 1770 astonished Europe. A series of land campaigns in the Balkans followed, eventually forcing the Sultan to cede swathes of modern Moldavia and Ukraine to Russia in 1774. That same year the suppression of Pugachev's revolt also provided opportunities for military glory – and the massacre of superior officers necessary for the promotion of ambitious young subalterns. But all this was no good for Rezanov, who had the misfortune to join the army right at the beginning of what was to be a fourteen-year outbreak of peace.

Every year, from 1 May to 1 September, the Izmailovsky Guards would take part in manoeuvres in the countryside around St Petersburg, tramping the roads of the Baltic coast in their green uniforms with red cuffs and collar, red waistcoat and breeches. In the winter the men retired to their log barracks at the regimental headquarters in the village of Kalininskoye, south of the capital, while the officers repaired to the city for the winter social season. This leisurely rhythm was doubtless a well-earned rest for the veteran senior officers, but for their ambitious juniors it must have been a tragic bore. The official regimental history is a perfect blank from the regiment's return from putting down Pugachev in 1774 to the start of Catherine's war against the Swedes in 1788.[3]

Just before his twentieth birthday, in the spring of 1784 after five years of peacetime soldiering, Rezanov decided he had had enough and resigned. He was a sergeant in the cadet corps – in fact the highest rank a cadet could reach, but nonetheless humiliating for an adult with years

---

* At least fourteen of Rezanov's regimental classmates are immortalized in the gallery of portraits of the victorious generals of the war of 1812 in the Winter Palace commissioned after the victory over Napoleon.

of soldiering experience. Yet promotion proceeded strictly by seniority, and with no enemies to kill off his superiors Rezanov would have to wait till they died of old age. Rather than waste any more of his life, the restless young former Guardsman struck out into the civilian world with few qualifications other than a good pedigree and some decent family connections.

On retirement from the regiment Rezanov was promoted to the rank of captain. It was a kind of consolation prize to get him started in civilian life. A captain was eighth in the table of ranks, the equivalent of a collegiate assessor and entitled to be addressed as 'Your High Nobleness'. The rank alone, however, carried no salary. Like many young men suffering career setbacks, Rezanov was forced to return to his mother's house in the country to compose himself for the next stage of his life.

During the summer months, when the court was absent from the capital, the nobility of St Petersburg habitually fled the malodorous, mosquito-filled and malarial city for their country estates. We can assume that the young Nikolai and his three siblings spent their summers among the orchards and hayfields of Demyaninskoye, their mother Alexandra Okuneva's estate. Demyaninskoye, near Pskov, had been part of her dowry when she married Rezanov's father.*

Pskov was a backwater in 1784. It remains a backwater today. The Empress, who visited in 1776, deemed it the ultimate in Russian backwardness and decline. 'Inoculate someone with your talent for development and send him here,' she wrote to her friend and confidant, the German author Friedrich Melchior Baron von Grimm, from Pskov. 'Perhaps he will be able to bring on its industry from its present sorry state.'[4] The town had enjoyed a heyday in the fifteenth century, when its burghers joined the Hanseatic League and traded amber, pine pitch, furs and lead up and down the Baltic. These merchant princes erected handsome, solidly built cathedrals and squat manor houses with steeply pitched roofs. The city's thick-walled kremlin withstood twenty-six sieges mounted by Poles, Lithuanians, Tatars, Teutonic

---

* Nothing, not even the name, remains of the estate today.

Knights and Russians from Novgorod, all eager to seize its wealth for themselves. By the end of the eighteenth century, however, Pskov had been bypassed by the currents of the world. Since Peter the Great had conquered neighbouring Estonia from the Swedes eighty years before Rezanov's arrival, Pskov's strategic value had been comprehensively eclipsed. Its commerce had been swallowed by St Petersburg, two hundred miles to the north, and Königsberg to the west. According to parish records the town's population in the 1780s was around 7,000, less than half of what it had been in the Middle Ages.

After the social whirl of a young guards officer's life in the fast-growing capital Rezanov must have felt that he had returned to an older, slower Russia. In Petersburg the papers were full of the latest ballet performances at the new Mariinsky Theatre. Literary types were buzzing about Derzhavin's newly published 'Ode to Felitsa', a witty and avant-garde work which addressed the Empress in a bantering tone which made gentle mockery of stilted literary classicism. In Pskov the big news was that work was starting on a new courthouse. Finished in 1790, it still stands today, a mediocre provincial echo of the capital's elegant neoclassical colonnades.

Everything about Pskov, from the architecture to the society, must have seemed stolid, squat and plain. To the young Rezanov it may have felt like failure. Or perhaps, more rationally, he considered it a necessary provincial apprenticeship before a triumphant return to the capital. Derzhavin, after all, himself recently retired from the guards, had just accepted the governorship of Olonets, a dreary northern province recently won from the Swedes.* Derzhavin would later be moved to the governorship of grain-rich Tambov, earning a steady reputation as an administrator as he bided his time for the wheel of fortune at court to turn in his favour. The young Rezanov must have fervently hoped that the same would apply to his own fledging career.

The Okunevs were, as prominent local landowners, inevitably close to the provincial administration, and a job was quickly found for the young Nikolai. His complete lack of legal training notwithstanding,

---

* Now known as Karelia, on the border with Finland.

Rezanov was appointed assessor to Pskov's recently opened civil court. As a favour to this promising local nobleman, a year of service was added to boost him up the bureaucratic hierarchy, qualifying him for an immediate judicial position. Two weeks before his twentieth birthday Rezanov took his place on the bench of the province's central court, one of five court officers who sat as judge and jury on the affairs of the thieving, philandering, foul-mouthed and light-fingered citizens of Pskov.

The records of Rezanov's time as a civil servant show a court roster of mind-boggling provincial tedium. About the time Rezanov joined the bench, some tragic proto-Gogolian clerk made a minute inventory of every piece of furniture in Pskov's courthouse. Worthy of record, in the clerk's view, were 'two brass inkstands, one bell, one sand scatterer, one Dutch stove with iron doors, eight brass candlesticks' as well as 'windows and several doors'.[5] The court met every day but Sundays and holidays from eight in the morning until two in the afternoon. Rezanov dutifully signed his name in the roster almost without fail every working day for four years. The president of the court, his two deputies and two assessors would process into the courtroom wearing their newly designed uniform of light blue kaftans with red trimmings, buff waistcoats and buff breeches. They all wore swords to signify their noble status. All morning they would hear a series of petitions, presented in descending order of social rank of the appellants, concerning extortion, debts, inheritance, the liberation of serfs, family feuds, slander and the complaints of prisoners in the town jail.

Before Catherine the Great the Russian judicial process had been simplified by the routine use of torture, usually branding and racking, which produced either neat confessions or dead suspects. The Empress's ban on such barbarous practices in 1767 attracted the praise of European liberals like Voltaire but made for messy hearings and interminable cases. Another, more welcome, innovation of Catherine's was the introduction of salaries for state employees. Previously the state's servants were expected to exist 'from their affairs', as an *ukaz* of Peter the Great coyly put it, or in plainer terms from the bribes of petitioners.[6] It is highly doubtful that Catherine's newfangled salaries eliminated the deeply ingrained habit of bribery – indeed using their official powers to extract money remains the universal practice of Russian bureaucrats today. Nonetheless, under the new system Rezanov's pay was 300 rubles a year. It was no fortune, but enough to keep a decent table and a modest household. The parish records of the church of St Sergius Zaluzhia in central Pskov for 1786 record Nikolai Rezanov living with his mother, two younger brothers Dmitry and Alexander and his patriotically named sister Ekaterina with just eighteen servants, rather modest by local standards. A goose at the Pskov market cost twenty-five kopecks, a pike or a pound of flour two kopecks. The court's watchman, an ex-soldier, got eighteen rubles a year; its president received twelve hundred.

The Hannibal family of Mikhailovskoye made regular appearances at the Pskov court both as defendants and plaintiffs for sword fighting, slander and assault as well as various petty territorial disputes with their neighbours. They were the litigious and unruly descendants of Abram Petrovich Hannibal, born Ibrahim Hannibal in Eritrea and sold as a slave to Constantinople. He was bought and rescued by the Russian ambassador's deputy, who brought him to St Petersburg in 1704. Peter the Great took a shine to the bright African boy and adopted him; Hannibal married into the Russian aristocracy and rose to the rank of major-general. The family's most famous son was Alexander Pushkin, Hannibal's grandson and still noticeably African of feature. Pushkin was to continue the hell-raising tradition by conducting public affairs with other men's wives and fighting twenty-nine duels, including his last one against Frenchman George D'Anthès over an insult to the honour of Pushkin's wife, in which the poet was killed.[7]

Such entertaining cases as the turbulent Hannibal clan provided were however relatively rare. Rezanov seems to have had a good head for figures and a certain pedantic flare for the nuts and bolts of administration. These talents landed him with an even more boring job, if that were possible, than that of court assessor. For six months a year he was seconded to the Pskov provincial treasury, housed in the mansion of the merchant Postnikov. The house still stands, a stolid seventeenth-century building which is now the town's historical library. Its domed ceilings, tiny barred windows and thick walls breathe the oppressive heaviness of medieval Russia, an impression reinforced by the fact that the house has sunk below the level of the modern street like a water-logged barge. One imagines the young Rezanov, surrounded by brass inkwells and massy medieval treasure chests left over from the town's more prosperous days, staring out of these windows towards the dripping pine forests and dreaming of escape.

By 1788 Rezanov, now twenty-four, had again decided that he had had enough. As in the army, Rezanov had served nearly five years without promotion. Unlike the army, however, there was no inbuilt mechanism for the wholesale slaughter of his superiors in the line of work. Furthermore, in 1763 the Empress had decreed that advancement in the civil service would come automatically through length of service rather than merit. It was a perfect formula for the institutionalization of mediocrity.

Given the remarkable imagination, energy and diplomatic skills Rezanov was to demonstrate later in his career, it seems likely that his talents had simply been buried under the dead hand of his placeman superiors. In any case, in February 1788 Rezanov applied to the court for a leave of absence and an internal passport for travel to St Petersburg. In May he wrote again for an extension of his leave – on full pay, collected weekly by his younger brother Dmitry – claiming that he was planning to rejoin his old regiment. This seems unlikely. The Izmailovsky Guards had been mobilized the previous autumn when the Ottoman empire declared war in an ultimately futile attempt to recover territories lost to Rezanov's swashbuckling grandfather, General Gavriil Rezanov. By spring 1788 the great fortress of Ochakov, on the shores of the Black Sea in modern Bulgaria, had fallen to a desperate Russian assault, and the regiment was moving on to further glories before the Ottoman fortresses of Bendery and Brailov. Rezanov had definitively missed them.

Instead the young nobleman-judge-treasury-secretary was busy advertising himself in the ministerial waiting rooms and salons of the capital, paying court, as contemporary Englishmen would call it, to the great and the good in search of a vacancy commensurate with his and his family's social traction. In this regard Rezanov had several obstacles to overcome. His first and most serious handicap was that his maternal grandfather General Gavriil Okunev, the old soldier who had been in charge of all shipbuilding on the Baltic, had died in 1781. Another was that his uncle Ivan Rezanov had inconveniently and quite suddenly fallen from royal favour.

Uncle Ivan had risen up the bureaucracy with giddying speed, first in the Ministry of Foreign Affairs and later as secretary to the chief procurator of the Senate, Prince Alexander Vyazemsky. Political decision-making in Russia rested solely with the Empress, but the Senate – essentially a talking shop for the senior nobility – drafted laws and petitions for Her Majesty's approval and controlled a network of judicial and bureaucratic appointments second only to the Palace itself.

Ivan Rezanov's social and, he doubtless hoped, political ace in the hole had been his beautiful daughter Maria. She soon became the mistress of Prince Vyazemsky, who was certainly powerful but, unfortunately for the Rezanovs, already married. This arrangement was not as prestigious for Ivan Rezanov as having Vyazemsky as an official son-in-law. But Vyazemsky's wife was wise enough to ignore the liaison, and the prince, in due course, did the right thing and found a wealthy and well-heeled husband for his pretty young mistress. In 1783 the girl became engaged to Lieutenant General Ivan Yakobi, the governor-general of Irkutsk. Thus Ivan Rezanov was poised to set up his daughter with a powerful and rising nobleman and advance his own career to boot.

Alas, the Empress disagreed. Despite having a vast and unruly empire to run, Catherine took an intense interest in the love lives of Russia's aristocracy and devoted a remarkable amount of time to matchmaking and, in the case of the Rezanova–Yakobi engagement, match-breaking. She seems to have wanted to punish Vyazemsky, who had incurred the Empress's disfavour by dragging his feet over her proposed Code of Laws. 'I don't want this Vyazemsky to give his Rezanova to Yakobi and present her with all Siberia as her dowry,' the Empress wrote at the beginning of the winter season of 1783. Catherine intended to offer Yakobi, a dashing and wealthy widower, as a marital prize to a more loyal courtier.

Both Vyazemsky and Yakobi survived this minor social debacle; only Ivan Rezanov's fortunes waned in the wake of the embarrassment. By the time his nephew came looking for a job in 1788 Ivan had disappeared from the Senate's records and retired from the civil service into genteel obscurity.

In December 1788 Rezanov went to work for the Treasury, presumably on the strength of his Pskov accounting experience. He remained at the post for nearly two years. Alexander Radishchev, a radical and one of the greatest oppositional minds of his age, was his colleague. Radishchev was thirteen years Rezanov's senior in years but one step below him in bureaucratic rank; he had studied at the University of Leipzig and returned full of Jacobin ideas.* Rezanov was either nervous of befriending such a dangerous mind or found Radishchev's radicalism distasteful. In any case, the two men never became friends. Instead Rezanov used his toehold in the bureaucracy of the capital to work on his late grandfather Okunev's connections. Belatedly these came through, even ten years after the old man's death. In 1791 the Admiralty finally offered a suitable position to the old shipbuilder's young grandson, as junior secretary to Count Ivan Grigoryevich Chernyshev, vice president of the Navy Board.[8]

Chernyshev had been one of the original backers of Catherine the Great's coup and had served as her ambassador in London for many years before returning to Russia and the gigantic estate of Alexandrino, given to him by a grateful empress.[9] He was a powerful patron, and Rezanov, showing a talent for both administration and ingratiation that would stand him in good stead in the future, quickly became Chernyshev's *chef de cabinet*. In less than three years Rezanov had moved from provincial mediocrity to within touching distance of the court itself.

---

* Radishchev's book *A Journey from St Petersburg to Moscow*, published in 1790, was a passionate condemnation of serfdom and feudalism. All copies were confiscated and Radishchev condemned to death, later commuted to exile in Siberia.

Catherine had seized the throne when Nikolai Rezanov was just six months old. In the intervening twenty-four years she had applied her extraordinary energy to remaking the Russian Empire in her own image. Born a minor German princess, she had not a drop of Russian blood. As a daughter of Europe, Catherine saw herself as the spiritual successor of Peter the Great's quest to bring Russia to civilization and greatness. Indeed she saw those two concepts as inextricably linked. The neoclassical palaces and boulevards of St Petersburg which took shape during her reign were a mirror to a larger civilized world that she was determined Russia should join.[10]

Like Peter she believed that only an enlightened absolute monarch, supported by an educated aristocracy, could reform Russia. But where Peter had indulged in impulsive, almost boyish, enthusiasms for the kind of grand engineering projects that brought instant gratification – his navy, for instance, his capital, or the Ladoga Canal – Catherine tackled the fundamental architecture of the state itself. In the early years of her reign she banned judicial torture and experimented with a nobles' assembly and a basic constitution. She undertook a massive codification of Russia's tangled mass of statute and common law, drafting many of the clarifications personally. 'Russia is a European State,' Catherine wrote in a preamble to her *Instruction on Laws* – written in French.[11] 'There are 20 peoples of various kinds in this town who do not in any way resemble each other. And yet we have to make a coat which fits them all. I might say that there is almost a whole world to be created, united, preserved,' she wrote to Voltaire, the leading public intellectual of the day, from Kazan in May 1767 during a barge cruise down the Volga. 'Imagine I beg you that these laws must serve for Asia as well as for Europe . . . Here I am in Asia.'[12]

The Empress considered the abolition of serfdom and attempted to canvas ideas internationally for reforming Russia. In 1766, at the behest of the palace, the Free Economic Society of St Petersburg sponsored a Europe-wide essay competition, offering cash prizes for the best answer to the question 'What is useful to society, that the peasant should own land or only movable property, and how far should his right over one or the other extend?' There were 164 anonymous entries, only seven of them in Russian. Voltaire submitted two, one in French and the other in Latin.*

However, the anarchic violence of Pugachev's revolt in 1773-4 dampened Catherine's reforming enthusiasms and put off attempts to end serfdom for nearly a century.[13] The American Revolution and the rise of Jacobinism in France further steeled her against constitutionalism. But Catherine's determination to bring Russia kicking and screaming into the eighteenth century by enlightened despotism rather than democracy continued unabated. For twenty years she conducted a semi-public correspondence with Voltaire. The old sage was delighted to be an unofficial adviser to the Empress and called his Russian penfriend the 'Semiramis of the North' after the great law-giving Assyrian queen.

Catherine also invited the Encyclopediste Denis Diderot to St Petersburg. Their daily talks became so animated that the Empress was forced to place a table between them to stop the Frenchman from grabbing her knees in his enthusiasm. In 1765 she had bought the impoverished Diderot's library and made him its salaried librarian for life. Like her correspondence with Voltaire, the purchase was partly driven by private intellectual curiosity and partly by a calculated public display of cultural diplomacy. The acquisition of the library was Catherine's grand reproach to a French society which had failed to support his genius. 'Would you ever have suspected fifty years ago that one day the Scythians would so nobly recompense in Paris the virtue, science, and philosophy that are treated so shamefully among us?' wrote Voltaire.[14]

In 1779 Catherine caused a similar sensation when she bought the art collection amassed by former British Prime Minister Robert Walpole from his spendthrift grandson. Its 204 pieces included works by Rembrandt, Rubens, Van Dyck, Hals and Guido Reni, and was probably the greatest single art purchase of the eighteenth century. It formed the basis of a new public museum attached to the Winter Palace that Catherine called the Hermitage. The English public was indignant, and

---

* An early example of what would today be called crowd-sourcing.

the export of the Walpole collection became a national scandal. 'How sad it is to see passing into the hands of Scythians things that are so precious that ten people at most will admire them in Russia,' wrote the French collector and art dealer Jean-Henri Eberts of an earlier purchase of Catherine's in September 1769.[15] It was not the last time that Russian money would buy great British institutions, to the titillated disapproval of London's chattering classes.

'You forget that we are in different positions – you work with paper which forgives all while I, the poor Empress, must work with human hide,' Catherine had written to Diderot after his departure from St Petersburg in 1774. That human hide had proved, by the late 1780s, less tractable than she had once imagined. By the time young Rezanov came to the capital to make his way in the world, the gulf between the Enlightenment enthusiasms of Catherine's early reign and the reality of the absolute personal power of the Russian monarch was clearly apparent.

Like the Empress Elizabeth before her, Catherine added a twist to the traditional carousel of patronage and vying for place: the possibility of gaining the heights of power via the imperial bed. This practice is probably the part of Catherine's life and world most misunderstood today. Catherine was a passionate woman lonely at the pinnacle of power she had seized for herself. She had been brought to Russia as a fourteen-year-old and married to the future Peter III, a psychologically crippled adolescent who preferred to play with toy soldiers rather than make love to his young wife.[16] By her own account, in a startling frank autobiography that was banned by her son Paul, Peter did not touch her for the first nine years of their marriage. When he finally did perform his marital duty, Catherine's three children were taken from her almost immediately and looked after by her domineering mother-in-law, the Empress Elizabeth. Small wonder that in later life Catherine's relationships with both her children and her lovers were complicated by her emotional neediness and by the fact that her absolute power made a truly equal relationship impossible. 'The trouble is that my heart is loath to be without love for even a single hour. If you want to keep me for ever then show me as much friendship as love and, more than anything else, love me and tell me the truth,' she wrote to her greatest favourite of all, Grigory Potemkin.

In all, Catherine had twelve lovers during her life. She had long, passionate and faithful relationships with great men such as Grigory Orlov, the man who had helped her depose her husband, with Stanislaus Poniatowski, the brilliant Polish magnate whom she would elevate to the kingship of his native land, and with Potemkin. The rest of her lovers were found, loved and fired with a rather Germanic no-nonsense briskness. Candidates were checked for signs of venereal disease by the Empress's Scottish physician Dr John Rogerson, and her lady-in-waiting the Countess Bruce would chat to them to assess their suitability as conversationalists, sending Catherine little notes with her conclusions.[17]

Prince Grigory Potemkin was the Empress's longest-serving favourite. He was also for a time virtual co-ruler of Russia. He caught her eye as a dashing young sergeant on the very day of her coup against Peter III. According to his own later account, Catherine was reviewing her troops in full (male) guards uniform in preparation for a march on the Palace of Peterhof, but lacked a sword knot. Impertinently, Potemkin rode out of the line to offer her his own, which was graciously accepted. He was subsequently rewarded with an officer's commission and the favour of the Empress. He persisted in his gallantry, and meanwhile rose to major-general and covered himself in glory in Catherine's wars against the Turks. Finally in February 1774 his persistence was rewarded and he became Catherine's lover – but not before he had threatened to retreat to a monastery in a fit of amorous anguish.

Their relationship was tempestuous. Catherine was frequently exasperated by Potemkin's tantrums and fits of jealousy, but she recognized that he was 'one of the great originals of the age'. Part of her was clearly happy to have found a man who was her match in terms of energy and intellect. In December 1774 Catherine privately referred to Potemkin as her 'husband' for the first time and continued to do so in twenty-two letters between 1774 and 1791. To marry officially would have been politically and dynastically complicated for Catherine, who despite her late husband's inadequacies had at least produced a legitimate heir, the future Paul I. But it is probable that Potemkin became her consort, at least secretly.[18]

Catherine showered Potemkin with wealth and titles, including that of prince of the Holy Roman Empire (*Reichsfürst*), and remained devoted to him until the end of her life. But their physical relations probably ended soon after Catherine took one of her secretaries, Pyotr Zavadovsky, as a new lover in 1776. Potemkin himself was spectacularly unfaithful, taking at least one of his nieces to his bed. But they remained close and affectionate allies, and despite his lingering jealousy Potemkin had to tolerate Catherine's taking a succession of young lovers.

In August of 1789 the sixty-two-year-old Catherine wrote to Potemkin that she had 'returned to life after a long winter slumber as a fly does'. A new friend, 'a dark, little one', had made her 'well and gay again'. The new favourite was twenty-two-year-old Platon Zubov, a pretty young aristocrat whose arrogance and corruption would appall even the hardbitten court of St Petersburg. Zubov played shamelessly on Catherine's maternal instincts. 'Our baby weeps when denied the entry into my room,' Catherine wrote to the long-suffering Potemkin. 'At last, the Empress has a "Platonic" relationship,' was the snide joke that went around the court. But Platon Zubov's rise was to play a defining role in the career of another ambitious young aristocrat – Rezanov – also desperate to push into the golden glow of the Empress's regard.

At first Potemkin paid little heed to the upstart lover, assuming that Catherine would tire of him as she had tired of others. But Zubov quickly established a strong hold on the Empress's affections and, increasingly, her exercise of power.[19] Potemkin was irritated and disappointed by Catherine's catastrophic lack of judgement, and set off on a tour of the newly conquered territories of New Russia. On 16 October 1791 Potemkin expired on a dusty roadside in the southern empire to which he had dedicated so much of his life.

Catherine was inconsolable. But with his greatest rival now dead, the path was now clear for the clever and utterly cynical Zubov to make his career in his predecessor's image. 'Count Zubov is everything here. There is no other will but his. His power is greater than that of

Potemkin,' the diplomat Fyodor Rostopchin reported. 'He is as reckless and incapable as before, although the Empress keeps repeating that he is the greatest genius the history of Russia has known.'[20] Catherine had regularly used her lovers as lieutenants even after they had stopped being her intimates – Stanislaus Poniatowski had been made King of Poland and presided over the division and then disappearance of his homeland into the Russian Empire; Potemkin continued as ruler of New Russia long after he had stopped sharing the Empress's bed – but Zubov took open advantage of his position as no other favourite had done before. Over his seven-year reign, Zubov accumulated thirty-four state posts and the titles first of count and then prince of the Holy Roman Empire. He succeeded Potemkin as governor general of New Russia and amassed a fortune in diamonds, serfs and lands lavished on him by the soft-hearted old Empress. He spoke of himself in the plural and was rude to the heir apparent, the Tsarevich Paul.

At court one took opportunities where they presented themselves. Gavriil Derzhavin, now governor of Tambov, quickly spotted the steel behind the foppish young Zubov's good looks and attached himself to the rising young favourite. He received his reward in December 1791, two months after Potemkin's death, when at Zubov's prompting the Empress appointed Derzhavin state secretary for petitions.

Her immoderate fondness for Zubov notwithstanding, Catherine remained a formidable administrator and judge of men. She liked her advisers to be frank; sycophants irritated her. 'I am very fond of the truth and you may tell me without any danger if it leads to good results in affairs,' she had instructed Count Vyazemsky on his appointment to procurator general of the Senate. 'And may I add I require no flattery from you but only honest behaviour and firmness in affairs.'[21] Derzhavin was certainly both firm and honest – so much so that he achieved the rare feat of being sacked by three successive sovereigns for his excessive candour.

Meanwhile, Derzhavin's new post was a hugely influential one in the semi-feudal government of Russia. A petition – a formal letter requesting promotion, funding or justice – was the principal form of interaction between the state and its citizens. Whether from a private citizen, noble or corporation, a petition would be approved by a governor, then by a governor-general, and then, with crisp banknotes changing hands at every stage, would make its way expensively to the desk of the secretary of petitions. He alone would decide whether to bring it to the Empress's personal attention or forward it to one of Russia's four chief ministries – Marine, Foreign Affairs, Education and Commerce. Derzhavin stood at the centre of a web of paper and patronage that governed the fate of fifty million people.

Immediately on his appointment Derzhavin followed the first principle of court life and remembered to reward his old friends and advance his young protégés. So he summoned the young Rezanov from the Admiralty to act as his private secretary. The twenty-six-year-old Rezanov was now ensconced in a small office in the Winter Palace, within yards of the empire's ultimate centre of power.

Like the Palace of Versailles, on which it was modelled, St Petersburg's Winter Palace was a small city in itself. With 1,050 rooms, 117 staircases, 1,886 doors and 1,945 windows, the place was a labyrinth.[22] Catherine ruled Russia from her apartments on the sunny south-eastern corner.* From her windows Catherine could look south across Palace Square towards Moscow, or east down Millionaya, St Petersburg's most fashionable street, where she could keep a watchful eye on the comings and goings of carriages at the mansions of her courtiers. Behind her apartments (rebuilt after a fire in 1837) is a staircase, now known as the Archive Staircase, which led up to the apartments of her current lover. The door could only be locked or unlocked from the inside.

The Empress habitually rose at six and lit her own fire. Her secretaries – led by Derzhavin – would arrive at eight and find her sitting alone, usually reading. Wearing a loose silk gown, she would receive advisers one by one until about eleven. Catherine held no council or collective discussions except at moments of national emergency. After she had dressed, the Empress often walked through the eight-room enfilade of her private apartments into the closest of her reception

---

* Today the suite houses the Hermitage Museum's collection of slightly bilious Poussins.

rooms, known as the Hall of the Chevalier Gardes, where privileged petitioners waited to present their cases to Derzhavin or to catch a glimpse of the Empress herself.

After a light lunch with between ten and twenty courtiers, usually including her secretary of petitions and visiting officers and ministers, the Empress would retire to her rooms to read or be read to. This was also known as 'the time of the favourite' or 'the time of mystery'. Government business was suspended, the door to the Archive Staircase would perhaps be unbolted, and the Empress's more personal needs were ministered to. 'I am doing the Empire a great favour by educating the young,' Catherine wrote archly to her old favourite Sergei Saltykov of her young lover Zubov.[23]

On winter afternoons she also liked to tinker with her collection of scientific instruments, including a 'small electrical machine' – a generator invented by the Bolognese Doctor Luigi Galvani – with which Catherine enjoyed electrocuting her servants. She also wrote political and philosophical tracts, producing essays for literary journals under the pseudonym Patrikei Pravdomyslov (a play on the Russian for 'right-thinking'). At five in the afternoon, 'I either go to the theatre or play [cards] or I gossip with the first people to arrive for dinner, which is over by eleven.'[24]

The shows were often of Catherine's own composition. She was an enthusiastic playwright, producing over thirty plays, several of which were made into operas. Her subjects ranged from tales of the witch Baba Yaga and other Russian folk stories to pseudo-medieval romances like *The Knight Orkideyevich* and allegorical pieces such as her ballet *Prejudice Overcome*, in which Minerva the Genius of Science conquers Ignorance and Superstition. The only opera her bumptious and militaristic son Paul enjoyed, however, was the battle scene in Manfredini's *Carlo Magno*.[25]

While the Empress and the more frivolous courtiers amused themselves with dangerous liaisons and amateur dramatics in one part of the palace, other corners of the great house buzzed with busy bureaucrats. The Ministers' Staircase, next to the annexe housing Catherine's art collection, linked a labyrinth of small offices on the second floor to the apartments of the Empress. This was the Office of Petitions over which Derzhavin – and Rezanov, as his *chef de cabinet* – ruled. The ministers' windows, as befitted humble functionaries, overlooked a courtyard. Rooms with a view were reserved for the Empress's ladies-in-waiting and the official lover, with whom Rezanov and his fellow scribes shared the second floor, the clamorous backdrop to the pageant of ambition and power that was the palace's life.

Location within the physical geography of the palace was a mirror of status. By that measure Zubov soon proved that he was a cut above the usual royal gigolo by leaving the modest apartments of the Empress' *cavaliere servante* and moving down into grander ones near Catherine's on the Palace's *piano nobile*. He also acquired his own wing of the Catherine Palace in Tsarskoye Selo, the imperial summer residence. Zubov also set about establishing his own private court, a motley confection of ambitious Russian aristocrats, foreign adventurers and court ladies attracted like flakes of glitter to the magnetism of his swelling wealth and power.

Nikolai Rezanov may not have glittered, but nonetheless the diligent young secretary caught Zubov's eye. Perhaps it was during one of the Empress's convivial staff lunches at the Winter Palace, or in the bustling upper floors of the palace, where distinctions between the court's worker bees and its social butterflies broke down in the rushed corridors. Doubtless Derzhavin, an intimate ally of the rising Zubov, commended his youthful protégé to his even more youthful patron. In any case, within a year of Rezanov's arrival at the Winter Palace Count Zubov had hired him away from Derzhavin's Office of Petitions to join his own growing household.

So what manner of man was Rezanov at this, the moment when he finally moved from the attics of the Winter Palace to take his own place on the court's crowded carousel of fortune? An energetic young bureaucrat, certainly. 'A dedicated scribbler',[26] good with numbers and ambitious. A man hard-working to the point of obsession: 'I have a headache from thinking that all my efforts are in vain; I wish I were not a loafer,'[27] Rezanov would write at the end of a life filled with furious activity. He knew how to make himself agreeable – at least to people he needed to conciliate. 'Rezanoff is a man . . . possessed of many amiable qualities,' according to the American Captain John D'Wolf, who travelled with him to California.[28] 'He was kind and affable to those around him and always ready to hear complaints and afford every redress in his power of grievances.' Rezanov's behaviour towards his subordinates was not always so charming – but that is a story for another chapter. At twenty-nine years old he was also still a bachelor. This, for a man of Rezanov's class and generation, was a measure of his social ambition rather than romantic failure. He was a man of good name but modest means. Wealthy heiresses often married poor aristocrats – but only successful ones, and Rezanov clearly judged his professional achievements too modest, as yet, to be cashed in on the marriage market.

Rezanov was loyal too, and eager to please. Certainly he pleased Derzhavin enough to earn a recommendation to Zubov. And beneath the sober exterior he was also a gambler. Leaving a safe job in the Office of Petitions to join Zubov's louche and corrupt court was a risky strategy, and not an entirely respectable one. Nonetheless, if fortune continued to favour the arrogant young favourite, his followers stood to reap large rewards. Yet in many ways Rezanov was also careful, and conservative. He would have no truck with political radicalism, for instance, and had stayed well away from Radishchev at the Treasury. And he was passionately patriotic – or at least he wrote of his patriotism often and at length. 'Love of country has made me spend all my energies,' he wrote later, 'I wish for nothing but the knowledge that I have been of some service to His Imperial Majesty.'[29] Rezanov's shipmates would report that he reduced the sailors to tears with his patriotic speeches, and wept himself as he drank to the Emperor's health. In later life Rezanov would come to see himself as an agent of Russia's greatness, a servant of the empire destined to bring glory and increase to his beloved Emperor. Sincere or not, a burning sense of duty to his sovereign was a central part of him – at least of the man he pretended to be.

It was at the glittering, venal court of Zubov that Rezanov met a man of a completely different world from his own who set his life on an utterly unexpected course. His name was Grigory Shelikhov, a millionaire fur trader, adventurer and explorer, known in St Petersburg society – with various overtones of sarcasm and envy – as the King of Siberia.

4

The King of Siberia

Their master has in him the same cruelty that we read of in the ancient
Spanish histories when he tries his sword and pistol on the unfortunate
Aleuts.[1]

Eric Laxman to Foreign Secretary Count Bezborodko

Had Grigory Ivanovich Shelikhov been of noble stock, or even at a
pinch a foreigner, he would doubtless have been recognized in his lifetime as one of the age's greatest explorers. But since he was the son of a
middling merchant from the backwater of Rylsk, near Kursk in central
Russia, Shelikhov's discoveries were tainted by the lowly motive of
commercial profit rather than the lofty scientific and imperial ambition
of gentlemen-explorers like Alexei Chirikov and Vitus Bering.

In the course of a tumultuous life Shelikhov became a millionaire,
the founder of Russia's first overseas colony and the most powerful man
in Siberia. But he never quite became respectable. He was like those
whom Englishmen of the time called nabobs – new men who had
enriched themselves in the colonies, men whose fortunes failed to mask
their primitive manners and a brutal way with subordinates. Like many
merchants Shelikhov arrived in Siberia as a young fortune-seeker.
Unlike most of his fellow adventurers, however, he had both a canny
way with money, a systematic mind and a burning ambition. 'His fiery
soul coveted not so much riches but glory. To him obstacles did not
exist,' wrote Ekaterina Avdeeva-Polevaya, the daughter of one of

Калумбы Росскіе презрѣвъ угрюмый рокъ,
Межъ льдами новый путъ отворятъ на Востокъ,
И наша досягнетъ въ Амери́ку Держава,
И во всѣ концы достигнетъ Россовъ слава

Frontispiece of Shelikov's memoirs of his voyage to Kodiak – with franciful 'sea dogs' to the left.

Shelikhov's business partners. 'He conquered all with his inflexible iron will; those around him labelled him "the Scorching Flame", for good reason.'[2]

Over fifteen years, first briefly as a fur trapper and then as a trader, Shelikhov built a powerful business empire that spanned north Asia from Irkutsk to Kamchatka. His first breakthrough came in 1763, when the newly-crowned Empress Catherine II abolished the state's monopoly on trade with China. Shelikhov would later have cause to regret Catherine's zeal for free markets, but initially at least the abolition sparked a boom in Chinese demand for Siberian furs that brought immense wealth to Shelikhov and his fellow Irkutsk fur barons.

Shelikhov's first recorded commercial partnership was with the trader Pavel Lebedev-Lastochkin,[3] a veteran Kurile navigator whom he met on a fur-trading trip to Kamchatka in 1774. By the next year the young Shelikhov had acquired enough cash and social standing – in eighteenth-century Irkutsk these were pretty much synonymous – to marry Natalia Alexeyevna Kozhevina,[4] daughter of a prominent clan of Okhotsk navigators and mapmakers. Shelikhov was twenty-eight, Natalia thirteen and a half.

It was an inspired match. Natalia was to prove every bit as formidable an explorer and administrator as her husband. That same year Shelikhov dispatched his first overseas fur expedition to the Kurile Islands. The ship he had built, the *Sviatitel' Nikolai,* was probably financed by Lebedev-Lastochkin and Natalia's dowry. It was crewed by shipmates and cronies of his new Okhotsk in-laws. The expedition was a high-risk venture: a decade previously four Russian expeditions had been massacred and their vessels burned by Aleuts angry at Russian inroads into their fur catch. But luckily for Shelikhov's fledgling business career, the ships returned unmolested and filled with pelts after a bumper season.

Shelikhov was joining a rush for the fur wealth of the north Pacific in which the world's maritime empires would soon take an intense interest. In 1763 the trapper Stepan Glotov ventured further than any of his predecessors and discovered Kodiak Island, just off the coast of the Alaskan peninsula. It was a key discovery because it was the first island found in the north Pacific with large stands of tall spruce trees suitable for planks, making Kodiak a vital staging post for shipbuilding and repairs. The following year the Empress Catherine sent her British-trained Admiral Vasiliy Chichagov to map the entire northern coast of Siberia as far as Kamchatka, an endeavour that was to take five years.

The British Royal Navy, always keenly interested in any maritime intelligence picked up by His Majesty's ambassador in St Petersburg, got wind of the supposedly secret expedition, possibly through Chichagov's English wife. London thought the matter important enough to send Lieutenant John Blankett to St Petersburg specifically to gather information on Russian Pacific navigation. The appearance of an English officer in her capital asking questions about Alaska spurred Catherine to take a keener interest in her Pacific backyard. In 1768 she dispatched another navy expedition,[5] this time to explore the coast of America with express instructions to scout out sites for future colonies.

Security evidently being none too tight at the Russian Admiralty, news of this second supposedly secret expedition soon reached Madrid. The Spanish government was understandably nervous at the Russians' probing at the fringes of their empire. Madrid therefore decided to reinforce its claim to the province of Nueva California* by founding a new settlement at the northernmost extremity of its New World possessions.[6] Thus it was in direct response to Russian ambitions that in 1776 the Spanish founded a new mission on the shores of a great natural harbour. They called it San Francisco, after the founder of the colony's dominant monastic order.

Russian attempts at keeping their discoveries secret, including publishing a deliberately inaccurate map of the north Pacific to throw their rivals off the scent, unfortunately succeeded in concealing vital information only from the Russians themselves. The industrious William Coxe, an Anglican priest who visited in St Petersburg in the 1770s as tutor to Lord Herbert, son of the Earl of Pembroke, collected various manuscripts of Russian travelogues as he travelled across Europe. The resulting *Account of the Russian Discoveries between Asia and America* included the Cossack Semyon Dezhnev's account of his passage through the Bering Strait in 1643 and was, to the Empress's extreme indignation, a far fuller record than anything the Russian Admiralty itself possessed.[7] It was published in London in 1780 and was keenly read by students, both amateur and professional, of Britain's expanding naval power.

Captain James Cook was already a celebrity in England as a result of his two voyages of discovery in the south Pacific. He had been the first European to make landfall in Hawaii, Australia and New Zealand. In 1778 he set out on a third expedition, his most ambitious yet, to explore the coast of Alaska and the Bering Strait. Cook's personal interest was a measure of how excited London's scientific, commercial and military circles were about the north Pacific, the last unexplored corner of the world's oceans.

---

* Later known as Alta California – roughly corresponding to modern California and parts of Arizona.

'A man of Oonalashka' as drawn by Cook's artist, John Webber.

Cook sailed up the craggy west coast of North America, mapping and naming geographical features as he went, and attempted unsuccessfully to pass through the Bering Strait to investigate the possibility of a passage between the Atlantic and the Pacific along the northern coast of Siberia. Prevented from sailing north by contrary winds and fog, Cook instead turned south to Hawaii and his rendezvous with death at the hands of an enraged native mob on the beach at Kealakekua Bay on St Valentine's Day, 1779. Cook's deputy Charles Clerke continued with the expedition without his chief,* sailing into the harbour of Petropavlovsk on Kamchatka in August 1779. The Russian authorities were deeply alarmed by his unexpected arrival – even more so when Clerke showed local officials the expedition's draft maps of the American coast, with English names attached to features long claimed as Russian.[8] Ingenuously, Clerke also allowed the Russian governor-general's

---

* Or rather almost entirely without his chief, for a few of Cook's bones were returned after his flesh had been eaten.

cartographers to copy his charts, which found their way to the Admiralty in St Petersburg and caused predictable consternation. Clerke himself was already gravely ill with tuberculosis picked up during a youthful spell in debtors' prison in London on his brother's behalf.[9] He died two weeks later, on his thirty-eighth birthday, and was buried in Petropavlovsk.*

Cook's third voyage of discovery had one wholly unexpected but revolutionary consequence. Officers and men from the HMS *Resolution* and *Discovery* had traded beads, copper trinkets and tobacco with natives in Cook Inlet in Alaska and the Aleutian Islands for the pelts of sea otters. These animals, five feet long and weighing up to seventy pounds, have the densest fur of any animal in the world. It is a deep rich brown, two inches thick and quite miraculously soft.[10] When Cook's ships docked at Canton, China's great trading entrepôt, the English were amazed to find that local merchants offered them one hundred Spanish dollars per pelt, nearly two years' salary for an ordinary seaman.[11] Lieutenant John Gore, the expedition's third commander, almost had a mutiny on his hands as the crews clamoured to return to the source of these pelts which the mandarins of Peking valued so highly. Conceived with high-minded scientific goals and partly funded by the millionaire naturalist Sir Joseph Banks, the main result of Cook's expedition was to spark a rush for the north Pacific's soft gold.

In Irkutsk news of the fantastic prices sea-otter pelts could command on the Canton market electrified Shelikhov. The time had come, he believed, for Russia – or at least a Russian – to claim America and the vast numbers of sea otters on her shores for the Tsar. And no Russian was better placed to do so, Shelikhov believed, than himself. In 1781 he embarked on what was to be the first of many trips to St Petersburg in search of money and patronage for a voyage of conquest and colonization in America.

Shelikhov's first investor was a Rylsk merchant and convicted embezzler named Mikhail Golikov. Golikov had recently been fined for

* The British Royal Navy erected a handsome granite monument to Clerke in 1914 which still stands by the esplanade at Petropavlovsk, overlooking a rusting fishing fleet and the sleek black hulls of Russia's nuclear missile submarines as they slip out of Avacha Bay.

attempting to smuggle cognac past Russian excise men in Riga and urgently needed to raise money. Shelikhov, evidently a formidable salesman, persuaded Golikov to gamble his last capital on the success of his American expedition.[12] The two men duly founded the North-East American Company, a slightly modernized version of the old Cossack joint-stock partnerships formed for a single voyage.[13] The new company was incorporated for ten years on the St Petersburg Stock Exchange. Another backer was Nikita Demidov, an aristocrat whose family had grown fantastically wealthy from the profits of iron smelting in the Urals. He was intrigued enough by Shelikhov's plan to contribute 50,000 rubles to the venture to plant a permanent Russian colony in America.[14]

Armed with Demidov and Golikov's gold,[15] Shelikhov again demonstrated his considerable powers of persuasion by assembling over 150 colonists willing to volunteer for his new colony on Kodiak. True, many of them were exiles and criminals with little to lose, but there were at least forty families among them, most with young children. One of the families was Shelikhov's own. Natalia Shelikhova, thought pregnant, nevertheless insisted on accompanying her husband on his voyage along with their two-year-old son Mikhail.* 'She wished to follow me everywhere and share all my trials,' wrote Shelikhov.[16] Two slightly older daughters were left behind in Irkutsk. Despite the fact that Shelikhov was now a man of property – on the eve of his voyage to Kodiak he owned shares in nine companies and fourteen ships and had sponsored twenty-one voyages – he was determined to found his new colony in person.

In the summer of 1783 the party made its way across 5,000 miles of Siberia from Irkutsk to the port of Okhotsk, where Shelikhov had commissioned three ships, the *Arkhangel Mikhail* (named for his infant son), the *Tri Svyatitelya* (*Three Hierarchs*) and the *Svyatitel' Simeon*. The colonists set sail on 16 August 1783 from the Urak River, near Okhotsk. The *Three Hierarchs*, with the Shelikhovs aboard, soon became separated from the other ships in fog and got as far as Medniy Island, 500

---

* He was the second of three Shelikhov sons named Mikhail, all of whom died in infancy.

miles to the north-east of Petropavlovsk on Kamchatka, before the end of the sailing season

Unlike the party of Vitus Bering, who mostly died of scurvy over the winter of 1741–2 on nearby Bering Island, Shelikhov's party survived the winter safely in bivouacs dug into the ground. Natalia gave birth to a baby girl named Avdotia.[*] In spring the now slightly enlarged party continued eastwards and rejoined the *Sv. Simeon* (the *Arkhangel Mikhail* was never heard from again). In a month they landed at Unalaska, site of an old Lebedev-Lastochkin Company settlement, and two months later they reached Kodiak Island itself.[17]

There are several, wildly differing, accounts of the two years Shelikhov spent on Kodiak. But they agree on one thing – the natives were none too pleased to see him and his colonists. The first group of Koniag leaders to come aboard the *Three Hierarchs* on 5 August 1794 was shocked and awed by an eclipse of the sun that serendipitously occurred while the chiefs were on the Russian ship. The omen was not, however, interpreted by the local shamans as a positive one. Within a week a native skirmishing party attacked Shelikhov's shore camp at the inlet he had named Three Hierarchs Bay.

According to a scurrilous account by Sergeant Miron Brityukov, a surgeon's assistant who later developed a deep hatred of Shelikhov and went to great lengths to blacken his former chief's name,[†] the Russians fought back and took several prisoners. Shelikhov personally tortured two of the captives for information (according to Brityukov), ordered a third speared to death and shot a fourth. Two more captives were summarily shot by Gerasim Izmailov, the ship's helmsman. Escaped Aleutian slaves – or possibly friendly natives from the Koniag village – brought more worrying news. The Koniags were massing on a nearby

---

[*] Avdotia grew up to be as forceful a character as her mother. Pavel Lebedev-Lastochkin wrote in 1787 that 'the girl Avdotia Grigoriyevna, "the American", is a great talker – you can see she began her life on the Islands'.

[†] Perhaps understandably. After he fired Brityukov during the return voyage from Kodiak in 1786, the notoriously tight-fisted Shelikhov deducted 370 rubles from his share of the profits for supplies consumed on the voyage, leaving him with just 47 rubles for two years' exertions.

headland, today known as Refuge Rock, apparently preparing for a major attack at dawn to wipe out the Russians.[18] Shelikhov, a modern man, promptly brought the latest technology to bear on the problem. He ordered the ships' five small cannon dragged into range of the cliffs and opened fire. Shelikhov later claimed that he fired at the rocks, not at the massed natives, and that his 128 men took 1,000 Koniags prisoner. Brityukov said that 500 natives were killed. Both versions seem equally far-fetched. Izmailov, when questioned by a commission of inquiry sent by St Petersburg in 1790, testified that Shelikhov and 'Russian workmen killed islanders, approximately one hundred and fifty or two hundred people, and that probably many more among them threw themselves off the promontory into the water out of fear'.[19]

Whatever the numbers, the massacre of Refuge Rock had important consequences: it brought an end to organized resistance to Russian rule by Aleut and Koniag natives, and heralded a century of shameless Russian exploitation. It also earned Shelikhov a reputation for blood-thirsty brutality which he was never to shake and which formed the basis for a distaste and distrust of merchants by the government that

'Man of Kodiak', a Koniag chief sketched by John Webber.

was to last until the end of Russian rule in America. Shelikhov spent the rest of his life talking up his colony as part of Russia's civilizing mission to the natives – partly to cover the original sin of its bloody birth, and partly to extract funds from the government.

There was, in Shelikhov's view, much to civilize. He found the Aleuts even more backward than native Siberians. Incest and polyandry were widely practised, and a special caste of boys was brought up as girls for the sexual amusement of tribal leaders. The Aleuts had no wheeled vehicles or writing. They were amazed by the concept of letters, which they called talking papers, and were convinced they whispered to their readers in a little voice when opened.[20]

Shelikhov and his wife took pains to baptize as many natives as they could. Shelikhov performed the rite himself on forty Koniags, there being no priest available, and both stood godparent to dozens of new 'converts'. They also set up a school, of sorts, for the natives – or specifically for the children of native chiefs, whom the Russians held hostage against their parents' good behaviour in a longhouse at Three Hierarchs Bay. He formally offered the Empress's protection to native chiefs who would swear loyalty to the crown, glossing over the fact that the threat they most needed protection from was probably Shelikhov himself.

Like Hernando Cortès at the other end of the north American continent two centuries earlier, Shelikhov quickly became adept at exploiting tribal feuds to divide and rule the Aleuts, a slave-owning society which used prisoners of war – known as *kalgi* – as unpaid labour. Shelikhov encouraged the Russian colonists to poach these with offers of better living conditions, creating a caste of Russian-owned slaves. Later complaints claim that Shelikhov regularly used these slaves as assassins to eliminate impertinent native leaders. The Russians called these captives *kaiurs,* from the Tatar word *gaiour*, or infidel,[21] tellingly exposing the old Siberian origins of the practice, when it was the Russians themselves who had been enslaved.

The Russians 'frequently quarrelled and fought with the natives and were on such bad terms with them that they never went to sleep without their arms ready loaded at their side', wrote English Captain George Dixon[22] – a former shipmate of Cook's – who visited the Aleutian

Islands in search of furs in 1787. But the Russian reign of terror was effective. Dixon was unable to find any natives to trade furs with because they were all too afraid of their Russian masters to go behind their backs. Dixon found the Tlingit tribes of the American mainland quite different, trading enthusiastically with all comers and, when the Russian showed up in the 1790s, refusing to pay tribute or give hostages.

Tlingits of Sitka Sound.

By spring 1786 Shelikhov had successfully subdued the natives of Kodiak, planted a permanent settlement on the island and founded several small redoubts – the maritime equivalent of Cossack *ostrogs* – on the north shore of Kodiak and on the nearby island of Afogniak. Shelikhov's men, led by the Cossack Konstantin Samoilov, liberally plied native settlements and canoes with their artillery. Satisfied with his work, Shelikhov set off for home on 23 May 1786 in the *Three Hierarchs,* leaving Evstrat Delarov, a Greek veteran of several Cossack fur-hunting voyages, in charge as his general manager.[23] Aboard were Shelikhov's wife and two children, a dozen mostly sick Russian colonists, including the already disgruntled Sergeant Brityukov, and almost

300,000 rubles' worth of sea-otter and other furs. A number of Alaska natives keen to see the wonders of Okhotsk formed the bulk of the crew, as well as at least twelve Aleut children, whose parents, according to Shelikhov, 'wanted them to learn the new Russian knowledge'.[24]

In early August they sighted the eastern shore of Kamchatka and made landfall near Bolshaya Rechka.* However, while Shelikhov and a small shore party were searching for supplies of fresh water and fish, a gale blew up. The *Three Hierarchs* dragged her anchor and was born helplessly southwards, with Natalia and the children on board. Shelikhov and his men made their way overland to Petropavlovsk and waited for the ship's return, but as winter set in he realized that the storm must have pushed the *Three Hierarchs* further south still, into the Sea of Okhotsk. Undaunted, he decided to strike out on foot across Kamchatka and through the lands of the Chukchi to rejoin his family at Okhotsk, arriving two and a half months later after a cross-country trek of over 1,200 miles.[25] Reunited with Natalia and his children, he rested only eight days in Okhotsk before setting out for the next gruelling leg of the journey to Yakutsk, where they spent only a day before pressing on to Irkutsk. Miraculously both the Shelikhov family and the native children appear to have survived this punishing journey.[26]

In Irkutsk Shelikhov found himself a celebrity – not least among his worried investors, who were beginning to fear that he would not return. From the proceeds of the Kodiak expedition the Shelikhovs bought themselves one of the largest timber houses in Irkutsk, complete with a separate 'barrack house' so that they could comply without inconvenience with the onerous duty of billeting soldiers, which was imposed on all members of the merchant class.[27] More importantly, Shelikhov presented his notes and maps to the governor, Ivan Yakobi (the same Yakobi who had once courted Maria Rezanova), and the two discussed how Shelikhov's new colony could become the foundation for a Russian Pacific empire.

Yakobi, a sixty-year-old widower and veteran of an embassy to China, as well as a hero of Potemkin's Crimean campaigns, was enthusiastic.

---

*   A strange name – it means in Russian 'Big Little River'.

Shelikhov's dream was to equip ships to trade furs and manufactures between Russia and Canton, Korea, India, the Philippines and United States, and to send thousands of colonists to occupy the wildernesses of north-western America. However such a scheme was possible, in Russia, only with the backing of the state. The reasons for this were primarily financial. The merchants of Irkutsk, or even the wealthy Demidovs, were good for financing single voyages, but, unlike in Britain or Holland, Russia's merchant class was neither wealthy nor bold enough to finance larger-scale longer-term ventures. Equally importantly, unlike Britain, Holland and even the fledgling United States, Russia had no system of maritime insurance. This made large ventures ruinous for their backers if they failed. Neither were there any state or private banks willing to lend significant capital to merchant adventurers. The aristocracy, with its vast collateral of land and serfs, had no problems running up vast debts with private bankers like Zubov's Scottish financier Baron Richard Sutherland. But lending-houses such as Sutherland's were not investment banks as much as glorified private high-interest mortgage lenders to the rich and spendthrift.

Shelikhov calculated that he needed a twenty-year loan of half a million rubles to expand his colony. Only the crown had the capital and the patience to offer that kind of credit. In November 1787 Yakobi forwarded Shelikhov's proposals to St Petersburg, with his enthusiastic personal recommendation.[28]

In theory the timing of Shelikhov's plan was perfect. Even before the publication of the account of Cook's *Third Voyage* in London in 1784, word was out that vast profits were to be made from sea-otter pelts in the northern Pacific. First to act was James Hanna, a British merchant based in Canton, who set out in spring 1785. Evidently not a believer in concealing his intentions, Hanna christened his brig the *Sea Otter*. Two more ships with robustly self-explanatory names – the *Experiment* and the *Captain Cook* – were being fitted out in the East India Company's port of Bombay to experiment with Captain Cook's newly-discovered fur grounds. By the next sailing season there were no fewer than six British ships from India and London – including two captained by Cook's former officers Nathaniel Porlock and George Dixon

– trading with natives for furs up and down the American coast. Their modus operandi was simple – travelling in pairs, the English would make a show of force by loosing off a few broadsides. Then, having impressed the natives with their firepower, they proceeded to barter manufactured goods for skins.

Europe's great powers had also begun probing the north Pacific with their navies. Clerke's unheralded arrival had been shock enough, but the last straw for St Petersburg was news in the summer of 1786 that a French navy squadron commanded by Jean François de Galaup, Comte de La Perouse, was also cruising the coast of Alaska. After offloading his furs at Canton at vast profit, La Perouse docked at Petropavlovsk in September 1787 and airily told his Russian hosts that he had claimed Lituya Bay in Alaska for France the previous August. By this time the Russian Empire was finally stirring. Catherine was sufficiently alarmed by Cook and La Perouse to authorize a major Russian naval expedition, the biggest and most ambitious yet, with the explicitly imperial objective of 'claiming that coast from [the] harbour of Nootka to the point where Chirikov's discovery [of 1742] begins as Possessions of the Russian State'.

The expedition, signed into existence by Catherine in December 1786, was to comprise no fewer than four ships-of-the-line, one transport, 639 crew and 34 officers. The Empress took a close personal interest in the provisioning and equipment of the squadron, checking details of the waterproof native-style parkas and woollen socks issued to the crew and insisting that a supply of lemons to fight scurvy be carried on board, as prescribed by Captain Cook. The commander, Captain of the First Rank Grigory Mulovsky, was ordered to destroy all shore installations built by foreigners but to treat the natives with 'kindness and forbearance'. The Russian Empire was now, in theory at least, finally in the business of asserting its empire in America by right of occupancy.

But it was not to be. War broke out with Sweden and Turkey in October 1787 as both powers sought – unsuccessfully – to reverse their losses in Catherine's earlier wars. Reluctantly, the Empress was forced to call off the Mulovsky expedition and redirect the ships to the Swedish campaign. So disappeared Russia's best chance of staking a claim to the Pacific coast of America from Alaska to California. *

In the wake of the cancellation of the Mulovsky armada, as a gesture towards her fledgling American empire the Empress ordered a series of numbered iron-and-brass 'possession plates' produced, each inscribed with a cross, a serial number and the legend *Zemlya Rossiskago Vladeniye* – 'Land Belonging to Russia'. These plates were distributed to Russian privateers to be buried in any new lands they discovered.[29] Their exact location was a state secret, and the intention was that they could be unearthed in the event of a later claim by a foreign power to prove the Russians had got there first. A single possession plate survives, dug up at St Michael's Redoubt just north of modern Sitka in 1934. The iron has almost rusted away, but the soldered brass words and cross still shine with the Empress's words.

Despite the abandonment of Mulovsky's expedition, the educated Russian public's imagination continued to be fired by the promise of Pacific conquests. In 1787 St Petersburg's Academy of Sciences produced a handsome map, more decorative than informative, of the north Pacific complete with pictures of a Russian, a native, a Chinaman and the god Hermes, with Bering's and Chirikov's voyages marked prominently on a rather vague rendition of the American coastline.[30] The time was ripe, Shelikhov calculated, for a public–private partnership to take over where the crown alone had failed.

The Shelikhovs set off for St Petersburg armed with their business plan in the new year of 1788, when the winter was coldest and the travelling fastest. Governor Yakobi, their self-appointed chief lobbyist, accompanied them. Arriving, they rented rooms in a fashionable quarter of town, complaining of the expense to their relatives back in Irkutsk. Shelikhov, after a visit to the capital's top tailors, began

---

* By the time Russia's claim was reasserted with the foundation of the colony of Fort Ross in Sonoma County, California, in 1812, both Spain and Britain had already established their own rival settlements on that coast. The crucial moment had passed.

energetically ingratiating himself with Demidov and Yakobi's friends and relations.

In late February 1788, after much lobbying and expensive palm-greasing, Shelikhov was finally received by the Empress at the Winter Palace to present and explain his petition. Shelikhov asked for a loan of 200,000 rubles (he had been talked down by Yakobi from his startling original request for half a million), together with a hundred soldiers, the right to buy native slaves and bring conquered natives under the Russian crown, as well as the right to hire and indenture Russians. Most crucially, he asked for a state-guaranteed monopoly on trade with Russian America.

Shelikhov was undoubtedly brave, energetic and charismatic – yet the audience did not go well. The Empress, for one, did not trust these would-be American entrepreneurs. Shelikhov's partner Mikhail Golikov was a convicted smuggler and excise evader, and his brother Ivan Golikov also owed the exchequer large sums in taxes. Thanks to the denunciation written by Brityukov the previous year, Shelikhov himself had already acquired his reputation as a butcher of natives. With so many foreigners sniffing around the north Pacific, Russia's fragile dominion depended on its ability to command the loyalty of the local population, which was being alienated and abused, Catherine suspected, by the barbarities of bucaneers like Shelikhov.

'In the North-East Ocean all commercial enterprises – one might better call them larcenous enterprises – are in the hands of Shelikhov, whose men are drawn from the ranks of the most depraved thieves and bandits of Irkutsk,' the distinguished explorer Eric Laxman wrote to Foreign Secretary Count Bezborodko. 'Their master has in him the same cruelty that we read of in the ancient Spanish histories when he tries his sword and pistol on the unfortunate Aleuts.'[31]

On the question of trading exclusivity, Shelikhov and Golikov had the backing of Yakobi and the Ministry of Commerce. But rival Irkutsk merchants who stood to lose their livelihoods in the event of a North-Eastern Company monopoly were, understandably enough, adamantly opposed. These merchants wielded plenty of influence of their own in the capital, thanks to their deep pockets. They now mobilized their friends at court to oppose Shelikhov's plans to seize the whole American trade for himself. The Empress also had ideological objections. A close reader of the Scottish political economist Adam Smith, she disliked monopolies in principle. Furthermore she was deeply alarmed by the revolutionary republicanism of the newborn United States of America. The Empress wanted no troublesome American colonists of her own.

A copy of Shelikhov's petition with the Empress's annotations survives in the papers of her private secretary Alexander Khrapovitsky. 'Exclusive concession is not at all compatible with the principle of the Empress for the elimination of every kind of monopoly,' was one of thirteen points Catherine wrote in the margin.[32] She found the idea of ownership of swathes of the Pacific 'ludicrous'[33] and pointed out that 'it is one thing to trade, quite a different thing to take possession'. As for the money, 'The proposed loan resembles the proposal of a man who wants to train an elephant to speak in thirty years,' wrote the Empress, a noted wit. 'When asked why such a long term he replies "the elephant may die, I may die, the person who lent me the money may die".'[34]

As a rather underwhelming consolation prize, Catherine gave Shelikhov a gold medal and silver sword. But even as she refused the merchant petitioner his monopoly, Catherine had nonetheless decided to keep a closer eye on Russia's interests in the north Pacific. That summer she sent a small expedition at government expense – nothing on the scale of the Mulovsky fleet, but rather a more modest mapping and surveying effort led by Joseph Billings, a British captain in Russian service who had also sailed under Cook, with another Englishman, Martin Sauer, as his cartographer.[35] It was Governor Yakobi who suffered the worst fallout from the failed bid. He was accused of bribe-taking – probably by allies of Lebedev-Lastochkin and other Irkutsk merchants opposed to the Shelikhov–Golikov monopoly – and was dismissed from his post.

The indefatigable Shelikhov did not allow these setbacks to throw him off his stride. If a monopoly was out of the question, Shelikhov would make sure several different companies were involved in the Pacific trade – all of them, however, would be controlled by himself or his associates.[36]

Shelikhov founded and registered a slew of companies on the St Petersburg Stock Exchange – a renewed North-Eastern Company, nominally head-quartered in Kodiak, the Predtechensky Company based in the Pribilov Islands and, later, the Unalaska and Kurile Companies.

He also took a leaf out of Catherine's book and hired talented foreign adventurers to build his American empire. He tried unsuccessfully to recruit the brilliant young naval engineer Samuel Bentham, brother of the philosopher Jeremy, when Sam was in Irkutsk in the summer of 1788 (see notes for the remarkable Russian careers of the Bentham brothers, two of the great original minds of the age).[37] But he had more luck with one of the talented English shipbuilders that Bentham had brought to Siberia with him, James Shields.

The launch of James Shields's ship, the *Phoenix*, in Voskresensky Bay, 1794.

Shields was the father of a technological breakthrough crucial to the future of Russian America: locally built modern sea-going ships capable of navigating the open ocean. Hitherto Russian navigators from Bering to Shelikhov had sailed in glorified Cossack riverboats, with shallow draughts and primitive rigging. The first of Shields' new deep-keeled, ballasted, swift-sailing, three-decked ships was a barque christened the *North-Eastern Eagle*, built at the Shelikhov-Golikov Company wharves at Okhotsk in 1790.[38] The following year the *Eagle*, under Shields, assaulted and took the island of Unalaska for the North-Eastern Company. The Englishman had a genius for improvisation. At Voskresensky Harbour on the Alaskan mainland in 1794 he created a kind of tar from pine resin and made cordage from vines. 'Although the Company has a shortage of iron and pitch . . . a solid paste from spruce pitch, flammable brimstone, ochre, and whale fat was made,' Natalia Shelikhova reported to Platon Zubov – though she attributed this invention to her husband.[39] The resulting three-masted, twenty-four-gun frigate *Phoenix* was the Company's first serious warship and by far the most powerful naval vessel then on the Pacific.* The Company now had the maritime clout it needed to resupply and protect colonies 11,000 miles from Okhotsk.[40]

By that time the north Pacific had suddenly become the unlikely focus of the world's attention and nearly triggered a major European war. The series of events that was to bring the Alaskan coast international fame had been set in train in late 1785 when the Comte de La Perouse, en route to the northern Pacific, made a brief victualling stop in Spanish-ruled Chile. News that France was planning to stake a claim to the regions to the north of New Spain caused alarm in Madrid (just as La Perouse's visit to Petropavlovsk generated deep consternation in St Petersburg the following year).

One by one, the powers of Europe proceeded to assert their own claims to the remote coastline. As we have seen, news of Perouse's voyage pushed Catherine the Great into ordering the Mulovsky expedition. News of Russia's threatening preparations, reported by a worried Spanish Ambassador to his chiefs in Madrid, stung the Spanish into action in their turn. The viceroy of New Spain, Manuel Antonio Flores, was ordered to dispatch an expedition from Spain's new naval base at

---

* She was also to be Shields' grave: she went down, with Shields aboard, during a storm off Afognak bay in 1799.

San Blas on the Pacific coast of Mexico* to repel the expected Russian invaders. The viceroy instructed Naval Lieutenant Esteban José Martinez to occupy Nootka Sound, at the foot of modern-day Vancouver Island, to build a settlement and fort, and to make it clear to all interlopers that the coast was Spanish territory.

On arriving at Nootka Sound in May 1789 Martinez found no Russians – the Mulovsky expedition having been cancelled the previous winter – but he did find one British and two American merchantmen moored in the natural harbour. Rashly, Martinez boarded the British ship *Iphigenia* and arrested its captain, William Douglas, at pistol-point before confiscating his vessel and her valuable cargo in the name of His Most Catholic Majesty. Martinez then seized two more English merchantmen, the *Princess Royal* and the *Argonaut*, as well as two American ships as they arrived at Nootka. The simmering international crisis was further inflamed when Martinez shot Callicum, a local Indian chief who had come aboard the *Argonaut* to protest against a settlement named Fort San Miguel which the Spanish were busy erecting on his ancestral land. Martinez ended his summer's work by taking the *Princess Royal* and the *Argonaut* as prizes of war and sailing them, along with their imprisoned captains and crews, to San Blas under armed escort.

When word of these acts of aggression against British trading vessels reached London there was predictable outrage. The government of William Pitt the Younger, receiving no apology or recompense from Madrid, began preparing a naval assault on Spain. A full-scale fleet was equipped at enormous cost – there was even talk of imposing an income tax to fund the war [41] – but in one of the few examples in history of an arms race with a happy outcome, Spain folded first. In October 1790 Madrid signed the humiliating Nootka Convention, which effectively ceded Spain's exclusive claims to the American coast north of the Colombia River to Britain. The British Admiralty, relieved to have preserved its fleet from war,† sent Captain George

---

*   Near modern-day Guadalajara.
†   Many of the ships built for the would-be Nootka war would eventually fight the Spanish at Trafalgar in 1805.

Vancouver (yet another of Cook's former officers) to the American Pacific coast to establish symbolic control in a very English way – to map it and name it.[42]

Shelikhov's reaction to the presence of foreigners in waters he considered to be Russian was belligerent. He urged his new general manager Alexander Baranov – of whom we will hear much more later – to take matters into his own hands. When Baranov reported that an English merchantman – the *Phoenix,* a namesake of Shields' new frigate – had called at Kodiak, Shelikhov wrote back to upbraid him for not seizing her and murdering the crew. Local Koniags could be blamed for the attack, he suggested. Baranov was insulted. He had enjoyed getting drunk with Hugh Moore, the *Phoenix*'s captain, and even accepted a young Indian servant boy called Richard from him as a present. 'The indoor theories of hot-headed intelligences do not always turn out in practice' was Baranov's sarcastic comment to a fellow Company manager. To Shelikhov himself he wrote, 'Your rebuke astonished me. It shows greed and cupidity without limit. How can you imagine that I would break the rules of hospitality? Instead of being civilized I would be called a barbarian.'[43]

Shelikhov's suggestion showed that the Empress's reservations were well founded – for all his airs he remained part-pirate. But Shelikhov had not given up hope of respectability, and of a royal charter. By 1793 it was clear that the time was ripe to renew his efforts at court. Five years before, when he had first tried to interest Catherine in his idea of a state-backed monopoly, the north Pacific had been a remote backwater, of interest only to the hardiest and most enterprising fur traders. Now, it seemed, the whole world was squabbling over the coastline. It was time, Shelikhov judged, to win the Pacific Great Game once and for all for Russia. He consulted his old backer, Urals iron king Nikita Demidov, on tactics. Demidov knew exactly the man who could persuade the Empress to change her mind: her darling and lover, Prince Platon Zubov.

5

A Nabob in St Petersburg

The Russian Columbus here buried crossed the seas and discovered
unknown shores. Seeing everything on earth is corrupt, he set his sail for
the Heavenly Ocean.

Gavriil Derzhavin, epitaph on Grigory Shelikhov's tomb, 1795

Men of ambition wishing to make their way in the world in the summer
of 1793 knew that the fastest path to wealth and advancement lay
through the favour of the Empress's most shameless and most powerful
lover. Zubov's court was a theatre of greed and ambition where favours
were traded, government appointments were bought and sold and
gossip was swapped. Nikolai Rezanov was one of its gatekeepers.

At his newly acquired apartments at Tsarskoye Selo, the twenty-
four-year-old Zubov behaved in the manner of a minor monarch. The
Polish Prince Adam Czartoryski, who attended Zubov's audiences in
the hope of recovering ancestral property confiscated by Catherine,
observed that they resembled nothing so much as 'the levees of the
mistresses of French kings'.[1] From the early morning anxious suppli-
cants rolled up to the palace leaving their carriages parked three deep in
the drive, as if outside a theatre. At eleven the folding doors of the
noble *Reichsfürst*'s private apartments were flung open, and Zubov
emerged from his bedroom in a flowing silk dressing gown.

As the full pageant of the prince's morning toilet was enacted by a
team of hairdressers and powder-puff-wielding valets, the suppliants

were shown in one by one. The most important of the petitioners were conducted in by the prince's principal secretary Andrea Altesti, a Sicilian-Greek scandalmonger and blackmailer. Rezanov, Altesti's deputy, was assigned to deal with lesser favour-seekers. Zubov heard them out while brushing his long hair in front of a mirror, his back to the visitor, and dismissed or approved their petitions with a casual nod or a grunt. Occasionally Zubov would address remarks to his buffoon or to a pet monkey, which sprang from head to head in the dressing room, dislodging minor avalanches of powder. Specially favoured guests were allowed to make him coffee. In this manner Zubov received princes, marshals, generals and the highest state officials, all seeking his favour and, through him, the ear of the Empress.[*]

'This Zeubov has the character of being an active little man,' wrote John Parkinson, a visiting Oxford don who met the prince at Tsarskoye Selo. 'Who however behaves with no small degree of hauteur, which in a person from the dust is no small offence.'[2]

Potemkin was dead. The new young favourite was 'flying high despite his years; he is minister of all parts of the administration', wrote the veteran courtier and former royal lover Pyotr Zavadovsky despairingly in July 1793.[3] Zubov surpassed Potemkin, Zavadovsky and indeed all the Empress's other lovers in the scale of his greed and corruption. Like Grigory Orlov before him, he shamelessly promoted his brothers to positions of power in the army – but unlike the talented Orlovs, the Zubovs were mediocrities. The ageing Empress loaded him with over 10,000 serfs, lands in Russia and Poland and marvellous jewels. Zubov shamelessly further added to his fortune by charging his petitioners heavily for his favours. Only the oldest and most venerable of Russia's grandees dared to challenge the new favourite. 'I do not like the tone of your orders, your addresses, your letters or your flunkeys,' was General Alexander Suvorov's acid comment to the young upstart. But Suvorov

---

[*] A century later these petitioners' spiritual (and doubtless actual) descendants would flock, similarly present-laden, to the apartments of the Siberian self-described holy man Grigory Rasputin, who, like Zubov, gained a powerful hold over the Tsarina and whose word decided appointments and favour.

was Russia's most decorated soldier and one of the few men who could get away with snubbing the Empress's beloved.[4]

Zubov's court became a magnet for adventurers, rogues and opportunists. Then, as now, Russia attracted foreigners fleeing failure or seeking adventure, advancement, quick fortunes in a land of infinite opportunity where they could be free of their background, disgrace or both. The enormous wealth of Russia's aristocracy was concentrated in St Petersburg, where the demands of the court and society forced them to flaunt and fritter it away in constant display. The Russian capital was a stage for a vastly expensive architectural and social spectacle, the Dubai of its age. Soldiers and builders as well as practitioners of softer arts from dancing masters and tailors to fly-by-night financiers and theatrical impresarios flocked to the land of open-handed patronage, where wealth exceeded taste by a considerable margin.

The Empress Catherine led the way, with her international essay competitions and her correspondence with the great public intellectuals of Europe, effectively declaring her country a vast laboratory for those who wished to experiment with their own versions of mankind's future. She recruited Saxon farmers en masse to revolutionize the farming of the Volga.* She hired French sculptors and painters and Italian architects to build her palaces and the cities of Potemkin's New Russia. Potemkin had hired bright young idealists like the Benthams. But Zubov's circle attracted a more dubious kind of adventurer. Zubov's secretary Altesti, for instance, obtained his entrée into Russian society by striking up a friendship – later cemented, the gossip went, by homosexual blackmail – with the Russian ambassador to Constantinople.[5] Altesti was a skilful spymaster and collector of what Russians today call *kompromat* – compromising information – on powerful courtiers. Catherine herself had tried to dismiss Altesti for embezzlement, only to be talked into reinstating him by Zubov.†

---

* Even after Stalin had them exiled to Kazakhstan as a potential fifth column, the Volga Germans' villages were famously orderly, sober and well kept.

† Catherine's son Paul, on acceding to the throne in 1796, immediately threw Altesti into solitary confinement in a dungeon in Kiev, where he would keep his secrets to himself. The old rogue was freed in 1801 and deported to Italy in a closed carriage,

Another Zubov crony was the half-Spanish half-Irish adventurer Don Giuseppe de Ribas-y-Boyons. De Ribas had attached himself to Alexei Orlov, commander of Catherine's Mediterranean fleet, in Livorno in 1770. He fought against the Turks at the battle of Cesme and became Orlov's trusted envoy, ferrying messages to his brother Grigory, Catherine's first favourite, in St Petersburg. By the time of Zubov's ascent in 1789 de Ribas was a brigadier general married to one of Catherine's ladies-in-waiting and the Empress was godmother to his daughters. He was as much in imperial favour as any foreigner could hope to be. Formally, it was Zubov who became de Ribas's patron, but it was the wily old adventurer de Ribas who doubtless gave the younger man a masterclass on ways to take advantage of his position. In 1794, with Zubov's backing, de Ribas was sent south to found a great new city on the recently conquered Black Sea coast. Catherine named it Odessa, and it became known as the St Petersburg of the south; its main street was named Deribaska, the Russified version of its founder's name.[6]

Somehow Rezanov did not seem to quite fit in among this dubious crew. For one, unlike his flamboyant colleagues at the court of Zubov, Rezanov did not get rich in the prince's service. In 1795, after four years in the household, Rezanov was still writing to his relatives asking for money. Was he too honest, too cautious? He does not come across as a priggish type, and his shipmates would later report Rezanov joking about how well he knew the art of lining his own pockets. More likely, Rezanov was just calculating. He was not a flash foreign fortune-hunter; he was a Russian-born nobleman of good family, a former officer and judge, a sober man good with figures whom great men like Derzhavin and Zubov trusted to organize their affairs. Rezanov's was a longer game. He was using his years in the service of Zubov to study the mechanisms of power up close: how advancement could be wheedled, lobbied and bought.

---

like a bacillus. He lived to be almost one hundred in comfortable retirement in his native Sicily.

Grigory Shelikhov arrived at Zubov's court in the autumn of 1793 through a convoluted chain of acquaintance. Nikita Demidov introduced him to his friend Alexander Zherebtsov, Zubov's brother-in-law, who brought him to the prince's notice. Shelikhov was already well known in the capital as a wealthy lobbyist reputed to pay top ruble for any political capital going. The Siberian nabob, with his dreams of fortune and empire and most importantly his ready cash, was most welcome in the infamous ante-chamber of Zubov's wing at Tsarskoye Selo.

Shelikhov had hit on a brand new angle to persuade the crown to support his colony. Leaving the idea of a monopoly aside for the time being, he instead planned to petition the government to send a fresh group of skilled colonists to Kodiak – and also a priest. The clergyman would be maintained in the colony at Company expense to educate and baptize the natives. Brityukov's old complaints of brutality – despite a positive report from Captain Billings – still tainted the Company. What better insurance against future calumny, Shelikhov calculated, than a priest to look after the education of the natives and hopefully knock a bit of the fear of God into the rowdy colonists? A party of settlers, family men and craftsmen would also help transform Kodiak from a community of plunderers into a permanent outpost of empire.

Perhaps it was the Nootka Sound incident that finally convinced the Empress that her American colonies were worth fighting for. Certainly Zubov's support played a key role.[7] But whatever the reasons, Catherine's attitude had changed completely since Shelikhov's unsuccessful lobbying of 1788. In a letter to the new governor-general of Siberia in late 1793 the Empress confirmed that Shelikhov's plans were 'wholly useful to the State' and wished him well in his endeavours. The recently-formed Holy Synod quickly fell into line, falling over itself to echo the sovereign's new-found enthusiasm for Shelikhov's American Company. Metropolitan Gavriil decreed that not one but eight monks would be sent, selected from the monastery of Valaam, renowned for its strictness and probity. The priestly party was to be headed by thirty-two-year-old Archimandrite Iosaf, a biblical scholar and missionary.[8] By January 1794 Shelikhov's petition had been formally granted, the Empress's letters of support drafted, and the group of monks was ready to depart on its long journey to the New World. [9]

Then, as now, political favours in Russia were a tradable currency: power was turned into money and vice versa. Zubov had expended political capital to further the interests of Shelikhov at court; now it was time for Zubov to collect the debt, probably in the form of an interest in the booming and highly profitable fur trade. But who would the prince send to supervise his new interests in Siberia? Who better than Rezanov, his trusted man of affairs, who must have played a key role in the winter's political manoeuvrings. Rezanov was duly appointed Zubov's personal representative, charged with taking royal letters from the Empress as well as 'personal dispatches' from Zubov to Ivan Pil, successor to the disgraced Governor Yakobi. Zubov also instructed Rezanov to report on how his orders had been fulfilled and, crucially, to ensure that they were, which made him more than a mere messenger.[10] Rezanov was to be dispatched to the Siberian town where his father had spent the last thirty years as emissary and plenipotentiary of Russia's most powerful man.

Shelikhov set out from St Petersburg for Irkutsk with his group of monks on 22 January 1794. Midwinter, when rivers were frozen hard and sleighs could make fast progress over snow-covered ground, was Russia's travelling season. In spring and autumn roads became impassable because of mud and rivers dangerous because of floating ice. The monks carried with them a collection of prayer books, crosses and a mobile altar to bring the word of God to the Empress's newest subjects and comfort to themselves. They also took a brand new icon of the Virgin and Child painted at Valaam in the modern taste.*

Rezanov set off a little later, probably in late spring; he never caught up with Shelikhov's fast-moving party. Zubov was famous for fitting his

---

* Unusually the Mother of God wears a red robe, as opposed to the traditional blue, and the background is a jaunty azure rather than gold. The icon still hangs in the Church of the Holy Resurrection on Kodiak Island, blank-faced and inscrutable as all icons are, her golden halo understandably battered by its extraordinary travels. A heavy iron penitential cross that Herman, one of the monks, wore under his robes all his life is also preserved in the church as a relic.

household servants out in liveries finer than many noblemen's own best clothes. It is likely, then, that Rezanov, a trusted secretary and the prince's personal representative, was sent off to Siberia in some style. Several of Catherine's long-distance coaches of the period are preserved in the Kremlin Armoury and at Tsarskoye Selo. The latest fashion was for travelling carriages of English design, with high axles and two pairs of enormous wheels six or even eight feet in diameter. The bigger the wheel, the less likely it was to get stuck in potholes. City carriages were sprung on steel arcs, but the springs of the time were fragile, and rugged long-distance vehicles were usually suspended from stout leather straps instead. Luggage, in heavy leather cases, was strapped to the roof. Armed footmen would have perched behind while Rezanov's valet and secretary sat inside. Four or six horses, ridden by Cossack postilions and changed up to three times a day, could haul such a carriage up to thirty miles between dawn and dusk.

A round-trip to Siberia entailed an absence of a year at least, most of it spent on the road. On the evidence of contemporary inventories of gentlemen travellers' luggage, Rezanov would have taken trunk-loads of summer and winter clothes, boots and shoes, bed linen, tents and furs, wet-weather gear of greased cotton canvas, storm lamps and candles, dry provisions and cognac, a medicine chest, a travelling library, a canteen of cutlery and pewter plates, a writing desk and in all likelihood a small arsenal of fowling pieces and pistols, dress swords and cutlasses.

Thus equipped, Rezanov's little expedition bowled along the beaten earth of the Royal Road from St Petersburg to Moscow reserved for government traffic and persons of quality bearing special passports. Lesser subjects trundled and plodded with their carts and nags along the road's rutted verges. At Moscow they joined the stream of humanity and merchant carts on the *Trakt*, the great road which linked European Russia to Siberia – not really a road at all in the modern sense, but a wide swathe of sandy tracks criss-crossing the flat farmland and pasture, dotted with clutches of peasant *izbas* – log houses – clustering around the stumpy bell towers of churches.

Rezanov had travelled before, of course, on manoeuvres with the

Izmailovsky Guards, but it was here on the *Trakt*, as it passed through the Volga towns of Nizhny Novgorod and Kazan and on into the emptiness of the steppes, that the bustle and traffic of Russia proper fell away and Rezanov first tasted the true vastness of his own country. Even today, without the dust and the bedbugs and the saddle sores, the thieves and the smell of horse dung and unwashed bodies and the clouds of horseflies, travelling by road across Siberia is almost hypnotic. The monotony of the landscape lulls you into an almost metaphysical state where you become acutely aware of your own insignificance. You are a mere human speck, crawling slowly across the face of a great and barely-changing land.

Shelikhov, with at least two months' head start, had made excellent speed. By early May he was already in Irkutsk, with the monks lodged at his newly built house, where their gravity and piety made a great impression on Shelikhov's six surviving children. Shelikhov's aura of celebrity had never been stronger now that he was in the favour of the Empress.[11] Irkutsk's new governor Ivan Pil' issued an order echoing Catherine's *ukaz* that Shelikhov's venture was 'useful to the State'.[12] Pil also hurried to fulfil Catherine's command to round up some colonists for the New World from 'among the exiles' – convicts for whom Irkutsk was an open prison to which they had been condemned for life. What Pil's criteria were in recruiting men for Kodiak is not clear, but judging from the reluctant colonists' later attempts to escape from, murder and rebel against their masters in the Company, it's safe to say that the governor did not send his best people. Shelikhov had requested 'skilled artisans', and in this at least his request was honoured – Pil selected eleven convict blacksmiths, coppersmiths, carpenters and their families to live out the rest of their lives in the Kodiak colony.

Russia's roads, such as they were, stopped at Irkutsk. Beyond lay rivers and trackless taiga – subarctic scrubland dotted with marshes and

---

* Pil was a former governor of Pskov and Rezanov's old superior in the Pskov bureaucracy. Pil became an enthusiastic supporter of the Russian American Company; he also befriended and helped Rezanov's old Treasury colleague Alexander Radishchev after he was exiled to Irkutsk for his radical 1790 *Journey from Petersburg to Moscow*.

small trees. Shelikhov, his little party reprovisioned and shriven, set out in the early summer of 1794 as great sheets of ice on Lake Baikal buckled and the floes jostled down the River Lena as it flowed northwards to Yakutsk, 800 miles to the north. The monks and their reluctant new flock, along with their equipment and supplies, were piled onto a flotilla of flat river barges of a design pioneered by the first Cossack settlers of Siberia. For two weeks the barges were punted, rowed and towed by sailing skiff up the 450-mile-long western shore of Baikal, the party camping every night on stony beaches on the edge of the forest. Local tribesmen – Buryats, then Lamuts and Tungus – would shyly emerge as the smoke of the party's cooking fires curled into the spring air to trade game for chunks of the Russians' tea bricks and hard bread. A two-day portage then brought them to the head of the Kirenga River, a tributary of the Lena, and from there the boatmen left the little flotilla to drift with the river's flow. They were carried north at the river's sedate pace, fending off flat islands in the stream and the riverbanks with long poles. They were in the hands of nature now, the land and the water pushing them forward relentlessly, further into the wild.

The forest gave way to taiga. The barges drifted past the felt yurts of the Yakuts, watched impassively by grazing oxen. After three weeks on the river, the summer days lengthened as they approached the Arctic Circle. The hypnotic monotony of the landscape was broken by the sight of the trading post of Yakutsk, founded as a Cossack *ostrog* a century and a half before and now boasting 362 Russian log houses and five wooden churches surrounded by an untidy huddle of native huts. Shelikhov and his party now transferred their baggage and provisions to packhorses for the two-month overland crossing to Okhotsk, since no wheeled vehicles could negotiate the Stanovoi Mountains. The Yakuts provided the horses as a kind of tax to the empire. Caravans of a hundred or a hundred and fifty horses were usual, with one Yakut leading a team of ten horses tied nose to tail. Goods thus transported to Okhotsk could increase in value up to forty times, such was the expense and difficulty of carrying them overland. In 1805 a *pood* – thirty-four pounds – of flour cost half a ruble at Irkutsk, one and a half at Yakutsk, ten rubles at Okhotsk and forty rubles in Kamchatka.[13]

The trail to Okhotsk wandered between royal post houses, dripping lonely huts manned by solitary Cossacks and their native concubines. Novice Herman reported that bears attacked the party in the Stanovoi foothills. They would have met mounted Cossack postmen coming in the opposite direction carrying leather post cases with one, two or three pigeon feathers fixed to the seal to signify the urgency of the mail. These official letters, written in the counting houses of Okhotsk or the chancelleries of St Petersburg, would be carefully placed for the night out of harm's way in special alcoves on the brick stoves while their bearers ate the government's soup and swapped news of floods and landslides, spreading bogs and Yakut war parties.

On 13 July, after seven months on the road, they reached the end of the world – or so it must have seemed as they trudged into Okhotsk. This ramshackle port on the Pacific coast was considered grim, violent and desperate even by the standards of contemporary Siberians. A few plank-built houses clustered around the remains of wharves built by Vitus Bering in 1742; a pine-built quay knocked together for Joseph Billings's expedition to the north Pacific in 1790 was already disintegrating.* Okhotsk was the ultimate, in every sense, wild eastern town. It was a place with no government officials and populated by fugitives, chancers and trappers so wild and tough that they seemed barely human to civilized men. The Shelikhov-Golikov Company headquarters offered the only half-decent accommodation and kept a good table for visiting managers, Company and naval officers. The taverns were a different story. Hunters and settlers came from a thousand miles around to swap the season's furs for gold, which they lost no time spending on vodka, native whores and gluttonous feasting.

'Most of the men who come here are depraved, drunk, violent and

---

* Okhotsk was also a poor harbour. Like Bering, Billings had built two ships on arrival in Okhotsk, but one had become stranded in surf while trying to cross a sandbar at the entrance to the shallow bay and stuck fast. Unable to move her and unable to continue without the supplies she carried, Billings had the brand new ship unloaded and burned to the waterline to recover the valuable iron used in her construction. Symbolically the ship that was burned had been christened the *Good Intentions*; only her sister ship the *Glory of Russia* made it out to the open sea.

corrupted,' Rezanov wrote later from Russian America. Out in the colonies 'hardship and work makes them behave more quietly and there are few opportunities to get drunk. But returning to Okhotsk they resume the old life again and in a few weeks spend on drink and debauch the products of four years' labour. Then they return to America. What example can we expect from them?' Some would bring their half-breed children to Okhotsk 'and after spending all money on drink leave them to shift for themselves. Being unused to the climate and the food, lacking clothes and exposed to smallpox, they die.'[14]

Archimandrite Iosaf was predictably shocked by the licence and brawling of Okhotsk's hard-drinking citizens. The unctuous Shelikhov was quick to assure him – entirely falsely – that conditions in the Company's outposts were far more regular. Indeed when Shelikhov stretched out in his pine-walled office after enjoying the Company's *banya*, or bathhouse, he would have read desperate and wheedling letters which awaited him from his chief manager on Kodiak, Alexander Baranov. They spoke of scurvy ravaging the settlements and of hostile natives enraged by the murdering and raping indulged in by rival trappers from the Lebedev-Lastochkin Company. Baranov pleaded for iron, for food, for his personal supplies of vodka to be sent, for sailcloth and money and trade goods. None of this grim litany of want and disaster was shared with Iosaf and his convict charges. Instead, Shelikhov fired off one of his customarily breezy letters to introduce the new settlers. 'You will lay out the convict settlement with taste and due regard for beauty of construction so that when visits are made by foreign ships it may appear more like a town than a village, and that the Russians in America may live in a neat and orderly way, not as in Okhotsk, in squalor and misery,' Shelikhov instructed his long-suffering manager, adding, high-handedly, that 'your work will be reviewed and discussed at the Imperial court'.

In August 1794 Shelikhov sent the party off in two Company-built brigs, a new *Three Hierarchs* named for the ship that had carried him and Natalia to Kodiak and back the previous decade, as well as an older boat, the *Svyataya Ekaterina*. In total there were 183 souls on board: the 52 settlers and 10 priests, together with 121 new hunters recruited from the stews of Okhotsk and a handful of natives. Shelikhov, encouraging the illusion of the high moral and intellectual tone of the colony, sent out books for Kodiak's school on 'classical, historical, mathematical moral and economic' topics.[15] He also sent seeds, with detailed instructions on planting, as well as dogs, rabbits, goats, pigs, two pairs of cattle and a mare and foal.*

The two ships reached Kodiak on 24 September but struck rocks at the entrance to St Paul's Harbour, so the passengers had to struggle ashore through the surf from their foundering ships. After this inauspicious start, things became considerably worse. The priests discovered the church, the school and indeed the town about which Shelikhov had spoken so enthusiastically did not, in fact, exist. Instead of a well-ordered settlement at Kodiak they found a collection of mean barracks, no candles and barely any food or shelter.

The general manager's house was the only decent building in the settlement. In 1788 the Spanish Captain de Haro found the house 'hung with Chinese paper, with a large mirror, pictures of saints and well-painted and rich beds'.[16] The rest of the settlers lived far less well. Baranov was able to offer the new arrivals accommodation only in communal barracks where the Russian settlers lived in sin with their native concubines. Iosaf and his priests preferred to camp in a lean-to on the beach, where they gathered clams for food while the colony's workers caroused drunkenly with native women in their crowded and stinking quarters. Daily services were held by the beleaguered monks in the lee of an upturned boat on the beach.[17]

The convict settlers found they didn't like Kodiak much either. Within a month Baranov got word that some of the newly arrived exiles were plotting to plunder the Company warehouse, seize a ship and sail home. The only detail that the would-be rebels were still debating was whether to cut Baranov's throat before they left or not. The manager had the plotters rounded up and soundly whipped, then sent the ringleaders in irons to distant outposts.

---

* Shelikhov's exalted ambitions for stockbreeding and agriculture would end up sacrificed to the more pressing demands of hunger: of all the animals on board, only the dogs escaped being eaten by that winter's end.

The priests did not, at least, plot to kill Baranov, but they nonetheless turned out to be nearly as big a nuisance as the convicts. The monks constantly complained to the general manager of the colonists' drunkenness, licentiousness and their cruelty to the natives. Baranov attempted to placate Iosaf with a personal pledge of 1,500 rubles of his own money – ten years' wages for an ordinary seaman – to build a church at Kodiak named for the Holy Resurrection.[18] Construction began on 21 November 1794,* but Shelikhov's idea to send priests to Russian America would become a terrible liability for Baranov, and for the Company, for decades to come.

---

* The church still stands today, much rebuilt, across the road from the old Company log-built storehouse.

6

To China

> This is a true desert – you will shudder to look at these bare hills with no vegetation with icy peaks or these forests as thick as reeds . . . Sometimes the silence is so absolute that one is afraid to wake the wilderness with the sound of one's voice.
>
> Ivan Goncharov, author of *Oblomov*, on crossing Siberia, 1855[1]

Rezanov's fine coach rolled into Irkutsk in early August 1794. Garbled accounts of a powerful messenger en route from the capital had been circulating for some weeks before he actually appeared. 'I have heard recently that there is a rumour in town that [Captain] Billings tattled on you to Her Majesty saying that you cheated Her in that you asked for a group of people [to go to America] for no reason,' wrote Natalia Shelikhova to her husband in Okhotsk on 5 August. 'Billings said he saw that you have nothing in America and that you made up everything and that you lied to Her Majesty, having made up things in your own mind. They say that Her Majesty became angry and sent a courier to bring you back from the road and take you to St Petersburg in chains. It is said the courier passed by in secret, and no one knows about him.'[2]

The truth was fortunately far less worrying. Rezanov and Shelikhov had in fact been corresponding furiously all year – between May and July Natalia Shelikhova mentions that she has forwarded at least four of Rezanov's letters. The letters themselves do not survive, but it is clear that Zubov's emissary and the head of Siberia's largest business had much of mutual interest to discuss. More important for Rezanov personally was the prospect of seeing his father, probably for the first time in his adult life.

Pyotr Rezanov had left to take up his post in Siberia in 1767, when his son Nikolai was just three years old. He had been appointed a judge at the civil court of Irkutsk, having satisfied the two major qualifying criteria, an ability to read and the possession of noble blood. By 1785 Pyotr had risen to the rank of collegiate councillor, the equivalent of a full colonel, and was the head of his own bench, the region's equity court responsible for settling civil disputes.

That year, however, the older Rezanov got mixed up in a scandal that was to taint his reputation for ever. The convoluted details are described in Irkutsk's surviving court records. According to a complaint of 22 January 1785, one Shirayev, a (presumably former) serf from Ustyug and worker at an Irkutsk glass factory, claimed his employer, the Moscow merchant Ivan Savelyev, had promised him 292 rubles, 33 and a quarter kopecks more than he had actually been paid for his work. The case was transferred to Rezanov's court, and rather than fight the claim Savelyev chose to settle, depositing the disputed amount with the court. But the money – about two year's wages for a working man – disappeared from the court's strongbox. An investigation by the local criminal court was launched. One suspects that presiding Judges Vedenyapin and Maltsev had axes to grind against Rezanov for reasons now lost to history. In any case Rezanov, as head of the equity court, was ruled to be legally responsible for the missing cash and, insultingly, was banned from leaving Irkutsk for the duration of the investigation of the theft.[3]

It is highly doubtful that Pyotr Rezanov himself was the culprit. He earned 2,000 rubles a year and lived modestly in the Parish of St Procopius in a house with just three stoves, served by only two housemaids and a stable boy. In order to close the case, however, Rezanov chose to return the money to Savelyev, almost certainly from his own pocket. But Savelyev was no longer in town, and his Irkutsk man of affairs was, in Judge Rezanov's opinion, 'untrustworthy because of his un-sober lifestyle'. Eventually, in 1787, Rezanov sent the gold by courier to Savelyev in Krasnoyarsk, but it took him a further five years to clear his name, obtaining a formal exoneration from the Senate in St

Petersburg only in 1793 – probably with his son Nikolai's help. This Dombey and Son-like legal nightmare drained the old judge, who died in 1794, soon after the arrival of his son in Irkutsk. As Nikolai was to find out for himself when he took over Shelikhov's business empire, the political intrigues of Irkutsk could be every bit as vicious as those of the capital, the passions higher even as the stakes were lower.

Irkutsk was the last outpost of Russian civilization before the true wilderness. By Siberian standards it was a well established town, boasting forty churches, a stone cathedral and a handsome governor's mansion, the neoclassical columns of its façade hewn from whole Siberian pines. The prominent citizens of Irkutsk, an eccentric collection of exiled nobles, merchants, frontiersmen-made-good and reformed criminals, marooned in their sea of forest, clung fiercely to their respectability and their brief history. But in reality it was a town on the make, a place where the class distinctions of St Petersburg faded and the merchants were the kings. The arrival of such a prominent personage as Rezanov – titular emissary of the Empress, actual emissary of her all-powerful favourite and the son, to boot, of a prominent Irkutsk judge, generated considerable excitement. Grigory Shelikhov hurried home from Okhotsk to greet Rezanov, arriving some time in early autumn to welcome the distinguished guest.

The Shelikhovs spared no effort or expense in entertaining the young nobleman. Shelikhov may have been a self-made millionaire and a ruthless operator who did not shy from using violence to impose his will on natives and rivals. But he was socially ambitious and keen to acquire the polish and graces of noble rank. He also needed to win over Rezanov for political reasons. The showman Shelikhov had told a number of lies when describing the Kodiak settlement to anyone who would listen in the capital – including Zubov – and would need powerful friends to protect his name when Iosaf and his colleagues eventually reported the shabby truth of the colonies' disorder.

But Shelikhov had not prospered in the lawless and violent world of Siberian commerce by being a bad judge of men. It's clear from his later writings that Rezanov was charmed and impressed by Shelikhov in equal measure. Furthermore, the two men had much in common, despite the differences in their social rank. Certainly both saw in the wide wilderness the promise of fortune, adventure and greatness. Rezanov, from his teenage years in the Guards to his brief career at court, had spent his life in a series of institutions governed by protocol and birthright. Now, in Siberia on the first independent journey of his life, he found himself in a world where tough, clever men like Shelikhov could rise above their station by bending nature to their will. Rezanov was a child of the Enlightenment. Here before him in Irkutsk, on the tables from which he ate and the roofs under which he slept, was arrayed the ample evidence of wealth that could be won if reason and order could be applied to exploit the apparently endless bounty of nature.

Shelikhov lost no time in introducing Rezanov to the intricacies of the Siberian fur trade. They toured the Shelikhov-Golikov Company's tanneries, warehouses, counting-houses, exchanges, armouries and the chancellery, where bearded prospectors, fur caps in hand, signed up for service in the Company by scratching a shaky X on their contracts. As the Siberian winter closed in on Irkutsk, Shelikhov prepared to dispatch convoys of furs in special closed sleighs under armed guard to the great annual trade fair at the entrepôt of Kiakhta, which had resumed the previous winter after being closed for seven years on the orders of the Emperor of China.

A view of Kiakhta, 1799.

The tiny Inner Mongolian frontier town of Khiatka was the only trading post where Russians could legally offer their wares for sale to Chinese merchants. China was the world's largest market for fur, while Russia was fast becoming China's largest market for the dried herb both countries called *chai* – tea – which over the last thirty years had gone from a fashionable beverage for the rich to a staple drink of nearly all social classes. By the 1780s a million cases of tea were coming across the border every year. Khiatka was therefore the heart of the Shelikhov–Golikov empire, of Irkutsk's trading wealth and of all Russia's Asian commerce.

For centuries both Russia and China had viewed the great Eurasian steppes with deep suspicion. Violent wandering nomads from Central Asia had raided east as well as west, and had plagued the Celestial Empire since the First Dynastic Period, 2,000 years before the birth of Christ. Of China's four great borderlands – Tibet, Sinkiang (known to the Russians as Turkestan), Manchuria and Mongolia – it was Mongolia which was always the most volatile and vulnerable. As the Mongol and Tatar empires crumbled and Russian Cossacks began to push eastwards in the sixteenth century, Muscovy put out tentative feelers towards its great southern neighbour. The Cossack Ivashko Petlin of Tobolsk became Russia's first emissary to the court of Peking in 1618. Ming officials assumed that he was a tribute-bringer from a hitherto unknown pale-skinned northern tribe and put Petlin up in a special guesthouse for such missions run by the Imperial Board of Rites. The following year Petlin reported to the court of Tsar Mikhail Romanov on the enormousness of the Emperor's palace and the Great Wall. He was not believed.[*]

As Russia expanded steadily across north Asia it was clear that the two empires were destined to become rivals.[4] Cossack raiding parties were rapidly encroaching on native Siberian peoples who had been

---

[*] Petlin's account, however, was republished in 1625 by the English cleric Samuel Purchas in the fourteenth volume of his bestselling compendium of travelogues *Purchas his Pilgrimage: or Relations of the World and the Religions Observed in all Ages and Places Discovr'd, from ye Creation unto this Presente*. It caught the eye of John Milton, who describes Adam's vision of 'Paquin of the Sinaean kings' and, as contemporary typography has it, the 'Ruffian Kfar in Mofcow' in Book XI of *Paradise Lost,* line 390.

Chinese tribute-payers for hundreds of years. And in China itself a series of peasant revolts and weakening Ming power allowed a new, warlike dynasty from Manchuria to seize power in Peking in 1644. The new Qing dynasty, also known as the Manchus, with their power base in the northern marches of the empire, were naturally more sensitive to the encroachment of the Russians on their historic homelands. Diplomatic relations of a sort were established with the Qing through a Muslim merchant, Setkul Ablin of Bukhara, who delivered polite letters from Peter the Great's father, Tsar Alexei Mikhailovich, to the Emperor of China during his fur-trading visits to Peking.

In 1670 the Manchus were forced to take notice of their upstart neighbours when Cossacks established an *ostrog* at Albazin on the Amur River, the Chinese empire's only natural northern boundary. The Cossack *voyevoda*, or leader, underestimating his opponent's strength, even provocatively wrote to the Chinese emperor suggesting he accept the suzerainty of the Tsar.[5*] At least one Amur native leader defected to the Russians, was baptized, and received a princely title from Muscovy by way of reward. In 1683 a punitive Manchu force of 3,000 was eventually sent north to demolish the upstart *ostrog*. It was barely a skirmishing party by Chinese standards – the Ming had maintained a permanent garrison of one million men guarding the Great Wall. Nevertheless it took the Chinese three years and two sieges before the Cossacks were finally forced out of the Amur River basin, Siberia's natural link to the Pacific. The Russians were not to return to the Amur until the middle of the nineteenth century.

To avoid further conflict, Asia's two great land empires needed to define a commonly agreed border. Peter the Great sent his childhood friend Fyodor Golovin to the Qing emperor in Peking with a guard of 500 musketeers and 1,400 Cossacks to negotiate a lasting peace. A treaty was drawn up with the help of two Jesuits fluent in Chinese and was signed in the frontier town of Nerchinsk in 1689. Monumental stones carved in Latin, Manchu, Chinese and Russian would mark the

---

* The Chinese translators were baffled by this concept and concluded that the Russians were confused because they 'do not have the benefit of Chinese education and culture'.

mutually agreed key border points. Crucially for the Russians, the Chinese had agreed to trade – though only at a single spot, the tiny settlement of Kiakhta on the steppes of northern Mongolia. 'The mutual trade at Kiakhta does not benefit China, but because the Great Emperor loves all human beings he sympathizes with your little people who are poor and miserable, and because your Senate has appealed to His Celestial Majesty He has agreed to approve of the petition,'[6] read the preamble in Manchu.* But for all the Manchus' high-handed bluster it was the first treaty ever to be signed by China which treated a foreign power as an equal rather than as a vassal.

'Two towns quickly arose upon the site appointed as an entrepôt and place of barter,' wrote Charles William Vane, Marquis of Londonderry, who visited the border in the 1830s.

> The one, Russian, was called Kiakhta, from the name of the little river which bathed its walls; the other, Chinese, was known by the appellation of Maimachine, which signifies 'the town of sales and purchase.' These two towns were separated only by an esplanade of small extent; on one side, to the north, appeared a gate of European architecture, a Russian guard and sentinels; on the other was seen one of those fantastical edifices which the Chinese erect at the entrance of their towns, having its walls covered with grotesque sculptures, inscriptions and paintings in gaudy colours. At Kiakhta regular streets are formed of those neat houses that compose the provincial towns in European Russia and near the vast storehouses belonging to the [Russian] American Company . . . behind them rise the cupolas and bells of several churches. At Maimachine the streets, gloomy and narrow, are formed by walls with no windows in them.'[7]

---

* Later scholars have noted that this and similar passages unflattering to the Russians were, not altogether surprisingly, omitted in the Latin version drafted by the Jesuit Fathers François Gerbillon and Thomas Pereira and signed by Golovin. No one noticed at the time, however, because the Jesuits were the only men present able to read both versions. Nor were any Chinese mandarins present – the journey could only be made on horseback, and since this was considered beneath the dignity of senior Chinese officials, they sent their scribes instead.

By late December 1794 the Siberian rivers were well frozen, and Shelikhov set off for Kiakhta for the traditional Sino-Russian winter trading fair. His party was carried south across the ice of Lake Baikal by fast three-horse troika, pounding across the powder snow as the passengers huddled under blankets of sable. The southern shore of Baikal is fringed with steep cliffs, now pierced by the tunnels and bridges of the Trans-Siberian Railway. In the south-east corner of the lake they subside to the lakeside, and the road snakes down to Ulan-Ude, tribal capital of the Buryat, the only Siberian people who knew how to write and forge iron when the Russians conquered them two centuries before. South of Ulan Ude the woodlands of Siberia give way to rolling grassland, then finally open steppe. In summer crossing northern Mongolia on horseback is mesmerizing. The land is so open that a day's travel appears not to change one's place in it at all, while underfoot an apparently infinite number of tiny gerbils scramble into their holes at the sound of a horse's hooves, making the ground tremble and seethe at the periphery of one's vision. The skies on this high plateau are a deep midnight blue; they seem as big as the world. In midwinter these steppes are an endless, featureless desert of snow.

We have no direct evidence that Rezanov accompanied Shelikhov to Kiakhta, but it seems likely that he did. There are no letters, or records of letters, between the two men for the winter of 1794–5 so they either broke off the furious correspondence that they had been carrying on all year or Shelikhov took his curious young protégé with him to the winter fair. In later letters Rezanov speaks of Kiakhta's prices and merchants with a familiarity that suggests that he saw it at first hand.

Kiakhta would have been Rezanov's first glimpse of Asia. The trading post still moved to the medieval rhythms of the Silk Road. The Chinese town was enclosed with high mud-brick walls and guarded by Chinese serf soldiers with long queues and halberds. In the Chinese trading rows were warehouses full of paper, lanterns, gunpowder, candles, brass lamps, nankeen cotton cloth, silk and of course tea. In the Russian town were pungent rows of carefully tanned sable, fox, mink, ermine, sea otter, marten, beaver, wolf, squirrel, hare and lynx. In the smoky fug of the Russian merchants' tea houses the great merchants down from

Irkutsk drank rough vodka with their employees and rivals and listened to the grumbles of the traders. By 1794 they would certainly have heard complaints about how the English were undercutting the Kiakhta trade by shipping Pacific furs direct to Canton.

Rezanov was a worldly modern man, brought up on the shores of the Baltic. His visit to Irkutsk and Kiakhta seems to have convinced him that the ancient land routes of Asia were inefficient and archaic. Sea trade, not land trade, was the future. The germ of the idea that was to dominate the rest of Rezanov's life was formed during the winter he spent on the Silk Road. If the Dutch could trade with Japan at Nagasaki and the English with China at Canton, why should Russia, the largest empire in Asia, not also trade across the Pacific – or, for that matter, dominate that Pacific trade?

Certainly trade with Japan had recently been a topic of much debate at court. At Tsarskoye Selo in 1791 Rezanov must have seen and perhaps even spoken to a most unusual vistor. The Japanese merchant Daikokuya Kōdayū had been shipwrecked on the Aleutian Islands eight years before, and was seeking the Empress's permission to mount an expedition to his homeland. Kōdayū, desperate to return home, had offered to help the Russians break the Dutch monopoly on trade with the hermit kingdom of Japan.

Catherine duly approved a trading expedition headed by the Finnish–Swedish Captain Adam Laxman.* Laxman landed at Hokkaido, the northernmost of the Japanese home islands, in 1792, but found the Japanese suspicious and disinclined to trade in any way with anyone but the Dutch. Laxman returned to St Petersburg empty-handed except for a passport from the Japanese authorities for a single further Russian ship to visit in the future. This document would play a fateful role in Rezanov's life.[8]

If Rezanov's thoughts were beginning to hum with visions of a grand Pacific triangle trade between Russia, the Alaskan colonies and Japan, then Shelikhov too was doing some strategizing of his own. In Rezanov he had found a clever, noble, well-connected political fixer in the capital

---

* Son of the explorer Eric Laxman who had so disapproved of Shelikhov.

to promote his interests at court. Shelikhov decided the time had come to bind the well-connected young nobleman to his house and join their fortunes more permanently. Anna Grigoriyevna Shelikhova, third of the Shelikhovs' twelve children, was fourteen and a half years old in January 1795, a year older than her mother had been when she wed Shelikhov. Rezanov was, at thirty-two, already an ageing bachelor. For a man of rank like Rezanov the match was technically a mésalliance. But perhaps his months in the freebooting world of Siberia had sown a healthy respect for the merchant class into which Shelikhov now proposed he marry. Moreover, Russia's class system was, even at the end of the eighteenth century, far less rigid than that of Western Europe. Russia's wealthiest aristocrat Nikolai Petrovich Sheremetev would soon push propriety to its very limits by marrying Praskovya Kovaleva, known as the Pearl, one of the serf actresses from his personal theatre troupe. Marriage to the daughter of the merchant King of Siberia, then, was by no means social suicide for Nikolai Rezanov.

It helped, of course, that Anna Shelikhova was staggeringly rich. Not only did she bring with her a hefty dowry, but she was also one of the heiresses to a company which had turned over three million rubles in the previous decade at a time when the entire budget of the Russian state was around forty million rubles a year. Trade wealth was admittedly not quite the thing in St Petersburg society, but the fabulously wealthy Demidov clan had completed the journey from blacksmiths to senior nobility inside a century without stigma. And as Rezanov was to argue – perhaps a little defensively – in coming years the modern world's greatest and most vigorous empires like Britain were rising on commerce, while those who snobbishly disdained it, like Spain, were wilting before the white heat of trade.

This was an age where marriage, even among the peasantry, was first and foremost a property transaction and very rarely a love match. Rezanov seems to have been lucky in achieving both. He wrote of the happiness of his marriage to Anna, 'my gentle angel',[9] and was, his contemporaries remarked, quite indecently distraught when she died in childbirth seven years later.

Their wedding marked the union of two worlds: not only of

aristocrat and merchant, but of an older, traditional Russia and a newer, westernized one, the provinces and the capital. Anna would leave the pre-Petrine world of Irkutsk for a new life among the powdered wigs and accented French of St Petersburg. We have few details of the Rezanov–Shelikhova wedding other than that it was considered a great and lavish affair. But other contemporary accounts of Siberian weddings show that they were deeply steeped in the Asiatic traditions of the Russian heartland. Rezanov would have appeared at the gate of his father-in-law's house in a new red Russian tunic and soft boots, while his bride, in a high *kokoshnik* headdress and heavy veil, would have prostrated herself in front of him in the yard. The tradition was for the groom to offer his bride a lock of his hair; she would hand him a bowl of bread and salt with bowed head. In merchant families well into the nineteenth century the bride's father would also strike his daughter with a specially made whip, pronouncing the words, 'By these blows you, daughter, know the power of your father. Now instead of me, your husband will teach you with this lash.'[10] The whip would be ceremonially passed from father to son-in-law. Shelikhov, a stern paterfamilias, certainly beat his wife and children (Natalia wrote about it in her letters), and it is not hard to imagine him fulfilling this time-honoured part of the ceremony. In any case, a three-day bout of general feasting, with barrels of vodka, was the norm, at which the local merchants would drink themselves insensible. Rezanov, for all his book-learning and foreign ideas, was marrying back into the Asiatic Russia of his grandfathers.

7

Empire Builder

Your son-in-law is not such a fool as you describe him.
Nikita Demidov to Natalia Shelikhova, 10 December 1795[1]

In eighteenth-century Russia all businesses were family businesses. With his marriage to Anna Shelikhova, Rezanov had become a de facto partner in one of Russia's biggest and most powerful trading houses. Fur, of course, was at the heart of the Shelikhov-Golikov Company's business, but as the largest logistics network in Siberia, the Company also controlled a vast general trade stretching nearly halfway across the world. Natalia Shelikhova's correspondence mentions whale baleen transported to Tomsk, walrus tusk brought from Yakutsk, frozen mammoth fur gathered on the northern Lena, Chinese plain cotton fabric, waxed paper and fireworks from Kiakhta, and even red millet brought from Turkey in scarlet leather sacks.[2]

Natalia Shelikhova was in many ways the keystone of the operation. She was family matriarch, manager of the Company's main office in Irkutsk and chief liaison with that city's fractious merchants during her husband's long absences. Company correspondence shows that Grigory was travelling for more than half of every year between 1788 and 1795. Supervising shipbuilding in Okhotsk, keeping his ear to the ground in the taverns of Kiakhta, showing a leg in the salons of St Petersburg, Shelikhov pushed the Company's expansion in every possible quarter. But it was Natalia, with her ledgers, keys and scales, who kept the whole vast operation going on a daily basis. The Irkutsk merchants and her sons-in-law would address her and refer to her in their letters as *matushka* – little mother – a respectful term reserved for priests' wives and the Empress. Natalia was in fact just thirty-three at the time of her daughter's marriage in January 1795. Rezanov was just a year younger than his mother-in-law.

Natalia was not merely a caretaker; she took decisions affecting tens of thousands of rubles. 'I have been told that in Moscow these commodities are dearer, but I thought that it would be better to catch a titmouse at home than to await a crane in a field,' she wrote to her husband in the summer of 1794 after disposing of thousands of furs in Irkutsk rather than sending them west.[3] She also chose and hired most Company employees. One Vasiliy Solodenkin signed a contract written in Natalia's own hand that pledged him to 'behave in a proper manner as an honest man and not drink alcohol'.[4] Tellingly, even Nikita Demidov, the family's most important patron and financier, addressed his letters to 'Grigory Ivanovich and Natalia Alexeyevna Shelikhov', a highly unusual double form of address in a world where business was usually a man-to-man affair.

The Shelikhovs' relationship was close, if stormy and sometimes violent. 'Believe me, my heart, I cannot forget you, day or night,' Natalia wrote to her husband in 1792. 'I can forget you only when I go into a deep sleep. I pray to God that you will come back to us soon. I myself often see you in my sleep: you were scolding me and beating me.'[5] Her every letter contains touching updates on their children's health. 'I know not what to do to protect little Vanya from the smallpox, it is roaming our land full of wrath at little children.' Ivan succumbed to the disease in 1777 aged six months. Of the Shelikhovs' twelve children, only five survived to adulthood.

But even this endless cycle of pregnancy, life-threatening childbirth and infant mortality did not stop Natalia from keeping herself attractive and pursuing the latest fashions. 'Gracious Sire, Dear Friend, Grigory Ivanovich,' she wrote to her husband in St Petersburg in March 1793. 'We with our daughters ask you to deign to buy good and fashionable hats for our heads like those that are worn there; two strings of best pearls, good quality that would be seemly. And a pretty snuffbox for myself.' She also asked for Italian printed silk and ostrich feathers. Even distant Siberia was following the fashion for large ostrich-feather hats set by Georgiana, Duchess of Devonshire, the previous season in London. Anna Shelikhova would probably have been wearing her grand new hat and pearls the first time Rezanov set eyes on her when he arrived in town.

Rezanov and his young bride set off for St Petersburg soon after their wedding. He had left the capital less than a year before, a promising courtier of middling means, a talented and well connected man with powerful friends for sure, but nonetheless still a servant to the capricious favourite of an ageing empress. He returned one of the heirs to Siberia's greatest fortune, a gentleman of means who no longer had to take orders from anyone – not even from Zubov himself. Rezanov installed Anna in a new house on the fashionable Liteiny Prospekt – number 24, not far from the Field of Mars.[6] They were, by Rezanov's account, happy. 'Eight years of our marriage gave me a taste of all the happiness of this life, as though its loss will poison all the rest of my life,' he wrote after Anna's death.[7]

Rezanov busied himself with Company business, working to build the vast edifice of contacts and bribes that would be required to secure imperial patronage for the further expansion of his father-in-law's business. Naturally his first port of call would have been on Prince Zubov – still Rezanov's employer in name, at least – who could be relied on to take a keen interest in any scheme likely to increase his fortune at no effort to himself. His old family friend and patron Derzhavin would be another. Derzhavin was now a senator and would shortly become head of the powerful Ministry of Commerce. But Rezanov was not to remain a mere lobbyist for the Company for long. In July 1795 grim news came from Irkutsk. Grigory Shelikhov had been stricken by some kind of poisoning. Anna, and possibly Rezanov too, rushed back to Irkutsk to be at his bedside.

Shelikhov was in agony for three weeks before he died. He 'has had extraordinary pain in the stomach and such an inflammation that he, in order to stop the fire for just a moment swallowed whole platefuls of ice', wrote one Irkutsk acquaintance.[8] Typhoid, a widespread disease in the insanitary towns of eighteenth-century Russia, produced similar symptoms, but typhoid's most visible symptom was red abdominal splotches recognizable to those familiar with the disease. It usually killed within days, whereas Shelikhov lingered for weeks. Shelikhov frequently exposed himself to various diseases, both local and exotic, in his capacity as a patron of various Irkutsk Church-run hospitals, which he often visited. He also imported and handled foreign goods, most of them preserved or tanned. It is conceivable that he contracted a form of anthrax from animal hides. He also often ate foreign foods sent to him as gifts.

But Shelikhov also had dangerous enemies. He was the wealthiest merchant in the fiercely competitive Siberian fur business, and had become so by ruthlessly cutting other operators out of rich otter-hunting grounds and hiring away their best people. This was reason enough for unscrupulous rivals to wish him dead. Shelikhov had also been accused more than once of unfair dealing. Only the previous autumn one associate had accused him of seizing some personal effects and 2,000 (or 200, according to conflicting accounts) fur-seal pelts arriving as part of a cargo in Okhotsk.[9] Certainly lesser merchants would murder each other for less. Whether Shelikhov was poisoned or not, his death exposed the extreme fragility of his business empire – indeed of any business in Russia whose strength lay not in the legal protection of the state but in the support of important patrons and the personal connections of its owners. Shelikhov, knowing he was on his deathbed, realized the vulnerability of his wife and heirs and drafted a long, heartfelt appeal to the Empress to protect their interests, which he dictated to his younger daughter on 30 June 1795.

In Your mercy that You have as a Mother, forgive me that I dared to bother the Sacred Person of Your Imperial Highness in the hope that, from Your good heart, Your protection may be requested for my wife and my children. Almost three days have passed since I have started to suffer from a cruel disease which gnaws at me. If I die my wife and children will remain orphans, possibly harassed because they will be bothered by relatives who desperately want my property, which I gained by my own work . . . Possibly ill-willed people will exert their forces using various means in order to put my descendants in disarray in order to acquire my vast trading places in Siberia and on the Eastern Sea [the north Pacific]. In consideration of this and in the matter that my wife, who followed me in my sea voyage for the acquisition of property and who helped me in the upbringing of my children and in maintaining my house and who deserves my full confidence, she with my children, but no one else, should have possession of my property, which is in trading and hunting areas under the American Company.[10]

Shelikhov finally expired on 20 July 1795; he was forty-eight years old. Just eight days later Natalia's nine-month-old daughter Elizaveta also died, of an apparently unrelated illness. In addition to this double bereavement, Natalia was seven months pregnant. But the greed of her Irkutsk neighbours, business partners, friends and enemies gave her little time to mourn. The Shelikhovs had five surviving daughters but only one son, Vasiliy, who was just four years old. Natalia's last child would be another son, named Grigory after his dead father, but given that three sons named Mikhail had already died, the Shelikhov inheritance was on shaky ground.[*]

Natalia lodged her claim to her husband's business empire at the Irkutsk Probate Court almost immediately, on the evidence of Shelikhov's explicitly-worded will. But just as Shelikhov had predicted when he dictated the petition to the Empress, local rivals attacked his suddenly vulnerable company. Several minor shareholders challenged the terms of the will. Debtors to the Company refused to settle accounts. Anonymous gossips circulated rumours that Natalia had poisoned her husband. Natalia, doughty as she was, needed energetic male kinsmen to defend her interests in Irkutsk and some political traction in St Petersburg to push through her inheritance rights to the Company.

Rezanov could at this point have made several choices. With his father-in-law dead and plenty of money in the bank, he could have distanced himself from the legacy of the roguish Shelikhov and settled down into the life of an idle and prosperous St Petersburg aristocrat. Natalia Shelikhova's other son-in-law, who had married Anna's younger sister Avdotia at the age of eleven, was Mikhail Matveyevich Buldakov, a merchant from the northern town of Velikiy Ustyug and one of

---

[*] In fact Grigory Grigoriyevich Shelikhov also died at the age of four, in 1799.

Russia's largest fur retailers. In most ways Buldakov was a far more appropriate leader for the Company than Rezanov. He was closer in class and background to the Shelikhovs, and indeed Natalia seems to have trusted him more than the aristocratic and educated Rezanov with his alien metropolitan airs. Buldakov was also a correspondent member of the Academy of Sciences and a man of solid intelligence. But Rezanov chose otherwise. In place of a Siberian family business, he saw the opportunity to turn the Company into a commercial empire that would change the world. The courtier, clerk and judge Rezanov was, it turned out, also a businessman, a visionary, and a gambler.

First and foremost, prompt royal assent for Natalia's right to inherit the Company was vital – not only to avoid a long and trying court case in Irkutsk but also to prove to its rivals that the Company enjoyed protection at the highest levels of the empire. But at exactly the moment when Rezanov was marshalling the Company's friends at court to petition the Empress, bad news came in from Kodiak. As Shelikhov had feared, Archimandrite Iosaf had sent a series of blistering letters to his colleagues at the Synod full of bitter criticism of the conditions he and his priests had endured over their first winter. He wrote of the lack of candles and buildings, of life in lean-tos on the beach, the drunkenness, and fornication, the endless clam suppers. 'Shelikhov used the name of Christ to deceive the government and entice thirty-five families to the savage shores of America, there to fall victim to his avarice,' Iosaf thundered.

Rezanov may not have known much about Arctic navigation, grading sable pelts or the intricacies of trans-Siberian finance, but he knew how to handle a crisis at court. Or rather, he knew exactly whom he needed to enlist to handle such a crisis. Zubov was now at the height of his powers, handling an ever-larger part of the ageing Empress's day-to-day decision-making. Rezanov, on his return from Irkutsk, had secured promotion to collegiate councillor – equivalent of a full colonel – from the prince. Solving the problems of the Shelikhov-Golikov Company was easily within Zubov's powers, but it would require suppressing the allegations of Shelikhov's poisoning from Irkutsk, placating the Synod's indignation at the treatment of its mission in Kodiak and persuading the Empress herself that Iosaf's complaints of the Company's moral turpitude were exaggerated. All this would take time and political capital. Rezanov would have to persuade Zubov that he would be well rewarded.

Natalia Shelikhova dispatched her husband's petition, as well as her own, to Nikita Demidov for presentation to Zubov and thence to the Empress herself. Naturally, a banker's draft for 10,000 rubles was also enclosed to assist the petition's passage to the Empress's ear. Shelikhova's tone was abject. 'I ask for forgiveness for interrupting Your Radiance's rest by my thoughts and requests,' read Natalia's petition to Zubov of 22 November 1795. 'To whom could I apply but you in your patriotic ardour? Being a widow and an orphan and having young children, from whom can I ask patronage comparable to Your Radiance?' Sensibly, she expressed her deep respect and reverence for Abbot Iosaf – 'no person could be found there whose dignity and position is higher' – and proposed that the monk be put in charge of the administration of justice in the colony. But, almost certainly on the advice of Rezanov, the Company's lobbyists refrained from immediately offering Zubov the 10,000 rubles to take the petition straight to the Empress. Rezanov had something far bigger in mind.

In Rezanov's vision, the company would be renamed the Russian American Company, and its brief would be to bring all of Pacific America, from Alaska to California, under the Russian crown. Shelikhov had of course lobbied for an imperial monopoly similar to the one enjoyed by the British Hudson's Bay Company, which traded furs in the territories that would later become Canada. But the scheme hatched by Rezanov in 1795 and brought to fruition over the next four years was far more ambitious in its scale and boldness.

Rezanov's model was the eighteenth century's greatest powerhouse of wealth and imperial expansion, the British East India Company. In 1757 an East India Company army and its Indian allies had broken the back of Mogul power in India at the Battle of Plassey. In the forty years since, the Company had brought almost the entire Indian subconti-nent under its rule, built fleets and cities and extended British dominion halfway across the globe. Other enterprises formed in its image included the Dutch East India Company, which had recently taken possession of New Holland (modern Indonesia), the Hudson's Bay Company of Canada and the French East India Company, which controlled areas of India around Pondicherry. The Danish, Austrian and Swedish East India Companies and the Scottish Darien Company had also, with lesser degrees of success, tried their hand at trade and colonization.

In all cases the basic formula was simple: a government charter granted a private corporation exclusive rights to trade across a specific piece of territory. The chartered companies were further licensed to build their own forts and ships, raise armies, issue money, fly their own flags and dispense justice to their employees and subject peoples. In exchange for their governments' protection of their monopolies it was understood that the lands brought under the companies' control would eventually be ceded to the crown. The costs of these ventures were born by shareholding speculators – now more politely termed investors. Thus eighteenth-century governments farmed out their imperial adventures to merchants and their hired armies.

Rezanov played not only on Zubov's greed, but on the Empress's fear. Larger matters than the missionaries' objections to the colonists' morals and to their own seafood diet were at stake. Interloping foreigners were challenging Russia's imperial destiny in America; indeed the post that had brought Iosaf's complaints also brought a batch of disturbing reports from Baranov: Boston traders had been appearing in ever greater numbers, endangering the Russian outposts by selling the natives liquor and gunpowder.* Another plaintive petition from the Aleuts – doubtless organized by the embittered Iosaf – complaining of ill treatment by the colonizers was turned by Rezanov into another argument for his hobby horse: only a chartered company under government supervision could bring the Empress's justice to these, her newest

---

* Two years before, George Vancouver's British expedition, dispatched in the aftermath of the Nootka Crisis, had also appeared, mapping the north-west coast of the Americas. The Spanish, too, in a small fleet led by Dionisio Alcalá Galiano and Cayetano Valdés-y-Flores had been spotted nosing around the north Pacific.

vassals. Clearly, a race for America's west coast was afoot, and Russia could lose no time in staking her claims to the land.

Queen Elizabeth I of England 'founded the greatness of her country' on trade, Rezanov wrote. Now the Empress had a chance to make her 'name of greater exaltation than Elizabeth's . . . if under Your happy reign Russians will shake off the yoke of foreign nations and reap an abundant harvest from great undertakings.'[11] The old Empress finally put her imperial imprimatur on a draft charter for the infant Russian American Company at the end of September 1796. Perhaps she was intrigued by the prospect of becoming a new Elizabeth I. More probably she had been swayed by the argument that foreigners were threatening Russia in her own backyard.

Demidov was impressed by the aplomb with which Rezanov had handled the family business and pressed his suit at court. 'Your son-in-law seems not as foolish as you describe him,' he wrote to Natalia Shelikhova. Rezanov should, counselled Demidov, be 'more respected at your home, and be endowed with a voice regarding your present situation made difficult by the atmosphere of [rival merchants'] greed'.[12] In securing the royal charter, Rezanov had proved to his sceptical ruble-counting mother-in-law that he was not merely a feckless aristocrat but a negotiator of the highest calibre.

But Rezanov's triumph was short-lived. On 6 November 1796 Catherine the Great, who had been on the throne of Russia since Rezanov's infancy, the patroness of all his political allies and the cornerstone of all St Petersburg's vast edifice of appointments, favours, alliances and political pacts, collapsed from a massive stroke on her commode at Tsarskoye Selo.[13] Zubov rushed to her bedside and found his royal mistress unconscious. As she lay dying he busied himself with burning the Empress's private papers and planning a hasty withdrawal from Russian politics.

8

Tsar Paul

He pretends to be a Prussian king, and every Wednesday holds
manoeuvres.

Count Fyodor Rostopchin.[1]

Catherine was succeeded by her dwarfish, emotionally crippled and
mentally unstable son, the Grand Duke Paul, who hated his mother
with a consuming passion. This dislike was not entirely irrational:
Catherine had deposed Paul's father, Peter III, who was subsequently
strangled by her supporters. Catherine, for her part, reciprocated
her pug-nosed little boy's dislike. In her memoirs, widely circulated
in secret in court circles after her death,* Catherine hinted strongly
that her first lover Sergei Saltykov was Paul's real father, despite a
striking resemblance between Paul and Peter in both appearance
and personality. She also labelled Paul 'weak' and 'dull-witted'. Nor
did she confine her opinions to the pages of her memoirs. 'Monsieur
and Madame are persons of the second sort,'[2] she wrote to a friend
of Paul and his wife. Paul's paranoia grew into full-fledged mania
during the 1790s, as the Tsarevich feared that his mother was trying
to kill him and publicly accused the Empress of having glass mixed
into his food.

---

* Alexander Pushkin purchased a pirated copy, making Catherine the mother of
Russian *samizdat* undergound literature.

As soon as Paul heard the news of his mother's stroke he rushed to Tsarskoye Selo and started rifling through her personal papers. Zubov had already wisely vacated the premises. The veteran diplomat Count Bezborodko claimed that Paul found a sealed packet in Catherine's papers marked, 'To be opened in Council after my death'. Russian monarchs, by order of Peter the Great, had the right to choose their successor, and Paul had long feared that his mother would pass him over in favour of his own eldest son Alexander, on whom the old Empress doted.* Catherine certainly considered this possibility and even discussed it with her advisers in 1794. But by the time of her death Alexander was only nineteen years old, still a little young to rule, and it is unlikely that Catherine would have left such a dramatic change of succession to a single piece of paper. In any case, Paul tossed the Empress's last testament on her study fire.

Cruel wits at court called Paul the Russian Hamlet. Like Hamlet's mother Gertrude, Catherine had lived with the murderer of her royal husband and marginalized her troubled and introspective son. Paul was forty-two years old when he finally succeeded his domineering mother, making him the oldest tsarevich in Russian history. A dozen years earlier Paul was already lamenting, 'I am already thirty and have nothing to do.' When his children were born Catherine took them away to raise them herself, just as the Empress Elizabeth had taken away Catherine's own children within days of their birth.†

Deliberately excluded from government by the Empress, Paul made his Palace of Gatchina a microcosm of the empire he would one day inherit. Paul's residence was itself a kind of cruel joke on Catherine's part: it had belonged to her lover Grigory Orlov, whose brother Alexei had killed Peter III, and was given to Paul after Orlov's death. Paul's first petty act of revenge was on Orlov's palace. He ordered the pretty French parterre torn up and replaced with a raked red-gravel parade

---

* Indeed Catherine designed the world's first all-in-one romper suit for the baby Alexander.
† Two of Paul's four sons went on to become tsars – Alexander I and Nicholas I – and two of his five daughters became queens, of the Netherlands and Austria.

ground. In place of garden pavilions he built barracks for a small army he dressed in Prussian uniforms and drilled mercilessly. He also had a 150-yard long escape tunnel built in case of attack by assassins sent by his mother. Catherine, so judicious and wise in her dealings with her advisers and correspondents, had bred a monster of a son.

Paul's boredom had fuelled a paranoia that was to destroy his reign after only four years, four months and four days. One of his first acts on acceding to the throne was to avenge himself on his mother's favourites. He ordered the mausoleum which contained the remains of Potemkin smashed and the prince's bones dug up and scattered. This was taken as a strong hint by Zubov, who fled the capital, though in the end he managed to escape the worst of Paul's wrath and was simply made to resign his offices and exiled to his estates in Lithuania but allowed to keep his wealth and jewels.

The Orlovs, as represented by Grigory's last surviving brother Alexei, were almost as lucky. Paul ordered his father Peter III exhumed from the tomb in the Alexander Nevsky Monastery where he had been buried thirty-four years before after the 'fatal attack of haemorrhoids' that remained the official explanation for the late tsar's death. Peter's bones, along with the boots and gloves recovered from the coffin, were conveyed in solemn procession to the imperial crypt at the Peter and Paul Fortress. Alexei Orlov was made to walk behind the coffin carrying Peter's crown. That night, on Paul's orders, Orlov also stood vigil with another of Peter's murderers, Catherine's former court marshal, Prince Baratinsky. Peter's killers were thus humiliated but hardly punished. Paul's reign began, as it would continue, with a display of both vindictiveness and weakness.

Paul's guiding principle was to systematically reverse every policy of his mother and ruin the men she had raised. He rejected Russia's alliance with the Austrian Emperor Franz II on the grounds that he was the nephew of his mother's old friend, the Emperor Joseph II. Despite his passionate hatred of Jacobinism, he ordered that Catherine's most radical critic, Rezanov's old colleague Alexander Radishchev, be returned from his Siberian exile. Paul revived the medieval tradition of full prostration before the Tsar, which his mother had scrapped as un-European, and banned his subjects from travelling without special passports.

This petulant destruction of Catherine's legacy boded ill for the fledgling Russian American Company, pet project of the fallen Zubov. After spending so much effort on getting Zubov to back the scheme, Demidov and Rezanov now had to back-pedal as hard as possible to distance themselves from the disgraced favourite. They were not alone in doing so. Derzhavin, wily old courtier that he was, quickly ingratiated himself with the new regime by writing one of his epic odes in praise of the new Tsar. Catherine had appointed Derzhavin to the Senate after firing him as her secretary of petitions in 1793; now he made himself useful by drafting a new bankruptcy law. Paul wisely decided that the irrepressible Derzhavin was too valuable and experienced an administrator to lose and appointed him head of the chancellery of the Imperial Council, with a diamond tobacco box to seal his successful transition into Paul's favour.

Once again Rezanov rode Derzhavin's ascending coat-tails. On Derzhavin's recommendation, Rezanov was appointed procurator of the First Department of the Senate. Russia's Senate was not a constituent part of a parliament – unlike, for instance, the Senate of the fledging United States of America or Britain's House of Lords. Rather, it functioned as the empire's highest court and was the body that controlled Russia's bureaucracy. Paul distrusted it as a stronghold of Catherine's appointees but evidently decided that dismantling the Senate would be more trouble than it was worth. So while it was not as powerful as the court, the Senate was nonetheless an important centre of patronage and power. It is an impressive testament to Rezanov's diplomatic skills that after only six months in the political wilderness he had gained such a promising position. He was now able to renew his efforts to hitch the Company's fortunes to the empire's.

By 1798 Rezanov had acquired a new weapon in his arsenal of persuasion: a newly printed three-volume copy of Captain George Vancouver's *A Voyage of Discovery to the North Pacific Ocean.* Paul may

---

* Rezanov had the French translation, dated 'Paris, Revolutionary Year III'.

have disdained all projects embraced by his mother on principle, but the published opinions of a foreigner, and an Englishman to boot, certainly pricked his interest. Rezanov was himself so impressed by Vancouver's strategic vision that he quoted it often in his later letters. The west coast of America, Vancouver argued, was a prize waiting to be taken from the lazy Spaniards by a vigorous maritime nation – meaning his native England. But his arguments applied just as well to Russia. 'The Spaniards . . . have only cleared the way for the ambitious enter-prizers of those maritime powers who, in the avidity of commercial pursuits, may seek to be benefitted by the advantages which the fertile soil of New Albion [California] seems calculated to afford,'[3] wrote Vancouver, author of some of the most convoluted prose of the eighteenth century. The Spanish had inexplicably neglected it, but 'the prosecution of a well-conducted trade between this coast and China, India and Japan [could] become an object of serious and important consideration to that nation which shall be inclined to reap the advantages of such a commerce'.[4]

Thanks to the patronage of Derzhavin, now heading the Ministry of Commerce, Rezanov was senior enough in the administration to make these arguments to Paul in person. America's Pacific coast was a jewel to be taken, Rezanov told the emperor, and the English were clearly planning to do so. An English settlement planned by Vancouver at Nootka Sound in Alaska would be, as Rezanov later wrote, 'a dagger held to the throat of the Russian East'.[5] It was an image judiciously chosen to appeal to Paul's assassin-obsessed mind. The colonization of America was, in Rezanov's analysis, an urgent issue of Russian national security. Finally, in what was perhaps his clinching argument, Rezanov reminded Paul that his mother had always been opposed to granting commercial monopolies – indeed the version of the charter that she had signed stopped short of granting such a monopoly. Rezanov knew his man. If Catherine had been against it, Paul would be bound to consider it a capital idea.

Rezanov's persuasive arguments planted the seed firmly in Paul's mind. In February 1798 Paul demonstrated his favour towards the Company by conferring noble rank on Natalia Shelikhova and her children, with the right to engage in trade. Rezanov had been just in time. Just two months after the Shelikhovs' ennoblement, a wild-eyed monk with a pair of Aleut natives in tow arrived in St Petersburg bearing fresh tales of drunkenness and cruelty from the American colony. This was Father Makarii, one of the unfortunate group of divines Shelikhov had dispatched in 1794. Like Sergeant Brityukov a decade earlier, Makarii had found an eager audience of jealous merchants in Irkutsk to sponsor any lurid tales likely to damage the Shelikhov-Golikov Company. These merchants' allies in St Petersburg ensured that the Tsar personally received Makarii and the Aleuts and heard their tale of woe. But Paul, by now firmly convinced of the strategic importance of the American colonies, was unmoved. He berated Makarii for leaving his post without his superiors' permission and sent the whistle-blowers away with only a gold coin each to buy themselves new clothes.

Tales of disorder and abuse had made Catherine wary of granting the merchant adventurers any government-like powers. Makarii's visit had the opposite effect on Paul. On 4 June he sent a *ukaz* to the governor of Irkutsk charging him 'to give strict orders to protect the inhabitants of the Islands from future oppression', the usual hypocritical bluster. But, crucially, he also stipulated that the colonists' affairs must be 'in accord with the interests of the State'. [6] Paul, as Rezanov had hoped and envisioned, was starting to consider the Company an extension of the Russian crown. And yet Paul did not sign the renewed Company charter that Rezanov so badly needed. The obstacle was Prince Pyotr Lopukhin, father of Paul's mistress Anna Lopukhina.

Anna had caught the Tsar's eye at a Moscow ball in 1796. Lopukhin's allies, noticing the attraction, told Paul that the girl was so in love with him that she was on the verge of suicide. Despite an attempt by Paul's wife Maria Feodorovna – born Sophie Dorothea, Duchess of Württemberg – to prevent the lovesick Anna being brought to St Petersburg, a passionate affair ensued. Lopukhina's father was, exactly as he had calculated, duly showered with honours. Paul made Lopukhin a prince, with the title His Serene Highness, and appointed him procurator-general of the Senate – and therefore Rezanov's immediate superior. Lopukhin had always disliked Zubov, who had with characteristic arrogance cruelly mocked his daughter's homely looks. This dislike extended to Zubov's old cronies, which included Rezanov and Derzhavin.

Despite Lopukhin's smouldering hostility, Rezanov buckled down to everyday Senate business. He busied himself drafting new laws on land and factories, for which he was given the Order of St Anne second class, which brought with it a modest 200-ruble-a-year pension. But Rezanov, who had learned his court politics at the knee of Derzhavin, was at the same time plotting a coup against Lopukhin. They just had to wait until Paul's ardour for Lopukhin's ugly daughter faded.

Anna Lopukhina's relationship with the irascible Tsar indeed deteriorated quickly. After less than a year as Paul's official mistress she asked for, and received, permission to marry her childhood friend Prince Pyotr Gagarin. With the end of the affair came the end of Pyotr Lopukhin's mayfly political career. On 4 July 1799 Commerce Minister Derzhavin recommended to Paul that he sign the charter of the new Russian American Company at a meeting of the Imperial Council. Three days later Lopukhin was relieved of his post in favour of Rezanov's ally General Alexander Bekleshev, former governor of Riga. On the following day, 8 July 1799, the charter was finally signed. It was Rezanov's thirty-fifth birthday. The Tsar's present to him was America.

The terms of the charter were more generous than anything Shelikhov had ever dared to ask for. The new company was 'Under His Majesty's Special Protection', meaning that it could not go bankrupt. Moreover, the state guaranteed its military security, in theory at least. 'All military officers of Our country as well as Our naval officers are to provide support wherever the Company may request it to do its business,' read the charter. And lest there be any doubt as to the backing of the state, the Company's official standard was to be the Russian imperial eagle on a tricolour background. Better still, the emperor himself became a shareholder with twenty shares with a face value of 10,000 rubles. The Tsarina Maria and Paul's younger son Constantine each bought two 500-ruble shares. The lion's share of the new company's capital, though, went to the Shelikhov family, who between them held an impressive

935,700 rubles' worth of stock. Four directors were appointed, including Rezanov's brother-in-law Buldakov and two former Irkutsk rivals-turned-partners, the brothers Mylnikov. Rezanov himself, as a government official, could not be a director, though he was by now the acknowledged de facto head of the Company. Officially he appeared on the books as the Company's 'High Representative in the Capital'.

On 16 September 1799 the new Russian American Company held its first board meeting at which its headquarters were officially transferred from Irkutsk to St Petersburg – symbolically, from the world of merchants to that of courtiers. Business was also booming. In October 1798 James Shields' Alaska-built brig the *Phoenix* had landed a bumper harvest of furs in Okhotsk which had fetched over a million rubles in the markets of Kiakhta and St Petersburg.[7]

'Please persuade Mother [Natalia Shelikhova] to be gracious to the Company's directors,' Rezanov wrote to Buldakov on 30 October 1799. 'Make sure to provide the directors with money. Do not forget about me either. But I am asking that they be provided with money first of all. Please forgive them. They did not have opportunities such as we did. You invested your money in your business, and I bought a village. So we have to thank God, and Mother.'[8]

Shelikhova's fortunes had improved along with her social standing. The grateful matriarch bought Rezanov and Anna a small country property twenty-six miles to the south of the capital where the Moika River (a different Moika River to the one in central St Petersburg) joins the Neva. There was a pleasant house on the estate, as well as a small hamlet of twenty-three adult male serfs – known as *dushi*, or souls – and their families. Modern Russians would describe such a suburban retreat as a dacha, albeit a rather grand one. Rezanov initially named his new property Rezanovskoe, but tactfully changed it to Annenskoye in honour of his young wife. Perhaps his fierce mother-in-law had a say in the matter.

Natalia Shelikhova also bought the young couple a more substantial estate in the Pskov governate comprising 241 souls and six villages. Like all her business dealings, the transaction was finely calculated. She purchased the estate from the Okunevs – Rezanov's mother's family

– who were evidently in financial difficulties at the time, thereby deftly combining social climbing with family diplomacy. Neither the Rezanovs nor the Okunevs showed any sign of being embarrassed by accepting the Shelikhovs' money. And though Natalia Shelikhova herself took an unladylike interest in the details of the property's inventory, she seems to have been resigned to her new role as cash cow to a clan of feckless aristocrats.

Flush with Shelikhova's money, Rezanov also bought a handsome new neoclassical building near the Blue Bridge on the Moika canal, just off Senate Square, for the new Company headquarters. It still stands today, number 72, renovated but empty, its historical status marked by a plaque to the revolutionary Kondraty Ryleev, who like many of the young liberals who fomented the Decembrist uprising in 1825 was an officer of the Russian American Company.

As Rezanov set up his grand new headquarters, the Tsar was quietly succumbing to paranoia. 'I came to the throne late and will not be able to bring order everywhere,' Paul feared. To help him impose the order for which he yearned, Paul recruited Pyotr Obolyaninov as head of his secret police and later as procurator-general of the Senate.[9] As well as supervising the legislative affairs of the Senate the post also involved running Russia's judiciary – the equivalent of a prosecutor-general. By happy coincidence, Obolyaninov also happened to be an old judicial colleague of Rezanov from Pskov days.

Paul had chosen well. Obolyaninov turned out to be one of the many geniuses of repression that punctuate Russian history. The Tsar had a yellow box installed at the side of the Winter Palace for petitions and denunciations. These were supposed to be anonymous, though in fact Obolyaninov's spies watched the comings and goings of the night-time petitioners. Paul would personally open the box with his own key at seven o'clock every morning, and the Tsar's replies were published in St Petersburg's newspapers. At first the most common complaints were about watered vodka in the capital's taverns, but as word spread of the Tsar's personal interest in the box on Palace Embankment jokers began posting obscene verse, pasquinades and caricatures. Paul had the box closed.

Like his mother, Paul was an obsessive micromanager of his subjects' lives, but he lacked Catherine's flair for administration and wasted his energies on regulating what he could see every day – the streets of St Petersburg. All the monarchs of Europe had been profoundly shocked by the execution of Louis XVI in 1792, but none went quite as far as Paul in stamping out every hint, real or imagined, of Jacobinism. Spotting the son of an English merchant on a St Petersburg boulevard wearing a peaked velvet hunting cap – the late-eighteenth-century equivalent of a baseball cap – Paul decided that this and indeed all round hats were a symbol of Jacobinism. There being no word in Russian for a hunting cap, Paul's ukaz forbade 'any person to appear in public with the thing on his head worn by the English merchant's son'.[10] Coloured tops to boots were also banned for the same reason, as was use of the word 'revolution' by scientists to describe the movement of planets. French was still widely spoken at court, but Paul worried about dangerous Gallic influences on the general public and ordered merchants to desist from French borrowings such as *magazin* to denote shop – the closest native Russian word was *lavka* meaning 'counter'.*

Less harmlessly, in 1800 Paul's terror of assassination fuelled a purge of politically unreliable courtiers. Paul's son Nicholas I was to become the true founder of Russia's modern police state, with its apparatus of secret political police, in-camera court hearings and prison camps, but Obolyaninov certainly laid the foundations of terror. 'In going to bed it was quite incertain whether during the night some policeman would come with a *kibitka* [a police gig] to take you off at once to Siberia,' wrote Prince Adam Czartoryski. Princess Dashkova, the former best friend of Catherine the Great, was dubbed by Paul 'a suspicious poltroon' and banished to a hut in Karelia. Obolyaninov's police also monitored the less exalted. 'If any family received visitors in the evening; if four people were seen walking together; if anyone examined a public

* Russian Prime Minister Viktor Chernomyrdin tried to ban foreign-language signs in Moscow in 1996, with similar lack of success. A campaign against foreign words was again mooted by the Russian Duma in 2012, until it was pointed out that this would mean changing the Russian words for Kremlin (a Tatar borrowing), President, Minister, Army, Navy, car and other key concepts.

building for too long he was in imminent danger,' Edward Clarke, an English traveller to St Petersburg, wrote in 1800. 'If foreigners ventured to notice any of these enormities in their letters, which were all opened and read by the police, expressed themselves with energy in praise of their country, or used a single sentiment or expression offensive or incomprehensible to the police officers or their spies they were liable to be torn in an instant from family and friends, thrown in a sledge and hurried to the border or to Siberia. Many persons were said to have been privately murdered or banished.'[11]

Paul was not the first ruler of Russia to suffer from paranoia, nor would he be the last. But unlike his more ruthless predecessors and successors he failed to destroy the powerful enemies he made, and they therefore destroyed him. One of the least wise acts of Paul's brief and self-destructive reign was to launch an assault on the military elite who had brought Russian arms to unheard-of heights during his mother's reign. Paul hated the Guards regiments as havens of idleness and luxury as well as for providing Catherine with lovers. He therefore humiliated the Guards' commanders and cut down their privileges, at a stroke alienating thousands of Russia's most socially connected, best-trained and heavily armed young soldiers. Paul also recalled all Russian troops from overseas, including an expeditionary force of 60,000 which Catherine had imaginatively dispatched to push the boundaries of her empire southwards through modern Azerbaijan and into Persia.

Grigory Potemkin and his brilliant eccentric protégé Alexander Suvorov had re-invented the Russian army to the highest modern standards, including the introduction of radical new uniforms which were comfortable and quickly put on. 'Get up, and you're ready to go!' was Suvorov's maxim. Paul considered the new loose-fitting uniform sloppy and ordered the entire army back into antiquated Prussian-style wigs and tall hats. He also introduced the Prussian goose-step, which Russian soldiers still use today.

Most eccentric of all was Paul's obsession with creating a universal Church uniting secular and temporal power, headed by himself. The origin of this idea came when he and his wife visited Rome on a grand tour of Europe in 1782. The young Tsarevich met Pope Pius VI, and they discussed uniting the Catholic and Orthodox wings of Christianity, split since 1054.* On coming to the throne Paul had himself declared head of the Russian Orthodox Church, the only Russian monarch ever to do so. He had the chapel of his new Mikhailovsky Palace built in the classical Italian baroque style with no iconostasis, the screen which traditionally separates the congregation from the altar in Orthodox churches. The Mikhailovsky chapel is almost indistinguishable from a Catholic church. Here Paul himself served as priest, gave communion and heard the confessions of his household.

When the thrusting young General Napoleon Bonaparte took Rome in 1798, Paul suggested the Pope move his headquarters from the Vatican to Moscow. Pius politely declined, but Paul had more luck with an invitation to the Knights of St John of Malta, whom Napoleon had recently evicted from its historic stronghold in Valetta as he seized Malta en route to Egypt. The Order's Russian years were one of the odder interludes in the knights' 800-year history. In exchange for his patronage and protection, Paul had himself appointed seventy-second Grand Master of the Order and moved its seat to St Petersburg. This was in fact the Order's fourth move, after Saracen and Turkish advances had forced them to abandon Jerusalem and Rhodes and now Napoleon had forced them out of Malta. Paul became passionate about the order's ancient chivalric ethos and incorporated the red and white Maltese Cross into the Russian state coat of arms.

Malta itself, though actually under French occupation, was made a province of the Russian Empire and assigned a garrison of 3,000, as well as an administration. All those notables in the rank-obsessed Tsar's favour were assigned one of thirty gradations in the Order's tremendously complicated hierarchy of knighthood. The white enamel Cross of Malta, worn on a ribbon at the throat, became the principal symbol of royal favour in Pauline Russia. Derzhavin, as an Actual Privy Councillor and second in the table of ranks, was granted the cross of a Knight Commander first class, which came with diamonds. Rezanov, a

---

* Paul was one of only two tsars to ever meet a pope – the other was his son Nicholas I.

mere Actual State Councillor and number five on the table, received the plainer Commander's cross in silver.

Paul had begun his reign by eschewing his mother's foreign military adventures in Persia, but he was so incensed by Napoleon's outrages against the Pope and the Knights that he ordered Russian troops to retake Rome and Malta for the Russian crown. Paul summoned the sixty-eight-year-old General Suvorov from his retirement in a monastery with a letter that said, simply, 'Come and save the Tsars.' Paul joined the first (of six) anti-French coalitions masterminded by England. Russia's new allies were Austria and, oddly, given Catherine's relentless wars against the Sublime Porte, Turkey. In the summer of 1798 an Anglo-Russian fleet under Admiral Fyodor Ushakov established an outpost on the Ionian Islands off Greece. The following year Suvorov's force invaded through the heel of Italy and took Naples and then Rome. The old general was preparing to invade France itself, through Piedmont and Savoy, but Russia's Austrian allies demanded that Suvorov's force join them in southern Germany instead and fight alongside another Russian army which was making its way through Poland to join the fray.

Suvorov therefore turned his 15,000-strong army north and fought his way through Switzerland. Traces of the extraordinary road that his engineers carved for the army over the St Gotthard Pass are still visible today, including the holes for pitons with which they secured ropes to the vertiginous Alpine cliffs. Suvorov stormed the French defences at the Devil's Bridge over the gorge of the River Reuss and pushed on. Unfortunately he arrived too late – the main Russian force, which had marched overland from Moscow, had been routed by the French at Zurich, and his Austrian allies sued for a separate peace with Napoleon.

Never before had a Russian army roamed so freely across the heart of the continent – though Russian troops had occupied Berlin in 1760 – and Suvorov was styled Prince of Italy, Prince of Sardinia, Count of the Holy Roman Empire, Field Marshal of the Austrian and Sardinian armies as well as Generalissimo of Russia's ground and naval forces. In an age filled with military prodigies, Suvorov's heroic crossing of the Devil's Bridge became a European legend. The French army nicknamed him the Russian Hannibal.

Perhaps predictably, Suvorov's successes threw Paul into frenzies of jealousy and suspicion. On his return to St Petersburg the Tsar stripped the old general of his titles and fourteen decorations. Suvorov died, disgraced, the following year. Derzhavin was the most senior official to risk the emperor's wrath by attending his funeral. Part of Paul's anger at Suvorov was based on a growing fascination with Napoleon, whom he began to imagine was a man of destiny almost of his own calibre.

Paul's hatred of Jacobin France had once been so manic that he decreed that Frenchmen would only be allowed into Russia if an official of the Ancien Régime had signed their credentials. But by the autumn of 1800 Paul's enmity towards the French Republic was clearly wavering. A Russo-British attempt to invade the Netherlands failed, and in October the British instead took Paul's beloved island of Malta – that is to say, the Russian province of Malta – from the French. In his rage at his ally's treachery, Paul dissolved Russia's alliance with Austria instead, a short step from wrecking the English-led coalition entirely.

Charles-Maurice Talleyrand, Napoleon's foreign minister, had made it his business to be kept informed of Paul's quixotic obsessions, and in 1800 he began to lay the groundwork for an alliance with the man who had until recently styled himself Revolutionary France's most implacable enemy. Talleyrand played his cards brilliantly. Six thousand Russian prisoners of war taken by the French army in the campaigns of 1799–1800 were returned to Russia not just excellently fed but in new uniforms run up by Lyons tailors. Talleyrand also sent Paul a ceremonial sword presented by Pope Leo X to Paul's predecessor as Grand Master of the Order of Malta. In addition he had his agents in St Petersburg emphasize that Napoleon had put the Jacobin excesses of the Revolution behind him.

'It is terrible to see the so unexpected collapse of great hopes,' wrote Charles, Lord Whitworth, Britain's ambassador to St Petersburg, to the foreign secretary in London as the First Coalition disintegrated. 'The Emperor [Paul] is obviously mad. And his illness is constantly progressing . . . With a man like him no one can feel in security under such circumstances.'[12] This letter, though written in invisible ink, was intercepted and read by Foreign Minister Count Fyodor Rostopchin's spies, further damaging Anglo-Russian relations.

By this time Paul was exchanging courteous letters with Napoleon. 'The duty of those to whom God has entrusted the power to govern nations is to devote themselves to the wellbeing of their subjects,' began Paul's first letter to the French First Consul in November 1800. 'Let us try to restore that peace and quiet to the world which are so much needed and which seem to conform so closely to the immutable laws of the Almighty. I am ready to listen to you and hear what you have to say.'[13]

Bonaparte answered enthusiastically. 'Under this, our union, Britain, Germany and other powers will drop their weapons,' he wrote. A Russo-French alliance was quickly sealed.

As recently as the previous year Paul had gone as far as to hire the German playwright August Kotzebue* to draft a letter to the 'Corsican usurper' challenging Napoleon to a personal duel.[14] Paul had also taken a strong interest in a scheme to restore the Bourbon monarchy and had hosted the exiled Louis XVIII, brother of the executed Louis XVI. Now Paul threw Louis out of the Jelgava Palace in Courland (modern Latvia) and reneged on the 200,000-ruble pension he had bestowed on the man who would be King of France. Instead a portrait of Napoleon, Paul's new best friend, was duly hung in the Tsar's bedroom.

Paul and Napoleon's correspondence quickly turned to the subject that interested both men most of all: world domination. After the collapse of the First Coalition Napoleon longed to decisively crush his arch-enemy England. He had taken Egypt in 1798 – why not India next? The idea had been floated in the days of Louis XVI, who had actually authorized a naval attack on Bombay in 1782, but with Russian support, it was finally – in Napoleon's mind at least – feasible to rob England of her most valuable overseas possession. Talleyrand presented Napoleon with a detailed plan 'for striking a mortal blow at the English power in India', combining a blockade of Britain with a naval assault on Bombay and Calcutta and a land attack across Afghanistan. 'Your sovereign agrees with me that if we take India away from England we will weaken her might,' Napoleon enthused to the Russian diplomat

---

* Whose boisterous young sons Moritz and Otto would play an important role in Rezanov's story as midshipmen on the round-the-world voyage.

Count Georg Magnus Sprengtporten. 'India, this fairy land, this Oriental diamond, has given much more wisdom to the world than this drunken and vicious England with its shopkeepers.'[15]

America too caught the hungry eyes of the would-be rulers of the world. Napoleon had recently forced Spain into an unhappy alliance and had demanded large swathes of what is now the southern United States to add to the French-owned Louisiana Territory centred on the Mississippi valley.* There was no reason, thought Talleyrand, why the Spanish territories on the Pacific coast should not be ceded to Russia, thereby securing a handsome new swathe of territory for France's new allies.

Paul took to the Indian scheme with an enthusiasm that unnerved even Napoleon. Ignoring French pleas to first devote his energies to the closer-to-home parts of the great project such as blockading England, the Tsar planned the coming conquest of Asia in minute detail. Paul, whose recreations still included playing with a huge army of toy soldiers, delightedly busied himself with the logistics of the great expedition. The cloth to be sold to the natives, he stipulated, was to be 'of the colourings most liked by the Asians', and the Cossack expeditionary force was to carry a large stock of festive fireworks to impress the locals.

In January 1801 Paul issued orders to Vasily Orlov (no relation of Catherine the Great's late favourite), ataman of the Don Cossacks, to assemble a 25,000-strong force with which 'you will invade India . . . drive out the English powers and ruin their commercial establishments'. The plan was for the Cossacks to join 35,000 soldiers of the French Rhine army under Suvorov's nemesis General André Masséna, who would sail down the Danube, up the Don, down the Volga, across the Caspian Sea and disembark at Astrabad in modern Turkmenistan, from where they would march on India. According to French calculations, the zig-zag route from France to Astrabad would take just eighty-three days, and the march to India via Herat and Kandahar fifty more. The combined Franco-Russian land and sea assault on Bombay was pencilled in for September 1801.

---

* Which Napoleon would sell to the United States in 1803.

Alas for Paul, his attempt at changing the destiny of the world was not to be.* Even as Ataman Orlov tramped with his Cossacks across the Kazakh steppes towards Khiva and Bukhara, a coterie of aristocrats around Paul was hatching the murder plot that he so feared but had done so much to provoke. Paul was so hated among the nobility that Count Peter Pahlen, governor of St Peterburg, found no shortage of willing conspirators. Count Nikita Petrovich Panin, nephew and namesake of the Emperor Paul's old tutor, was delegated to speak to Tsarevich Alexander about the possibility of deposing his father. Panin was so nervous of Obolyaninov's police spies that they met in a bathhouse. Alexander was persuaded to 'relieve the injustices and tyrannies' of the father he feared and detested, and agreed to the coup, but, he protested later, did not acquiesce in his father's murder. 'To make an omelette you must break eggs,' Pahlen told the prince.†

Despite Panin's security precautions, Pahlen's plot was soon the talk of the town. Paul even asked Pahlen directly whether a plot against his life existed. 'Impossible, Sire,' replied Pahlen, with impressive sang-froid. 'There could be no conspiracy unless I belonged to it.' Fiendishly, Pahlen used Paul's fear against him, persuading the unstable emperor to issue a warrant for the arrest of his charismatic and popular son and heir. It was a trap. The warrant became Paul's suicide note, forcing the hands of Alexander's allies into action.

———

On the night of 3 March 1801 Nikolai Zubov – brother of the exiled favourite Platon – threw a dinner for 120 conspirators. They ate off gold plate. Zubov stood to solemnly announce that the Tsarevich Alexander had been informed of the arrest warrant and had consequently approved the overthrow of his father. A general toast was drunk. The same evening Paul himself dined with General Mikhail

———

* Alas for Napoleon too. In exile in Elba he would claim that if Paul had not been assassinated he would never have made the fatal mistake of invading Russia in 1812.

† This ruthless phrase is often wrongly ascribed to Joseph Stalin – it was in fact Walter Duranty, the *New York Times'* Pulitzer Prize-winning Moscow correspondent, who used Pahlen's line to describe Stalin's purges.

Kutuzov and members of the royal family, including Alexander himself. Conversation was, understandably from Alexander's point of view, more than usually strained. The Tsarevich complained of illness and retired early while Paul, in a chilling premonition of his death later that night, looked in the mirror as he left the dining room and remarked, 'I see my neck, wrung.'

Pahlen, who had been waiting with Alexander for the Tsar to go to bed, rushed from Paul's grim neo-Gothic Mikhailovsky Palace to Zubov's house to report that the time to strike had come. The dinner party broke up into two groups, one under Pahlen, which headed for the Mikhailovsky's main gates, another under Levin August von Bennigsen and Nikolai Zubov, which entered though a side entrance. Ten of the conspirators climbed the seventy-four spiral stairs to the imperial bedroom and forced the door.

They found Paul trying to hide behind a fire screen. The conspirators attempted to 'force him to abdicate', according to Bennigsen's – obviously self-serving – account. Bennigsen claimed that he told the terrified Paul, 'Remain calm, Your Majesty! This is a matter of your life or death.' Paul failed to remain calm. A scuffle broke out, and Nikolai Zubov struck Paul on the left temple with a gold tobacco box – the dented box, with a handwritten account of its role on the fateful night carefully folded inside, is now in the Hermitage Museum. Other conspirators piled in and strangled Paul with a silk officer's sash.

The Guards regiments of the capital at first refused to believe that the Tsar was dead. Two old sergeants had to be taken to the bedchamber to check the beaten corpse. 'Pavel Petrovich is dead, firmly dead,' they reported back to their comrades. When Alexander heard the news he burst into tears. 'Stop being a child and start being a tsar,' Pahlen snapped at him. As news of Paul's 'fatal apoplectic attack'* spread further there was general rejoicing on the streets. By the end of the day, reported Edward Clark, there was not a single bottle of champagne to be found in the shops of St Petersburg.

---

* This remained the official cause of death until censorship was partly lifted in 1905.

9

Russia's East India Company

Our mission, our civilizing mission in Asia . . . a new Russia will be
created which shall in time regenerate and resurrect the old one.

Fyodor Dostoevsky[1]

Having lost two difficult and volatile royal patrons to old age and
murder, Rezanov must have felt on safer ground with the third, the
twenty-four-year-old Emperor Alexander I. Rezanov had been on good
terms with the Tsarevich Alexander since his appointment to the sena-
torial staff in 1798 and possibly before. To the relief of the court, the
young Tsar quickly showed himself temperamentally closer to his
grandmother Catherine the Great, who had raised and doted on him,
than to his paranoid father.

Alexander had Paul's killers, including Pahlen and Zubov, quietly
exiled, neither rewarded nor punished. Most of the old hands of Paul's
administration were allowed to keep their posts, but Pyotr Obolyaninov,
the feared prosecutor-general and author of Paul's terror, was considered so dangerous to the new regime that the plotters arrested him
within hours of the murder. Alexander removed him from his position
and reinstated his benign predecessor, Alexander Bekleshev, who was
popular with the nobility and another ally of Rezanov. Like his grandmother, who had herself come to power as a result of a noble-led coup
in 1763, Alexander understood that the supposedly limitless powers of
the Tsar were nothing without the broad support of the aristocracy.

Both Alexander's father and his grandfather Peter III had ignored this principle and had paid with their lives.

Russia may have been the largest empire in the world, but St Petersburg was still a village with the Tsar as its squire. Alexander and his brothers Nicholas and Constantine were intimately connected with the lives and gossip of the capital's salons and palaces. The two brothers, along with a group of young progressive Anglophile nobles became the new Tsar's eyes and ears in the capital.* They formed an informal council they jokingly referred to as the Committee for Saving Society. The group met in a suite of rooms on the western side of the Winter Palace that Alexander had had decorated in the fashionable neoclassical style, with round Roman arches and walls painted deep Pompeian red. These impressive and rather pompous interiors survive to this day; the view, across the street to the Admiralty and over the Neva to the Stock Exchange, is also unchanged.

Alexander had been taught the humanitarian principles of Jean-Jacques Rousseau by a radical tutor, Frédéric-César de La Harpe, who by the time of his pupil's coronation was leading a French-backed Jacobin government in his native Switzerland. Catherine the Great had employed La Harpe to teach her young grandson despite her own misgivings about Jacobinism – perhaps she wished the frustrated liberalism of her own youth to be resurrected by a future generation. Alexander now determined to impose a version of La Harpe's liberal ideas on the empire he had inherited. The committee's plans were as radical as they were familiar from the reformist days of the young Catherine – the establishment of a constitutional monarchy and the abolition of serfdom. Derzhavin, though something of a free thinker himself in his youth, was shocked by some of the ideas coming from the inexperienced 'band of Jacobins' that now surrounded the Tsar.[2]

For Rezanov and his newly chartered Russian American Company, Alexander's questing ambition could only be good news. Rezanov had sold the idea of Russian America to Paul by appealing to his paranoia. He now set out to sell the idea again to Alexander, this time appealing

* Victor Kochubey, Nikolai Novosiltsev, Pavel Stroganov and Adam Jerzy Czartoryski.

'A dynamic fellow, hot tempered, a dedicated scribbler…' Nikolai Petrovich Rezanov in the uniform of a Court Chamberlain and wearing the Order of St Anne First Class; this portrait was painted just before he left Russia for the last time in July 1803 and hung in the boardroom of the Russian American Company in St Petersburg.

Russian adventurers opened up Russia's New World by zig-zagging across Siberia's three great river systems. The Cossack river-pirate-turned-conquistador Yermak Timofeyevich (*left*) led a raiding party of renegades into Siberia in search of fur and gold and overthrew the Tatar Khanate of Sibir in 1582. The Eastern Sea (*below*) was Russia's final frontier: Peter the Great sent captains Vitus Bering and Alexei Chirikov to explore the 'Great Land' rumoured to lie beyond it – and claim it for Russia. Chirikov made landfall in modern-day Alaska in July 1741.

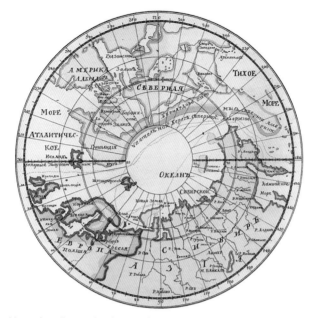

The world seen from the top, showing America as a natural extension of Siberia. This map was drawn in 1763 by Mikhail Lomonosov, a leading proponent of further exploration and conquest of the Great Land.

The natives of the Aleutian Islands had hunted sea otters with spears from kayaks made of sealskin stretched over a wooden frame for centuries. Russian colonists put them to work and quickly devastated the sea otter populations of the region.

The deep, lustrous fur of sea otters is the thickest and warmest of any mammal. In 1780 a single five-foot-long sea otter pelt was worth more than an ordinary seaman's annual salary in the markets of Canton, a discovery which triggered a fur-rush to the North Pacific.

Born into a humble merchant family in Rylsk, Grigory Shelikhov became the millionaire master of Russia's greatest fur-trading empire as well as one of the boldest explorers of his age. He founded a colony on Kodiak, but his reputation was forever tainted as a butcher of natives. His daughter's marriage to Rezanov was Shelikhov's bid for respectability – and for influence at court.

The Empress Catherine the Great shared Peter the Great's ambitions to expand Russia's Empire into America – but was wary of ruthless merchants like Shelikhov.

The Bronze Horseman – or the Copper Horseman in Russian – was Catherine the Great's monument to Peter the Great. The casting took French sculptor Etienne Falconet twelve years and was the talk of St Petersburg as Rezanov grew up; it was finally unveiled (*below*) in 1782. The Horseman through Japanese eyes (*right*): a sketch by the sailor Kankai Ibun who accompanied Rezanov to Japan in 1806.

The Courtiers. Gavriil Derzhavin (*above left*), poet and politician and family friend of the Rezanovs, was Nikolai's unfailing patron. Count Nikolai Rumiantsev (*right*) was one of Russia's great magnates, a cousin of Tsar Alexander I, who ran the powerful Ministry of Commerce. He recognised the political and commercial potential of a Russian round-the-world expedition.

Prince Platon Zubov was Catherine the Great's last, and most cynical, lover-favourite. When they met, the Empress was sixty; he was twenty-two. She showered him with money and titles. Zubov's morning receptions 'resembled the levées of a French Royal mistress' and his private court was a carousel of bribery and favour. Rezanov became one of Zubov's secretaries in 1793.

Tsar Paul sent Russian armies deep into Europe and planned a joint Russo-French land and naval assault on British India with Napoleon. *Above*, an army of 20,000 Cossacks was en-route to India when Paul was assassinated in 1801; *Below*, General Alexander Suvorov is greeted by cheering crowds as Russian troops occupy Milan in April 1799.

Catherine the Great's dwarfish, paranoid son Paul hated his mother and when he finally succeeded her in 1796 set about undoing many of her reforms. His disastrous reign lasted just four years, four months and four days before he was murdered by discontented aristocrats.

Happily for Russia, Tsar Paul's son Alexander took after his grandmother, Catherine the Great. He began his reign as an enthusiastic reformer and backed Rezanov's grand plans for pushing Russia's empire into southern Alaska and beyond. He made Rezanov's son a royal page.

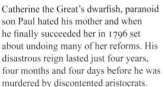

Modelled on Britain's East India Company, the Russian American Company would, Rezanov believed, make the Pacific a Russian sea. The Company had the power to issue money and have its own armed forces, and its Royal Charters – from both Paul I and Alexander I – allowed the Company to fly a flag almost identical to Russia's own.

to the young man's ambition. The idea of extending Russian dominion to the mouth of the Amur River and sending Russian 'trading ships to Canton, Macao, Batavia, the Philippine and Maram islands with products and productions obtained in America'[3] had originally of course been Shelikhov's. But Shelikhov had failed because his sovereign had been wary of merchant adventurers in general and suspicious of Shelikhov's tainted reputation in particular. Rezanov had no such problem. He was an insider, an experienced courtier and a nobleman whose motives were – by his own account at least – loftily strategic rather than basely commercial. And his tsar was young, intelligent and zealous about expanding and improving the empire.

The Company's charter was renewed by the new monarch in the early summer of 1801. The Grand Duke Constantine, Alexander's younger brother, had been a shareholder since 1799. Now Rezanov, salesman extraordinaire, also persuaded Alexander himself, as well as his wife and brother Nikolai to invest their personal money. With such luminaries at the head of the list of shareholders, and with the Company again claiming to be 'Under His Imperial Majesty's Highest Protection', fashionable St Petersburg flocked to subscribe to Rezanov's initial public offering of shares.

The Russian American Company had a considerable way to go before it could rival the numbers of ships, men, guns and capital that the British East India Company had built up over its two centuries of trade. By 1801 the EIC was wealthier and more powerful than most European states, ruling 90 million Indians with a standing army of 200,000 men. It controlled trading posts in India, China and Singapore, and dominated world trade in cotton, silk, indigo dye, saltpetre and tea from its headquarters in Leadenhall Street in the City of London.[4] But the Russian American Company did have one great competitive advantage against other great nations' chartered companies of the day: it already possessed, according to its own charter at least, a swathe of American territory to rival India. Paul had granted the RAC a monopoly on all trade and minerals found 'on the shore of America from 55° latitude [roughly the southern border of modern Alaska] to the Bering Strait and beyond and also on the Aleutian, Kurile and other islands lying in the Northeastern [Pacific] Ocean'. Continental Russian America, not counting the Aleutian Islands, stretched 1,400 miles from its eastern tip (today called Cape Prince of Wales, by Little Diomede Island in the Bering Strait) to its southwestern boundary near Sitka. If laid on top of the continental United States, the territory – which closely corresponds to the modern state of Alaska – would stretch from California to Florida. Moreover, unlike the British in India or China, the Russians did not face organized enemies, only belligerent natives and – if Vancouver was to be believed – indolent Spanish colonists. The Spanish settlements were 'wide from each other and unprotected in themselves', Vancouver reported, creating 'irresistible temptations in the way of strangers to trespass over their boundary.'

Rezanov's grand design, then, was nothing less than to make Russia the all-powerful master of the whole northern Pacific.[5] He proposed the further expansion of Russia along the west coast of America including California, to the Hawaiian Islands and also the island of Sakhalin, north of Japan. He argued for a new naval base at the mouth of the Amur River to guard against Chinese aggression[*] and proposed a new road connecting Irkutsk to the Pacific.[†] For Rezanov, the fate of Russian America was nothing less than a litmus test for Russia's worthiness to succeed in the new nineteenth century. As Rezanov wrote to Count Nikolai Petrovich Rumiantsev, who had recently succeeded Derzhavin as minister of commerce,

'As decidedly as I am convinced of the success of this proposed undertaking just as positive am I that if its merits are not recognized and embraced in the time of Alexander I we never need expect to reap the potential benefits, missed by not being seized in time. Then it will be evident to the world that the Russians, recognized for initiative and possessed of a faculty for surmounting obstacles – our national traits – must have submitted to circumstances and sunk into inactivity with

---

[*] Advice the government eventually took in 1858 when it founded the port of Vladivostok.

[†] A project only finally completed under President Vladimir Putin in 2002.

souls dead to everything meritorious and of moment. In a word, we shall be compared to a worn flint from which wearied hands struggle to strike a spark which, if secured, is impotent – a flint whose original potent fire was not utilized.'

The point was taken. Alexander considered himself a new emperor for a new century and did not share his grandmother's aversion to merchant monopolies. He was inspired almost immediately with the idea of expanding Russia to the Pacific and beyond, ensuring that no enemies could threaten his empire's backyard. It was a rare moment when imperial power combined with visionary imagination.

News of the Tsar's nocturnal discussions over the map table became the talk of St Petersburg. The worried Spanish ambassador, desperate for information about Alexander's intentions, scattered bribes among Winter Palace servants for scraps of gossip.[6] The rumours that he gleaned sped by packet boat back to the gloomy corridors of the Escorial outside Madrid, where courtiers were so alarmed that orders were sent to Mexico City and thence to San Francisco to fortify the settlement's defences in anticipation of Russian attack. Ripples of Rezanov's vision were spreading round the world as fast as trade winds and galloping couriers could carry them.

Rezanov, however, was not the only man in St Petersburg with a head full of ideas and high hopes of the new regime. Alexander's reformist enthusiasms had triggered a stampede of petitions from bright young men from all over Europe who believed their schemes would transform the empire's commerce, arts and sciences. Rumiantsev's papers are filled with projects for canals, shipyards, roads, crop rotation, steam-powered mine lifts and swamp-drainage systems.

One of these petitioners was thirty-one-year-old Captain Adam Johann von Krusenstern, known in Russian as Ivan Fyodorovich, the scion of an aristocratic Swedish family which had retained its estates in Estonia after it was ceded to the Russian Empire in 1710. Krusenstern had entered the Russian Naval Academy at Kronstadt in 1785 at the age of fifteen and served under both Chichagov and Mulovsky, the greatest Russian admirals of the age, in action against the Swedes in 1788.

In 1793 Catherine the Great, horrified by news of the execution of Louis XVI of France, had sent Krusenstern and nine other promising young Russian officers to the British Royal Navy to help fight the Jacobins at sea. The young Russians visited America, India and China on British ships and in the process became the best-trained officers in the Russian service.[7] On his return to St Petersburg in 1799, Krusenstern penned a treatise on how and why Russian ships and shipbuilders should be dispatched to Kamchatka to build a Pacific fleet as powerful as the Baltic force. But, more practically, Krustenstern suggested that a round-the-world naval expedition could supply the colonies in America and also begin a Russian fur trade between Alaska, Japan and China.

In early 1802 Krusenstern's proposal caught Rumiantsev's eye and imagination. He passed it to the minister of the navy, Admiral Nikolai Mordvinov, who also liked the idea. Since the proposed round-the-world voyage focused on resupplying Russian America, Rumiantsev also showed the plans to Rezanov – and made a delicate enquiry as to how much of the vast cost of the proposed expedition the Russian American Company would be willing to meet.

Rezanov took the proposal to the Company directors and browbeat the conservative Buldakov into agreeing to finance the venture.[*] On 13 July 1802 Rezanov rode to Rumiantsev's magnificent family mansion on the English Embankment to inform the minister that the Company had approved financing for the bulk of the projected 700,000-ruble cost of the expedition as long as the state lent the Company 250,000 rubles up front. Rumiantsev agreed, and the following month the emperor formally approved the rest of the funding and appointed Krusenstern head of the expedition.

In September Rezanov and Krusenstern met for the first time to discuss the timing of the voyage and the practicalities of bankers' drafts for the purchase of one of the expedition's two ships. The Company, as principal backers, had set the departure date for the following June. Already the misunderstanding that was to be the cause of deep rancour

---

[*]   A decision which, by 1805, came close to ruining the Company and necessitated the directors to make personal loans to keep the RAC from bankruptcy.

between the two men was appearing. To Rezanov, the main purpose of the expedition was 'the trade of the RAC, at whose expense the vessels were bought, armed and supplied with appropriate cargoes'.[8] He believed, therefore, that he was interviewing a captain who would be carrying out the Company's wishes. Krusenstern, for his part, considered he was serving his tsar and that Rezanov was merely the money man Rumiantsev had lined up to part-finance the naval expedition that he had conceived and would command.

Krusenstern, armed with the RAC's letters of credit as well as gold from the Treasury, sent Lieutenant Yury Lisiansky, an old comrade from British Royal Navy days, to Hamburg to buy two ships. Russian-built ships of the time were by no means bad, and had acquitted themselves well in the Russo-Swedish war of 1788, but the Baltic shipyards founded by Rezanov's grandfather General Okunev worked slowly and were famous for theft and corruption. Pressed for time, Krusenstern judged that buying foreign keels would be cheaper and quicker.

Lisiansky, accompanied by Vasiliy Shelikhov, Grigory's elder brother and a Company naval architect, together toured the shipyards of Hamburg. However Lisiansky professed himself unhappy with the vessels on offer and insisted that he continue on his own to London with the bankers' drafts. At Gravesend, guided by wily Royal Navy ship agents, Lisiansky inspected various second-hand English frigates. He settled on the 430-ton, 16-gun *Leander* and the 14-gun, 373-ton *Thames*.[9] He paid £22,000 sterling for the two ships.

Lisiansky was either duped or – in the widely-held opinion of his shipmates – accepted a handsome kickback in exchange for overpaying. 'On his return he was impressed with himself, because he had filled his pockets with the money of others,' wrote Lieutenant Hermann Ludwig von Löwenstern. Both ships were built in 1789, though Lisiansky reported to St Petersburg that they were considerably newer.[10] The *Leander*'s foremast had been badly cracked by the impact of two French cartouche balls and had to be replaced. The ships needed a further £6,000 worth of repairs and fitting out before they were seaworthy for their voyage to St Petersburg and a new life. Lisiansky returned with them with hired British crews in the spring of 1803. The larger vessel was rechristened the *Nadezhda – Hope –* and the smaller one *Neva* after St Petersburg's principal river.[11]

While Lisiansky was negotiating his deals in the shipyards of London, tragedy struck the Rezanov household. Anna Rezanova had given birth to the couple's first child, a boy named Pyotr, in 1801. On 7 October 1802, after a traumatic two-day labour, a second child was born, a girl named Olga. Infection set in and after eleven days Anna died. She was buried under a simple classical column among the greatest soldiers and courtiers of her age in the fashionable Lazarus Cemetery of St Petersburg's Alexander Nevsky Monastery. Curiously, there are almost no traditional Christian crosses to be seen in the graveyard. The Russian nobility of the period preferred to commemorate their dead with broken Roman pillars, weeping muses, empty classical armour, pyramids and steles.

Even in death Anna was defined in relation to the men in her life – husband, father and son: 'Here lies the governing Senate's Ober-Procurator and Knight Nikolai Petrovich Rezanov's wife, Anna Grigoriyevna Rezanova, born Shelikhova, mother to Peter aged one year and three months,' reads her epitaph. Rezanov was devastated – so much so that even six months after Anna's death the Tsar and Rumiantsev remarked that the widower still appeared crushed. 'I have lost all my life's happiness with Anna's death, and though my two little children are pleasing to me they only open my wounds,' he wrote to his friend Ivan Dmitriev.[12] 'My true love is still with you, at the churchyard of Alexander Nevsky under a piece of marble,' Rezanov wrote later to his brother-in-law Buldakov, even though he was by that time engaged to Conchita Arguello. [13]

While Rezanov grieved, the round-the-world expedition that he had underwritten was catching the imagination not just of the Tsar but also of the navy, the recently founded Russian Academy of Sciences, the Foreign Ministry and St Petersburg's beau monde. The expedition's goals quickly multiplied. This was not to be just a naval sortie to support the Russian American Company's American settlements, but something much grander. The voyage of the *Nadezhda* and the *Neva* would be a great scientific expedition of conquest and exploration as well as the first Russian circumnavigation of the world. Rumiantsev decided that it would also, crucially, make an attempt to open the closed markets of Japan to Russian trade. The voyage would therefore carry the first ever embassy from the Tsar to the Japanese Shōgun* at Edo.

The emperor's emissary for such an important mission would obviously have to be a nobleman, a native Russian, a courtier, preferably a man with a stake in the success of the mission. To Rumianstev and the Emperor, if not yet to Rezanov himself, it was clear there was only one man for the job. In April 1803 Alexander summoned the unsuspecting Rezanov to Tsarskoye Selo for a private audience.

'The Emperor kindly sympathized with my grief and at first advised me to do something to distract myself,' Rezanov wrote to Dmitriev. 'At last His Majesty offered me a voyage and then, gently leading me to agreement, announced to me His will that I should take upon myself the Embassy to Japan.' The offer, judging from Rezanov's letter, came as an unpleasant shock. The expedition would be at sea for at least three years, and Rezanov would be forced to leave his two motherless infant children behind. Nonetheless, one did not refuse the Tsar. Alexander made the offer more attractive by promoting Rezanov to the court rank of *kamerheer*, or royal chamberlain, equivalent to a major-general and fourth in the table of ranks, and upgrading his Order of St Anne to first class. Whether he liked it or not, Rezanov was now launched on a new career as a diplomat and inspector of the Russian American colonies. He would be exchanging the world of the court for one of the remotest wildernesses on earth.

Rumiantsev rushed to back up the Tsar's offer with assurances of the embassy's success. The two men probably met in the study on the first floor of Rumiantsev's mansion; its windows overlook the Neva and Peter the Great's Kunstkammer Museum on the far side. Rezanov would be in overall command of the expedition, Rumiantsev promised, and indeed the Instruction the Emperor issued to Rezanov in July

---

* The de-facto ruler of Japan, though technically subordinate to the demi-god Emperor at Kyoto.

clearly stated in its first paragraph that the chamberlain was 'in command of all the officers' – including, by implication, the captain himself. We will hear much about this controversial document in coming chapters. In Russian America Rezanov would, according to these written orders, also be the Tsar's viceroy, with full authority 'to administer courts and punishments . . . as much as possible remove all burdens from the inhabitants . . . [and] lay firm foundations of good order'.

As for the embassy to Japan, the ships would be sailing under the authority of the document the Japanese authorities had granted to Adam Laxman in 1792 – though perhaps the minister omitted to mention that the Laxman document allowed only a single Russian ship to trade at Nagasaki and was ambiguous about the possibility of political contact. Rumiantsev also announced that a parallel embassy to Rezanov's was to be dispatched overland to China, with a brief to overturn the restrictions on Russo-Chinese trade imposed by the Treaty of Nerchinsk and open trade at Canton to Russian shipping. Furthermore, Rumiantsev promised, the Treasury would provide ample diplomatic gifts for the Japanese Shōgun and even relieve the Russian American Company of the cost of buying the *Nadezhda*.[14] For good measure, and since this was now to be a government mission as much as a Company one, Rumiantsev attached a priest nominated by the Holy Synod to report on the state of spiritual affairs in Russian America. Rezanov, for his part, launched an appeal for books for the enlightenment of the Tsar's newest subjects. Fashionable St Petersburg flocked to become patrons of the expedition. 'Many vied with each other to serve their country and sent many things and books,' wrote Rezanov. 'When I reach Kodiak I will put in the American museum in eternal memory for generations to come of those who patronized the enlightenment of the region.'[15]*

---

* Part of the library Rezanov took to Kodiak surfaced in San Francisco in the early 1930s, when a Russian émigré offered twenty-four books on economics, navigation and husbandry to Father Andrew Kashevarov, a historian of Alaska. He was unable to buy them and they have been never heard of since. Another volume ended up in the Library of Congress – a tome by Nikolai Ilyinsky on the history of Pskov, which one imagines was of limited usefulness to readers in Kodiak.

If Krusenstern was annoyed by all these additions to his expedition, he was careful to conceal his resentment from the navy and from Rumiantsev. Crucially, Krusenstern still believed that he, not Rezanov, was the expedition's commander. He busied himself selecting his officers and crew, which as captain was his time-honoured personal prerogative. In the early summer of 1803 both Krusenstern and Rezanov were inundated with petitions and requests from society hostesses and powerful bureaucrats to find places on board for their children and protégés. By the time Hieromonk Gideon of the Alexander Nevsky Monastery, the Synod's representative on the voyage, reported for duty at the naval base of Kronstadt there were no cabins left on either ship. Only when Admiral Chichagov, deputy minister of the navy, and Rumiantsev himself came to inspect the preparations were various hangers-on – including seven members of Rezanov's suite, one of them a nephew on the Okunev side – dismissed. 'Some of the staff and senior officers not needed for the voyage were taken off,' reported Gideon. 'There was plenty of altercation.'[16] The priest was eventually assigned a cabin on board the *Neva* with the painter Prichetnikov, despite the ship's captain, Lisiansky, himself the son of a priest and a man of deep anti-clerical convictions, 'fighting hand and foot' against it.

Rezanov himself first visited the *Nadezdha* on 2 June, in the company of Rumiantsev and RAC directors Buldakov and Evstrat Delarov, the veteran Greek manager of Kodiak. Rumiantsev, introducing Rezanov as 'Ambassador' to Krusenstern and his officers on the quarterdeck of the *Nadezhda*, did not mention to Krusenstern that Rezanov was also to be the head of the expedition. This duplicity was motivated by realpolitik. Rumiantsev needed both captain and ambassador to make the expedition work, yet he knew that neither would consent to be subordinate to the other, so he made them both believe they were in charge, a surely deliberate omission that was to have disastrous results during the voyage.

It is unlikely that even as powerful a courtier as Rumiantsev would have played such a double game without the knowledge of the Tsar; it may well have been Alexander's idea. Many who had dealt with Alexander certainly would not put such deviousness past him. 'Alexander was clever, pleasant and educated but one cannot trust him.

He is a true Byzantine . . . subtle, treacherous and cunning,' Napoleon was to write of the Tsar from his exile in Elba. 'Alexander is acute as a pin, sharp as a razor, and false as the foam on the sea,' wrote the Swedish ambassador to Paris, Count Gustaf Lagerbielke.[17]

Guilty or not of hoodwinking Rezanov, in mid-June the Tsar came in his personal yacht from Oranienbaum to inspect preparations, 'found the tubs to his liking'[18] and complimented Krusenstern on the *Nadezhda*'s sturdy new Russian masts. Again, there was no mention of Rezanov as the voyage's new chief.

The navy officers watched the luggage of Rezanov's embassy and the presents for the 'Emperor' of Japan arrive at the dockside with growing trepidation. On 29 June Löwenstern reported that 'thirty large crates and chests with the gifts for the Emperor of J arrived today . . . immediately another boat arrived with more crates, presents for Japan. And three apothecary chests, and thus it continues endlessly to a point where you cannot move on shipboard.' An inventory of the presents lists

4 pairs of vases from the Imperial porcelain factory; 71 glass mirrors from the Imperial glass factory; 15 glass place mats from ditto; one portrait of Alexander I in tapestry from the Imperial tapestry factory; three other carpets and tapestries from ditto; furs – one black fox, one ermine; 300 yards of watered silk; 356 yards velvet; 11 lengths of English felt; Spanish felt; bronze mechanical clock in shape of elephant taken from the Imperial Hermitage; 5 ivory boxes; 100 ivory cups; pistols; muskets; dagger and sword; folding steel table; 4 chandeliers, 8 cut glass vessels w gold mountings; 12 glass jugs; 2 lamps with multiplying mirrors for lighthouses; 25 gold coronation medals; 200 silver ditto; 39 yards of blue medal ribbons; 142 yards of St Vladimir ribbons; 2 sets of steel buttons.

One wonders who compiled this strange collection of gifts, or who imagined it would be a good idea to send so much glassware and crockery across both the Atlantic and Pacific oceans. Rumiantsev was particularly proud of having wheedled the elephant clock out of the Winter Palace's high chamberlain, Count Pyotr Tolstoy; it was probably Tolstoy who made the selection of surplus palace lumber and sold it to the expedition for high prices.[19]

Rumiantsev also judged that five Japanese sailors who had been ship-wrecked on Kamchatka three years before would help the success of the expedition. Returning the men to their homeland would make a favourable impression on the authorities, it was decided, as well as strengthening the Russians' excuse for exceeding the terms of the Laxman letter. The sailors were duly outfitted with new suits, presented with silver watches by the Tsar as proof of Russia's goodwill, and added to the *Nadezhda*'s crew. 'Five Japanese to whom the Emperor has given watches came aboard,' sniffed Fourth Lieutenant Hermann Ludwig von Löwenstern. 'They are ugly people who guzzle like hedgehogs and have a lot of pretentions.'

The Emperor paid a final visit in mid-July, conferring his blessing on the crew. A dinner party hosted by Krusenstern's wife Juliane Charlotte was held for the officers and their wives on board the *Nadezhda*. Rezanov had arranged for his children to be looked after by their aunt, the late Anna's younger sister Avdotia Buldakova. Rezanov took his last leave of his son and daughter on 21 July and boarded the *Nadezhda*, which had moved out into the sea-roads off Kronstadt in preparation for sailing.

10

From Newgate to Brazil

And the Oceans parted for him, opening the path before his feet.
Gavriil Derzhavin, 'Ode on the Taking of Ismail', 1791[1]

At midsummer in the northern Baltic there is no night. Sleep comes fitfully, and the sun never takes its pale eye off the earth. Early on the morning of 26 July 1803 Hieromonk Gideon sang a Te Deum on the quarterdeck of the *Nadezhda* before returning to his quarters on the *Neva*. 'At 8 o'clock after midnight,' under fresh wind at twelve versts an hour,[2] the two ships nosed out of the shelter of the fortified island of Kronstadt at the mouth of the Neva and into the open Baltic. Behind them the golden spire of the Peter and Paul Fortress caught in the sun like a bright splinter even after the rest of the city had disappeared in the haze. It was the last Nikolai Rezanov would ever see of his birthplace.

'As I glanced with heartfelt emotion at the waves playing around the ship their momentary elevation and immediate descent I imagined the uncertainties and even mysteries of human fate,' wrote Gideon. He recalled the Book of Proverbs, which compares man's fleeting existence on earth to 'the way of an eagle in the air; the way of a serpent upon a rock; the wake of a ship in the midst of the sea'.[3]

At 3 p.m. – the end of the first afternoon watch – the *Nadezhda*'s officers, the expedition's scientific and artistic attachés, officials of the Russian American Company and members of Rezanov's embassy sat down to their first dinner together in the ship's Great Cabin, which doubled as Captain Krusenstern's private quarters. Of the twenty-two gentlemen who dined at the captain's table, only nine were Russian. Almost all the ship's officers were Lutheran Germans from the Baltic. Both Lisiansky, captain of the *Neva*, and Löwenstern, fourth lieutenant of the *Nadezhda*, were former British Royal Navy men;* indeed the Estonian-born Löwenstern 'spoke not a word of Russian' when he quit George III's navy for the Tsar's in 1797. Lieutenants Romberg, Löwenstern and Bellinghausen, Midshipmen Otto and Moritz Kotzebue and Marine Lieutenant Otto von Bistam were all either Krusenstern's relatives, friends or friends' children. August von Kotzebue, father of the two midshipmen and the popular playwright who had composed Tsar Paul's challenge to Napoleon, achieved the impressive feat of marrying three of Krusenstern's cousins in succession before being stabbed to death by a religious maniac in front of his family in 1818. First Lieutenant Makar Ratmanov and Second Lieutenant Pyotr Golovachev were the only Russian officers aboard.

The men of science were Dr Karl Espenberg, of Hobeda, Estonia, the Krusenstern family doctor and the illegitimate son of a friend of the captain's. The natural scientist Fyodor Brinkin of Moscow had also joined the expedition on the recommendation of the Russian Academy of Sciences. Two more Germans, astronomer and physics professor Dr Johann Caspar Horner of Göttingen University and Dr Wilhelm Gottfried Tilesius of the medical faculty of Leipzig University, were due to join the expedition at Copenhagen. From the Russian American Company were manager and cargo supervisor Fyodor Shmelin, an older man with a weakness for drink, and Filipp Kamenshikov, chief quartermaster and First Mate, who was a navigator of the twelfth rank, equivalent to a naval lieutenant.

Rezanov's ambassadorial suite, in its trimmed-down version, numbered five. Major Hermann Karl von Friderici was a cartographer and astronomer and member of St Petersburg's Academy of Sciences. Court Councillor Fyodor Fosse – equivalent of a lieutenant-colonel

– was a former police officer. Stepan Kurliantsev, a silver-medal-winning graduate of the Imperial Academy of Arts, was the expedition's official artist. Last but not least was Lieutenant Count Fyodor Ivanovich Tolstoy of the Preobrazhensky Guards.

Tolstoy was not meant to be on board. When Rezanov's embassy was being assembled, the Tolstoy family's considerable social traction was applied to secure a place for Fyodor Petrovich, the young sailor of the clan, a graduate of St Petersburg Naval Academy. However Fyodor Petrovich himself had not been consulted and was in fact keen to remain in the capital since he was discovering artistic gifts that were in later life to place him in the forefront of Russia's painters.[4] His first cousin Fyodor Ivanovich, on the other hand, had a long and growing list of urgent reasons to leave town. His military career had started badly when, soon after being commissioned into the Preobrazhensky Guards at the age of sixteen, he challenged the regiment's commanding officer to a duel. Colonel Baron Fyodor Vasiliyevich von Drizen declined the meeting – wisely, it turned out, because even as a teenager Tolstoy was a superb swordsman and pistol-shot who went on to kill eleven men in a lifetime of duelling.

The twenty-one-year-old Tolstoy was already known in St Petersburg society as a 'dangerous madcap . . . whatever anyone else did, he did ten times over.'[5] But professionally and socially he was in a squeeze. He had already been demoted to an inferior battalion of the Guards for unrecorded misdemeanours. Gambling debts loomed, and by his own (highly unreliable and contradictory) later accounts, a complicated love affair with a married woman made his continued presence in the capital inadvisable. So the two Tolstoy cousins agreed to swap. Rezanov approved the last-minute substitution, evidently unaware of the replacement Tolstoy's psychopathic tendencies. Of all the arrogant drunks in this most mismatched of ship's companies, Tolstoy was to be the most dangerous and disruptive. Even before they set sail Tolstoy began as he meant to continue. He and two other junior officers 'did not deny themselves the opportunity of staging a drinking bout into the night . . . they are a lively bunch, jumping around, laughing, climbing, making noise. Count T. is primus.'[6]

The first day's sailing was not a success. The *Nadezhda* was top-heavy because of the luggage stowed on deck: she rolled dangerously and eventually developed a list to starboard. Rezanov and half the officers were struck down with seasickness. It was also discovered that in the confusion of departure Ratmanov's gold watch, Tolstoy's gold snuffbox and Shmelin's pipe had been stolen, prompting a general if fruitless search of everybody's effects. The Japanese, whom Rezanov had exempted from the search lest these live diplomatic gifts take offence, were universally suspected. At dusk the gentlemen retired to their tiny sleeping cabins to commence their journals, letters and diaries.

Almost every one of the literate men on board wrote a diary, recording the querulous table talk in more or less detail. Several – notably Krusenstern, Lisiansky, Tilesius and Langsdorff – published their journals, lavishly illustrated, to great international acclaim at the expedition's end. But it is the diary of Hermann Ludwig von Löwenstern, the *Nadezhda's* fourth lieutenant and map-maker, which is by far the frankest and funniest. Written mostly in German but with an admixture of Russian and English, it was edited by a German-speaking relative in the late nineteenth century, who excised some references to the crew's womanizing in the South Seas but – hilariously – failed to censor Löwenstern's frequent use of Russian obscenities.[7] It was not published until 2004. 'Well my dear ones, you who will in future leaf through my diary, have to be kind to the writer,' wrote Löwenstern wryly. 'My passionate character has led me to conclusions that I have written as they occur to me.'

By the time the *Nadezhda* reached Copenhagen on 3 August the ship's company was in better spirits, despite the loss of Usov, a sailor who fell overboard and became 'the unhappy victim of ferocious Neptune', an oddly pagan reference by Hieromonk Gideon.[8] Rezanov took the largest suite at an inn on Copenhagen's main square and set about entertaining himself and his fellow officers in style.

'Par curiositet R is visiting all of the dance halls and wh[ore] houses,' wrote the prudish Löwenstern of one exhausting afternoon spent ashore in the company of his chief. 'I could not decline R's polite invitation to lunch . . . That afternoon in the Summer Garden R forgot himself so completely that he with Star [of the Order of St Anne] ran after street girls and later climbed to the top floor of several houses. We followed as if pulled by the hair . . .'

Löwenstern's shock was not too great, however, to prevent him from dining with Rezanov that evening and lunching with him the day after as well. A more decorous expedition, with Hieromonk Gideon in tow, took the Russians to the royal palace, where the monk was deeply impressed by the Hall of Mirrors, 'so remarkably arranged that the spectators see themselves and their surroundings in infinite distance'.

Rezanov was clearly enjoying himself thoroughly and didn't care who knew it. 'From the balcony of his inn he does not let a single girl cross the market square without throwing her a kiss, calling to her, and laughing loudly at his own jokes,' Löwenstern noted in his diary. 'At about noon a young girl went by with her handiwork. R called and waved her in. Then R got a girl for Friderici, but since he did not want to she had the honour of being kissed by His Excellency. That takes the cake! R can talk of nothing else but girls and bawdy.'

Doctor Georg Heinrich Baron von Langsdorff, newly arrived post-haste from Göttingen, would have had no trouble locating the high-profile Russian party at the Hotel of Sieur Rau. There he presented himself on the morning of 24 August, neatly dressed in the black frock coat of a man of science. The twenty-nine-year-old doctor of medicine was also a keen amateur naturalist. In 1797 he had travelled to Portugal in the suite of a German prince, and had stayed on as surgeon major to the British Regiment of Castries. Fascinated by botany, Langsdorff corresponded with some of the greatest natural scientists of France. He was also a correspondent member of the Imperial Academy of Sciences in St Petersburg.[*]

For many hungry young men of science Russian service repre-sented a fast track to advancement, an opportunity to leapfrog the academic hierarchies at home. Langsdorff was no exception, and he

---

[*] Though since Rezanov's uneducated brother-in-law Mikhail Buldakov was also a correspondent member, one wonders how high the fledgling institution set the bar for membership above the ability to write a civil letter.

had written repeatedly to the Russian Academy of Sciences in an attempt to attach himself to the great round-the-world expedition, only to be politely rebuffed. Undaunted, Langsdorff rushed to Copenhagen to press his suit in person and begged Rezanov 'to be received as a sharer in the voyage'. He promised to pay his share of mess bills and offered to act as Rezanov's personal physician. A portrait engraving in Langsdorff's memoirs, published in London in 1811, shows a slight, angular young man with a likeably intelligent expression. Both Rezanov and Krusenstern seem to have been charmed (even though Langsdorff, though German, was surprisingly not related to the captain) and, despite the lack of space, assigned him a small cabin near Shmelin's in the hold.

By 1 September the ship's water casks had been refilled and the holds repacked for the journey across the Atlantic, round Cape Horn and thence across the Pacific. Rather than lose any of the Emperor of Japan's precious presents 300 *puds* – nearly half a ton – of flour was unloaded in order to trim the ship for the open sea.

The crossing of the North Sea proved a traumatic experience for the newly formed ship's company. Shmelin almost blew the vessel up by using candles near the powder magazine, and a violent storm saw all the inmates of the great cabin 'elbowing, jostling, crying out . . . a scene entirely new to most of our company',[9] wrote Langsdorff. 'The moaning and throwing up is endless,' observed Löwenstern, less delicately.[10] After the storm had abated, Langsdorff gazed at a spectacular aurora borealis: 'streams of light rose like pillars of fire'.[11]

In the English Channel the *Nadezhda* and *Neva* were stopped repeatedly by British men-of-war hoping to take a lightly armed French prize. Krusenstern, Löwenstern, Lisiansky and several other Russian officers were reunited with old acquaintances on the British ships. Captain Berrisforth of the frigate *Virginia*, an old shipmate of Krusenstern's from his days in Canton, offered to run Rezanov and his suite to Sheerness. They would rejoin the *Nadezhda* and *Neva* in Falmouth by post-chaise after a brief look around London.

Rezanov also needed to visit London on a fact-finding mission. As the future head of a major colony to be peopled primarily by convict labour, Rezanov was anxious to glean as much as he could from the British about their fifteen years of experience transporting prisoners to Botany Bay in Australia. He was cordially received by the governor of Newgate Prison and shown a shipment of convicts ready to be transported. Rezanov was impressed at how humanely the English treated their prisoners – a far cry, he wrote, from the brutalities inflicted on the Russian convicts he had seen en route to Irkutsk, who regularly had freezing water poured onto their shaven heads as a punishment.

But the talk in Newgate in 1803 was not of Botany Bay but of an exciting scientific experiment that had been performed in the jail earlier in the year by an Italian physician named Professor Giovanni Aldini, nephew of the biological electricity guru Dr Luigi Galvani. Following his uncle's pioneering work with beheaded criminals in Bologna, Aldini had wowed London by apparently animating a body using an electrical generator. The victim, or subject, was one George Foster, hanged for drowning his wife and youngest child in the Paddington Canal.

'The jaws of the deceased criminal began to quiver, and the adjoining muscles were horribly contorted, and one eye was actually opened,' observed the *Newgate Calendar*. Mr Pass, the beadle of the Surgeons' Company, 'who was officially present during this experiment, was so alarmed that he died of fright soon after his return home'. So fashionable were Dr Galvani's amazing machines in the courts of Europe – it was with an early model that Catherine the Great had electrocuted her staff – that Rezanov bought one and had it stowed in the hold of the *Nadezhda* as an additional present for the Shogun. Thus would Rezanov bring the wonders of science to the savage shores of Japan.

While Rezanov was investigating modern penal and Galvanic practices in London, Langsdorff explored the 'dry, desert and unfruitful aspect' of Cornwall, his interest excited only by the deep tin mines, which to his amazement extended under the seabed. The officers amused themselves as best they could with the social whirl, or perhaps slow rotation, of the Falmouth gentry. Rezanov, Tilesius and Horner returned from London in a carriage groaning with sextants, snuffboxes and other kit requested by their fellow officers from the fashionable shops of the metropolis.

The ships' companies reassembled, the two vessels set sail across the Bay of Biscay, bound for the Canaries. Giant sacks of fresh cabbages were hung from the stern rails. In one of them a wagtail had unwisely nested, 'but whistled, unafraid, its innocent song'[12] until one of the Japanese caught it and squeezed it to death, upsetting the sentimental Löwenstern. Tilesius and Friderici set up a convivial-sounding private bivouac in the ship's longboat, where they would read, sketch and smoke undisturbed. By Langsdorff's rose-tinted account, the voyage began to resemble a kind of floating Platonic symposium. 'In an expedition such as ours among a numerous society of learned and scientific men in search of knowledge, it is impossible to experience ennui.' Krusenstern's well-stocked library was available to all who asked. 'The mornings passed in reading, writing, drawing, taking the height of the sun and calculating the distance to the moon . . . all these things furnished abundant matter for pleasant and instructive conversation, even sallies of wit and mirth.' The men of science also busied themselves with observing the dolphins, flying fish, sharks, birds and whales. In the evenings, after 'a table spread with very excellent provisions' there were 'cheerful conversations over a bowl of punch'[13] and concerts 'with Romberg violono primo, Rezanov secundo, Tilesius basso, Langsdorff viola, Friderici flute primo, Horner flute secondo'. [14]

With the ships sailing in tandem, visits were exchanged. Hieromonk Gideon, dining on board the *Nadezhda*, got so drunk with Tolstoy that the priest fell sound asleep on deck. Tolstoy then proceeded to stick the prelate's beard to the boards with a large blob of wax impressed with the captain's seal, which he purloined from Krusenstern's cabin.[15] When Gideon came to, Tolstoy told him not to move because breaking the imperial seal would be treason. The clerical beard had to be cut off and left, sealed to the deck.

This agreeable idyll was disturbed only by the nascent but increasingly difficult-to-ignore rift between Rezanov and Krusenstern. Like many Lutheran German Balts, Krusenstern had a conflicted attitude to Russian rule and to the courtiers of St Petersburg who ran the naval ministry. The idea of putting together an expedition to circumnavigate the earth had been Krusenstern's and he clearly resented Rezanov's last-minute inclusion, even though it was thanks to Rezanov's great Russian American scheme that the expedition had received imperial patronage and Company funding. But the fundamental problem was that both men had effectively been given mutually contradictory instructions on who was to lead the expedition. 'We left Russia with the firm conviction that R was a passenger aboard,' wrote Löwenstern, a firm backer of Krusenstern. When 'Rezanov produced his Orders with the Imperial signature, [he] thereby suddenly robbed the captain of the incentives on whose account he had left the Fatherland.'[16] Rezanov, in the view of the officers, was attempting to hijack the expedition of which Krusenstern 'was the originator, recognized throughout Europe' – and moreover waited till the ships were three months out of port before revealing the full extent of his imperial authority.

This conflict, which was to resurface endlessly and with increasing rancour throughout the voyage, got its first full-blown airing as the *Nadezhda* approached the Spanish Canary Islands. Krusenstern wanted to dock at Tenerife; Rezanov attempted to insist that they put in at the Portuguese island of Madeira. It is not clear why. Löwenstern gives his version of their conversation verbatim.

REZANOV: What reason can you give me for not going to Madeira? I have to know in order to report to the Emperor.

KRUSENSTERN: No other than ones I considered good. And by the way, the Emperor will not care to know why we have sailed to Tenerife and not Madeira.

Rezanov fell silent.

Krusenstern's decisive response seems to have stung Rezanov into increasing bumptiousness. 'R behaves coarsely and harshly towards his fellow countrymen and is polite, well behaved and obliging towards foreigners,' complained Löwenstern. 'It is impossible to imagine being on board ship a long time with him. He has often enough been thoughtless, mean, partial and roaring.'[17]

Tenerife provided some respite from the claustrophobia of the Great Cabin, with the added piquancy that this was the last outpost of Europe that they would see. They found the town neat and clean. Langsdorff was sent to gather geraniums for transport to Kamchatka while Rezanov and Friderici went in search of 'bold women and rabble'.[18] The Russians found the Spanish 'exceedingly un-neighbourly'. A group of local rowdies stole the *Nadezhda*'s jolly boat after drunken Russian sailors left it unguarded, and Löwenstern was charged a shocking four dollars for twenty-five pieces of laundry. 'Tenerife is said to be for Spain what Siberia is for Russia,' complained Löwenstern. 'One finds more rascally faces here than anywhere else.'

They had a more friendly reception at the salon of Mrs Armstrong, 'a coquette of the highest degree'. Captain Lisiansky was much taken by the British hostess: 'he is like a cat prancing around a bowl of hot porridge with her', reported Löwenstern. A ball was thrown in the Russians' honour, with Lieutenant Fyodor Romberg taking over from the terrible local musicians and playing a Scottish reel on a Spanish guitar. The ladies of Tenerife, 'infected with their hostess' coquettish-ness', danced wantonly. Poor young Moritz Kotzebue was so smitten by one Delphine Kuwe that he considered deserting ship to be with her until talked out of it by Löwenstern. Instead Kotzebue climbed to the top of the mainmast in tears as the ship sailed for Brazil so that he could see his beloved one more time.[19]

But despite the fresh tropical produce bought at Tenerife, tempers began to fray when back in the close confinement of shipboard life. Dr Espenberg found the tea too strong and the coffee too weak, and irritated the officers by shaving at breakfast and appearing on the quarterdeck in his dressing gown. The wind failed and the *Nadezhda* drifted in the late-summer equatorial heat. The sun and humidity made the sleeping cabins too hot, so the gentlemen spent all day around the table. Rezanov loudly recited Japanese verbs; Friderici drew a map of Santa Cruz; Brinkin read Latin out loud; Dr Espenberg drilled the two young Kotzebues in arithmetic; Bellinghausen sketched ships; Romberg leaned against his cabin door playing his violin with a damper while the painter Kurliantsev 'leaned against the cabin wall staring vacantly at these goings on'.[20] Löwenstern, absenting himself from the crowd and sweating over his diary in his airless and lightless cabin, wrote, 'There is no place else where men can become so estranged from each other as on a ship. Little annoyances build up, vexation grows bigger and bigger . . . if mistrust has crept in, the step to discord is not much further.' [21]

A small lapdog Romberg had bought in Copenhagen had made friends with a sailor's cat and provided much amusement to the *Nadezhda*'s crew. 'They play together so hilariously that we often form a circle around them and simply enjoy it.'[22] Now, becalmed in mid-Atlantic, the little dog came into heat and began to whine and yap incessantly. Krusenstern ordered the animal thrown overboard, much to the distress of Romberg – and its friend the cat, 'which cannot stop looking for the little dog in all the cabins and crannies of the ship . . . meowing pitifully to call her playmate'.[23] One of the ship's pigs, driven mad by the heat on the becalmed ship, broke from its pen and jumped overboard. Unlike the dog, however, it proved such an excellent swimmer that Krusenstern ordered all the pigs thrown overboard for a good wash. The terrified squealing and shitting provoked by getting the pigs in and out of the water were distressing to the more highly strung passengers. The ship's hens were less fortunate: Langsdorff observed that the terrible heat and salt dust off the decks had blinded them all.

The captain insisted that full uniform be worn at table and reprimanded Tolstoy for appearing in a shirt. 'Perhaps the Russian custom of using the vapour-bath so much allowed [Krusenstern] to support the heat,' observed Langsdorff dryly.[24] Nonetheless, the crossing of the equator was celebrated in traditional style. The sailor Kurganov, dressed in sheepskins and carrying a harpoon in place of a trident, appeared as a sweaty Neptune and doused the ship's company in warm seawater. Rezanov made a patriotic speech on the occasion of the Russian flag flying in the southern hemisphere for the first time and presented every member of the company with a Spanish dollar. Krusenstern was tossed in the air, then Rezanov, and multiple salutes fired. 'Rezanov got completely drunk . . . everyone was joyous and only the *Nadezhda* was sober.'[25]

In early November, after nearly four months at sea, the *Nadezhda* approached the coast of Brazil. Violent rain showers made 'the whole ship smoke . . . the dampness makes everything rot, moulder and spoil.

Whenever the sun comes out everyone carts their belongings out to let them dry and our ship is festooned with clothes and bedding,' complained Löwenstern, ever the fastidious officer. Rezanov's simmering feud with the captain was stepped up a notch when he casually 'let drop a word at table that he was the leader of the expedition. Without a word, everyone left the table.'[26] 'Everyone' presumably meant Löwenstern and the ship's officers; Rezanov's own entourage would have stayed firmly put.

Rezanov attempted to regain the initiative by having the ship's company assembled on deck to hear him reading part of his orders from the Tsar. 'He probably wants to let us know how important he is,' remarked Löwenstern testily. 'Rezanov, the Russian Pinetti [a famous contemporary illusionist], has told several of us confidentially that he had already complained about Krusenstern from Tenerife. He also complains that the further we get from Europe the more the proper respect he deserves is lost . . . he shies from daylight and appears less and less often.'[27] Rezanov spent more and more time in his cabin, drafting and redrafting querulous letters to the Tsar and to his many allies in St Petersburg, an activity which in time was to become something of a mania. The polished metropolitan courtier who had successfully maintained himself in the favour of three successive monarchs had given way to someone altogether more pompous, argumentative and, increasingly, unhinged.

Sixty sea miles off the coast of Brazil the *Nadezhda* was greeted by a vast number of butterflies which had been blown out to sea by a squall and settled over every inch of the ship. Closer to port a dugout canoe brought Portuguese customs officers and a pilot who guided the *Nadezhda* to an anchorage opposite the fort of Santa Cruz, twelve miles from the city of Nossa Senhora do Desterro* some five hundred miles south of Rio de Janeiro. Rezanov attempted to forbid Tolstoy from going ashore as punishment for his constant high jinks and lack of respect. Krusenstern, humiliatingly, overruled him. 'If this is the way you act you won't say anything if someone hits me in the face,' Rezanov

---

* Modern-day Florianopolis in the state of Santa Catarina.

fumed before disembarking to take up the local governor's invitation to stay at his residence.

The *Nadezhda* was overhauled and the crew busied themselves filling water casks and purchasing provisions. Dozens of barrels of salt pork, pickled beetroot and sauerkraut were thrown overboard to make room for fresh pineapples, lemons and oranges. The cannons were lowered into the hold to add stability during the coming rounding of Cape Horn and the 'black' laundry boiled with lye soap in huge pots. The expedition's rival chiefs spent their time ashore penning letters to St Petersburg. 'My, the Emperor will be surprised by so many petitions from Brazil!' quipped Löwenstern. 'The captain is requesting protection and justice. R is making no secret of his intention to denounce us all . . . May the hangman take him!'[28]

The many letters Rezanov sent from Santa Catarina in November of 1803 are a convoluted confection of complaint and unexplained innuendo. They make for bizarre reading. 'I am ashamed to repeat here what I have had to endure,' he wrote to Admiral Pavel Chichagov, the assistant minister of the navy, without at any point explaining what exactly it was he was enduring. 'At least the beneficial consequences of this disorder might result in the future in the realization that without respect for rank nothing can be accomplished.'[29] It is not clear quite what Rezanov expected any of his correspondents to do about his predicament as the *Nadezhda* sailed towards the Pacific like some kind of faulty satellite, shooting off a flurry of garbled distress signals every few months to a puzzled St Petersburg.

'Every day R seeks out something new to anger our captain with,'[30] complained Löwenstern, who made a point of cutting off Rezanov halfway through every sentence the councillor addressed to him. 'R is the object of our general hatred.'[31]

Krusenstern, for his part, sent multiple copies of his letters to the Emperor, Chichagov, Rumiantsev and other luminaries, attaching a note to each explaining that the copies were 'to make it impossible for Rezanov to intercept them'. Tolstoy, collected 'attests' to his good character from his fellow officers to defend his reputation against the complaints he imagined Rezanov would be making against him – pointlessly, it seems, for Rezanov barely mentions Tolstoy in any of his surviving letters, though he had evidently threatened Tolstoy that he would.

For most of the company, though, there were more interesting things about Santa Catarina than the escalating Rezanov–Krusenstern feud. Langsdorff was 'wholly transported' by his expeditions to catch insects and butterflies. The human fauna were no less fascinating. 'They dance, they laugh, they joke, they sing, they play,' wrote Langsdorff of his expedition to Nossa Senhora do Desterro. 'The females are not ugly; among the higher classes we saw some who even in Europe might be called handsome . . . they are well-made with dark complexions, coarse dark hair and dark eyes full of fire.'[32] To the delight of the Russians, 'the most insignificant presents of European merchandise – tinsel, ribbands, ear-rings, are always thankfully received'[33] by the women. Friderici copied a local practical joke which involved crushing a wax ball full of perfumed water on the breast of a passing young lady – and dabbing the girl dry with a large handkerchief while chatting her up.

Langsdorff, free of the status anxiety which so gravely afflicted his superiors, went to special efforts to observe the black slaves dance 'despite the not very agreeable smell of so many Negroes shut up together in a confined space, heated up with the exertions of jumping and leaping . . . Their leader stood like a hero in the midst of his followers, his head ornamented with gold paper and feathers and his body with glass, gold, bangles and stars and suns in silver paper.' The conditions in the slave market, where Langsdorff saw 'wretched helpless beings lying almost naked about the streets for sale' for a hundred to a hundred and fifty dollars – fifty times more than the cost of a young steer – depressed him. But he soon discovered fellow gentleman-naturalist, Señor Matteos Cardoso Calideiro, and together they caught 'butterflies as big as birds' with a giant two-man net.[34] So taken with Brazil was Langsdorff that he returned in 1813 as Russia's consul general in Rio de Janeiro. He later acquired a farm, hosted and entertained foreign naturalists and scientists and led expeditions into the interior.[*]

---

[*] A recent study found that Langsdorff has 1,500 descendants in Brazil, among them Luma de Oliveira, a carnival queen who holds the world record for appearances on the cover of *Playboy* magazine.

Catholic Christmas and New Year were celebrated with feasts of mangoes and pineapples, their Orthodox equivalents in the Julian calendar following thirteen days behind. The *Neva* required extensive refitting, including a new foremast. Löwenstern was convinced that Lisiansky had deliberately put off these repairs to avoid awkward questions at Kronstadt about the extravagant cost of the two British frigates, supposedly in tip-top condition. 'Lisiansky certainly played under the same hat as the seller,' Löwenstern wrote.[35]

On board the *Nadezhda* Krusenstern was doing a little refitting of his own. The latest row had been sparked when Rezanov, getting his own back for being overruled on the matter of Tolstoy's punishment, refused to allow Krusenstern to ban the painter Kurliantsev – a member of the embassy and not a military officer, unlike Tolstoy – from the Great Cabin for insubordination. Krusenstern's ingenious solution was to order the ship's carpenters to erect a panelled partition down the middle of the cabin, one side for himself, the ship's officers and most of the gentlemen, and the other side for Rezanov. 'He will be wide-eyed when he arrives,' crowed Löwenstern.[36]

Rezanov's reaction on returning from his two months ashore, opening the familiar door to the cabin and finding it divided in half is, surprisingly, unrecorded. But we can safely speculate that it was not positive. Meanwhile below decks confusion reigned. Dozens of boxes of Langsdorff's specimens, including bullfrogs, lizards, crabs, snakes and butterflies, jostled for space with sacks of watermelons and vegetables as well as other crew members' live pets, including two raccoons, Löwenstern's green parrot, which could say '*Durak*!' – Russian for 'fool' – and a monkey purchased by Tolstoy.

In such disarray, and with the rival chiefs of the *Nadezhda* ensconced in their separate halves of the Great Cabin separated by an inch of good English oak, the two ships set off southwards into the most dangerous waters in the world.

Cape Horn to the Court of the Hawaiian King

L'enfer, c'est les autres.

Jean-Paul Sartre, *Huis Clos*

Rezanov has caused me very sad days through his personal hate, his countless deceptions as well as his offensive insults, his unjust, despotic and tyrannical control over me. He misused the authority and confidence of the Monarch.

Wilhem Gottfried Tilesius, 6 October 1805[1]

As the *Nadezhda* ploughed towards the earth's roughest seas, strong following winds drove Rezanov ever further into a cold and unfamiliar world. He was trapped in a wooden tub shorter than three London buses with sixty men, most of whom made no secret of their hatred for him. Rezanov was poorly equipped to deal with this strange and frightening predicament. He was a creature of the court and the capital. Intrigues, gossip, the vicious betrayals men were ready to contemplate in order to win fortune and power: these were things Rezanov knew well. He was a master of the game of politics. His skills were diplomacy, flattery, the ability to appeal to men's greed or ambition, to paint a grand and seductive picture for his royal masters, to bully, bribe and cajole subordinates into line. But these arts were for a world governed by a powerful and unrelenting gravitational force that centred on the monarch. Out here the rules were different; appeals to the Tsar in St

Petersburg were useless. Alliances and allegiances were fixed: on board the *Nadezhda* there was only one monarch, and it was not Rezanov.

The ambassador was cold-shouldered by the ship's company. The naval officers would not speak to him and moved away when he came onto the quarterdeck. 'The cold at Cape Horn cannot be colder than the cold which R meets from us.'[2] Löwenstern drew a sketch of Rezanov in 'optima forma' as the ship headed towards the Cape wearing a fur hat, baggy breeches, tall boots and an unbuttoned jacket, huddled in his lonely corner of the deck. The company in the cabin had no doubt been vexing, but it was ostracism that proved harder to bear. 'R goes round the ship like a water-shy dog, with lowered head.'[3] Already Krusenstern had resolved not to stop in Chile but press on to the Sandwich Islands – modern Hawaii – in order to deny Rezanov the chance to send more poisonous letters home. The officers also eagerly discussed Rezanov's tendency to seasickness. 'Irresponsible of me, I know, but I am hoping for a storm at Cape Horn,' Löwenstern observed.[4]

Löwenstern's sketch of Rezanov 'optima forma' on the *Nadezhda*'s quarterdeck.

On 4 February, in heavy seas, the *Neva* struck a whale. The blow was so powerful that her captain thought they had hit a rock. The whale also came out of the encounter badly. Langsdorff, on the nearby *Nadezhda*, observed whale fat spreading for hundreds of yards across the surface of the ocean and reflected on 'Dr [Benjamin] Franklin's idea that the waves of the sea, violently agitated, might be stilled' by the application of oil.[5]

The Cape proved a disappointment, at least to those officers who had been hoping to shake up the ambassador. The *Nadezhda* cleared it in under a week at a spanking nine knots in favourable winds. The only casualty was Löwenstern's parrot, who was found, squawking in distress, with its feet frozen to the ship's rail. The three-month slog north towards Hawaii was made tougher than it would otherwise have been by a lack of fresh food and water. Rezanov was blamed – though it is not clear if he was aware that the captain had decided on this course expressly in order to keep him from posting letters in Chile. 'The unpleasantness we have had, the cold weather and the permanent stress have converted our voyage to an eternity,' complained Löwenstern. 'I shudder, as does everyone else, at the thought that one has to spend three more years together with these people.'[6]

Even the usually affable Langsdorff managed to get into a screaming row with his fellow scientist Tilesius. Langsdorff refused to share some drawings of unusual jellyfish he'd spent all night catching in a net made of silk stockings. Rezanov came down with an unspecified malady and did not emerge from his cabin for days on end. 'Conversation, the spice of life, is completely gone of course . . . Our behaviour towards each other is less than upright.'[7] Only Tolstoy – 'that depraved fellow'[8] – had the spirit to continue his pranks. A Brazilian monkey he had bought in Santa Catarina broke its harness and ran amok in the Great Cabin, amusing itself by spilling ink over Krusenstern's maps and papers. Tolstoy, sent in to retrieve his unruly pet, was badly bitten on the hand and hit the creature so hard its injuries were deemed untreatable and it was thrown overboard.

On 24 April land was sighted. 'It was rocky not lush, with burnt peaks as though scorched.'[9] The *Nadezhda*'s English charts called the island chain Nukakhiva; it is now known as the Marquesas, part of French Polynesia. Krusenstern ordered crates of trade goods and trinkets hauled out of the hold, along with the cannon, which were mounted and loaded with grapeshot. Gunners filled cartridges and mounted racks of muskets and pistols on the gun deck. But instead of the expected fleet of canoes a single dugout paddled out to meet the Russian ship.

'How much we were surprised when instead of a South Sea Islander we saw a European,' wrote Langsdorff. 'He was entirely in the costume of the country with only a piece of cloth around his waist,' and greeted the ship's company in English. The mysterious sailor introduced himself only as Roberts and announced the imminent arrival of the island's King Katenua. (Edward Roberts' memoirs, published in 1974, revealed that he had deserted from an English whaler in 1798 and lived among

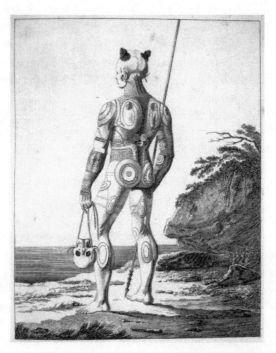

A native of Nukakhiva from Langsdorff's *Voyages and Travels.*

the natives of Nukakhiva until 1806 before working a passage to India, where he died in poverty in 1832.[10]) Reassured by Roberts via a signal that the visitors were friendly, the royal canoe duly appeared bearing Katenua and his brothers. The king was 'a large, robust man with his body tattooed all over. He was entirely naked, as were his attendants, and had no badge or characteristic by which he could be distinguished from them.'[11] The Nukakhivan men shaved their heads except for two patches above the ears, giving them the appearance of having horns. Löwenstern thought them 'a handsome people: each savage could serve as a model for the Apollo in Belvedere'.[12]

The king and his retinue shinned athletically up the side of the *Nadezhda*. Krusenstern, Rezanov and the embassy and officers, all in full ceremonial dress, formally greeted them.* Accompanying Katenua was another European renegade, Jean-Joseph Cabri (or Cadiche), a Frenchman who had almost entirely forgotten his native language and who was covered in native tattoos. The king was presented with presents of nails, knives and a piece of red cloth. In return, with Roberts translating, he promised pigs, crabs and fish. Apparently well pleased with the new arrivals, His Majesty took his leave by diving into the sea and swimming home, his presents in his teeth. [13]

Katenua's subjects on the shore took this as a general signal that the foreign ship was no longer taboo and could be safely approached. 'An extraordinary spectacle: a shoal of black-haired heads just above the water . . . some hundred men, women, girls and boys all swimming towards the ship, having in their hands coconuts, breadfruit and bananas to sell. The cries, laughter and romping of these mirthful people is indescribable . . . it exceeded any I have heard at our most numerously attended fairs.' To the delight of Löwenstern, and doubtless every other crew member, 'the female savages, naked, came onboard wearing only a few leaves to cover their privy parts. The goats on board smelled this greenery and hurried over to rob the naked girls of their last bit of cover.'[14]

---

* One is reminded of Mahatma Gandhi's quip about being underdressed for tea with King George V at Buckingham Palace: 'His Majesty was wearing enough clothes for both of us.'

This may have been an in-joke among South Sea sailors – a very similar story also involving goats, girls and grass skirts is repeated by the missionary Captain Wilson of the *Duff* as well as in other accounts.

Goats or no, Langsdorff recounts that the girls, 'their oratory illustrated with pantomime gestures, gave us to understand that they were making the most liberal and unreserved offers of their charms . . . Their menfolk did not show the slightest symptoms of jealousy but rather seemed pleased and flattered when a wife, daughter or sister attracted our particular attention.' Note the 'our'. Did the gentlemen take advantage of these 'topsy-turvy, wild girls'[15] some as young as eleven, 'such is the precocity of nature here'?[16] Langsdorff, in his published account, demurely notes that 'the Goddess of night with her dark veil covered everything which may have happened', and the puritan hand of one of Löwenstern's descendants has neatly excised the relevant passages in his diary with scissors.[17]

In the morning 'our new Venuses' slipped over the side of the ship carrying presents of 'bottles, pieces of broken china, coloured rags . . . one [sailor] tore the lining from his breeches and wrapped it

Interior of a native hut at Nukakhiva.

around the neck of his beloved – she was no less delighted and no less proud than a knight with the ribbon of a new Order and hastened home, no doubt thinking *honi soit qui mal y pense* . . .'[18] Having no pockets, the natives' habit was to carry articles of value in their mouths. Some experimentally minded sailors followed their paramours overboard 'in order to try it [intercourse] in the water, to see if it can be done'.[19] (Apparently it could, especially with the support of the anchor cables.)

A dinner was arranged on board for the royal family – of whom Cabri was a member, having married one of the chief's daughters. Muhaw, the king's brother, made an impression at table by casually punching a hole in the top of a coconut with his knuckle, drinking the water, then crushing the rest of the nut between his knees. One of the king's retainers, fastidiously measured by Tilesius as being six feet eight inches tall with ten and a half inches from his navel 'to the parting of the legs', further impressed the ship's company by climbing to the top of the mainmast and diving into the sea cannonball-style, his knees tucked under his chin.

The community's leading tattooist, an elderly woman who swam over holding her tools and dyes in her mouth, tattooed all comers from dawn until dusk in exchange for nails and cloth. Her bird's-quill needle with its blue-black ash-based dye was 'as much sought after as among us a particularly good tailor – though if the garment be spoiled in the making the mischief is irreparable and must be worn, with all its faults, the whole life through'.[20] Even Krusenstern submitted himself, though sadly exactly where and with what he was tattooed has been lost to history.

Tolstoy naturally went the whole hog and sat for tattoos every day. They eventually covered his whole back, arms and torso. In later life Tolstoy was to make much social hay of his ten days' stay on Nukakhiva. He enjoyed showing off his tattoos, especially to young ladies. His cousin Maria Kamenskaya recalled a dinner in 1842 at which Tolstoy, after not much persuasion, 'undid his shirt studs and bared and swelled out his chest. Everyone at the table stood up in their places and stared – it was completely covered in tattoos. In the

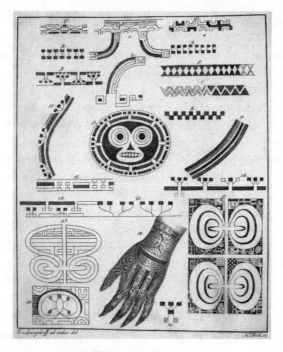

Langsdorff's drawings of Nukakhivan tattoos.

very middle sat in a ring some sort of big multi-coloured bird rather like a parrot in a blue and red hoop . . . The ladies sighed and gasped without ceasing and asked solicitously "Wasn't it very painful, Count, when those savages tattooed you?"'

Among the more extravagant lies Tolstoy told about his South Seas adventures was the claim that he was about to be eaten when another tribe attacked and treated him as an idol instead 'because of his beautiful white legs'[21] – though it is true that the Nukakhivans did occasionally eat enemies slain in battle. He also claimed that Krusenstern marooned him on a remote island, whence he made his way to the land of the Tlingits in Alaska, where he led hunts in his Preobrazhensky Guards uniform. In Alaska, Tolstoy told breathless listeners at St Petersburg dinner tables, he 'became as adept with a harpoon as he had been with foil or sabre' and the natives 'begged him to become their tsar'. He also claimed that Queen Pomare of Tahiti, which he never visited, was his daughter. In truth Tolstoy visited only one South Sea island – Nukakhiva – and thereafter remained on the *Nadezhda* until she reached Kamchatka, whence Krusenstern sent him home to St Petersburg in disgrace.

Rezanov was one of the few members of the ship's company not to join in the fun. He was showing signs of severe strain from the months of confinement in his lonely half of the Great Cabin with only a few sycophants from his embassy for company. He appears to have become more than slightly mentally unbalanced by this ordeal – at least by the account of Löwenstern, his determined enemy. Certainly a crisis broke soon after Lisiansky and the *Neva* joined the *Nadezhda* at Nukakhiva on 11 May. The tiff began with a disagreement between Rezanov and Krusenstern about the purchase of coral. Krusenstern had categorically forbidden the purchase of any items from the natives until his quarter-masters had finished their negotiations to fill the *Nadezhda*'s holds with meat and vegetables – his sensible intention was to prevent inflation which might be triggered by private transactions. Rezanov objected: his people had a warrant from the Academy of Sciences in St Petersburg to obtain as many natural specimens as possible, and should be exempted from the ban on trading.

During the shouting match that ensued over this apparently minor disagreement 'Rezanov allowed himself more freedom than his rank, the emperor's order and a carte blanche would permit him,' reported Löwenstern. 'The open threats, the insults and wrongs towards the Captain will have to be straightened out publicly . . . Who dares to cast insult into a Captain's face in front of his entire crew?'

Lisiansky was summoned, and once again Rezanov's tact appears to have deserted him. Lisiansky then gathered all the officers of both ships in the *Nadezhda*'s Great Cabin and announced that 'His Excellency the Chamberlain has said to me publicly that "You are acting childishly and will be demoted to common sailor." In light of this I cannot continue to command.'[22] Ratmanov suggested that Rezanov 'be considered crazy and locked in his cabin'. The ambassador was fetched from his quarters, from which he emerged 'looking pale and white with his [imperial] Instructions'. Without entering the cabin Rezanov reread his precious *ukaz* aloud from the safety of the companionway stairs. As is clear from the many complaints he would later address to the great and the good of St Petersburg, Ratmanov's threat to imprison him deeply shook Rezanov's already-bruised pride.

With neither side willing to back down or apologize, the row continued to fester unresolved. The officers acknowledged that the Tsar's signature on Rezanov's mandate was genuine, but all of them, except the *Nadezhda*'s Second Lieutenant Golovachev and First Mate Kamenshikov, declared that they would never have joined the expedition if they had known that Rezanov would be in charge. The two dissenters supported Rezanov for reasons of self-interest. The previous year Rezanov had hatched a plan to give one of the ships – probably the *Neva*, which was after all Company property – to the RAC's general manager, Alexander Baranov, for use as a private Company warship permanently stationed in Kodiak. It is not clear quite how Rezanov planned to transfer authority over the vessel to the Company, since regardless of who had paid for them both the *Neva* and *Nadezhda* were travelling under naval command and flew the St Andrew's Cross, the navy standard. In any case, Rezanov had privately offered command of the *Neva* to Golovachev and promotion to Kamenshikov, and as a result both men chose to publicly stand by the ambassador against their fellow officers. The result of breaking ranks was to be devastating for both men.

The two Russian ships set sail in the teeth of a growing gale on 18 May. Jean Cabri had come on board to say his farewells, but soon found that they had been blown too far for him to return to shore, where his native wife and children awaited him. 'He seemed however soon to reconcile himself to his fate and was an extremely useful sailor. As for the rest, he was but a *mauvais sujet*, very ready for laying plans for stealing, lying and cheating and no less adroit in executing them.'[23] Or as Löwenstern put it, 'only his nasty character and the few vulgar ballads he knows show him to be a Frenchman'.[24] Cabri's failure to disembark from the *Nadezhda* in time was the beginning of a disastrous decline. He made his way overland from Kamchatka to St Petersburg with Tolstoy, and by 1806 he was scraping a living teaching naval cadets at Kronstadt to swim. He ended up in a travelling freak show in Brittany showing off his tattoos. On his death in 1818 there was talk of raising money to preserve his skin for the anthropological museum in Paris, but too few people came forward and Cabri's tattoos were buried with him in a pauper's grave.

On 7 June the expedition sighted 'Owyhee', the largest of the Sandwich Islands. Discovered by Captain James Cook in 1778 and the scene of his murder the following year, Hawaii had become something of a Pacific metropolis by the turn of the nineteenth century. In 1795 King Kamehameha the Great of Hawaii had led a force of 960 war canoes and 10,000 warriors to bring most of the neighbouring islands in the archipelago under his rule, and by the time of the Russians' arrival had further built up his wealth and power by supplying the European and American ships which were frequenting the north Pacific in ever-greater numbers in search of whales and fur. He had also bought a fleet of fifteen Western-built brigs and frequently exchanged cordialities and gifts with Baranov in Sitka, 2,700 miles to the north-east. 'Baranov's fame stretches across the whole Pacific,' Rezanov noted with satisfaction.

When the Russians anchored off Hawaii the wily and obese monarch was away campaigning against the rebellious northern island of Kau'ai – where the Russians would later establish a short-lived colony. But a motley pair of English deserters known as Mister Davie and Mister Young who served as Kamehameha's advisers passed on some disturbing news. The Russian Fort St Michael, on Norfolk Sound just north of modern Sitka, had been sacked in November 1802 by Tlingit natives. Its Russian garrison had been massacred or taken into slavery, according to American ships that had picked up a few survivors and delivered them to Kodiak. The loss of the RAC's newest and most southerly possession posed a serious strategic threat to the Company's position. Rezanov immediately penned instructions to Baranov to retake the fort and avenge the loss of face the massacre represented to Russian power in the region.

The original plan had always been for Lisiansky and the RAC-owned *Neva* to break away from the *Nadezhda* in the north Pacific and head to Kodiak to drop off supplies and collect furs. But Lisiansky and Rezanov, though now barely on speaking terms, both realized that the *Neva*'s fourteen guns would be needed to retake Sitka. Lisiansky made ready and set off north on 31 May, with orders to rendezvous with Rezanov and the *Nadezhda* back in Kamchatka at the end of summer.

The *Nadezhda*, meanwhile, took on pigs, fruit and sugar. Langsdorff's ever-more-experienced eye for native breeding found the Hawaiian inhabitants 'naked, dirty, or middling stature, not well made . . . covered with bruises and sores, and many had lost front teeth'. Nonetheless the crew was disappointed when Krusenstern ordered his first mate to shoo away the crowds of curious half-naked native girls who approached the ship on outrigger canoes and clamoured to be allowed on board.

Rezanov's brief stay on Hawaii was not entirely ruined by the news of the sack of Fort St Michael. The temperate beauty of the island overwhelmed him. 'The fine woods of birch and grassy hills resemble a European landscape so much that we might believe ourselves in our native country,' wrote Langsdorff of a long walk he and Rezanov took into the interior.[25] It also occurred to Rezanov, as it had to Baranov shivering in Alaska, that the plenteous agriculture of Hawaii could be the key to solving Russian America's chronic food supply problems. 'All Siberia might be supplied with sugar from Owyhee,' Rezanov noted.[26]

The final leg of the *Nadezhda*'s journey across the north Pacific quickly became nightmarish. The fresh Hawaiian food quickly ran out, as did the ship's supplies of mustard and, more seriously still, brandy. Krusenstern had already threatened to leave Tolstoy on Hawaii for continued drunkenness and insubordination, but the unstable young count now descended into psychotic outbursts. 'Now he is saying he is going to kill Rezanov and then set fire to the *Nadezhda* and some other crazy stories.' The young man was by now so clearly insane that the captain ordered him to take sick leave on Kamchatka rather than punish him. Rezanov's psychological health appears to have been not much better. He stayed in his cabin, brooding and drinking, barely appearing on the quarterdeck between the *Nadezhda*'s departure from Nukakhiva in May and their arrival in Kamchatka on 3 July, when he emerged unsteadily from his cabin 'in full ornata' to take a seven-gun salute from the garrison of Petropavlovsk.[27]

View of Petropavlovsk on Kamchatka, 1811.

The gentlemen of the *Nadezhda* found this remote outpost of the empire miserable in the extreme. The Kamchatka peninsula may be physically joined to continental Russia, but in practice it was (and remains) an island, with no roads linking it to the rest of the country. Even today locals speak of Russia proper as 'the mainland'. Kamchatka is a land of volcanoes, forests, black sand and heavy sea fogs. In 1805 Petropavlovsk comprised no more than thirty log houses clinging to the steep sides of Avacha Bay, where the Mulovsky volcano plunges into the sea. It boasted a half-built church, barracks, fish-drying sheds, a stinking convict corral and guardhouse, and a small commander's house, where Rezanov installed himself. Packs of huskies roamed wild after being turned loose for the summer to fend for themselves.

The tiny settlement was home to a garrison of 150 soldiers, a company of artillerymen, some Cossacks and a handful of officers of the Russian American Company. It was surrounded by 'impenetrable grass almost as tall as ourselves, bogs and forests'.[28] In 1799 the Emperor Paul had sent a contingent of 800 troops to Kamchatka on a whim, and in the process nearly destroyed the fragile human ecosystem of the peninsula. The soldiers, 'dirty, stultified, negligent and entirely ignorant of husbandry . . . drained the Kamchatkans in every way and laid the foundation of both physical and moral depravity', complained a shocked Langsdorff.[29] Even the usually indifferent Löwenstern was moved. 'Pox and fever have decimated the [native] people; where one hundred once lived there are now barely five.'[30]

Interior of a native hut on Kamchatka, from Langsdorff's sketch.

Despite the peninsula's extraordinary natural abundance – 'three casts of the net and the [*Nadezhda*'s fish] barrels were full of turbot, cod, herring, salmon and a dozen crabs' – everything other than fish was in desperately short supply. So expensive was powder and shot that the native hunters were permanently in debt to their Russian masters. 'No soldier goes out of his house without taking a Kamschatkadal as his companion to carry all burdens without pay.' Rezanov attempted to ease the locals' lot by fixing a new list of prices, but they were still outrageously high – five rubles for an iron teapot, pig iron fifteen rubles a pound, soap two rubles a pound, when the average wage for a Russian labourer in Russian America was just 150 rubles a year.

On 30 July, with the *Nadezhda* on her side in the harbour being scraped down and re-rigged, Kamchatka's governor-general, Pavel Koshchelev, returned from an expedition to the other side of the peninsula. His arrival was the signal for the final showdown between Rezanov and Krusenstern as both rushed to complain to this, the first Russian of comparable rank to their own they had seen in nearly a year. Rezanov was overheard in the bathhouse, or *banya*, complaining to the general that he had been 'held prisoner on board for seven months'[31] and that 'all the officers except Golovachev and Kamenshikov should be treated as rebels'.

Rezanov also gloatingly told Tolstoy and – oddly – Tilesius that they would be sent to the salt mines for the rest of their lives for their various misdemeanours on the voyage.[32] Krusenstern, for his part, was prepared to resign his commission and return overland to St Petersburg rather than continue to Japan in the company of Rezanov. After delivering this threat Krusenstern broke down in tears. 'I curse the moment I had anything to do with the American Company,' he stormed in a rare moment of anger.[33] Rezanov responded by threatening also to resign and abandon the expedition – a bizarre Mexican standoff that would, logically, have resulted in the *Nadezhda* continuing on her voyage minus both captain and ambassador.

After three days of shuttle diplomacy by the alarmed General Koshchelev between Krusenstern's quarters in the *banya* and Rezanov's in the superintendent's house a compromise of sorts was brokered. Mostly it involved a humiliating public apology by Rezanov. Krusenstern demanded that the ambassador 'leave the discipline of the ship absolutely to me'[34] and write 'a letter to the Emperor stating that he is at fault and report our having made peace with one another'.[35] Since the *Nadezhda* had no chance of reaching Japan without her captain or officers, Rezanov had little choice but to acquiesce. 'He confessed he had acted rashly, and he asked that everything be forgotten,' reported Krusenstern in an unpublished portion of his diary. 'He intended to let me read anything he wrote the Emperor and I could seal his letter myself and give it to the governor. All of the officers witnessed the negotiations. A general reconciliation occurred.'[36]

The result was a jaunty and upbeat dispatch from Rezanov that glossed over the hardships of the voyage and instead concentrated on the shortcomings of Kamchatka, including 'lack of bread, salt, vegetables, powder . . . and a shortage of women, which makes the young men desperate and tempts the women to corruption'. Referring to his last doom-filled message from Santa Catarina, Rezanov apologized for referring to any 'discord between me and the naval officers. We felt sorry and upset during this whole journey thinking that this disagreeable news would make Your Majesty sad and that you would think that we put our petty personal ambitions above the interests of the State. I have to confess that the only reason for this was our great ambitions, which blinded the minds of all of us to such an extent we became jealous of one another . . . I feel guilty in sending a report that was premature and humbly beg your pardon for myself and all our navy officers.'[37] This grovelling draft was agreed upon by Krusenstern – 'this most experienced and prudent officer,' according to the letter.

Rezanov read his letter out to the assembled officers. 'The whole thing was very well written,' thought Löwenstern. 'After having read the letter to the Emperor, Rezanov's satisfaction with himself shined out of eyes with a volubility of his own. Rezanov asked us if we had any criticism of the letter and asked us to state our opinion freely. We all were silent, and our silence was interrupted by the appearance of schnapps and breakfast.'[38]

Rezanov certainly wrote a groveling letter. But did he actually send it? Löwenstern had his doubts.

> Rezanov put his letter away again and went on land in order to seal it (as he claimed?) together with his other dispatches. Krusenstern excused him by saying that Rezanov's friendliness, his flattering personality, sealed through his frequent kisses, were proof of respect and friendship that give his appearance the varnish of sincerity. Does Rezanov understand and know how to be sincere? Doesn't he have new tricks and traps lurking in the background? . . . May we not regret believing this two-faced man can be honest.

Was Rezanov capable of such an underhanded trick as swapping the letter he had just read for another, less humilating version? The next year, when the *Nadezhda* returned to Kamchatka, Governor Koshchelev also claimed that Rezanov had replaced the letter of apology with a different one, full of complaints against his opponents.[39] Yet a long letter from Rezanov, with grovelling aplenty, was logged in the Imperial Chancellery and is quoted above; it sounds exactly like the one which Krusenstern and Löwenstern described and approved. Rezanov, in all probability, was traduced by Löwenstern and Koshchelev.

After such a public climbdown, Rezanov's own injured pride would have to be massaged a little. Koshchelev's opportunity to stage-manage a public reconciliation came when letters arrived from St Petersburg confirming the promotion of First Lieutenant Makar Ivanovich Ratmanov[40] to the rank of captain-lieutenant. Koshchelev asked Rezanov, as the senior official on the island, to read the news of the appointment to the assembled officers. They duly assembled in full uniform outside the Rezanov residence – not, as Rezanov claims in his own diary, to apologize en masse but to hear the imperial letter of promotion read out. Ratmanov was duly congratulated and Krusenstern made a short speech of a conciliatory nature 'making peace' with Rezanov. Apology or not, it was enough to convince all parties that honour had been satisfied. 'Our story has a beautiful theme: the victory of Justice over Vice,' crowed Löwenstern.

Tolstoy was sent home, a 1,500-ruble loan from Rezanov in his pocket as a thinly disguised bribe to ensure he gave a good account. The artist Kurliantsev, who was suffering from gallstones, was also let go, as was Doctor Fyodor Brinkin, for unknown reasons. Perhaps he had also cracked in the Great Cabin's febrile atmosphere – in any event, Brinkin poisoned himself soon after his return to St Petersburg.[*][41] Travellers who met Tolstoy en route in Siberia reported a crazed man in a weather-stained Preobrazhensky Guards uniform. 'His eyes, probably as a result of heat and dust, appeared bloodshot, his rather melancholy expression

---

[*]   Of the twenty gentlemen who sailed with the *Nadezhda,* two – Brinkin and Golovachev – would kill themselves, a suicide rate of 10 per cent.

appeared troubled and his very quiet manner of speaking frightened my companion.'[42] Tolstoy went on to become a hero of the 1812 war against Napoleon and scandalize society by marrying a Gypsy singer with whom he had eleven children, all of whom died in infancy. The count came to believe that this was divine punishment for the eleven men he had killed in duels, though that did not stop him from continuing to provoke them.

The *Nadezhda*'s ship's company, meanwhile, prepared to continue their fractious journey. Minor problems remained: the officers' dirty underwear was sold by the local sub-surgeon, who drank the proceeds before he was discovered. The *Nadezhda*'s spectacular leaks could not be adequately fixed because of a lack of seasoned wood, nails and copper. But the seismic rift between Krusenstern and Rezanov, which had threatened to destroy the whole expedition, had, for the time being at least, been patched up. Krusenstern ordered his carpenters to take down the partition that had divided the Great Cabin since Brazil.

12

Nangasac

I most humbly entreated His Majesty that I should be conducted in safety to Nangasac. To this I added another petition, to excuse my performing the ceremony imposed on my countrymen, of trampling upon the crucifix . . . The Emperor seemed a little surprised; and said he believed I was the first of my countrymen who ever made any scruple in this point.'

Jonathan Swift, *Gulliver's Travels*, 3.xi: 'The Author leaves Luggnagg and sails to Japan', 1726

The *Nadezhda* was given a rousing send-off from Kamchatka for her historic voyage to Japan. Company Director Evstrat Delarov, Shelikhov's old Greek shipmate, was freshly arrived from Okhotsk. He and General Koshchelev played hosts. A feast of goose, wild sheep, ox steaks and roasted reindeer was prepared, followed by a ball in a tent set up by Rezanov. The company consisted of the governor's wife, the wives of subalterns and soldiers and 'some Kamchatkadale women in silks, nankeens and satins'.[1] Rezanov took a turn playing quadrilles on the violin. Langsdorff was less impressed by the Kamchatkadale dances 'which consist of imitations of bears, dogs and birds'.

On 22 August the *Nadezhda* set sail with her heavy freight of imperial ambition. She soon ran into heavy seas. The cast-iron fireplace in the Great Cabin broke loose and crashed through a partition, demolishing four smaller cabins and smashing dozens of bottles and pots as it went. Nonetheless on 11 September the gentlemen were in good enough humour to stage a small 'Round the World' concert, even though 'the creaking of the ship outshouted the instruments and the storm played counter-bass'.[2]

A few days later, on the occasion of the anniversary of the Emperor Alexander's coronation, Rezanov addressed a rousing speech to the assembled officers and crew. 'Love of Fatherland, skill, dignity, disdain of danger, subordination, mutual respect and meekness are the main characteristics of the Russian seaman and of Russians in general,' he declared. He praised the sailors, telling them that 'you have already acquired a degree of renown which jealousy herself can never deprive you'.[3] And to his 'cavaliers and associates of the Embassy, my worthy companions and assistants, it remains to us to accomplish the brilliant objects on which we are set: the opening to our country of new sources of wealth and knowledge'. This speech reduced 'all the sailors to tears'.[4] Rezanov then distributed medals to all the seamen. The mood of high patriotic fervour was marred only with a by-now-predictable altercation with Krusenstern, who asked Rezanov if the medals weren't meant for loyal natives and foreigners rather than his own crew. To which Rezanov replied, 'I say nothing: fuck your mother.'[5]*

Krusenstern did not take this remark well.

'I demanded to be arrested and shackled and taken to St Petersburg in irons if Rezanov's charges were to be accepted,' Krusenstern wrote in an unpublished portion of his diary. 'A mutineer – for this is what Rezanov called me – cannot be in charge of a ship of war.'[6] By his own account, the captain only abandoned his threat to have himself imprisoned because without his leadership the expedition would be 'destroyed' and 'all of Russia would suffer because Rezanov insulted me'.

The following evening the weather turned even worse. The *Nadezhda* ran into mountainous seas, whipped up by the tail end of a great Pacific typhoon. One giant wave engulfed the *Nadezhda* completely from the stern, smashing her boats and filling the Great Cabin with three feet of churning water. 'The waves rolled in frightful masses, rushing over one

---

* The exchange was recorded in Cyrillic in Löwenstern's diary, hence escaping the editorial hand of his censorious descendants.

another with the swiftness of an arrow . . . every strike seemed to threaten to be the finishing stroke of our existence. Expensive books, chairs, tables maps, mathematical instruments, clothes, all swam together about the Cabin and seemed to give a foretaste of what was to follow.'[7] 'All were preparing for death. They held each other and asked for pardon . . . one sat like a stone, another praying and preparing to give up the ghost.'[8] The next morning the lower decks were found to be three hands' deep in sand and shells, showing how close they had been to an unknown shore and perdition. The soaked damasks for the Japanese Shōgun were unpacked and draped over the stays in an attempt to dry them.

Undaunted by this near-fatal experience, Rezanov pressed on with preparations for meeting the Japanese. Chief among these were getting the guard of marines he had picked up at Kamchatka to practice drum rolls and presenting arms on the quarterdeck, preparing stocks of vodka, wine and tobacco, and mustering all the officers in full-dress uniform. He also prepared a written question-and-answer pamphlet for the benefit of any Japanese curious about Russia. 'Russia occupies half the world and is the greatest Empire in the Universe,' it began, boldly but perhaps not terribly tactfully, [9] Rezanov, unconsciously echoing the Chinese emperor's grandiloquent letter to the Russians at Nerchinsk a century and a half previously, went on to explain that 'The Great Russian Emperor, seeing the deficiencies suffered by other lands, out of human compassion permits the use of the State's ample resources and our borders are open to all merchants.'[10]

He also pored over his copy of the letter given by the Japanese to Adam Laxman eleven years before, which Rezanov hoped would be his warrant to pursue both trade and diplomacy. In this Rezanov was either deluded or highly optimistic, because the text left little room for misunderstanding. 'Our Empire offers neither respect nor disrespect for your Empire,' wrote the chief shogunal councillor at the time, Matsudaira Sadanobu. 'We expect no further negotiations. As for establishing friendly relations, it is impossible to do so locally and it is forbidden to travel from here to [the shogunal court at] Edo.' Nonetheless, the Laxman letter – known as the Nagasaki Permit – did provide permission for a single Russian ship to come and trade.

Through this loophole, as well as the humanitarian pretext of returning the five shipwrecked Japanese, Rezanov hoped to climb, aided by his hold-full of gifts. He was also armed with an elaborately illuminated letter in Russian and Japanese from Alexander I assuring the 'Emperor' of Japan of his 'sincere respect' and 'reaffirming Our unshakeable friendly disposi-tion'. Alexander also mentioned the 'clock in the shape of a mechanical elephant, mirrors, fox furs, ivory vases, guns, pistols, steel and glass arte-facts . . . produced in Our manufacturing plants'. This was less than the full truth, as evidenced (as Löwenstern acidly observed) by the word 'London', which featured prominently on the clock's face.* Never mind. Alexander hoped that 'though these gifts are of no great value I wish that Your Majesty will find something from within my borders to your liking'.¹¹

On 26 September they sighted a fishing boat crewed by 'men like savages, naked but for their belts',¹² who attempted to shoo the *Nadezhda* away, but seeing the foreign ship with Japanese aboard retreated in confusion. The Russians, with marines beating to quarters, sailors hauling the cannon out of the hold and officers scrambling into their dress uniforms, continued into the mouth of Nagasaki Bay. The *Nadezhda* thus became the first – but by no means the last – Russian man-of-war to enter a Japanese harbour.¹³

Ahead, the Russians saw a town of low wooden houses dominated by hills covered in terraces to their very summits. An official war barge, manned by forty rowers and flying a black-and-white pennant, inter-cepted them. Two officials on board, after reading an edict from a scroll which no one on the *Nadezhda* heard, indicated that the Russians should anchor four miles offshore. It was a bad anchorage, exposed to the open ocean swells and in forty fathoms of water, but Rezanov was nonetheless delighted. 'He hugged us for joy and kissed me and Bellinghausen,' reported Löwenstern.¹⁴

Two large barges carrying local notables and a small party of Europeans – evidently the local Dutch representatives – approached to

---

* This timepiece made it all the way round the world and was eventually returned to the Winter Palace collection from where it was originally obtained by Rumiantsev. Alas this well-travelled clock is no longer in the Hermitage Museum's inventory.

inspect the Russians but did not hail them or acknowledge their signals. As night fell twenty small sampans bearing curious picnicking sight-seers edged out into the bay, illuminated by paper lanterns 'of great size and beauty bearing two very bright and clear lights and highly orna-mented with transparencies of coats of arms'.[15] The *Nadezhda* settled down to her first night in Japanese waters moored in a sea of bobbing paper lanterns and wreathed in the smell of frying fish.

The next morning an official Japanese delegation of thirty elabo-rately dressed officials, armed with swords, and their attendants came aboard. The head official was shown into the Great Cabin to the accompaniment of well-drilled drum rolls. The Russians, following the Dutch-speaking Japanese interpreters, called him a *banyoshi* – apparently a corruption of the Japanese title *bugyo,* best translated as 'civil servant.'[16] The senior *banyoshi* and his two subordinates imme-diately seated themselves, cross-legged, on the cabin's divan. Attendants with symbolic lanterns arranged themselves on one side; on the other more servants bearing 'an apparatus for smoking, a vessel with hot embers, another for tobacco and a small one for spitting' knelt at the *banyoshi*'s side.

Rezanov, after bowing to his distinguished visitor in the European manner, settled himself opposite in a carefully-placed armchair. He attempted to use his hard-won Japanese but was politely cut off by one of the officials' team of interpreters, who apologized that it was not permitted to address the *banyoshi* except through an official translator.[17] The senior Japanese translator, *oppertolk* in Dutch, was Motoki Shozaemon. He was to become the Russians' principal liaison with the Japanese authorities for the first three months of their stay. Since Rezanov spoke no Dutch he needed a *tolk* of his own, but there being no Dutchmen aboard the *Nadezhda* this service was performed by Dr Langsdorff, who knew some Low German. Revealingly, Shozaemon knelt as he addressed Rezanov, but when he turned to the *banyoshi* he fell forward on his hands and knees and humbly addressed his transla-tion to the cabin floor.

After a period of chit-chat during which the Japanese enquired about the visitors' journey, three European visitors were announced by the cabin sentry. Hendrik Doeff was the twenty-seven-year-old head of the Dutch trading mission in Nagasaki. He was accompanied by Captain Mousquetier of the Dutch trading vessel *Gesnia Antoinetta*, out of Batavia, and Baron von Pabst, a Dutch traveller.[18]

Löwenstern's sketch of the Dutch bowing.

'They had only just begun to greet me, when the chief interpreter abruptly shouted for [Doeff] to make a compliment' to the *banyoshi*, wrote Rezanov. 'The interpreter fell onto his knees and bowed, and the Dutch had to do the same, bending at the waist before the *banyoshi*, placing their hands on their knees, while glancing to the side to see if the interpreter had finished his lengthy speech.'[19] Eventually Doeff enquired, '*Kan ik wederom upstaan?*' – 'May I stand up?' – and was given permission to unbend. The performance made a deep impression on Rezanov, sensitive as he was to questions of status, who devoted many pages of his beautifully penned diary to the incident. 'It was extremely distressing to the Dutchmen to have us all as witnesses to their unprecedented degradation,' he wrote. 'The Japanese did not dare to subject us to such demeaning acts.' Rezanov himself did 'not even bow to God, except in my own mind'.

Rezanov, in his own estimation, had saved face while the hapless Dutch had lost theirs. He was quite wrong. For one, Doeff did not consider bowing degradation at all. 'I myself cannot understand in what this self-abasement consists,' he wrote after Krusenstern's account of the Dutch 'humiliating demonstration of submission' before the Japanese was published in London in 1813. 'The courtesies that we use in our relations to Japanese are the same that they use among themselves . . . in whatever part of the world one finds oneself one has to adapt or agree to the reigning customs and ceremonies. Otherwise, one need not go there at all.'[20]

Doeff's attitude was not a species of early multiculturalism but rather, came from a hard-headed desire to do business. Unlike the Russians, the Dutch traders in Nagasaki were integrated into the neo-Confucian social structure and hierarchy of Japan's feudal system, known as *bakuhan*. The head of the Dutch trade mission, the *opperhoofd*, was recognized as a vassal, or *kashin*, of the Shogun, with the right to an audience at the palace in the capital of Edo. The fact that the Dutch were foreigners excused them from having to make the full prostrations that Japanese lower officials – such as translators – had to perform to their superiors.[21]

Two centuries earlier many Spanish and the Portuguese traders and military officers had also taken Rezanov's attitude that prostration was undignified – and had been summarily expelled by Shogun Tokugawa Ieyasu between 1624 and 1639. The humbler Dutch, on the other hand, traded successfully and without interruption from 1609.[22] The issue revealed a deep gulf of understanding between Rezanov and his Japanese counterparts, a gulf that was only to grow over the coming six months.

Another wrangle over protocol followed the next day. A shipload of Japanese notables hove into view, kettledrums banging and standards fluttering. A small boat was dispatched to inform Rezanov that the rank of the visitors dictated that he personally approach their craft in *Nadezhda*'s jolly boat and invite them on board. This, the ambassador considered 'beneath his dignity',[23] sparking the first of many tedious back-and-forth negotiations over the minutiae of precedence which were to cause the Japanese much confusion and the Russians much frustration. Eventually a compromise was hit upon: Rezanov's senior officers would go in the boat to invite the Japanese dignitaries, while Rezanov himself stood on the *Nadezhda*'s forecastle – in a commanding position above the ship's latrines – and greeted his distinguished visitors from there.

After more tea-drinking, pipe-smoking and decorous spitting, Rezanov presented his credentials in the form of his emperor's letter written in Russian, Manchurian and Japanese. The *banyoshi* regretted they were unable to read the Japanese because 'the handwriting is very bad and the language only that of the vulgar use'[24] – hardly surprising, since the translation was penned by a former Japanese fisherman living in Irkutsk. The five shipwrecked sailors from Sendai – who to Rezanov's frustration were illiterate – were duly produced for the *banyoshi*, dressed in silk clothes and each brandishing the silver watch given to him by Alexander I as a sign of the Russians' generosity. However, the *banyoshi* were less interested in their own countrymen than in the *Nadezhda*'s charts and a small globe made by Adams of London, on which the Russians traced the line of their two-year-long voyage. More impressive still was the spark-producing galvanic machine, which 'excited the attention of the Japanese more than any other'. Indeed during the Russians' entire stay 'very rarely did a *banyoshi* come to visit without desiring to feel the effect of the electricity'.[25]

Rezanov had little choice but to agree to the *banyoshi*'s chief demand that the ship be fully disarmed before being allowed to approach within cannon range of the city. The only exceptions Rezanov and Krusenstern were able to wring from the Japanese were that the officers were allowed to keep their swords as 'a necessary part of their uniform',[26] Rezanov's personal honour guard their muskets and the *Nadezhda* her cannon – as long as they were stowed in the hold and all powder unloaded into Japanese safekeeping. Rezanov considered these concessions a great diplomatic victory. As it turned out, he was instead in his stubbornness sowing the seeds of disaster for his mission.

The Russians 'unloaded every grain of gunpowder and every arm down to the smallest midshipman's dirk'.[27] Thus disarmed and securely attached, like Gulliver in Lilliput, by many ropes to a fleet of fifty small rowing barges, the *Nadezhda* weighed anchor and was towed inshore to a safer anchorage with rhythmic cries of '*O! Ossi! O!*' As she anchored, a provision boat arrived piled with duck, rice and fresh vegetables, a gift from the governor.

The visitors now settled down to wait for answers from the *banyoshi* – when they would be allowed ashore, when they would be able to have an audience with the governor, when Rezanov would travel to Edo to present his compliments to the Shogun. None were immediately forthcoming. During their first negotiations Rezanov had been told that Edo would have to be consulted even on the matter of whether he would be able to bring his sword ashore. This did not bode well for a quick and successful outcome to the embassy.

Löwenstern's sketch of Rezanov and the *tolks*.

Langsdorff, who spent as much time speaking to the various *tolks* assigned to the *Nadezhda* as Rezanov, was struck by 'their excessive closeness and the circumspection with which every step is taken; it seemed as if the least error would cost the life even of the person highest in rank'. He found them obsessed with secrecy: 'every thought, every question, every word was weighed in the nicest manner'.[28] The *tolks* refused even to tell Rezanov the name of the reigning emperor, which they claimed was hidden even from his own people until his death, though they did tell him the name of the current shogun, Tokugawa Ienari, as a deadly secret.[29]

Löwenstern was more concerned with observing the local women-folk through his telescope. He found the Japanese married woman's practice of blackening her teeth disgusting, but was charmed by 'her clothing, which is very comfortable, one nightgown upon another, like a book one can open'. The prospect of doing just that was evidently much on his mind. 'The Dutch awaken hope that according to Japanese law everyone will be given a girl, the officers two and the captain four,' he wrote, joking that the captain's famous uxoriousness meant four more for the other officers.[30]

Doeff, coming aboard a second time, told Rezanov frankly that he was pessimistic about the success of the Russian mission. 'The laws and customs of this people do not allow them to enter into ties of friend-ship and trade with other nations,' Doeff wrote in his memoir after twenty years as the Dutch East India Company representative in Nagasaki. 'Until the fundamental laws of the state, by which Japan has fared so well for two centuries, are repealed, all such proposals from any nation will receive a negative reply. If we Dutchmen were not settled there already, we would never be allowed in.'[31]

Both Langsdorff and Krusenstern later became convinced that the Dutch were scheming to sabotage the Russian mission, but the truth is that there was a dire shortage of trading hulls in the Pacific because of the Napoleonic Wars, and the Dutch badly needed ships – even Russian ships – to carry wares from Nagasaki to Batavia, Canton and Europe. Doeff himself says that though he and Rezanov were only allowed to meet twice, they maintained a warm (if secret) correspondence, and claimed that he often spoke in the Russian's favour.[32]

The *Nadezhda* was still moored an uncomfortable distance from the shore, with autumn squalls and swells gathering, and the eupho-ria of arrival soon turned into irritation. 'It is a kind of incarceration,' wrote Löwenstern. 'All we have learned from the Japanese is through the telescope.' Rezanov vented his frustration on his messmates, ordering Horner to take off the nightcap he wore against the cold and bawling at Tilesius to sit up straight at table. To the *tolks* he was scarcely more diplomatic, shouting at their mumbled apologies and excuses. Had Rezanov been 'an insignificant personage like Laxman he would have been ashore long ago', they explained. 'But for so great a man they must wait the commands of the court as to the manner in which he must be received and to make the necessary preparations for his rank and dignity.'[33]

A rumour circulated that a recent Chinese ambassador had waited eight months on his ship while suitable arrangements were made; Rezanov, with his higher rank, might have to wait even longer. This was probably true, tempting though it is to imagine that the *tolks* came up with the explanation as an ingenious way to needle the rude Russian. Rezanov's insistence on his own exalted status had backfired badly. 'The Japanese were astounded to hear Rezanov making so much noise, since for them patience and calmness are the first qualities of a distinguished man.'[34] The *tolks*, for their part, were so unfailingly courteous that Langsdorff found that 'we might have supposed ourselves among the most polished Europeans'.[35]

The Dutch ship *Gesnia Antoinetta* left harbour in mid-October, firing a thundering 150-gun salute as if in mockery of the Russians' lack of gunpowder, while the *Nadezhda* and her unhappy inmates found themselves an involuntary tourist attraction. Every fine day a flotilla of sampans and noble barges would cruise past to observe the Europeans and their ways. Boatloads of children, 'a whole school brought out to be treated with a sight of the Russians', women with infants at the breast, young girls with stringed instruments and gawpers with telescopes. The grandest was the yacht of the 'Prince of Fisen' – more correctly the Daimyo of Hizen – 'decorated with a variety of flags, staves, bows, arrows, muskets and other insignia of honour'.[36]

Meanwhile, Rezanov, in Löwenstern's phrase, 'fools away the respect of a nation' by his habit of appearing on deck in a loose jacket and pissing off the side of the ship – an act commemorated in a sketch in

Löwenstern's diary wryly entitled 'Rezanov shows himself to the people of Japan'. Rezanov 'loses a great deal in the eyes of the Japanese who observe etiquette so strictly,' Löwenstern observed in a low moment. They 'hold us Europeans in contempt – and rightly so'.[37]

13

Humiliation

God grant us patience to bear Japanese ceremony and Russian caprices.

Hermann Ludwig von Löwenstern

While the Russian ambassador was relieving himself into the Bay of Nagasaki, furious debate was unfolding in Edo over the very nature of Japanese civilization and its relationship to the wider world. Unbeknown to Rezanov, his arrival had precipitated a power struggle between the noble supporters of the Tokugawa Shogunate, a hereditary clan who had ruled in the emperors' names since 1603, and a growing class of magistrates, officials, interpreters and merchants who stood to benefit from trade with the Russians.

But the matter of opening diplomatic relations with Russia was much more than a simple commercial matter – it went to the heart of the regime's legitimacy. The principle which came to be known as *sakoku* – literally 'closed country' – had been proclaimed by Iemitsu, the third Tokugawa shogun, in 1633–9, after he had cemented his power by finally expelling the Jesuits and Portuguese.[1] *Sakoku* was a fundamental plank of Tokugawa power – indeed, when the Shogunate did finally reluctantly agree to fully open Japan to the West in 1858, it would last only ten more years.[2]

The Dutch were tolerated because of their willingness to integrate themselves into the Japanese social hierarchy. An influential Japanese philosophy of the age was *kokugaku* – 'national learning' – the notion of the innate superiority of Japanese culture relative to all others. When they bowed to the *banyoshi* the Dutch acknowledged their submission to the Shogun, and, by implication, *kokugaku* also. Rezanov, by contrast, was clearly unwilling to do so. What he failed to understand was that the rites and rituals that he disdained were more than simply courtesy; they were the outward manifestations of the neo-Confucian vertical hierarchy that formed the ideological underpinnings of the Shogunate. To conservative noblemen in Edo, Rezanov embodied not only a reprise of the threat from the Christian West that the ancestors of Shogun Tokugawa Ienari had repulsed in the early seventeenth century but also a challenge to Japanese civilization on an elemental spiritual level.[3]

Back in Nagasaki, the *tolks* told the ambassador little of these machinations, replying to his urgent questioning with cascades of apologies. Rezanov therefore tried a different tack to get attention. Taking to his bed, he sent word to the *tolks* that he was angry at being treated 'not as a friend but rather detained as a criminal and State prisoner' and that his deteriorating health made it 'absolutely necessary to walk on land'.[4] This gambit seemed to do the trick. Frightened as the Nagasaki authorities were of acting without orders from Edo, the prospect of their distinguished guest perishing in the harbour worried them even more. Swarms of workmen appeared in an uninhabited corner of the bay on the Cape of Megasaki known as Umegasaki or Plum-Tree Point. A bamboo house was erected and just as quickly concealed from view by a bamboo palisade. The little ambassadorial compound was ready three days later. With the sailors in the rigging saluting him, together with the usual drummers and honour guard, Rezanov descended to the jolly boat to be rowed ashore to enter his new residence on Japanese soil, the first official ambassador of a foreign government ever to do so.

The compound built for the Russians was 'small beyond all idea',[5] just twice the length of the ship and with every blade of grass torn away and replaced by perfectly levelled packed sand. By strict order of the governor, no more than nine Russians were allowed to stay ashore overnight. Nonetheless, shore duty was eagerly looking forward to, even in these spartan conditions. Ratmanov asked the *tolks* when they would be getting their rumoured quota of Japanese girls. Rezanov, settled in a large armchair decorated with a double-headed eagle crest, which he had had brought from the *Nadezhda*, found this request very funny. The Japanese 'drew breath and remained silent'.[6]

This mean bamboo hut, Rezanov decided, was no place for an ambassador of His Imperial Majesty to reside. With Krusenstern planning to run the *Nadezhda* aground and tip her over to repair her fouled and damaged bottom, grander accommodation had to be found quickly. An old Chinese junk was rejected out of hand as too being cramped and low-ceilinged (not to mention her poor sailing qualities: 'no ship so illogical, fat and big can exist anywhere', thought Löwenstern). Therefore work began to convert a larger storehouse on Umegasaki into in a compound in which Rezanov and his suite could winter in greater comfort. As the *Nadezhda* was stripped of her rigging, masts and spars in preparation for her overhaul, the tantalizing sound of the Japanese carpenters' hammers again drifted across the water.

December was punctuated by excuses that couriers from Edo had been delayed by floods – as well as grovelling and apparently pointless enquiries from the *tolks* as to the appointments of the new residence. 'How many casseroles, pans and kettles does he need? . . . They will probably come again in five days to enquire if the ambassador drinks tea or coffee, if he wants to sit on chairs or benches, if he will be wearing boots or shoes, how many girls should be held in readiness for him,' wrote Löwenstern in frustration. 'God grant us patience to bear Japanese ceremony and Russian caprices.'

The gentlemen of the *Nadezhda* amused themselves by sketching, writing, reading and translating. On the quarterdeck above the great cabin Espenberg taught the Kotzebue brothers fencing. Rats, it was discovered, had got at the last of the wine barrels, leaving the Cabin nothing to drink but bad Kamchatka rum. 'Our ill humour was increased by very cold, stormy weather,' wrote the usually cheerful Langsdorff. 'There is scarcely a soul on board who does not feel great impatience and indignation at being trifled with.'[7]

The Japanese, when finally ready, certainly put on an impressive show. After the usual elaborate negotiations over protocol, the Daimyo of

Hizen's barge was sent to collect Rezanov and his embassy to view their new accommodation. The ambassador was installed in the barge's state apartment, whose laquered walls were draped in lilac silk and decorated with the prince's arms in gold, his marines carrying the Russian flag standing behind. Though the barge had places for sixty rowers it was towed by smaller boats as a sign of further respect. The new residence itself was an improvement, at least, on the first, though by no means impressive: a single-storey house with walls of varnished paper and with fine woven mats on the floor in a compound forty paces by fifty, surrounded on three sides by sea and on the fourth by a high bamboo screen. Rezanov and his 'cavaliers' found a fine dinner of venison, ducks, rice and fowl prepared. As dusk fell their Japanese hosts took their leave and the 'doors of our new habitation were close shut and locked and we were surrounded by a guard on all sides'.[8]

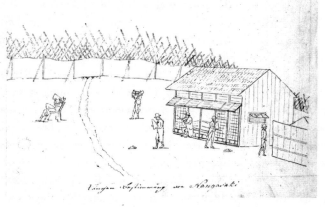

The Ambassador's compound on Megasaki, by Löwenstern.

On board the *Nadezhda* the officers celebrated. 'The plague of the Embassy is now raging on land.'[9]

Rezanov decorated his new quarters with the *Nadezhda*'s cargo of official presents – the six-foot mirrors, the galvanic machine, the elephant clock, the woven picture of Alexander I and all the rest. He busied himself with learning Japanese from the *tolks* and compiling a

Rezanov pacing his new compound at Megasaki.

dictionary of the language. On 24 December Rezanov declared that he was dissatisfied with the work of Motoki Shozaemon and asked for a different interpreter, Sukezaemon, with whom he got along better. This could suggest that Rezanov by this point understood Japanese well enough to be able to judge the accuracy with which his words were being conveyed – or that his peevishness and frustration was expressing itself in aggression towards the only Japanese he saw on a regular basis.

A brief attempt to break out of the compound and mingle with ordinary Japanese was less successful. By Löwenstern's hearsay account (he was on board the *Nadezhda* at the time 'enjoying peace and quiet'), Rezanov 'stormed out of the house, got in with a crowd of rough Japanese porters who had more to do than to make way for our fool . . . Rezanov was bent, pummelled shoved and thumped, then went back to his house.'

Relations within the compound were also less than perfectly harmonious. 'You rogue, fuck your mother, I will order the soldiers to shove your head down the shitter,' Rezanov told Fyodor Shmelin, the Russian

Löwenstern's sketch of Rezanov falling in the mud at Megasaki.

American Company's supervisor, after the disappearance of a narwhal horn which Shemelin had been using as a walking stick. (This gem of authentic Rezanov was again recorded in Russian by Löwenstern, who was present.) Rezanov ordered the soldiers to get dressed and guard the drunk Shmelin 'lest he damage the valuable presents'. Later that night the ambassador was heard pacing his room, swearing to himself. Löwenstern's sketch of the scene shows Rezanov in a padded Japanese robe thoughtfully sent by Doeff, clutching his head as Shmelin is dragged away.[10]

Rezanov's mental state seems to have once again deteriorated rapidly during the freezing, drizzly days in Umegasaki. Cannon fire from a saluting Chinese junk had him screaming that the *Nadezhda* was under attack. Friderici joked that 'shooting is nothing – it's when they start building a gallows next to our house that we have to worry'. Löwenstern passed the time by bringing over captured rats from the *Nadezhda*'s hold and electrocuting them to death with the galvanic machine. Ratmanov and Friderici fell out and even asked to borrow Löwenstern's dueling pistols before realizing there was no powder with which to shoot each other.

No doubt influenced by the pervasive dark mood, Madsuira, one of the five Japanese who had accompanied the Russians from

Kronstadt, attempted to cut his throat with one of the soldiers' razors. The Japanese guards would not allow Langsdorff to treat Madsuira, and the bleeding man had to wait until the afternoon before a Japanese doctor arrived with an impressive laquered medicine chest and made an antiseptic gargle for the would-be suicide. The Nagasaki authorities would not accept the Japanese sailors back without authorization from Edo, so the unfortunate men lived on with their Russian companions, separated only by a bamboo wall from their homeland and families.

'After encountering many storms and inconveniences, we had at least reached an interesting land where we hoped to be received if not as friends then at least as strangers of distinction, entitled to all possible deference and respect,' lamented Langsdorff, who peered at the natural and human wonders of Japan through the compound's slatted fence. Japanese peered back 'in the manner that in Europe we look at wild beasts carried about for a show', enjoying the spectacle of Rezanov moping around the compound 'in a long dressing gown and nightcap, without trousers'.

Löwenstern's view of the Embassy on Megasaki, observed by wild dogs.

Deprived of specimens to examine, Langsdorff and Tilesius took to dissecting and sketching the fish they were brought for supper before they disappeared into the kitchens. Using the 'very thin, light and strong paper of this country', Langsdorff also passed the days in pasting together hot-air balloons. His early trial balloons, fuelled by straw soaked in spirits, proved such a success that the Japanese guards and interpreters asked him to repeat the trick. Rising to the challenge, Langsdorff created a monster balloon ten feet in diameter and fifteen feet high, with a sketch of Russia's two-headed eagle on one side and the monogram and crown of the Russian emperor on the other. The balloon rose up impressively high and flew over the rooftops of Nagasaki before crash-landing on the thatched roof of a merchant's house, causing panic. The city magistrates sent polite word to Rezanov that future ballooning experiments were to be conducted only when the wind was blowing out to sea.

Around the end of January, just as Rezanov was sliding into genuine illness with rheumatic pains and tightness in the chest, the *tolk* Tamehachiro confided 'a profound secret'. Two hundred of the 'highest dignitaries' had been summoned to Edo by the Shogun to consult upon the expediency of establishing trade relations with Russia. Whatever the existential dangers to the Tokugawa regime

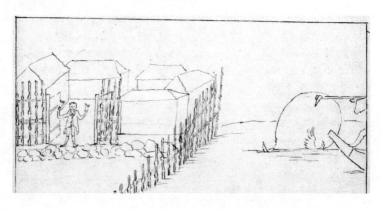

Löwenstern's sketch of Langsdorff's balloon experiments.

posed by Rezanov, contemporary accounts suggest that nonetheless large sections of Japanese society favoured more contact. The Nagasaki *tolks* and guards repeatedly told Rezanov that the local people wanted to trade with the Russians. Mogami Tokunai, a celebrated explorer of Japan's northern frontiers, wrote later that 'people all over the country sympathized' with the Russians. The artist Shiba Kokan argued that rice was both cheap and abundant in Japan and should be traded. Many members of the samurai class, Japan's largest landowners, who would become even richer by selling surplus grain, shared his view. The state too stood to gain tax funds to fund a pet shogunal project, the development of Ezo, the wilds of northern Japan.[11]

News of this 'great debate among the ruling circles of the country' thrilled Rezanov – and filled him with agonized anticipation. When he was told that it would be at least thirty more days before the governor of Nagasaki could see him because special ceremonial robes would have to be prepared, he flew into a rage. 'I shit on the governor and all of his clothes,' he shouted. 'I will not be led around on this fool's rope any more!' The *tolks* attempted to pacify Rezanov with gifts of lacquer boxes. 'Your constant complaints could have dire consequences,' they warned. 'Do you want our governor to receive a sword from Edo to cut open his stomach with?'[12]

Suffering from cold and rheumatism, the ambassador built himself a

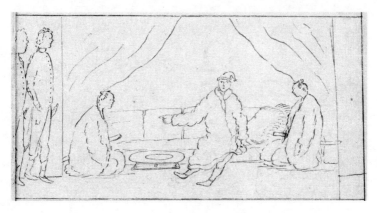

Rezanov ill in bed.

small tent from rugs, sailcloth and straw mats inside his room and spent much of the day huddled inside with a pan of hot coals. When he emerged his companions were dismayed that 'none of us wears our shirts so dirty or such torn stockings'. Extreme lethargy and disregard for personal appearance are of course classic signs of depression. So is paranoia. 'He is so crazy that he has set up a written plan for war,' reported Löwenstern. Rezanov repeatedly threatened the long-suffering translators, his only Japanese interlocutors, who bore the full brunt of his disintegrating psyche. 'If I killed ten of you *tolks* then my business would go faster and better!' he raged. Japanese doctors were summoned. Their diagnosis, entirely correct, was that their Russian guest was suffering from 'ill will and ill humour'.[13]

On 1 March Rezanov was informed that there was no question of his travelling to Edo for a personal interview with the Shogun; an emissary would be sent instead to Nagasaki. Yet even as the Russians scrambled to prepare for their long-awaited audience, Rezanov oscillated from fatalistic anticipation of failure to wildly optimistic fantasies of a Russian Pacific empire. One day he chatted excitedly of a circular trade in Alaskan furs, Chinese manufactures, Japanese grain and rice, all centred on Kamchatka. The next, Löwenstern bitchily reported, he was having whispered discussions with Shmelin on how to steal some of the emperor's presents. Krusenstern reported that all the repairs to the *Nadezhda* had been made; Löwenstern drew cartoons of the ambassador doling out money from a box marked *Kaznya* – 'state funds' – to his crony Shmelin.

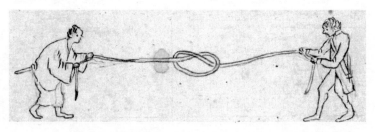

Rezanov and the Japanese 'pulling the knot [of misunderstanding] tighter'.

On 27 March, as the cherry trees around Nagasaki came into full blossom, the *Groote Heer* – the emissary from Edo – finally arrived in Nagasaki. The *tolk* Shozaemon's advice to Rezanov was to be 'like pure water – one may pour water into whatever vessel one wishes and the liquid takes the form of the vessel'. Sadly, this Zen approach was not the Rezanov way. Predictably, long negotiations on protocol ensued. Would only Rezanov be carried in a litter or his whole party? Would he kneel, sit or stand? Would he wear shoes or be barefoot? Sword or no sword? Honour guard or not? And so on. The *tolks* were near their wits' end. 'If your Embassy is unsuccessful because you did not wish to bow, will you tell your Emperor that too?' asked one of the Japanese in a rare moment of open frustration.[14]

On the appointed day the Daimyo of Hizen's state barge – festooned with the customary flags, hangings, drummers and rowers – again made her stately way to the Russian compound at Umegasaki. Rezanov emerged in his carefully-cleaned chamberlain's uniform with his Cross of Malta and glittering Order of St Anne prominently displayed. He was swordless and wore light shoes. Four of his cavaliers followed – Friderici and Fosse in their green-and-red army officers' uniforms, Fyodorov in his blue regimentals and Langsdorff in his plain black academic uniform – accompanied by two soldiers, one bearing a standard and the other brushes to clean the gentlemen's boots on arrival. A crowd of Japanese and 'a rooster who had placed himself in front' quietly watched the ceremony of the Russian marines presenting arms.[15]

The party disembarked at Nagasaki's 'Mussel Stairs' (probably the Ohato embankment) to find the town transformed. The bustle they had observed through their telescopes had disappeared. Every door and shutter was firmly closed and the side streets shut off by screens of cloth and matting. 'Here and there only we saw a head, urged on by insatiable curiosity, peeping from behind the hangings,' wrote Landsdorff. 'The *tolks* told us that the common people were not worthy to see so great a man as the Ambassador face to face.' Preceded by an honour guard of forty-eight Japanese officials and soldiers, Rezanov was carried in a litter through the streets while his cavaliers followed on foot 'still and slow like a funeral procession'.[16] Unlike the muddy and pestilential streets of European cities of the era, Langsdorff found Nagasaki's highway 'broad and clean with wide gutters to carry away water' and lined with finely built one-storey wooden houses.[17]

Rezanov, in 'full omata', presents his credentials to the Japanese.

At the governor's house the Russians were prevailed upon to remove their shoes and boots and shown into an anteroom with paper walls furnished with a large porcelain spittoon, where they were given pipes of tobacco and tea which 'in the general judgment of our company was by no means good'. The ambassador was shown into the presence of the emissary from Edo and the governor of Nagasaki. Behind them stood guards with drawn swords. Rezanov, as agreed, did not kneel but sat on the floor with his legs to the side.

The audience did not go well. Slowly and patiently, the Shogun's man explained that an embassy had been expressly forbidden in the letter given to Laxman and that Rezanov's presence was 'absolutely inconsistent with propriety'. Rezanov protested that he was simply an instrument of his emperor's will, delivering the letter which showed the Russian emperor's 'inclination to goodwill and friendship'. The official nodded gravely and observed that their Russian guest 'must be unused to sitting in such an uncomfortable position', bringing a polite end to the half-hour audience. A written answer would be delivered to Rezanov in two days.[18]

Spring rain poured from a low sky on 24 March, the day of the second interview. The tide was low and the boats ferrying the party to Hizen's barge ran aground; all the Russians were soaked apart from Rezanov, who had the embassy's only umbrella. Once they had crossed the bay, Rezanov insisted that litters be found for every member of his party, causing a two-hour delay which the Russians passed agreeably drinking tea and smoking on board the barge, warmed by braziers while their escorts waited in the rain. A Japanese artist had been sent to sketch the strangers; he seemed particularly fascinated by 'Rezanov's three-cornered feathered hat, his star and ribbon, the officers' insignia, their buttons, scarves, keys of office, watch-strings and seals'.[19]

In the governor's residence Reazanov was presented with a scroll that the *tolks* held to their foreheads in reverence and opened 'with a deep awe'. This letter, from the court of Edo, was 'an extraordinary instance of favour' from the Shogun, the *tolks* explained. However, its contents were anything but favourable to Rezanov's ambitions. 'The chain of friendship cannot be but disadvantageous to the weak members included in it,' wrote the shogunal chancellery. 'Japan has no great wants and therefore has little occasion for foreign productions. Her few real wants . . . are richly supplied by the Dutch and Chinese, and luxuries are things that she does not want to see introduced,' the court explained. 'Also our products are, unfortunately, very limited . . . all of Japan does not possess enough laquerware to fill your great ship.'[20]

More crushingly still, the Shogun regretted that he could not accept Tsar Alexander's gifts or even his letter, since to do so would oblige him to reply in kind by sending an embassy to Russia 'and we have no large vessels for such an undertaking, nor the gifts.' In short, 'The basic laws of Japan forbid us from making foreign acquaintances, and the breaking of this law could disturb the peace of Japan.' To make the point absolutely clear, the *tolks* presented Rezanov with two further scrolls, one signed by every member of the shogunal council, confirming the ruling, and the other from the governor of Nagasaki, advising him that he was free to leave and that provisions would be sent out to the *Nadezhda* to ready her for her return to Russia.

There was little Rezanov could say or do. He attempted to get the Japanese to agree to accept payment for the food, firewood, copper, timber and cordage that had been so generously supplied. The answer was an absolute refusal. 'If we accept one thaler or five hundred, it is still trade.' The Japanese also rejected Rezanov's suggestion that Russian ships could return shipwrecked Japanese sailors; in future, they stipulated, such survivors should be handed over to the Dutch for repatriation.

The Japanese, with their experience of Rezanov's moods, were desperate to placate their guest's volcanic temper. The Shogun's representative offered twenty-four coats as a parting gift for Rezanov. As they left the audience, Shozaemon 'asked very urgently whether the Russian emperor would declare war on Japan'. Rezanov assured him that he would not. The party set off back to the barge in the pouring rain, this time with no escort, their path back to the quay lit with waxed paper lanterns on poles. In the event it would not be the Russian emperor who declared a war of revenge on Japan but Rezanov himself.

'Just as a body cannot be reunited with its sweat, just as little can the ancient laws of Japan be rescinded,' Rezanov was told by Shozaemon , who had been – or at least told Rezanov he was – a keen advocate of opening trade.[21] 'All Japan is talking of you and saying that you are different from the Dutch, prouder, more heated and that you look down on the Japanese,' lamented the translator, who had seen more than his fair share of just how proud and heated the ambassador could be.

It remained only to take on provisions and pay a farewell call on the Nagasaki authorities. At Rezanov's third and final audience the Shogun's emissary assured him that the long delay in considering his embassy has been 'a proof of great friendship because other nations would have been refused much more quickly'. Rezanov, though he had promised not to, answered in Japanese. 'I need and would like to buy a lot of things,' he told them. 'But since you are so hard as to refuse to give me permission to do so I am leaving here in great need.' By Löwenstern's account, 'these unsuitable remarks were silently ignored'. Rezanov attempted to refuse the governor's gift of twenty-five cases of silk wadding, but was told that Edo would have to be again consulted on what was to be done with the presents. 'To obtain our liberty, therefore, our Excellency was obliged to accept.'[22]

A party of sailors painstakingly repacked the elephant clock, rugs, portrait, galvanic machine and all the rest, and hauled them back once again into the *Nadezhda*'s hold. The mirrors, judged too fragile to transport further, were left as a present for the Dutch, along with several candelabra and, oddly, a collection of steel coat buttons. To the long-suffering Japanese sailors, who were finally to be allowed to part company with their Russian companions, Rezanov ('the personifica-tion of greed', according to Löwenstern) gave three kisses and twenty ducats in addition to their navy pay of 300 Spanish thalers (pronounced 'dollars' by English sailors). The *tolks* accepted, after much persuasion, some tiny gifts – the Adams globe, a world map from Arrowsmith of London, a spyglass.

'The Japanese seem to fear us now because Rezanov has talked of war and animosities,' wrote Löwenstern. 'They hope to get rid of us soon with goodwill . . . since Rezanov is not in his right senses.'[23] A flotilla of thirty sampans carrying armed men appeared to guard the *Nadezhda* while a 'superabundance of provisions' was delivered, courtesy of the nervous Nagasaki authorities. The inventory complied by the careful Shmelin is indeed impressive reading: 1,627 eggs, 88 chickens, 85 ducks, 20 oysters, 1,982 pounds of white bread – plus '12 balls of twine, 8 giant snails, two pieces of seaweed and one bunch of parsley'. Three *banyoshi* who had accompanied the Shogun's emissary from Edo came aboard to have what they believed was the last glimpse in their lifetimes of live Europeans and their craft; 'unlike our local *banyoshi* these are free and bright with their looks, fresh and flexible in their bodies and have a thirst for knowledge'.[24]

These were not the only Japanese sorry to see the Russians go.

'Mademoiselle Apsha', a thirteen-year-old girl who lived in a house near the Russians' compound, sent a small portrait of herself to Moritz Kotzebue, along with a bouquet of white, green and red roses. Sadly, apart from a couple of lines in Löwenstern's diary, we have no other description of this would-be Madame Butterfly and her crush on the young Kotzebue. In a fit of righteousness, or perhaps simple malice, Rezanov confiscated the picture of the infatuated girl. The barge of the 'Prince of Tschingodsi' – probably the Daimyo of the fief of Chikugo, who shared the duty of defending Nagasaki Bay – a far inferior craft to Hizen's, ferried the embassy and its effects back to the *Nadezhda*. This time there was no ceremonial escort.

'Rezanov, quiet and still, speaks neither of the past, present or future,' observed Löwenstern. 'He was always niggardly [with his drink] the whole trip; now every morning at breakfast a double bottle of schnapps gets emptied . . . at noon one or two bottles of Madeira or Cheres, and at tea he offers the finest Jamaica [rum].' This sudden impetuous generosity was taken by his shipmates as a disturbing sign of Rezanov's deep despair.

At four o'clock in the morning of 5 April 1805 a flotilla of boats manned by soldiers in the livery of the 'Prince of Tschikusa' took the Russian ship under tow and rowed her out into the sea-roads four miles off Nagasaki. Only there, safely out of cannon shot, was the *Nadezhda*'s powder returned, along with the swords and muskets. With the powder was a final parting gift for the ambassador: a beautifully-wrapped packet of seeds for the Empress of Russia so that she might have Japanese flowers in her northern gardens.

14

The Voyage of the *Maria*

Authority is a solvent of humanity.

Patrick O'Brian, *HMS Surprise*

Most of the men who come here are depraved, drunk, violent and corrupted to such an extent that any society would consider it a great relief to get rid of them.

Nikolai Rezanov to the directors of the Russian American Company, 1805[1]

The *Nadezhda* stopped briefly at Sakhalin Island before returning to Petropavlovsk on 24 May 1805. Two other ships rode at anchor in Kamchatka's Avacha Bay, the Company brig *Maria Magdalena* and the imperial transport *Theodosia*. An unidentified disease had broken out among the crew of the *Nadezhda* and Rezanov himself was running a high fever. Sick and humiliated, he installed himself in the log cabin of Major Krupskoi, the senior officer of the settlement. General Koshchelev was once again absent from Petropavlovsk. Rezanov fired off a quick letter to him announcing the *Nadezhda*'s return and expressing his anger at his treatment by the Japanese. Their refusal to accept the Russian embassy 'will cost them dear', Rezanov blustered.[2]

All was not well ashore. Lieutenant Andrean Mashin, captain of the *Maria*, presented himself to Rezanov without his uniform, drunk. Rezanov, not in the best of moods, ordered his valet to throw Mashin out of the house and not admit him again until he was properly dressed.

When Mashin reappeared it was to admit that he had failed to deliver supplies to Alaska the previous autumn. Furthermore, a boatload of would-be colonists the *Maria* had brought from Okhotsk had revolted: twenty-four of the eighty-strong party had already deserted, preferring to take their chances in Kamchatka's wilderness to risking the privations of Russian America. 'They are rebelling, they want to attack me,' a tearful Mashin, again drunk, confided to a fellow naval officer in Company service, Lieutenant Nikolai Khvostov. Löwenstern formed no good opinion of the few colonists who remained. 'The subjects of the Russian American Company are known scoundrels and rascals, because who wants to go to Kamchatka as a prospector if he can find bread in St Petersburg or Moscow?'[3]

There was more bad news from America. The previous autumn Mashin had got as far as the Aleutian Islands, where he picked up mail from Baranov, who confirmed that Fort St Michael on Sitka Sound had indeed been raided and destroyed by natives.

The letters from St Petersburg Rezanov found waiting for him did little to improve his mood. The Tsar himself had written with advance congratulations on the embassy's success in Japan. A worried Rumiantsev asked about the situation at Fort St Michael. Buldakov reported falling Company profits. There was also five-month-old news from Europe: Napoleon had crowned himself Emperor of France, and the continent was once again preparing for war. Worst of all, friends in St Petersburg wrote to inform Rezanov that the Tsar was delighted by news of his reconciliation with Krusenstern and was planning to award the Order of St Anne First Class to the captain, to match Rezanov's own. The other officers were also to be handsomely decorated on their return.

This was too much for Rezanov's battered pride to bear. The previous year he had sent a series of bitterly critical reports of Krusenstern and his officers, finally accusing them of mutiny.[4] Now news came from the court – his very own stamping ground and spiritual home – that these officers were to be rewarded while he, Rezanov, would suffer the humiliation of reporting the absolute failure of his diplomatic mission to Japan. In his own eyes, he had stood up single-handedly for the honour and authority of the Tsar in the face of the arrogant German officers who had tried to defy it. Now the Tsar was ignoring the word of the man he had appointed to head the expedition and instead rewarding the mutineers.

In this angry frame of mind, still in bed with fever, Rezanov composed a long letter to the Emperor which bristled with indignation, spleen and barely-concealed accusations of betrayal. Penned between 9 and 12 June 1805, the twenty-page report blasts Koshchelev's administration of Kamchatka and complains about Krusenstern's insubordination. In a frenzy of self-pity, Rezanov even threatened to leave government service altogether: 'I will stay in America for a century. Rank and decorations are not necessary in America and I will send them back with pleasure on the first available transport.' Rejecting the tokens of the Tsar's favour was just about the most insulting thing a courtier could do. Rezanov's petulant letter surely deserves a place alongside the rashest political suicide notes in history.

Nor did Rezanov keep his anger to himself. 'Using very bitter expressions,' recorded Lowenstern, 'Rezanov said he intended to move totally to Kodiak' and even claimed that he had asked Rumiantsev 'to send his children there when they turn thirteen', though there is no trace of this request in any of Rezanov's surviving letters.[5] He also bawled at Tilesius, who reported that Rezanov 'tried openly to kill me with the most dishonourable of swear words, so that I sought the protection of the governor of Kamchatka'.[6] The fateful dispatches to the Emperor were sealed and handed to Councillor Fosse, who was returning to Okhotsk and St Petersburg on the *Theodosia*.

At some point in eastern Siberia Rezanov's blistering letters must have found themselves under the same post-house roof as the emperor's missive to Rezanov, heading the other way. It was the warmest, friendliest and most supportive letter the emperor had ever sent to him; it would also be the last. 'As a sign of Our particular good wishes towards you I send you a diamond tobacco case with Our monogram,' wrote Alexander in his own hand. 'I have also taken your son as a Page at court.' One can only imagine Rezanov's anguish at the knowledge that his apparent reply to this honour and kindness would be his own angry outburst, now heading inexorably towards the imperial Chancellery in Fosse's waterproof document case.

There was some comfort amid the bad news. Rezanov was alone at last in a relatively spacious room for the first time in a year and a half, and finally free of the company of the officers of the *Nadezhda*. Despite his physical and emotional exhaustion, the old gambler's belief that the next play could make everything right – silence his critics at a stroke with a single, glorious stroke of genius – still ran strong. He knew he had to somehow save his reputation and career, or he would never be able to show his face at court again. A crossroads, then. There was no way to explain away the disaster of Nagasaki in which the Tsar and the RAC had invested so much treasure and hope, he decided, except by holding out the promise of a greater victory. 'Not through petty enterprise but by great undertakings have mighty bodies achieved rank and power,' he would write the next year to Rumiantsev.[7] The time had come for a bold stroke.

Rezanov informed St Petersburg that the *Nadezhda* would continue her voyage without him. He would instead sail on the *Maria* back east to Russian America, take the new territories in hand after the disaster of Sitka and lay the foundations of the Pacific empire about which he had spoken so passionately at court. The consolidation and conquest of America would be Rezanov's redemption.

Rezanov's long-suffering valet Alexander was dispatched to clear out his cabin on the *Nadezhda* and remove a selection of the Japanese present fund from the hold. The *Maria*, in a terrible state after a winter being buffeted by Pacific gales, was to be readied for sea again, her foul berths sluiced out and all available cordage, supplies, sailcloth and tools scrounged from Petropavlovsk and loaded aboard.

Rezanov, 'not judging it expedient to wander among the rugged, uncultivated and inhospitable coasts of America without the attendance of a physician, made very advantageous proposals to me to accompany him', wrote Langsdorff.[8] The doctor, excited by the prospect of natural-historical discoveries in America and perhaps less than keen on returning to the pox-ridden *Nadezhda*, agreed. His letters written and orders issued, and with Langsdorff at his side with his bleeding bowl and scalpel, Rezanov retired exhausted to his bed to let his illness run its course.

Meanwhile the brawling, ill-disciplined daily life of Petropavlovsk raged unchecked. A brief mutiny on board the *Maria* was quelled by navy officers Khvostov and Davydov: one smacked the rebels' leader over the head with a hefty stick while the other slapped each mutineer in the face in turn.[9] A fight also broke out among the commanders of the garrison of Kamchatka. Major Krupskoi, nominally the governor's chargé d'affaires and Rezanov's host, had lost all authority over his unruly subordinates. Army Lieutenant Falkin attacked Krupskoi with a knife in a local alehouse, shouting, 'Get out of here if you love life.' Krupskoi succeeded in having Falkin arrested, but when he was called away on government business Falkin's allies dismantled the major's house and attacked his children.[10] 'In the summer the soldiers are lazy and catch no fish for winter supplies; in the winter they starve with their dogs,' complained Löwenstern. 'They would rather chop up fences that do not belong to them than cut down wood which is growing in front of their noses.'[11]

On the morning of 14 July 1805, with Rezanov's fever past and the mutinous sailors subdued, the *Maria* raised anchor and turned towards the rising sun. The *Nadezhda*'s officers celebrated Rezanov's departure with a drunken party, amusing themselves by taking turns to impersonate 'Petrovik's' humiliation at the hands of the insolently polite Japanese *tolks*.[12]

Rezanov was grateful to be, finally, in undisputed charge of a vessel – albeit one that began to disintegrate almost as soon as she left harbour. The 150-ton, two-masted *Maria* was, complained Rezanov, 'the newest and supposedly best Company ship', but her bowsprit fell off and her topmasts had to be lowered because they threatened to split in the freshening wind. 'Such is the shipbuilding at Okhotsk. The ignorance of the shipbuilders there and the shameless robbery by Company representatives produces worthless ships that cost more than ships built anywhere else.'[13] The ship's company also left much to be desired. The *Nadezhda*, for all its jealous officers, hard-drinking priests and pranksome counts, was at least a Chatham-built Tsar's ship crewed and commanded by professional sailors. The Okhotsk-built *Maria* contained the scum of the earth. 'From the moral point of view they may be called the refuse of mankind,' sniffed Langsdorff.[14] This band of desperadoes, adventurers, cut-throats and Siberian half-breeds were in various stages of scurvy from a diet of 'dry and frozen fish, the fat of whales and sea dogs [seals] as their principal nutrient'.[15] They also sported an impressive variety of venereal diseases. 'Our crew consisted of adventurers, drunkards, bankrupt traders and mechanics or branded convicts in search of a fortune.'[16] However, as Löwenstern wryly noted after the *Maria*'s departure, discipline could only improve as they sailed east. 'Even though the RAC hires the worst scoundrels [in Kodiak], they are forced to behave. He cannot escape – except into the hands of the [native] Americans, who would seldom let a Russian live.'

The ship was so overloaded – in part by Rezanov's four jolly boat-loads of luggage – that 'the greater part of the crew were obliged by turns to remain on deck'.[17] This overcrowding and the 'great want of linen' meant that the fastidious Langsdorff rarely ventured out to 'the place where fresh air might be inhaled' because 'these dirty disgusting men were sitting about it everywhere, disencumbering themselves of their unwanted guests'. The carpet of dead lice, ticks and fleas kept Langsdorff 'in a constant fever of disgust and horror at the sight of them'.[18]

The officers were little better. 'In Captain Krusenstern and other companions on the *Nadezhda* I had been accustomed to the society of upright and enlightened friends,'[19] wrote Langsdorff. The officers of the *Maria* were, apparently, neither. The Company had always had trouble recruiting good officers, and the few graduates of the Naval Academy that the Company was able to hire were to be retained at all costs, whatever their drunken and slovenly behavior. Khvostov and Davydov told Langsdorff – almost certainly pulling the prim German's leg – that one of the Company's officers had been 'exiled to Siberia for incest with his own mother'.[20] It's a measure of the low esteem in which their fellow officers were held that the German doctor believed them.

Nikolai Khvostov had been passed over for promotion after a dispute with the Admiralty and had recruited his younger protégé Midshipman Gavriil Davydov for service in America with the promise of fortune and adventure. Both were on their second tour to Russian America. 'I do not know if it is good or bad fate which let us come together with N. P. Rezanov in this the remote point of the Russian state,' wrote Khvostov in June 1805.

Nonetheless, Rezanov was hopeful. Piled above the stinking bilges of the *Maria*'s hold were the accoutrements of civilization – books, charts, navigational instruments donated by the flower of the St Petersburg scientific world and the Tsar's ministers for the betterment of the empire's future subjects, and even Dr Galvani's (evidently rather sturdy) electric machine. He was finally to see the wild coasts of which he had spoken so enthusiastically and for so many years but never visited.

Rezanov's first sight of Russia's offshore empire was magnificent, but appalling. Through the mists off the Pribilov Islands the *Maria*'s crew saw a land teeming with brown slippery bodies, the largest seal rookeries in the world. But as they approached the bleak black-sanded harbour of St Paul Island, Rezanov was almost felled by the wave of putrefaction from piles of rotting seal carcasses. 'The number of seals on this island is unbelievable. The shores are covered with them. It is very easy to kill them,' wrote Rezanov. 'Before I arrived 30,000 male seals had been killed in a single day. Their pelts had been discarded.'[21] Only the animals' penises had been removed for the Canton market, where they were much prized as aphrodisiacs. The Russian colonists had been encouraged in this practice by visiting Boston boats. Twenty had called over the previous season alone, buying up thousands of air-dried seal penises and slaughtering more seals themselves.[22]

'More than a million fur seals had been killed by the time I arrived,' a shocked Rezanov reported to Company headquarters. 'Even at that I was told that there are only a tenth as many as there used to be. These islands could be an inexhaustible source of wealth if only the Bostonians did not compete with us on the Chinese market.'[23] Already the sea otter, once so plentiful on the Pribylov Islands that 3,000 pelts were taken in a single recent season, had disappeared from those waters. Steller's sea cow, once a favourite food for sailors and colonists, had also been hunted to extinction within twenty-five years of its discovery; the last known specimen was caught in 1768. It was the old paradox which had driven Russia's imperial expansion in the first place, restlessly probing east in search of the retreating fur-bearing animals. 'The Russians for momentary advantage kill all they meet with – old and young,' wrote Langsdorff. 'Nor do they see that by such a procedure they must soon be deprived of their trade entirely.'[24]

Langsdorff led a scientific expedition into the seal rookeries, noting that the animals seemed to have no fear of man, an evolutionary lapse that had proved disastrous to their species. The noise and smell were overpowering. 'From many came a tone not unlike a person vomiting, and others cried like little children.'[25] Rezanov allowed the *Maria*'s men to kill eighty seals for meat and then 'ordered the killing be stopped lest they be exterminated and set the men to obtaining walrus tusks instead'.[26] The meat was 'very like veal' as long as the seals had fed only on their mothers' milk; otherwise Langsdorff found it disagreeably fishy.

The fifteen Russian colonists on the Pribilovs lived in dugouts and earth huts with their roofs held up with whale ribs, there being no timber on these windswept islands. 'The climate is cold and ungenial and it appears scarcely comprehensible how any persons not natives of the country can have resolved to fix their abode in so confined a spot, separated almost entirely from the rest of the world.'[27] Despite this, the Russian settlers 'fell at the Chamberlain's feet',[28] pleading not to be sent home and to be allowed to remain with their Aleut wives. Rezanov was unmoved, ruling that all employees of the Company must observe the regulations set down by Shelikhov and leave for the mainland after fifteen years' service.

The *Maria* lumbered on eastwards along the Aleutian chain. 'In winter the seas are covered with vast rocks of ice, in summer subject to perpetual fogs.'[29] At St George's Island the cannon fired to announce their arrival set such a large number of seabirds into flight that 'literally a thick living cloud spread itself around us; the sea as far as our horizon reached was blackened by birds'.[30]

It was on Unalaska that Rezanov had his first sight of sea otters, the lifeblood of the Company's business. Fur seals and walruses could be clubbed on land where they lay, and the resulting market glut meant their fur was cheap. The sea otter, on the other hand, was a far more elusive beast. Sea otters hunted fish in small groups up to half a mile offshore. They were also, unlike their seal cousins, deeply wary of humans.[31] The Aleut had hunted them for centuries from light two- or three-man canoes made of a light driftwood frame covered with seal-skin. The Russians called these craft *baidarkas*, a Siberian term for a bark boat; the Aleuts called them *iqyax*. They are now better known by their Inuit name, *kayak*. Langsdorff called them 'the best means yet discovered by man to go from place to place in the quickest, easiest and safest manner possible'.*[32]

Women sewed the skins but only men were allowed to handle the finished *baidarkas*, which were considered living things and members of the family. Paddling into range of the otters wearing special peaked wooden caps to keep the sun out of their eyes, the hunters could cast javelins extraordinary distances with the help of notched eighteen-inch-long throwing planks to give their arms more leverage. The Aleuts' hunting skills quickly proved their undoing. After local onshore communities of sea otters were exhausted, the Russian managers began to press-gang male Aleuts into months-long long-range hunting expe-ditions, leaving no one at home in the villages to catch and dry fish. This staple of the islanders' diet, known as *iukola*, now had to be bought at inflated prices from the Company, trapping whole families in cycles of debt from which it was impossible to escape.[33]

As the *Maria* progressed along the stations of the Aleutian archipel-ago, Rezanov found himself, in the Russian phrase, 'both Tsar and God' – or at least the closest to either the locals were ever likely to see. At each stop the natives prostrated themselves before him and the colo-nists met him bareheaded, not daring to raise their eyes before this great eminence. At Unalaska, the largest settlement on the archipelago before Kodiak, Rezanov set himself to dispensing justice. He ordered the Aleut hunters to give an account of their Russian masters. The local *toions* – Aleut elders – dutifully (and improbably) reported that

---

* 'The natives observing our astonishment at their agility and skill paddled in among the breakers which reached their breasts and carried their boats under water. They sported about more like amphibious animals than human beings,' wrote Martin Sauer, *The Billings Expedition*, pp157–8.

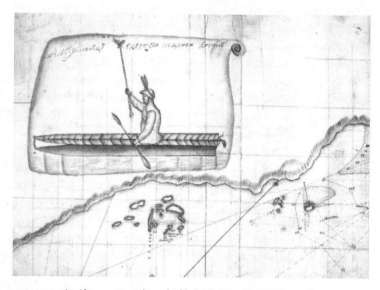

An Aleut carrying a brass double-headed Russian eagle on a pole.
Sketch by Martin Sauer, 1792.

Unalaska's manager Emilian Larionov was 'as a father to them . . . they had only one request to make and that was that the manager to be as good to them in the future as he was in the past'.[34] Later reports by Company officers depict Larionov as vicious and almost deranged, making the *toions'* praise all the more curious – or perhaps all the more understandable, given that the great chamberlain was passing through wheras Larionov was there to stay. Deserved or not, Rezanov duly presented a gold medal to Larionov and a silver one to his interpreter.

Demid Kuliakov, the RAC's foreman of the Pribilov Islands, was less fortunate.[35] Kuliakov lived on the island of Akhta, where he had a native wife and half-breed son, but was visiting Unalaska on Company business when he seems to have got into a bit of drunken bother. The exact circumstances of his crimes in Unalaska are unclear because only Rezanov kept a brief record of the justice he summarily dispensed. But Kuliakov was clapped in irons on Rezanov's orders 'for the inhuman beating of an American woman and her baby son'[36] and sent to Russia for trial.

Although Rumiantsev had breezily entrusted Rezanov with administering justice in Russian America, in truth neither Rezanov nor any other officer of the RAC had any formal judicial authority over the natives or colonists. Indeed for this reason there was still not a single prison or courthouse in Russian America when the colony was sold in 1867. In theory all felons and witnesses in capital cases had to be shipped to the nearest crown courts, six months' travel away in Irkutsk. But in practice local managers freely doled out corporal punishment. Most common was public flogging with baleen staves taken from the mouths of beached whales. RAC managers also forcibly impressed natives into working on distant islands as a matter of course. Men like Kuliakov were used to exercising casual brutality and absolute, feudal authority over their native charges.

Whether Kuliakov's behaviour in Unalaska was truly out of the ordinary or Rezanov was simply using his case as a way to display his power in front of the assembled *toions* is unclear. Löwenstern, who later saw Kuliakov in chains in Kamchatka, noted that 'his head for business and usefulness has caused the Company managers to wink at his many cruelties'.[37] In any case, for Kuliakov being sent away from the colony for trial was punishment enough. He never returned to Russian America or saw his native wife or son again. Langsdorff was 'very much overcome by the manner in which I saw the colonists' lives sported with'[38] and felt 'such repugnance to the scenes of horror which seemed to be in store for me that I almost resolved to shut myself in my chamber lest by communication I should come to be like those with whom I was principally surrounded . . . The distant islands are commonly under the supervision of a Russian colonist, in other words, a rascal, by whom they are oppressed, tormented and plundered in every way.'[39] Rezanov also formed no good opinion of the colonists. 'Those of depraved minds go nowadays to America solely with the aim of growing rich and then upon their return journey fritter it away in a few days, scattering like dust the riches obtained by many years of other people's tears. Can such desperate people respect their fellow beings? They have given up family life altogether and have no good example to follow. Therefore the poor Americans are (to Russia's shame) sacrificed to their debauchery.'[40]

Langsdorff also found the outposts filthy and disorderly with no medicine and little food.[41] 'The natives are so completely slaves of the Russian American Company that even their clothes and the bone tips of their spears belong to the Company,' he wrote. The 'oppression under which they live at home, the total want of care and the change in modes of living'[42] plus the Company's practice of sending away the best hunters from their home villages for months at a time had diminished the population severely since Shelikhov's day.

Langsdorff described the Aleuts as 'a kind of middle race between Mongol Tatars and North Americans . . . they have a pleasingly benevolent expression of countenance, their character is generally kind hearted, obliging, submissive and careful, but if roused to anger become rash and unthinking, even malevolent . . . The colour of their skin is a dirty brown to which perhaps their habits of life and a great want of cleanliness may well contribute.'[43, 44] The Aleut habit of washing their hair and clothes in human urine, kept in large open buckets at the entrances to their underground abodes, did not help sweeten their smell. They were both polygamous and polyandrous: 'boys if they happen to be handsome, are often brought up entirely as girls and instructed in all the arts women use to please men. Their beards are plucked, chins tattooed like those of women, they wear ornaments of glass beads and bind and cut their hair as women and supply their places with the men as concubines.' Langsdorff found it a 'shocking, immoral and unnatural practice.'[45] Incest was also widely practised, 'the nation in this respect following the example of sea-dogs [seals] and otters'.[46, 47]

Their villages of half-buried houses 'resemble a European churchyard full of graves'. Their dwellings – *barabaras* – 'consist of a large room with a door three foot square and an opening in the roof to let out smoke. The middle a large hole is dug for a fire . . . it answers the purpose of courtyard, kitchen and, when required, a theatre,' wrote Lieutenant Davydov. 'All household chores are done here, cleaning fish repairing *baidarkas*. Around the main hall are individual dwellings reached by separate holes in roof hatches covered in translucent fish skin.'[48]

Left to their own devices, the Aleuts were perfectly adapted to their environment. Every part of the seals they hunted was put to good use

– the oesopahgus for leggings and boots, the fat for light, the entrails for waterproof parkas and 'carters smocks ornamented with glass beads, exquisitely made, taking up to a year to make and decorated with little red feathers'.[49] Seal intestine was also used instead of glass on windows, the bones for household utensils. Local bilberries, raspberries, cloud-berries, cranberries and whortleberries were eaten by children and the sick, the Aleuts never having made the connection between the fact that 'a vegetable diet was not much esteemed' in their culture and their chronic seasonal scurvy.[50] They had become addicted under Russian influence to snuff, and would work as much as a day for a pinch of it. Alcohol, the other great Russian vice, was to decimate Aleut communi-ties in the twentieth century, but in this period was so scarce that Baranov seldom saw a barrel of brandy from year to year, and with barley or other grains almost unknown on the islands even producing decent home-brew was nearly impossible.

In early July the Company transport, the *Svyatoi Alexander*, sailed into Unalaska harbour, bringing Rezanov good news from the south: Baranov had recaptured Fort St Michael the previous summer. The *Neva*, under Lisiansky, had participated in the battle. In celebration of the victory the Unalaska natives amused Rezanov – or perhaps didn't – with their dances, accompanied by the rhythmic rattle of small stones in sea-dog bladders. 'The only motion consists of a kind of hop.'[51]

The *Maria* sailed for Kodiak on 10 July 1805, leaving 'some of the most unruly and diseased . . . of our half-starved, miserable crew'[52] to the care of Larionov, while taking in their place some of the healthiest and best Aleut hunters, as well as Mrs Larionov's last cured ham, several salted and smoked geese and a large supply of fish pastries. One imag-ines there were mixed feelings in the Larionov household concerning Rezanov's flying visit.

Shelikhov's original settlement at Three Hierarchs Bay on Kodiak Island had been badly damaged by a tsunami in 1792, and its harbour rendered useless by a sandbank swept inshore by the giant wave. Baranov relocated to a promontory on the north-eastern shore of Kodiak he called St Paul's Harbour. Even today, it seems an odd place for a town. The settlement stood clustered on a small plain overlooking a narrow channel, with sea inlets on two sides. But unlike the aptly named Anchorage, a day's sail to the north, Kodiak's twin harbours are shallow, prone to currents and barely sheltered from the massive storms which barrel in from the Pacific. Even on relatively calm days the swells breaking on Armoury Point to the north of the town throw spray forty feet in the air. The modern Kodiak, like most of small-town America, is widely spaced and huddles low to the ground. In winter, when the sport fishermen and cruise ships have gone and only a handful of bear hunters are in town, it has an abandoned air. Sea winds howl across the wide empty spaces between the giant downtown Wal-Mart and the locked fishing-boat sheds on the shore. The heights that loom over the town beyond the modern-day Rezanov Drive are bleak and covered in gorse and brush, like the Scottish Highlands, and beyond are tall stands of spruce and pine.

It was these forests that had attracted Baranov to this desolate place. No timber grew on the windswept Aleutians, and the woods at Kodiak were the first supply of straight pinewood between Kamchatka and the Alaskan mainland. The giant spruces, towering up to 120 feet into the air, were perfect for shipbuilding, while the less springy and denser redwoods were good for houses. The colonists mostly hailed from north Russia and Siberia, so naturally enough they built Siberian-style houses in their new colonies – one-storey, two-roomed log cabins made of whole timbers and caulked with moss. In the centre, dividing the structure in half, stood a large brick or stone stove at least two yards square reaching from the foundations to the roof. The design was perfect for extreme, dry, Siberian cold, less so for the mild, rainy winters of Russian America.

Nonetheless, the old Company storehouse, built in 1808 and incorporated into a later plank-built house, survives. The massive timbers are three feet wide, hand sawn down two sides and morticed together at each corner. In its heyday literally millions of rubles' worth of sea-otter pelts were stored in the house, enough to buy several ships-of-the-line or run the imperial court for months. Now the Baranov Museum, it contains a few tangible remains of Rezanov's period: a bronze bust of Alexander I brought by Lisiansky as a present from the Company; various corroded small-bore cannon; the Company's locally-issued money printed on squares of sealskin because of the shortage of metal.

By the time Rezanov made landfall, on 31 July 1805, Kodiak already boasted thirty houses, including a brick manufactory, a forge, barracks and storehouses, docks, vegetable gardens and even an iron smelter. But it was hardly the 'regular and well-ordered town' envisaged by Shelikhov. The main 'magazine' held the Company's collected wealth, the thousands of cured pelts stored for transport to Okhotsk. On their first voyage for the RAC two years before, Khvostov and Davydov had collected 18,000 sea-otter pelts from Kodiak, as well as fox, marten, black bear and 'sea bear' valued at two million rubles.

Kodiak was at least better appointed – in terms of accommodation and manufactures if not food – than many Siberian *ostrogs*. Moreover, despairing of seeing any ships from St Petersburg or Okhotsk and in spite of a desperate shortage of tar, cordage, nails and tools, Baranov had succeeded in building his own. The English shipwright John Shields' three-masted brig *Phoenix*, had been built on an uninhabited bay on Prince William Sound in 1793. But Shields' smaller, single-masted ships *Olga* and *Delfin* were built on Baranov's new slipway in Kodiak in the two subsequent summers. It was a remarkable achievement – in nearly two centuries on the Pacific coast of the Americas the Spanish had not yet succeeded in building a single ship there.

This progress had come at a high cost, largely to the local population. According to a census of Kodiak and the Aleutian Islands taken by Joseph Billings during his tour of inspection in 1791–2, the native population stood between 4,797 and 5,995 souls.[53] In the first seven years of Baranov's rule in Russian America one in ten of the Aleut population was killed, most of them during dangerous hunting expeditions far from home into which they had been press-ganged by Russians.

'The Company rounded up the Aleut hunters for the Sitka hunting party in the following manner,' reported Hieromonk Gideon, who had arrived in Russian America with Lisiansky on the *Neva* in 1804.

The Russians equipped themselves with leg irons, manacles, wooden neck-yokes and whips (for the young ones) and sticks (to beat the older ones), a boat was sent with a light cannon and muskets to the western edge of Kodiak. The armed Russians formed a line and said to the Koniags, 'Well, anyone who does not wish to go may speak up now and be shot.' Who under such threat could express his objections? On arrival at Sitka the Russians discharged a cannon, then put out all the manacles and yokes on the deck and stood with loaded guns. 'Whoever does not wish to go may choose one of these irons for himself.' The first man to try to talk himself out of going was immediately seized, clapped in irons and whipped until he could barely say the words, 'I will go.'[54]

Gideon estimated in his subsequent report to the Holy Synod in St Petersburg that between 1792 and 1805 'One hundred and ninety-five Aleuts have been captured or killed by Tlingit,' the natives of mainland Alaska, ethnically and culturally distinct from the Aleuts. A further 290 had drowned accidentally and 135 died as a result of shellfish poisoning. Langsdorff believed that depopulation had been more radical still. Evstrat Delarov estimated the population of Kodiak and its neighbouring islands at 3,000 souls in 1790. By 1805 Langsdorff found that no more than 450 able-bodied men were at the Kodiak manager Ivan Banner's disposal. 'The spreading of unusual diseases, oppression and ill usage – especially compulsory fatiguing hunting parties – cares and sorrows and insurrections have, like a pestilence, depopulated the countries to an almost incredible degree.'[55] The Company's activities were proving almost as devastating to the region's human inhabitants as to its wildlife.

The monks of Kodiak became the Aleuts' most vocal – and indeed only – defenders. As early as 1796 reports by Archimandrite Iosaf of abuses by Russian colonists had hindered Shelikhov's attempts to get Catherine II to grant a monopoly and a state loan. Even after Iosaf's death in the wreck of the *Phoenix* in 1799 his monks continued the dead prelate's complaints. This attitude did little to endear the clergy to the RAC and its officers, who concluded that the snitching monks were bad for business. Gideon, for his part, reported that the Company's Russian employees also 'use the monks as their tools against the Manager'.

Rezanov's attitude was more nuanced. On the one hand he found the rank-and-file monks venal and brutal, and he complained about them at length to both Company and emperor. When news came in late summer 1805 that the newly founded outpost on Lake Ilamna had been overrun by Yakutat Tlingits and all the Russians massacred, Rezanov placed the blame squarely on the Church rather than on the Company's manager Stepan Larionov, brother of the Larionov of Unalaska, who was massacred along with his family. [56]

'The monk Juvenaly . . . baptized the natives forcibly, married them, took girls away from some and gave them to others,' Rezanov wrote to the directors of the RAC with news of the massacre.

> The [native] Americans endured his rough ways and beatings for a long time and finally held council decided to get rid of the Reverend and killed him. He does not deserve pity. But the natives in exasperation killed the whole crew of Russians and Kodiak people . . . I told the Holy Fathers that if any of them took another step without first getting the managers' approval or if they meddled in civil affairs I would order such criminals deported to Russia, where for disrupting the peace of the community they would be defrocked and severely punished to make an example of them. They cried and rolled at my feet and told me it was the government employees who had told them what to do. . . . I admonished them thus privately in the presence of Father Gideon but in public I have always showed respect for their dignity. [57]

At the same time Rezanov thought highly of Gideon. He wrote to the Hieromonk with great civility, asking him 'what is required annually for the upkeep of the clergy and beautification of the temple of God . . . I deem it one of my first duties to understand the present situation of the spiritual mission.' Rezanov evidently found Gideon both an intelligent companion and ally in his mission to bring enlightenment to the new colonies. The thirty-five-year-old Gideon, born Gavriil Fedotov in Orel, was, with Langsdorff and Rezanov and the three naval officers, one of only a handful of educated men in the colony. Gideon had studied rhetoric, logic, geography, physics and geometry at the

Belograd seminary and taught French and mathematics in St Petersburg; his mission from the Synod was 'to inspect the new converts in the Christian settlements in America'.[58]

In Rezanov's view the Orthodox Church in America should be an arm of the Company, to be used by the authorities as an instrument of social control, just as the Church had for centuries been an arm of the state in continental Russia. The Company was founded on the exploitation of natural resources – which meant not just the local fauna but the natives and Russians too. The RAC was, in this respect, feudal in its organization and philosophy. The priests' role was to pacify the locals and persuade them to resign themselves to their fate. The monks should, in Rezanov's opinion, refrain from joining the RAC's managers in abusing the natives – but neither should they take the natives' side against the Company. 'I ask you to ensure that obedience to the management is preserved among the Americans,' he urged Gideon. 'Or else in this region all may unravel and be lost . . . and the knives under which we live will again be used to annihilate Russians.'[59]

But the Company was more than just a glorified Cossack raiding cartel. Its officers, and especially Rezanov, also believed, or claimed to believe, in Shelikhov's ideas of a civilizing mission. Efforts to educate native peoples were unknown, for instance, among the Cossack fur traders of Siberia. The Company also employed some of Russia's finest ethnographers and geographers. The mission of the *Neva* and *Nadezhda* was in part a voyage of discovery on the lines of Cook's and Vancouver's. Several naval officers employed by the Company – notably Lisiansky, Davydov and later Vasily Golovnin – took considerable interest in native customs and welfare. Lisiansky's magnificent collections of native artefacts formed the basis of the Kunstkammer Museum in St Petersburg's unrivalled native American collections. Langsdorff's detailed ethnographic accounts of the native traditions became a bestseller when republished in London in 1813. Even Hieromonk Gideon was a man of science as much as of the cloth and sent detailed descriptions of the culture of the Kodiak peoples back to Russia. He described the natives' shamanic rites – *igrushki*, 'little games', as he called them – with curiosity rather than censure. He also took a keen interest in native herbal cures and Aleut cosmology and myth.

Importantly, Gideon shared many of Rezanov's criticisms of the slapdash practices of the local clergy. 'Our monks have never followed the path of the Jesuits of Paraguay by trying to develop the mentality of the savages,' wrote Gideon. 'They have just been "bathing" the Americans, and when, due to their ability to copy, the latter learn in half an hour how to make the sign of the cross our missionaries return, proud of their success, thinking their job is done.'[60] Gideon moved quickly to remedy the situation. A school of sorts for fifteen native children had been founded by Shelikhov himself in 1784–5 and continued by Archimandrite Iosaf. But it was Gideon who created the first semblance of systematic education, opening a two-class school for up to a hundred part-time native pupils, who learned writing, reading and catechism in the junior classes and arithmetic, grammar, Church and state history in the senior.

One of Rezanov's less attractive habits was taking credit for the achievements of others. He told the Company that it was he who had ordered this school opened; he hadn't. Gideon mentioned it in a letter to his superior Metropolitan Amvrosii five months before Rezanov's arrival. Nonetheless it is clear that Rezanov took a lively interest in the place, handing out 'personal awards' to the best students after examining fifty pupils in their grammar and prayers. Rezanov also claimed that he had, in the course of a three-week stay in Kodiak, knocked out a seven-language dictionary of several hundred entries detailing the various dialects of the Aleut language, which he enclosed for the directors' perusal.

'I commissioned [the monks] to make a dictionary so as not to be at the mercy of interpreters [but] because a work of this kind looked as big and forbidding as a bear I began to make one myself,' wrote Rezanov breezily. 'The dictionary took quite a bit of work and enclosing it here I beg you to publish it and send bound copies here [for the] American schools.'[61] This dictionary was also in reality largely the work of Gideon, who was the first to translate the Lord's Prayer into the Alutiiq language.

For all his complaints about the clergy, it was the Fathers, not the Company, to whom Rezanov entrusted the agricultural experiments that were a strategically vital part of Russian America's future. As long as the colony could not feed itself it was at the mercy of the erratic transports from Okhotsk and therefore inherently insecure. Without vegetables the Russians sickened and died from scurvy. The monks dispatched by Shelikhov in 1794 had attempted to grow potatoes, radishes, poppies, turnips, tobacco, cabbage, cucumbers, watermelons, melons, green peas, sunflowers and beets. Of that ambitious *potager*, only the potatoes, winter radishes and turnips grew, plus a bit of barley on manured ground.[62] Rezanov reported that he 'gave Father Herman twenty [native] boys to be trained in agriculture. They will be taken to Spruce Island, to the north of Kodiak, to experiment with sowing wheat, planting potatoes and vegetables and learning how to make preserves of mushrooms and berries.'

Herman was to remain on Spruce Island for forty years and achieve sainthood there. His wheat, despite years of trying, did not take root. But Orthodoxy did. Long after the sea otters had been hunted to the edge of extinction and the Company's lands sold to the United States, the Russian clergy and the native faithful remained. Today the majority of the indigenous population of Alaska is still Russian Orthodox. That, and chronic alcoholism, are the two most visible legacies of Russian America. The most prominent landmark of almost every town in coastal Alaska is still a distinctive Russian onion-domed church topped with an Orthodox cross.

In Kodiak's Cathedral of the Holy Resurrection, a late-nineteenth-century building just off Rezanov Drive, the congregation still takes communion from the handsome silver chalice brought out by Gideon on the *Neva*. Its base is inscribed, 'Minister of Commerce Count N Rumiantsev sent this chalice to America in the Year of Our Lord 1803.' There is the handsome icon of the Virgin and Child from Valaam, and the set of heavy iron chains and four-pound iron cross worn by Herman under his clothes for his whole life. Today the priest is a Washington-State-born American, the inscriptions on the modern icons and the service are all in English. But the robes, the smell of incense, the low chanting of the choir, the huddle of bowed Aleut congregants, these are all clear echoes of the hut in which Rezanov must have taken communion from those same vessels for the first time in 1805.

It is on Spruce Island, though, that the spirit of those early monks most perceptibly lingers. The island is separated from Kodiak by a mile and a half of choppy sea, which the three modern-day monks navigate in a sturdy steel open boat. They are skinny, bearded and wear robes their eighteenth-century forebears would immediately recognize: long black cassocks and black cloth monk's caps. Only their rubber boots and bright North Face backpacks might baffle Herman. The beaches of Spruce Island are of black volcanic sand, carpeted with shiny black kelp. Inland the woodland landscape is surreal. To a height of five or six feet every tree, rock and shrub is covered with a thick layer of vibrant green moss, several inches thick. This dense living carpet has the odd effect of dampening all sound, like snow, and one moves through the forest in a strange silence. The constant rainfall and damp of the forest floor also cause huge pale mushrooms to flourish.

For their first year on the island Herman and his twenty orphan charges lived in a large hole in the ground; it must have been damp. Later he built a simple hut next to a small clearing where he conducted his agricultural experiments. He is buried below the hut he built, now replaced by a plank-built church that attracts hundreds of pilgrims on his saint's day on 9 August. The Orthodox Church in America beatified him as St Herman of Alaska in 1969, and he is considered by the Orthodox to be the patron saint of the Americas. Today Herman is the Russian most widely remembered and revered in Alaska, not Shelikhov, Rezanov or Baranov.

In the crude shack on Kodiak where Archimandrite Iosaf had lived before his demise Rezanov ordered shelves to be put up. On these he carefully arranged the beautifully-bound, if now slightly mildewed, books donated by St Petersburg's grandees. Onto the walls he tacked prints of the royal family, and on the top shelves he placed the scientific instruments he had brought. In pride of place was the long-suffering galvanic machine, battered by its travels but still functional. Russian America, Rezanov proudly reported apparently without irony, now had its very own branch of the Academy of Sciences. [63]

15

Baranov

The wilderness found him out early, and had taken vengeance for the fantastic invasion. I think it had whispered to him things about himself which he did not know, things of which he had no conception till he took counsel with this great solitude – and the whisper had proved irresistibly fascinating. It echoed loudly within him because he was hollow at the core.

Joseph Conrad, *Heart of Darkness*

If somebody could count what these sea otters cost in human lives perhaps they would push their caps made of these same sea otters lower on their brows to hide their faces in shame.

Nikolai Rezanov, *Diary*[1]

Kodiak and the Aleutian Islands are scraps of land in a hostile ocean, remote and windswept chunks of Siberian taiga scattered across the Pacific. But as you approach Sitka by sea it is the land, not the water, which dominates. Granite cliffs rise straight up from the water topped with tall pines, unbowed by sea winds. Out on the Aleutians you are seldom out of earshot of the Pacific, but Sitka is protected by a thousand-mile stretch of sea-islands sheltering a convoluted inshore channel which Vancouver called the Inside Passage. Here the water is still, and it is the forests rather than the sea that pitch and hiss. After months out on the roaring ocean, the silence must have been deafening. Sitka

Sound itself is dotted with strange little wooded islands and dominated by the vast, snow-topped triangular bulk of Mount Edgecumbe.* This was, unmistakably, the edge of a great continent: finally a place worthy of Rezanov's grandiose imperial visions.

The *Maria* lumbered into Sitka Sound on 26 August 1805. Alexander Baranov hurried to meet the highest eminence yet (or indeed ever) to set foot in Russian America. Baranov was fifty-nine years old, 'of thickset build . . . upright, strong and agile. He walked with a quiet tread. His eyes shone with a lively and penetrating gaze.'[2] He wore the uniform of a collegiate councillor, equivalent of a provincial governor, and at his throat was the Order of St Vladimir third class (with his name misspelled as 'Boranov' on the back). Both honours had been awarded to him in the summer of 1802 for 'extraordinary services to the Tsar and Empire' – in fact both promotion and decoration had been lobbied for by the Company to forestall Baranov's regular attempts to resign from his post. On his high bald head was a wig of antique design, 'held in place by a black band under his chin'.[3]

Alexander Baranov had been a central figure in Rezanov's life ever since his first involvement with the Company back in 1794. Like Shelikhov, Baranov had been born into a modest merchant family in a town with a long commercial tradition. Cossacks and merchants from Kargopol, in north Russia, had traded along the Arctic coast of Siberia for centuries. Baranov had shown early initiative by inventing a mechanical tractor but had found no backers among the conservative town fathers. In his early twenties he left Kargopol behind to seek his fortune in Irkutsk, setting up a factory producing glass beads and bottles for the colonial market. By the late 1780s he was, like Shelikhov, a man of standing in the Irkutsk merchants' guild, and was able to borrow capital from his fellow traders to finance a fur-gathering venture in the far-flung territories north of the Sea of Okhotsk, which remained unexplored. In 1789, driven by an insatiable wanderlust, Baranov abruptly left his Irkutsk home, his wife, two daughters and a foundling

---

* Named by James Cook after a hill overlooking Plymouth harbour – the Russians called it Mount St Lazarus.

boy who had been left on the family's doorstep and headed further east. He would never see them again. With borrowed gold he trapped and bought furs in the then barely explored north of Kamchatka and the Chukchi peninsula beyond.

Winter transportation on Kamchatka, sketched by Langsdorff.

The Chukchi tribesmen were the only native Siberian tribe violent and warlike enough ever to fight the Russian invaders to a negotiated peace, concluded in 1778. Even after the Russian withdrawal from the *ostrog* of Anadyrsk under the terms of the treaty, the Chukchi remained notorious raiders of Russian settlements and caravans – including Baranov's. In 1789 a Chukchi attack robbed Baranov of an entire season's caravan-load of furs and left the once-prosperous merchant deeply in debt to the backers of his Kamchatkan venture.

Shelikhov had been trying to entice the enterprising frontiersman Baranov into his service since 1787.[4] Now he stepped in to pay Baranov's debts, and offered him employment as general manager of the North-East American Company territories in the New World. Whatever misgivings Baranov may have had about embarking on a life of risk and hardship on the islands were assuaged by Shelikhov's generous offer of four full shares in the Company and a percentage of the profits, to be paid in furs.[5]

Baranov turned out to be an inspired choice. He was to remain in Russian America for twenty-nine years, and his doggedness and bravery were to transform the Company's settlements from a series of precarious temporary trading posts into permanent and thriving settlements. Under his leadership the colony was brought, kicking and screaming, from the world of medieval privateering into the bureaucratic age of high empire.[6]

Before he even arrived at Kodiak Baranov showed his mettle in the wake of a disastrous shipwreck off Unalaska in the autumn of 1790. Shelikhov's old barque the *Three Hierarchs* ran aground and broke up in Koshigen Bay. Ordering the forty-four survivors to build native-style dugouts near the beach, Baranov wintered on the island. They lived off shellfish and seabirds when the weather was too rough to fish. 'At Lent we all fasted a proper fast and on Whit Monday by the Lord's Providence part of a whale was washed up on the beach and we broke our fast with that . . . I no longer think about either bread or sugar,' Baranov later reported to Shelikhov. Despite his desperate situation Baranov used the hungry winter months to plan improvements to the colony's shipping, its relations with the natives and the organization of sea-otter hunting. 'My first steps here were visited with misfortune by a cruel Fate . . . But privation and boredom I can bear with patience and I shall not rant at Providence, especially when I sacrifice to friendship.'[7]

By spring Baranov and his men had built and bought enough *baidarkas* for his entire crew and a handful of Aleut guides to continue their journey. This fragile flotilla set off across 750 miles of the north Pacific, bivouacking on unknown shores every night. The party eventually made landfall at Three Hierarchs Bay on Kodiak on 27 June 1791. He had not lost a single man on the way.

Even more important than Baranov's personal toughness and organizational skills was his ability to control the drunken and frequently violent colonists placed in his charge. 'You cannot spend a month without enmity and inflicting insult on your comrades and masters by second-guessing your masters' every step,' Baranov berated the assembled colonists on Kodiak after an abortive revolt in 1801. 'In your own village you did nothing but feed pigs or sit in the tavern, but here you become wise, a judge of all and a high-minded minister.'[8]

Baron Ferdinand Wrangel, general manager of the Russian American colonies in the 1830s, would dismiss Baranov as the '*ataman* of a band of brigands', and indeed the colony's early correspondence is full of stories of Baranov's fistfights – including one with James Shields – and his many amorous exploits with Aleut girls. Yet Baranov, more than any other Company officer, was able to turn a rabble of cut-throats and ne'er-do-wells into a workforce disciplined enough to ship a staggering three million rubles' worth of furs back to the North-East American Company's Irkutsk warehouses between 1794 and 1799.[9]

Shelikhov had pioneered Russian America, but it was Baranov, the Company's tough, hard-drinking manager, who made the colonies a permanent reality. In the late summer of 1799 Baranov was ready to execute his plan to expand the Russian settlements to the rich hunting grounds of Sikta Sound, 650 miles to the south of Kodiak. His war party, led by twenty-two Russians, set sail in the *Phoenix* and another smaller vessel. They led a giant, if fragile, flotilla of armed Aleuts in 200 *baikarkas*. As they rounded the tip of what is now Baranov Island into Sitka Sound itself a sudden storm swamped thirty of the canoes and ran the *Phoenix* aground. Baranov and the remains of his party struggled ashore in the teeth of the gale. Sixty men had been lost.

As the survivors lay half-dead on the beach amid the wreckage of the expedition Baranov heard 'a terrible war cry which echoed from the forests and made our flesh creep'. A desperate battle in the dark and wind ensued, Baranov and the handful of Russians fighting hand-to-hand as their Aleut hunters fled for their lives. Loading their muskets from a single flask of powder that had stayed miraculously dry, the Russians drove off the attacking tribesmen. In the morning the indestructible Baranov ordered his men to head further into hostile territory in the remaining *baikarkas*, where they were confronted with the unnerving sight of the massed braves of the Tlingit tribe, their faces painted half black and half red, their hair sculpted into fantastic shapes with grease and birds' down.[10]

Baranov went ashore for a powwow with the Tlingit chief, Skatleut. Outnumbered and negotiating for his life, he managed to convince Skatleut of his peaceable intentions and was granted permission to build a stockade on a tiny patch of ground on the north coast of the Sound. The chief agreed to be christened Mikhail and accepted Baranov's own chain-mail shirt as a gift. The exhausted colonists began to cut timber for the settlement that was to become Fort St Michael. Baranov duly buried one of the Empress's iron possession plates – the only one to have ever been rediscovered – under a wooden Orthodox cross overlooking the sea.

The life of the colonies was a desperate hand-to-mouth existence largely because of the precariousness of the supply chain from Okhotsk. Between 1797 and 1802 no Russian ships at all reached America. A second *Three Hierarchs* was wrecked in spring 1797 and the *Orel* in August that same year. Baranov's beloved *Phoenix* was lost in 1799 returning from Okhotsk with vital supplies – and the less vital, in the eyes of Baranov at least, newly anointed Bishop Iosaf. Only the arrival of the Boston ship *Enterprize* under Captain George Winship in 1800 saved Kodiak from starvation after she bartered $6,542 of goods – mostly food – for furs, which Winship then went on to exchange for trade goods such as tea, silk, cotton and porcelain in Canton.

The Atlantic triangle trade, the basis of many great British and American trading fortunes, involved shipping British cloth and manufactures to Africa and exchanging them for slaves, which were then transported to the West Indies and bartered in turn for rum and sugar for sale in England. The less well-known Pacific triangle had been pioneered by Boston men in the late eighteenth century. Bartering American manufactures for Alaskan fur, fur for China tea and selling the tea back in New England exponentially increased the profits of any merchant who could master it.

In February 1784 the Boston ship *Empress of China* docked at New York with China tea bought with $120,000 silver dollars in cash and cleared a profit of $30,727. But by trading cheap goods – tin, iron, copperware, brass kettles, wire beads, muskets, looking glasses, rum, molasses powder, flints, lead, knives, nails and dry goods – for furs on the north-west coast of America and bartering those same furs for tea in Canton the Boston men could fill their ships with the same amount of tea for an outlay of just $17,000.[11] That meant seven times more profit. By 1800 an average of ten Boston ships were trading in Russian America every year. The availability of cheap credit and maritime insurance, sound ships and plentiful manufactured goods meant that American merchants could deploy more ships to the north Pacific in a year than the Russian Empire was able to send to its colonies in two decades.

For Baranov the Boston men's arrival meant good conversation, solid shipboard fare and plentiful supplies of rum, enlivening an otherwise grim life punctuated only by outbreaks of scurvy, news of native attacks and shipwrecks. Baranov took no notice of the grave warnings against contact with foreigners periodically issued by the Company, which seemed to think if the interlopers were ignored they might go away. But it was John O'Cain, an Irish-American seaman with an eye for the main chance, who proposed a revolutionary idea to Baranov that would bind the Russian colonies to the Bostonians in a close alliance.

O'Cain had been first mate of the Boston boat *Phoenix* (no relation to the Company ship of the same name) under Henry Moore and had struck up a friendship with Baranov when the vessel called at Kodiak in 1794–5. By 1803 he had returned in his own ship – the *O'Cain* – with the usual trade goods. But this time he offered Baranov an intriguing joint venture: O'Cain would borrow a party of trained Aleuts and take them on a long-range expedition to the rich hunting grounds of California. The RAC would provide the hunters, O'Cain the transport, and the two would split the bag fifty-fifty at the season's end. It worked. O'Cain returned the Aleuts safe and well at the end of the season along with a large crop of sea-otter pelts. Thus by ignoring Company instructions and making friends with the Bostonians Baranov kept his warehouses full of furs.

However, these far-ranging expeditions, whether by Boston ship or under the hunters' own paddle power, carried special dangers. The

Tlingit of mainland Alaska were far more dangerous to the Russians and Aleuts than the Koniags had ever been.[12] The Tlingit had been trading sea-otter pelts on their own account with visiting Boston ships for a decade before Baranov's arrival at Sitka in 1799. Crucially for the gathering showdown, the Yankees were willing to pay for pelts in guns and powder. A single pelt could be traded for a good New England musket worth two to three pounds sterling or nearly fifty Spanish dollars. But by 1802 the Russians' devastatingly efficient parties of Aleut hunters based at Fort St Michael on Sitka Sound were having the usual fatal impact on the local otter population. The Tlingit leaders of south Alaska resolved to put a stop to the Russians' depredations and protect their threatened hunting grounds.

Hostilities began on 12 June 1802 when the Tlingit of Kake and Kuiu Island attacked a Russian-led hunting party on the shores of Yakutat Bay. A hundred and sixty-five Aleut hunters were killed; only the Russian commander, Urbanov, and twenty-one hunters made it back to Kodiak alive. A few days later, on the morning of Sunday, 26 June 1802, a large war party led by Katlian, nephew of the Sikta Tlingit chief Skatleut, without warning attacked and overran the unfinished palisade of Fort St Michael. The hunter Abrosim Plotnikov returned from a nearby pasture with the community's small herd of cattle to find 'buildings on fire and the storehouses looted'. As he later told Company officers in Kodiak, 'I saw Navaskin jump over the balustrade from the upper balcony and start to run. Perhaps his clothes caught in the brush because he fell and four Kolosh [the Russian term for the Tlingit] lifted him on their spears and carried him to the barracks where they cut his head off.'[13] Ekaterina Pinnuina, the (presumably native or mixed-race) wife of the Russian hunter Zakhar Lebedev, tried to take refuge in the main storehouse.

'The Kolosh broke the shutters and began shooting continuously through the windows. Soon they smashed the door leading to the back porch and cut a hole in the main door . . . Tumakaev fired the cannon which was aimed at the main door and killed several Kolosh.'[14] There was no time or gunpowder to reload the cannon so the men escaped to the upper floor through a hole hacked in the ceiling, but the building was already on fire. The men were forced to jump from the upper floor of the burning building and were all speared one by one. Pinnuina and the other women, who had hidden in the cellar until the door was broken down, were divided as slaves among the Tlingit warriors.

Plotnikov himself was seized by a party of Tlingit braves but escaped by slipping out of the jacket they were holding him by and hiding in a hollow tree trunk. He and a handful of fellow survivors lived in the woods for eight days without food, emerging only when they heard cannon fire roll across Sitka Sound. An English ship, the *Unicorn* under Captain Henry Barber, had anchored in the bay and sent a boat ashore to survey the still-smoking ruins of the settlement. All of the twenty-nine Russian and fifty-five Aleut men who had been in the camp at the time of the attack had been decapitated; their heads were stuck on sticks along the stony shore.

The Company's directors often suspected that the subversive, republican Americans had not only sold guns to the Tlingit but also encouraged them to eject the Russians from their shores. This was unfair: the reality was that commercial rivalry was forgotten when fellow white men were threatened, as the Sitka Tlingit found to their cost when they tried to sell the 4,000 sea-otter pelts they had looted from Fort St Michael to British and Yankee ships.

Barber acted quickly and ruthlessly. When the Sitka Tlingits' supreme chief 'Mikhail' – Skatleut – came alongside asking warily whether there were any Russians aboard, Barber assured him there were none but seized Skatleut and his nephew Katlian as soon as they were aboard. Two more ships, the *Alert* and the *Globe* of Boston under Captains Ebbets and Cunningham, sailed into the Sound the next day and took two other Tlingit trading parties prisoner as well, firing grape-shot for good measure to keep the rest of the tribe at bay. Barber demanded the return of all Russian and Aleut prisoners in exchange for their hostages. To speed negotiations, Cunningham had one of his Tlingit prisoners tried for murder by a kangaroo court convened on the *Globe*'s quarterdeck. The man was hanged from the yardarm in full view of the Tlingit braves ashore. The Tlingit, getting the message, surrendered their captives and retreated into the forest.

Abandoning his trading mission, Barber sailed to Kodiak with five (or eight, depending whether you believe Barber or Baranov) Russian men and eighteen women and children he had rescued from Tlingit slavery. European solidarity went only so far, however. Barber demanded a reward – or ransom – of 50,000 rubles' worth of furs in compensation for choosing to hang the locals rather than buy stolen Russian pelts from them at a discount. Otherwise, Barber told Baranov, he would destroy the village of St Paul with the *Unicorn*'s twenty guns. Even under such disadvantageous circumstances Baranov still managed to bargain Barber down to 10,000 rubles, sealing the deal with a celebratory dinner.

News of the massacre resonated across the Pacific, reaching the ears of the *Nadezhda* and the *Neva* in Hawaii on their outward journey to Japan. Revenge would have to be taken, but without warships Baranov was powerless. The keels of the brigs *Svataya Ekaterina* and *Svyatoi Alexander Nevsky* were hurriedly laid at Kodiak. By April 1804 Baranov had assembled an impressive war party – 300 *baidarkas* under 36 loyal chiefs, over 800 natives in total, plus 120 Russians. Baranov himself captained the *Yermak*, a shallow-draughted, 51-foot oared galley perfect for inshore attacks, carrying the heaviest guns in the colony mounted on her prow.

They began by ravaging the Tlingit villages of Kake and Kuiu in revenge for the attack on the Urbanov party in June 1802. The villagers had wisely deserted their homes on the approach of the Russian party, and Baranov was able to collect a large number of Tlingit ritual objects such as battle masks, wooden armour, a shaman's raven rattle and intricately carved halibut hook. Lisiansky later took the artefacts to St Petersburg, where they are now on display in the Kunstkammer Museum.[15]

On arriving at Sitka on 19 September, Baranov, to his surprise and relief, found the *Neva* waiting for him. Lisiansky had missed Baranov at Kodiak, but on hearing that the manager was already on the warpath he had raced the *Neva* directly across the open sea to Sitka and spent four weeks mapping Sitka Sound. The canoe party had taken the slower but safer Inside Passage. Despite the arrival of a warship, the Sitka

Tlingit were nonetheless in no mood to bargain. A stray Kodiak *baidarka* was captured by Tlingit braves and its two Aleut hunters beheaded on the spot before their seaborne companions could come to the rescue. O'Cain, who had come down from Kodiak in his eponymous ship with Lisiansky, attempted to trade but got his boat shot up for his pains. O'Cain himself got a musket ball through his uniform collar, doubtless causing the Bostonian to rue the high quality of the muskets he had sold the natives over the years.

The Tlingit had spent the two years since their raid on Fort St Michael making themselves as hard a target as their sketchy understanding of ballistics and fortification allowed. Having had a taste of the effects of naval gunfire from the *Unicorn* and *Globe*, Chief Skatleut had abandoned the old tribal stronghold on a natural promontory dominating Sitka Sound and moved his settlement half a mile up the shallow inlet to what is now called Indian River. They constructed a high palisade built of whole redwood trees 'so heavy that a man and even two men could not encompass them, placed both horizontal and vertical'[16] with two openings for cannon (also acquired from Yankee traders, it emerged) and a small gate for sallies. Inside were timber-covered dugouts in which the See'Atika clan of the Sitka Tlingit prepared themselves for the coming attack.

The Russians quickly occupied the abandoned heights of the old Tlingit citadel of Sitka, where they would remain until the ceremony of handover of the colony to the Americans was enacted on the same hill in 1867. Lisiansky's men dragged their largest cannon to the top, from where they successfully sank a large canoe bringing gunpowder and supplies to the Indian fort – it exploded impressively, boosting Russian morale. A hundred *baikarkas* then towed the *Neva* up the shallows of the sound as close to the Tlingit fort as Lisiansky dared without running aground. But even the *Neva*'s nine-pounder guns could do little damage to the fort – the cannonballs just bounced off the five- and six-foot-thick logs. Meanwhile the Tlingits' small-bore cannon 'did much damage to our rigging',[17] forcing the *Neva* to retreat out of range.

The war party of 'our new countrymen', as Lisiansky called the flotilla of Aleuts,[18] Chugach and Koniags, readied for a frontal assault.

The Chugach chiefs – a mainland tribe culturally close to the Tlingit – performed war dances using an old brass kettle as a drum, their hair covered in grease and bird down. On the morning of 1 October Baranov personally led an amphibious assault with his 120 men, struggling through the shallows onto a stony beach that offered the Tlingit cannon a clear field of fire. The defenders showed impressive discipline, holding their fire until the Russians were within fifty yards of the walls before unleashing a devastating volley of musket fire which felled nearly thirty of the attackers, including fourteen of Lisiansky's twenty sailors. Baranov himself was shot through the arm.

The Tlingit, pressing their advantage, poured out of the fort in full warpaint and musket-ball-proof armour made of hoops of hardwood covered in elk hide. Prominent was Katlian, who wore a wooden helmet in the shape of a raven and carried a heavy blacksmith's hammer looted from the smithy at Fort St Michael – both articles are now in museums in Alaska. Only a fierce rearguard action by the surviving sailors and covering gunfire from the *Neva* prevented the Tlingit from driving the Russians into the sea and capturing their field cannon. As they retreated to the fort the Tlingit dragged at least one wounded Russian with them. The unfortunate sailor was ritually impaled on the fort's walls.

The Russians had failed to take the fort, and Baranov, to whom most of the Aleut force were personally loyal, lay seriously wounded. But the Tlingit were also exhausted, many of their best warriors cut down by the *Neva*'s grapeshot on the beach. More seriously, they had used almost all their powder and would not survive another assault. 'If it were not for the want of powder and ball . . . they would have defended themselves to the last extremity,'[19] wrote Lisiansky, now acting Russian commander.

Skatleut and Lisiansky began cautious negotiations, interspersed by bombardment from the *Neva*'s guns. One Aleut slave released by the Tlingit as a gesture of goodwill reported that the chief was playing for time until reinforcements came from the north of the island. None arrived. A week after the attempted assault, the Russians heard the prearranged signal that Skatleut was ready to leave – a cry of 'Oo – oo

– ooo!' – which raised a feeble answering cheer from the Russians. All night a shaman woman keened in mourning. In the morning Lisiansky entered the fort to find it abandoned except for one old woman and a little boy. Piled in the centre of the settlement were the bodies of thirty Tlingit warriors killed in battle. More horrifying were the bodies of infants and dogs, killed to ensure that the Tlingit retreat would be silent. 'O man, civilized or uncivilized, [of] what cruelties is not thy nature capable?'[20] lamented Lisiansky.

The RAC flag flying over Castle Rock at Sitka, sketched by Langsdorff.

In this place of blood and horror, on the bluff overlooking Sitka Sound, Baranov decided to re-found the capital of Russian America. He called it New Archangel in memory of the lost Fort St Michael, a mile and a half up the Sound from the new settlement. Baranov kept his war party close, putting them to work erecting a stockade on the rock, then storehouses and barracks. The Tlingit did not return until the following summer, when a party in a canoe bearing peace offerings of white feathers, which they cast on the water, approached the fort. A nephew of Skatleut, held hostage by the Russians through the winter, was returned to his people. A peace feast followed, at which the natives were drunk under the table.

'So much honour did they do the feast that in the evening they were carried to their apartments in a state of perfect inebriety,' reported Lisiansky.[21] Skatleut accepted one of Baranov's copper double-headed eagles, mounted on a pole, as a gift – though almost certainly not as a sign of fealty, as the Russians intended. Katlian even appeared, and Baranov had him carried into the Russian stockade on the shoulders of Aleut hunters, a Tlingit custom for welcoming an honoured guest. Rather than hang the warrior for his actions, as Captain Cunningham would had done, Baranov wisely chose to behave as one chief would to another. Their two tribes had fought, and now they made peace through a ritual exchange of gifts.[*][22]

By late August 1805 the *Neva*, loaded with furs from Kodiak and New Archangel, was provisioning for her delayed onward journey to Canton. Despite the drama of the recapture of Sitka, the previous hunting season had been good: Lisiansky carried over 450,000 rubles' worth of furs. The Canton trip was a gamble, however, because no one in Russian America had any way of knowing if the diplomatic mission to China had been successful or even if Rezanov's efforts in Nagasaki had borne fruit.

The *Maria Magdalena*, bearing Rezanov and his party, arrived just after the *Neva* left. They missed each other by a week. Three hundred native canoes came out to greet the new arrival. The courtier who had brought Russian America to the attention of Napoleon, the Tsar and St Petersburg society finally met the man who had actually forged Russian America in blood. To a ragged salute of cannon fire, Rezanov was shown ashore to his humble accommodation. The most solid structures in

---

* The local Tlingit came to believe that Baranov was a wizard, and that the rockets fired from Sitka were in fact Baranov himself rising to the skies to spy on the Indians' plans. Baranov, who always wore chain mail, reinforced his reputation for invincibility by inviting Tlingit prisoners to fire arrows into his heart, which bounced off.

New Archangel were its impressive stockade with two squat towers, and the manager's house, and it was here that the chamberlain was installed. The colony was ringed with cannon – pointing not at the sea, but towards the endless threatening forest around.

16

Hunger, Disease, Shipwreck and Death

Truly in all my life I have never witnessed such drunkenness and debauch . . . drinking as they do and letting the hunters drink I would not be surprised if one day they would cause the Company more ruin than the Kolosh did.

Nikolai Rezanov, letter to the directors of the Russian American Company[1]

Russians are everywhere hated by the natives and murdered whenever the opportunity arises.

Georg Heinrich Langsdorff, *Voyages and Travels*[2]

After 'several days passed in festivity and mirth, during which business was entirely suspended,'[3] Rezanov's party, with the officers of the *Maria*, settled in for the winter. They squeezed into what primitive huts were to be had at New Archangel. 'The habitations are for the most part unfinished, small chambers without stoves and with so thin a thatch that the rains which we had continually often came through,'[4] complained Langsdorff. Most of the Russian hunters were even worse off, still living in tents. 'As soon as the roof is on a new building, the men move straight in.' Baranov himself lived scarcely less miserably than his men.

'We live quite crowded here but the winner of this land lives worse than any of us,' Rezanov reported to the Company on 5 November. 'He inhabits a kind of plank yurt that is so damp that the mildew has to be wiped off every day. The shack is so full of holes that with the continuous rains it leaks like a sieve. A wonderful man! He thinks only of the comfort of others but is so careless of his own that once I found his bed standing in water and asked him "perhaps the wind tore off a board somewhere". "No," he replied calmly, 'it seems to have run in under the floor," and went about his business.'

Despite the feasting and exchange of presents with the Tlingit earlier that summer, the Russians considered themselves to be in unequivocally hostile territory. 'We live on the rock with some men armed at all times and the cannon primed,' Rezanov wrote to Gideon in Kodiak on 11 September 1805. 'I fear . . . the knives under the threat of which we live here will again be used to annihilate the Russians. It is amazing how barbaric the local people are. They are at the moment held in check by fear, but malice remains and indescribable inhuman acts we hear are being committed against our people who are held prisoners by them.'[5]

Rezanov's fear was not mere paranoia. That summer, while Skatleut's shamans had been scattering chicken feathers on the waters as peace offerings to the Russians, a tribe of Tlingit to the north of Sitka had attempted to seize a Boston ship. The *Atahualpa*, under Captain Lemuel Porter, had come inshore in Milbanke Sound to trade. Once on board, the Tlingit chief stabbed Porter in the belly. Producing pistols from under otter skins they had brought aboard, his men shot down two American sailors as more Tlingit swarmed up the companionway. The Bostonians escaped only by raking their own deck with grapeshot from a falconet – a small cannon – mounted on the quarterdeck. Every officer was killed in the melee and only six crewmen remained unwounded; Captain Porter also narrowly survived. In the five years Boston men had been trading on this coast, six ships had been lost to such native attacks. Rezanov was understandably unconvinced by the Sikta Tlingits' professions of friendship. 'Our cannons always loaded . . . even in our rooms weapons are considered the best and most valuable part of our furnishings. Strict military discipline is upheld and we are ready to receive our "dear guests" any minute.'[6]

The Russians rarely ventured outside their stockade. When they did they found a hostile world. The forests of southern Alaska are damp, dark, weirdly quiet and as impenetrable as jungles. 'The forest is so dense that I think until the Russians came the sun never shone within it from the day of Creation,' wondered Rezanov. 'Their wildness is frightening. A few steps in the woods and one sees curious sights: piles of stumps lying one on top of the other and big trees growing out of them.' Rezanov found cavities full of water 'which seem to have no bottom . . . in these woods one has to crawl and climb instead of walk'. The Russians attempted to clear some of the redwoods and hemlock thickets around their settlement, but even after felling 10,000 trees they had 'barely made perceptible clearings'. The wood was too damp to be burned for charcoal and too hard to be easily sawn for planks. Stacks of firewood rotted instead of drying in the constant drizzle. 'Autumn is the worst season,' complained Rezanov. 'From October on the rains pour continuously day and night . . . Our life here is very tedious.'

Rezanov may have been suffering from a lack of amusements, but Baranov faced a more pressing existential problem. As Langsdorff delicately put it, 'however agreeable for the governor von Baranov to receive as his guest a plenipotentiary of the Company of such high distinction as the Chamberlain von Rezanov . . . Yet he was put to no small embarrassment by the wholly unexpected arrival of so large a train of visitors.' Both parties had evidently been expecting the other to furnish supplies. When the Aleut and Russian hunting parties returned to camp at the end of the season's hunting, Baranov found himself having to cater for over 200 people when he had supplies for no more than fifty.

Salvation arrived in the form of the *Juno*, a 250-ton brig from Bristol, Rhode Island. Her New England owners had provisioned her the previous summer specifically with the Russians of Sitka in mind. She carried a cargo of rum and tobacco (of course), molasses, sugar, rice, ship's biscuit and fine white flour, as well as the usual manufactured trade goods. It was the Americans, with an eye to profit, rather than the chancelleries of St Petersburg, who had responded to the needs of Russian America with impressive speed and efficiency. The *Juno*'s captain, twenty-six-year-old John D'Wolf, had already sold Baranov a third of his goods on arrival in Sitka that spring. Now, after a tense summer trading with the unpredictable natives up and down the coast with five other Boston boats – and helping the stricken *Atahualpa* after the Tlingit attack – D'Wolf returned to New Archangel to make urgent repairs to his hull after running into rocks near the modern-day city of Juneau.

Baranov, much as he needed both ships and provisions, had neither the cash nor the authority to buy an entire ship like the *Juno*, along with all her cargo. But Rezanov could. His signature, as de facto director of the Company, was as good as a cheque. It was D'Wolf who first suggested the deal. His cargo was for sale, and why not the ship too, if the money was right? Rezanov agreed – but before closing the deal he seems to have told the New Englander a few white lies to bring down the price. Rezanov claimed, for instance, that the Russian navy was on its way to patrol the coast and the Bostonians would soon be banned from trading with the natives.

D'Wolf's main difficulty, however, was not the threatened appearance of the Russian navy but how he and his crew would continue their journey to Canton with their haul of furs.[7] The solution presented itself at the beginning of October with the arrival of the *Yermak*, Baranov's old sailing galley, from Yakutat. The Russian American Company, in the person of Rezanov, bought the *Juno* and her remaining cargo for a total of $68,000 – close to what the Company had paid for the unladen *Neva* and *Nadezhda* together in London – and threw in the *Yermak* plus 572 sea-otter skins to the value of $13,000, as well as $300 in silver, representing almost all the cash available in the colony at the time.[8] Rezanov drafted a bill of exchange – a promissory note – for $54,638 to be drawn on the main office of the RAC in St Petersburg. In addition the *Yermak* was to be loaded with a hundred days of supplies, four of the *Juno*'s six falconets, plus two sets of sails, thirty muskets and ammunition. The *Juno*'s heavy guns – six full-bore cannon and eight dummy wooden ones – would now be part of the Company's arsenal.[9]

On 5 October, after mutual cannon salutes, D'Wolf ceremonially lowered the flag of the United States – the newest version, with fifteen stars and fifteen stripes to mark Vermont and Kentucky's new status as states of the Union – and raised the tricolour of the Russian American

Adam Johann von Krusenstern (*left*) conceived the idea of a Russian round-the-world voyage while serving with the British Royal Navy in the Pacific. The expedition was approved by the Tsar in 1803 – but with the addition of Rezanov as Ambassador to Japan. Both men believed they were in charge of the voyage, with fateful results. Krusenstern recruited his old friend from Royal Navy days, Yury Lisiansky (*right*), to buy two ships.

Hermann Ludwig von Löwenstern (*left*), scion of a German Baltic family in Russian service, was the *Nadezhda*'s fourth lieutenant and cartographer. He wrote an uncensored diary of the voyage, dedicated in large part to denunciations of Rezanov's arrogance. Georg Heinrich von Langsdorff (*right*) was a medical doctor, naturalist and anthropologist who attached himself to the expedition in Copenhagen by agreeing to serve as Rezanov's personal physician. He followed his chief all the way to San Francisco.

The *Nadezhda* reached the Pacific island of Nukakhiva in April 1804. Natives swam out to the ship; to the delight of officers and men the Nuhakhivan women were happy to dispense sexual favours in exchange for iron trinkets, which they held in their mouths as they swam home.

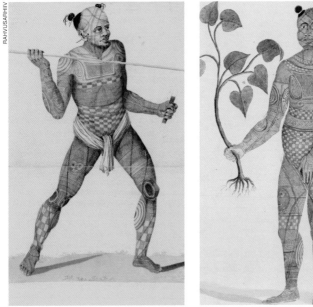

Langsdorff, with his cultivated eye, found the tattooed natives 'handsome and well-made … a model for the Apollo of Belvedere'.

The French renegade Jean Cabri deserted a merchant ship and married into the Nukakhivan royal family. He abandoned his native wife and children when a squall swept the *Nadezhda* out to sea with him on board.

Count Fyodor Tolstoy, 'The American', 'a dangerous madcap' whose drunken pranks almost got him clapped in irons. At Nukakhiva he had himself tattooed; in later life he killed thirteen men in duels.

The *Nadezhda* moored in Avacha Bay by the settlement of Petropavlovsk on Kamchatka, the remotest port in continental Russia.

The *Nadezhda* in Nagasaki Bay, disarmed of all her gunpowder, is towed to a safer anchorage by Japanese oared barges as her sailors salute from the yardarms.

'Rezanov shows himself to the people of Japan' – Löwenstern's sarcastic caption to his cartoon of the Ambassador urinating into Nagasaki harbour in full view of Japanese gawkers. Rezanov 'loses a great deal in the eyes of the Japanese who observe etiquette so strictly,' he wrote.

Dr Wilhelm Gottfried Tilesius's sketches of Japanese skiffs and official translators – known as *tolks* – whose impenetrable politeness Rezanov found so exasperating.

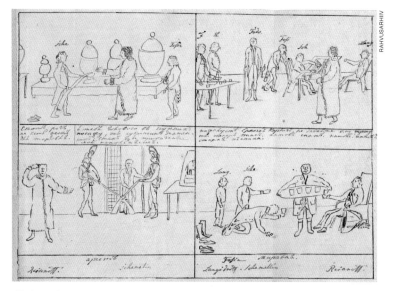

Clockwise from top left: Rezanov at Megasaki, loafing among the Tsar's presents for the Japanese Emperor in his dressing gown; drinking brandy with his cronies; ordering his Marine guard to arrest a drunken Fyodor Shmelin.

Rezanov as the Japanese saw him, resplendent in his Chamberlain's uniform and decorations. His visit to Nagasaki spurred fierce debate at the highest levels of Japanese society over contact with the outside world. Eventually advocates of *sakoku* – the philosophy of isolation – prevailed and the Russians were sent home empty-handed.

San Francisco was the northernmost outpost of Spain's American Empire, founded in 1776 in direct response to Russian Imperial ambitions in California. Rezanov arrived there in April 1806, scurvy-stricken and starving in his finery. The Russians found the settlement 'small and mean', but Rezanov fell in love with the Spanish governor's daughter.

Rezanov dreamed of turning the Russian American Company's precarious and slovenly Alaskan settlements into a well-ordered empire stretching far into California. But ships, men, food and even iron was in short supply – there was not enough spare metal to mint real coins, so the Company printed its own rubles on squares of seal hide (*above*). Alexander Baranov (*left*) was the Company's general manager for nineteen years and founded the colony in blood.

Russian America on a US map printed in Washington in 1860. In the aftermath of the Crimean War it became clear that Russia's navy could no longer defend her American possessions. The Tsar offered the vast territory to the British but Lord Palmerston refused; in 1867 Alaska was sold for $7.2 million – or about 2 cents per acre – to the United States.

The Russian American Company's colony at Fort Ross, in modern-day Sonoma County in California, was the southernmost outpost of the Russian Empire between 1812 and 1842. Today it is preserved as a state park.

Company in its place.[10] To general jubilation, the first instalments of the *Juno*'s cargo of 1,955 gallons of molasses, 3,000 pounds of sugar and – especially welcome – six hogsheads of rum were carried ashore. The colony's heavy smokers were also delighted to have six gigantic bales of Virginia tobacco, each weighing 1,800 pounds.

D'Wolf, it is clear from the cheery memoir he penned in deep old age of his youthful travels in Russian America and Siberia, was a man in search of adventure. Having exchanged his ship and her cargo for a piece of paper, he now decided – or allowed himself to be persuaded by Rezanov – to remain in Alaska and return to St Petersburg with the ambassador the following year. D'Wolf was 'agreeably disappointed to find that various reports that we should find the Russians little advanced from the savage state' proved untrue. He clearly hit it off with Langsdorff, a fellow questing spirit. D'Wolf gave George Stetson, the *Juno*'s first mate, command of the *Yermak*. The fifty-five-foot long craft, with most of the *Juno*'s Boston crew and their season's haul of furs aboard, sailed for Canton on 27 October.

'After taking a long, parting look at the little vessel fading on the horizon I returned to the village. I would take things as they came and make the best of them,' D'Wolf vowed. He kept on one man as a valet: 'Edward Parker, one of my ordinary sailors but a very useful man of work. A barber by trade, he was also a tolerably good tailor and performer on the violin and clarinet. This latter accomplishment might be useful in dispelling the Blues if we should at any time be troubled with that complaint.'[11] Thus equipped, D'Wolf settled in 'for a long siege'.

The *Juno*'s first mission for the Company was to go on a provisioning run to Kodiak, skippered by Lieutenant Khvostov. Johann von Banner (also known as Ivan Banner), the Company's manager at Kodiak, loaded 70,000 dried fish on board – yet she arrived with only half that amount. Rezanov accused Khvostov of selling the missing fish en route, or allowing his men to do so. A stand-up row ensued which ended in Khvostov retreating angrily to the captain's quarters of the *Juno*, where he would stay for much of the winter. But this tiff was soon forgotten in the excitement generated by *Juno*'s passengers, a number of Koniag women sent on Banner's orders for the amusement of the lonely colonists at New Archangel.

Langsdorff was indignant. 'It is obvious that the Aleuts are the complete slaves of the Company; no Aleutian of Kodiak would ever remove to Sitka' without coercion. But Banner knew his business. The arrival of a party of tarts did wonders for flagging morale. Baranov ordered a barrack cleared for dancing to celebrate the new arrivals. 'They made out bravely in cotillons and contradances' with the Kodiak women, who wore Russian-style clothes. Rezanov and Langsdorff played their violins, with George Parker – a Yankee deserter who had settled at Sitka and survived the massacre of 1802 and no relation to D'Wolf's man Edward – playing the clarinet. 'With plenty of good resin for the stomach as well as the bow we made a gay season of it.'

Winter closed on the settlement, bringing with it constant rain and strange atmospheric effects. 'For many hours together in the darkest nights a bluish green electrical light called St Helens or St Elm's fire may be seen on bayonets fixed to muskets or on the metal heads of the flagstaffs on the fortified hill,' reported Langsdorff, who kept himself busy with ornithology.[12] Like all accomplished naturalists of his day he was a superb shot with his English rifle. He obtained a *baidarka* by 'assuming an authoritative tone' – politeness, he noted dryly in his memoir, didn't seem to work on Russians – and used it to 'carry on hunting and water parties'. The meat of the birds he shot was for the table; the skins he stuffed 'for benefit of science'.[13]

Most of New Archangel's officer class was not so energetic. Naval Lieutenant Alexander Sukin,* who had skippered the *Yermak* down from Kodiak, appeared to be slipping into depression. 'His recreation is drink and sleep,' Langsdorff noted. 'He has done no work or exercise of any kind, visits nobody and nobody visits him. He lives so quietly it is almost as if he did not exist at all.' He shared a room with Lieutenant Mashin of the *Maria*, but the two men never seemed to speak. 'They

---

* This must have been a hard surname to live with. *Suka* in Russian means 'bitch', and *sukin* means 'of a bitch'. The insult *sukin syn* – 'son of a bitch' – has been in colloquial use in Russian for centuries.

are both so preoccupied with either the present or the future that they do not find matter for conversation with each other.'[14]

But it was Lieutenant Khvostov, brooding and drinking out in the foggy Sound aboard the *Juno*, who was becoming dangerous. He already had a reputation as an angry drunk. Soon after his first arrival in Kodiak two years previously, Khvostov had smashed windows in a murderous rage and fired a pistol at von Banner, who had had to lock himself in his office to avoid being murdered. Now, Rezanov reported to the Company, Khvostov 'began a drinking bout which lasted three months steadily. He drank, as you will see from his store account, 9 ½ buckets of French brandy and 2 ½ buckets of strong alcohol.' A 'bucket' was four gallons, meaning that the lieutenant apparently got through the equivalent of 272 bottles of strong drink in a hundred days. This combination of Khvostov's heavy drinking and his command of the *Juno*'s artillery was unsettling for the men ashore. 'All the time the drinking went on, swearing and threats to all. At nighttime there was shooting from cannons.'

Fortunately Khvostov's young protégé Davydov was on hand to rein in his superior's attempts to actually open fire on the colony, and also to thwart his frequent drunken attempts to abscond with the *Juno*. 'Davydov, who was always of sober behaviour, [confides] the ceaseless drinking was affecting Khvostov's mind so much that every night he wanted to raise the anchor,' complained Rezanov. 'Luckily the sailors were always too drunk' to carry out the order. [15]

When he wasn't under fire from the Company's own artillery, Rezanov was pondering the future of Russian America. Clearly, there was much room for improvement. The colony was at the mercy of American boats for supplies and, increasingly, for its core business of otter hunting too. The Company's shipping was in the hands of alcoholic naval officers, some manic-depressive and others murderous. 'I am trying to write to you in a polished style,' he wrote to his old patron Rumiantsev, 'but am obstructed by many obstacles of a physical and moral nature. Sometimes the bark roof over my quarters begins to leak, sometimes illness, alarm over the Kolosh, or our privileged class gets drunk and starts a disturbance... after two years of travels with immoral men I have become used to abominations of all kinds. I am disturbed almost every hour by abuse and turbulence.'[16]

Nonetheless Rezanov was able to present the Company's directors with a strategic vision of striking boldness. As the success, flexibility and ubiquity of the Boston merchants showed, the future of the colony depended on having a reliable fleet, both to trade across the Pacific and to keep the Bostonians away from the coast. Rezanov envisoned Company ships travelling not only to Canton but 'Cochin China, Tonkin [modern Vietnam], the Burmese Empire and India'. But though his letter was borne by the *Elizaveta*, with half a million rubles' worth of furs in her hold, Rezanov saw that 'notwithstanding this rich cargo . . . the Company as it is organized now will fail'. The current system of sending sporadic cargoes 'is only a palliative, nothing more – it cannot be the backbone of your business'.

Kamchatka should be made the major entrepôt for Boston traders. There they would avoid the dangers of trading direct with the natives and exchange their West Indian and American goods for the furs of Russian America, which they would sell in Canton, neatly bypassing the Chinese restrictions on Russian ships. In addition, Rezanov planned personally to pioneer a Russian version of the Bostonians' triangle trade by taking a ship from California to Batavia and Bengal and back to Russia. It would be, he boasted, the 'first experiment in trade between India and Okhotsk'. The Spanish shipyards of Chile, currently supplied by the English and Americans, could be furnished with Siberian and Alaskan timber instead. Most striking of all, Rezanov also anticipated the vastly profitable whaling business by half a century. 'Whale oil is used everywhere in India and we can count on Japan to buy all of it,' he enthused, proposing that the Russian bases at Aniva Bay on Sakhalin be turned into the centre of a Pacific whale fishery.

Rezanov believed that Russian control should be extended south at all costs, into lands where the natives were less hostile, the climate gentler and the soil more fertile. As a first step, he envisaged a settlement at the mouth of the Columbia River, near modern-day Portland, Oregon, 'from which we can spread little by little further south to the port of San Francisco . . . in ten years' time our strength will increase so much that we will be able to keep an eye on the California coast in order, the moment that political events in Europe are favourable, to make it a Russian possession'.

Since the Seven Years' War half a century before, every major European conflict had been fought in the New World as well as the Old. The Napoleonic Wars would surely be no different. And if the maps of Europe could be so dramatically redrawn, why not the maps of America?

> The Spaniards are very weak in this country and if in 1798, when war was declared, our Company had forces adequate to the size of our possessions it would have been easy to occupy California down to the Santa Barbara Mission . . . Nature itself prevents them from sending reinforcements by land from Mexico. The Spanish do not use this fertile soil themselves and moved north only to protect their boundaries. Leaving now the future hidden by Fate, however, I will continue to write about the present.[17]

Crucially, Rezanov argued, if Russia did not act to secure and expand her Pacific empire then others would soon come to fill the gap the collapse of Spain would leave.* 'If we do not make haste we can be sure that we have the Batavians [Dutch] as close neighbours in Kamchatka,' he wrote. And a victorious France – the 'New Empire,' as Rezanov called it – could soon return to follow up on La Perouse's discoveries. 'It would be a pity for Russia to lose out at a time so advantageous to her and let some other power get a hold in these parts and by that cut off a vast and profitable trade.'[18] At the same time, to the personal friends among his correspondents Rezanov admitted the overwhelming

---

* The crisis of Spain's empire was much closer that Rezanov imagined. Within two years of writing those words the empire would be effectively decapitated by Napoleon. Indeed the events that would lead to its collapse were already underway. Napoleon had been allied to an unwilling Spain since 1796, but it was Napoleon's 'continental system', an attempted blockade of English trade, which led to a British invasion of Spain. By 1807 British and French armies were fighting on Spanish territory, and Napoleon occupied Madrid and deposed the Spanish King Charles IV.

gap between his vast plans and the drunken, miserable reality of Russia's southernmost American possession. 'Sometimes the spirit of enterprise and ambition make me very resolute in my actions. At other times they seem to me an inexcusable folly,' he confided to his brother-in-law Buldakov, growing sentimental as he exercised his talent for self-dramatization and self-pity. 'Leaving behind me everything, sacrificing all, I do not expect nor want to receive praise or reward. Perhaps I will die here but I will die contented because . . . my Sovereign has bestowed on me the honour of being one of the first Russians to rove along the edge of a knife.'

Rezanov was very aware that none of his grand schemes had any chance of working without putting the chaotic affairs of Russian America itself in order. 'All the Company's actions are disorganized,' he stormed – the colony is 'an orphan left to the will of Fate'. Even the basic fabric of the settlements was, in Rezanov's view, wrong. Houses made of solid logs heated with large brick stoves were perfect for Siberia's dry cold, but in the warm drizzle of coastal Alaska 'the damp quarters with wet walls and the exhalation of many people create a putrefied atmosphere'. Rezanov recommended frame-and-plank houses built on raised cobble foundations, insulated and roofed with clay and chopped grass and heated with open fireplaces to provide ventilation in every room and dry clothes quickly – exactly the kind of houses that later American colonists were to build in coastal Alaska.

Rezanov found it 'very seldom cold here' – something only a Russian could write of Alaska, but relative to Siberia it was perfectly true. He worried also that thanks to the Yankees the natives were now better armed than the Russians. The guns sent from the Okhotsk stores proved 'defective and worthless', a constant and deadly reminder of the shoddiness and endemic corruption at the Company's base camp. 'It is hard to forget the rascals in Okhotsk. It is not enough to make them pay for the damage but it would be right and just for the Company to exile them to America for ever so that they can see all the harm from their swindling for which many here have paid with their lives.'

But it was the human factor that worried Rezanov more than humid buildings, scarce ships and bad guns. Recruiting good officers and men for colonial service had always been a problem for the Company. If Rezanov had ever believed that free, skilled Russians could be persuaded to come voluntarily to Russian America, observing the miserable conditions in the colony persuaded him it was impossible. Seeing 400 convicts being readied for transportation to Australia at Newgate prison had clearly given Rezanov food for thought. Having spent a year in the company of the kind of free-born riff-raff the Company had been able to attract– 'here, for a cup of vodka they are ready to cut anybody's throat'[19] – he decided that convicts would be preferable.

An English-style law in Russia implementing penal transportation to the colonies would do wonders for the fortunes of Russian America, Rezanov believed. 'All traders convicted of fraudulent bankruptcy should be shipped to America. In this way the State is getting rid of its unwelcome citizens and at the same time is building towns in the colonies . . . in brief, all criminals and men of bad morals will of necessity improve here and become useful.' It was only the dregs of society who ended up in Russian America anyway. Troublesome serfs – legally regarded as the chattels of their owners – would also do. Rezanov suggested that the directors 'ship over here skilled workers who are drunkards but otherwise fit for work, persuading the landowners who own them to cede them to the Company on favourable terms . . . Here hardship and work makes them behave more quietly and there are few opportunities to get drunk.' He suggested that the RAC advertise in the newspapers, offering a bounty of twenty-five to fifty rubles yearly for each man, with their owners ceding the right to demand their serfs' return. 'Moscow alone could supply enough men for this country and still have half the idlers who are now there.' Womenfolk, he added as an afterthought, could be shipped in from Unalaska. For all his enlightened principles Rezanov was a slave owner – just like many of the liberty-loving gentlemen who had recently framed the Constitution of the United States – and he remained an aristocrat and a landowner in whom the feudal instinct ran strong.

Langsdorff was profoundly shocked by the casual brutality he found in Russian America. 'The Russian subject here enjoys no protection of property, lives in no security and if oppressed has no one to apply to for

justice. It is revolting to a mind of any feeling to see these poor creatures half-starved and almost naked as if in a house of correction when
at the same time the warehouses of the RAC are full of clothing and
provisions.'[20] The Company ran a credit system whereby it sold food
and clothes to his own employees at inflated prices, to be deducted
from their salaries. The result was that the employees were 'debtors
rather than creditors' to their employers. 'Detained as hostages for the
payment of their debts, they strive to drown their cares in brandy . . . they
must esteem themselves fortunate if after years spent in hardship and
privations they return home at last with empty pockets, ruined consti-
tutions and minds wholly depressed and broken down.'[21]

Langsdorff was a gentleman of science: he had volunteered to come
to Russian America to document its natural wonders, and took his self-
imposed mission seriously. Just before Christmas a delegation of Sitka
Tlingit came to offer the Russians of New Archangel a feast. Visiting
'formerly their own abode, they did not venture any external show of
enmity, yet it can scarcely be supposed that they are free from it in their
hearts'.[22] Tents were pitched outside the stockade and a feast prepared
with an 'astonishing variety of things' from berries preserved in seal fat
to smoked geese and fermented salmon, mocking the Russians' inabil-
ity to feed themselves from the abundant land they claimed as their
own. The chiefs were invited into Baranov's compound but, wary after
the last time, refused brandy, 'afraid that, deprived of their senses, they
should fall into [the] power of [the] Russians'.

Langsdorff lost no time in securing an invitation to the Tlingit camp.
Perhaps unsurprisingly, he found no Russians who were willing to
accompany him. (Rezanov firmly believed that 'only the terror which
had been inspired by the European artillery . . . made [the Tlingit]
assume an outward show of friendship'.[23]) Only the irrepressible
D'Wolf was game. Accompanied by a former slave of the Tlingits who
spoke both Tlingit and Russian, the little party set off down Sitka
Sound in three three-man *baidarkas* paddled by Aleuts and was treated
to three days of feasts and native dancing.

The detailed anthropological observations Langsdorff made on his
travels were as important as Cook's and Vancouver's. His 1813 *Voyages*

and Travels became an anthropological classic. 'When their skins are clean and purified from the dirt they consider ornamental [the Tlingit] have complexions as fair as Europeans and by no means unpleasing features,' Langsdorff observed. Tlingit women have 'the most extraordinary, the most unnatural idea of increasing their beauty that the fertile imagination of man has yet invented'. They would pierce their lower lip in childhood and insert increasingly larger pieces of polished wood as they grew. 'The women thus all look as if they had large flat wooden spoons growing in the flesh of their lower lip.' The highest-ranked ladies wore pieces up to five inches broad. But Langsdorff found this no more absurd that contemporary European fashion. 'Why, when we would appear in great state, we rub the finest flour into our hair?' The main disadvantage to the practice, in Langsdorff's opinion, was that 'it is wholly impossible for the fair sex to receive a kiss'. The men were no less fastidious about their appearance. For ceremonies they made their hair up with the powdered down of eagle and painted their bodies with cinnabar, chalk and ochre. This process took 'as much time as a European lady spends at her toilette', aided with Boston mirrors, which allowed each man to decorate himself twice as fast as in old times, when they could only make each other up.'[24]

Within days of D'Wolf and Langsdorff's return from their social visit, chilling news came from Kodiak. The settlement of *Slava Rossii* – Glory of Russia – at Yakutat had been destroyed by a Tlingit war party. Of forty settlers at the fort only eight native men and two women survived. The Tlingit captured four cannon. Even worse, most of the large Aleut hunting party based at Yakutat was also lost. Seeing the burning colony from out at sea, the hunters in 100 out of 130 *baidarkas* panicked and attempted to make a run for Kodiak, right into the teeth of an advancing gale. Two hundred Aleut hunters and their season's catch were shredded on the unforgiving rocks of Yakutat Bay's eastern shore. Only the expedition's leader, Timofei Demyanenkov, and the thirty *baidarkas* that had stayed with him survived. The only good news was that nearby Fort Konstantinovsk was saved by the timely intervention of 'Matvei', a local Chugach chief loyal to the Russians. An escaped Chugach prisoner warned the chief that a 200-strong war party headed by the Tlingit warlord 'Fyodor' was on its way to destroy the fort. When Fyodor entered Chugach territory Matvei invited him and seventy of his Tlingit braves to a feast, where he had them all murdered.

Baranov, not a man to take bad news lying down, prepared to set out on a punitive mission on the Kodiak-built *Rostislav* with twenty-five men and four cannon. This despite having just had two bone splinters removed from his arm, a legacy of his wound from the battle of Sitka. Rezanov managed to talk him out of this suicidal mission.* Despite the loss of life, money and strategic reach that the Yakutat raid represented, Rezanov managed to remain sanguine about the future of relations between the Company and the Tlingit. 'Studying the mentality and morality of the savages I find them kind-hearted but revengeful, quick-tempered, lazy, moderate in their desires, capable of learning,' he wrote to Gideon, ruefully acknowledging that the colonists made poor role models. 'Their education is overlooked and they have few good moral examples to guide them.'[25]

As Christmas approached, the naval officers' behaviour became more drunken and violent. 'Everywhere they stay windows are broken and clerks powerless to stop them. Some [officers] owe a year's salary for vodka they drank and charged to their accounts. They drink two to three bottles a day. Mr Sukin to date owes the store more than 300 rubles,' Rezanov reported. The officers had long made a point of insulting Baranov as a social inferior and ignoring his orders. Ordered to take the *Maria* on a hunting expedition, Sukin had torn up Baranov's orders and eaten them. He then threatened to have Baranov tied to the mainmast of the *Maria* and flogged if the manager dared to step aboard. When relieved of his command by Rezanov for this egregious insolence, Sukin was sullen and disrespectful. 'Truly in all my life I have never witnessed such drunkenness and debauch,' wrote Rezanov. 'Drinking as they do and letting the hunters drink I would not be surprised if one day they would cause the Company more ruin than the Kolosh did.'

---

* The Company eventually ransomed the ten Aleut survivors from Tlingit slavery the following year.

But with the sailing season over and the *Maria* and *Rostislav* pulled ashore as makeshift barracks for the men, the officers were left with little to do except drink, brood and fight. Mashin, Sukin, Khvostov and Davydov went completely out of control, starting drunken gunfights and openly insulting Rezanov himself. 'They are losing their minds from too much drinking . . . One day they behave and listen to me, the next day they are drunk, curse without mercy and one day started a fight. I ran to stop them and they almost shot Baranov and me. We were lucky to snatch the loaded pistols from their hands.'

After this incident Rezanov ordered further supplies of alcohol to the *Juno* – still at anchor in Sitka Sound – stopped. That at least brought Khvostov immediately on shore, cursing from his longboat as he came. Bursting into Baranov's office, Khvostov managed to insult the Company's men so seriously that Baranov, his deputy Ivan Kuskov and all the clerks all immediately resigned in protest, even offering to forgo their salaries in exchange for immediate transfer back to Russia. Rezanov refused to accept their resignations and had Khvostov locked in the bathhouse to sober up. The following day, Christmas Eve, a hung-over Khvostov shuffled to Rezanov's hut to attempt an apology. Rezanov refused to open the door. The long-suffering Baranov was more forgiving.

'Toward evening Khvostov sincerely begged the Manager's pardon,' which Baranov gave. However, their tearful reconciliation triggered a further bout of Christmas revelry. 'Having drunk too much, [Khvostov] and Ivan Koriukin started carving each other.' Khvostov attacked the *Maria*'s shipwright with a knife. As the stabbed Koriukin was taken to his lodgings, Khvostov staggered in the direction of Baranov's sleeping quarters. Word went round the Aleuts that their manager was in danger, and sentries later discovered an impromptu bodyguard of four hunters hiding on Baranov's porch with knives in their hands ready to protect their chief from the rampaging Khvostov.[26]

Food grew scarce. Severe winter storms prevented the shooting of seals, the colony's staple meat. 'We gathered snails and clams during full moon when they are edible; at other times we have shot eagles and crows. We have been eating everything we can get. Occasionally we get a cuttlefish . . . from January on, thank God, seals reappeared and sea lions, which have been our main diet ever since,' wrote Rezanov. The ground froze hard, and work on a new wharf and a sixteen-gun brig ground to a halt. 'We did little else but sleep and long for spring,' remembered D'Wolf.[27] Even the busy Langsdorff became depressed. 'Buried in this remote part of the New World my only consolation has been to sigh and long for the old one,' he wrote in a rare mournful moment.[28] Rezanov missed the two children he had left behind in St Petersburg. The *toion* Akilkak from Ugatotsk brought his son to meet him, and Rezanov recorded in his diary that 'I kissed the boy, and while I was holding him close to my breast his hair became so tangled with my coat buttons that I had great difficulty in untangling it. The *toion* proclaimed that fate had decided I was the boy's second father.'

The men, naturally much worse off than the officers, were 'tormented by hunger [and] ready to give their last shirt or garment of any kind for fresh food'. By February 'many walked around in only stinking dirty sheepskins full of vermin'.[29] On weekdays the colonists were fed the rancid fat of a beached whale, on Sundays a thin soup of salt meat and rice, a glass of brandy and molasses. The officers kept luxuries such as flour, biscuit and sugar to themselves. 'While so large a portion of the people lay in a state of wretchedness the directors and other overseers, clerks and friendly officers and their hangers-on fed sumptuously on wild ducks, fresh fish and pastries . . . in short whatever was afforded by nature or storehouses.'[30]

Rezanov told the Company that he had 'ordered [the sick] given wheat molasses and beer made from fir cones. We all drank this as an antidote to scurvy.' A Tlingit fisherman set traps in the Sound, landing several 'excellent holybutts'. He went home 'a very rich man in his way, canoe loaded with shirts and breeches'.[31] But it barely helped. In the spring of 1805 Baranov had chosen 150 of the youngest and healthiest men in Russian America to retake the Sitka colony. Now, as winter of that year drew to a close, eight were dead of scurvy and sixty lay exhausted and covered in scorbutic sores in a barrack with no windows 'warmed only by their own pestilential breath'.[32] The Russians considered being carried to the sick house 'an infallible indication of being the end, as if a sick person yet living was carried to the churchyard'.[33] Aleut dead were given no funeral at all; the Russians were 'thrown carelessly into the earth . . . with scarcely a friend or comrade following his deceased fellow countryman to his grave'.

Boston ships would not arrive before early summer; Kodiak had been twice tapped for supplies, and Yakutat was destroyed. New Archangel faced starvation unless resupply could be arranged. The nearest prospect was the Spanish colonies of California. Despite the risk of storms at the winter equinox, Rezanov ordered the *Juno* made ready for sea. Eighteen of the healthiest and fifteen of the sickest men went on board. Khvostov was finally forgiven after tearfully begging Rezanov not to report his behaviour (on the grounds that 'the disgrace would kill his elderly parents'[34]) and put in command. 'All quitted with joyful hearts the miserable winter abode to which they had been doomed,' wrote Langsdorff.[35] On 25 February 1806, provisioned with the last of the colony's carefully hoarded salt meat and biscuit, the *Juno* nosed between the odd little islands of Sitka Sound and turned south towards the warm waters of California.

17

Conchita

With the advantages which so great a line of coast presents, it would be in the power of Russia not only to open new sources of commerce in that region of the world [California], but to command a complete monopoly of commerce of those seas.

Morning Chronicle, London, 1817[1]

The *Juno* reached the mouth of the Columbia River, the boundary between modern-day Washington State and Oregon, after twenty days in heavy seas. The fifteen men lying sick in the forecastle 'infected the air of the ship with their unwholesome breath'[2] and the ship's provisions were running out. Vancouver's chart proved impressively accurate: Mount St Helen's was spotted through driving rain, and also Cape Disappointment.* A sandbar made the approach to the Columbia notoriously difficult and dangerous. As the *Juno* tacked to and fro waiting for favourable winds, Rezanov was 'already sketching plans for removing settlement from Sitka to the Columbia river and was busied with building ships there in the air'.[3] They saw smoke from campfires rising in the thick forests south of the river, but there was no response to the *Juno*'s signals.

Though neither party had any way of knowing about the other, Rezanov on the *Juno* was less than five miles away from Meriwether Lewis

---

* So named by a British fur trader, John Meares, who failed to find the entrance to the Colombia river just to the south of the Cape in 1788.

and William Clark, the leaders of the United States' first transcontinental expedition.[4] Two years previously Thomas Jefferson, the third president of the United States, had bought 828,000 square miles of territory from France for $15 million. Part of this vast piece of real estate had been originally colonized by the French, but more of it had been wrested from the Spanish after their defeat by Napoleon. In any case the French emperor had little use for this wilderness. A bloody slave revolt in the French Caribbean had consumed precious French armies and resources that Napoleon needed to consolidate his conquests in Europe. And thanks to the sale of the Louisiana Territory in 1803 Napoleon had been able to keep the United States, with its large merchant navy, out of an alliance with England.

Many American merchants and industrialists opposed the Louisiana Purchase as a reckless extravagance – even at three cents an acre.[*] Nonetheless Jefferson managed to scrape the deal through Congress. The acquisition comprised not only the modern state of Louisiana but all or part of fifteen other present-day US states and two Canadian provinces, stretching from the Gulf Coast through the Midwest and westwards to the Rockies. The deal almost doubled the size of the United States.

In 1804 Jefferson commissioned Captain Lewis and Lieutenant Clark, both Virginian gentlemen and veterans of Indian wars in the Ohio valley, to explore the newly bought lands and beyond. They were not the first men to cross the continent by foot – a Scotsman, Sir Alexander Mackenzie, had managed it in 1793 – but Lewis and Clark were the first Americans to do so. They were given a large number of medals to distribute to native chiefs as tokens of subjection, just as Shelikhov and Baranov had handed out their copper double-headed eagles. More importantly, Jefferson charged Lewis and Clark with pushing beyond the Louisiana Territory – which extended as far as modern Montana – and continuing through unclaimed land to the Pacific in order to find a 'direct & practicable water communication across this continent, for the purposes of commerce with Asia'.[5]

After two exhausting years pushing up the Missouri River and down

---

[*] Similar objections would be made in 1867 to William Seward's proposal to purchase Alaska from the Russians for just two cents an acre.

the Columbia, Lewis and Clark finally reached the Pacific in November 1805. They made their winter camp on the Netul River, a couple of miles to the south of the Columbia on the edge of Chinook tribal territory. They built a stockade and called it Fort Clatsop, and there they spent a hard winter subsisting on berries and smoked elk. Clark led a mission south down the coast to find salt just before Langsdorff ventured ashore near Havre de Grey, north of the Columbia, in a *baidarka* to try to make contact with the natives. He found none and spent a terrifying night looking for the *Juno* as a heavy fog descended. In the final days of March 1806, as Rezanov was tacking to and fro in an attempt to enter the Columbia, Lewis and Clarke's expedition was preparing to turn back eastwards and head home. Lewis sent a last scouting party to the bluffs overlooking the shore to see if they could spot any merchant ships; they saw none. The *Juno* must have been just out of sight. The pioneers of Russia's and the United States' fragile new empires would never meet.

On 22 March, the day before Lewis and Clark left Fort Clatsop, one of the *Juno*'s sick sailors died of scurvy. Eight more were, in the opinion of Dr Langsdorff, just days away from death. 'The sick grew more diseased from want of anti-scorbutic remedies . . . no hope seemed to remain unless by the wholesome animal and vegetable productions that might be obtained on the shore.'[6] The *Juno* was then very nearly wrecked as strong winds pushed her towards the lee shore. Khvostov – evidently a decent enough sailor when sober – saved her by dropping both anchors, which caught in just eighteen feet of water a pistol shot from the shore. It was time to stop sailing up and down trying to cross the Colombia's sandbar and follow the wind south. To cheer everyone up Rezanov ordered the last cask of brandy on board opened. 'He gave [the] whole crew a good bowl of punch made with brandy of the Russo-Americans which I endeavoured to make more palatable by the assistance of acid of vitriol and sugar,' recorded Langsdorff. 'This beverage was universally admired.' Vitriol being the contemporary name for sulphuric acid, one wonders how the Company's brandy originally tasted if vitriol improved it.

On the evening of 27 March 1806, running before favourable winds, the *Juno* approached the entrance to San Francisco Bay. Vancouver's charts proved so accurate on every point that 'we could have run into the harbour in the dark',[7] but Khvostov decided it would be prudent to heave to until daybreak. The *Juno* had arrived at the northernmost extremity of the Viceroyalty of New Spain.

The Spanish-born Pope Alexander VI had first separated the globe into Spanish and Portuguese hemispheres in 1493, with the dividing line running longitudinally through modern Brazil. All non-Christian lands to the west of this meridian were – in the eyes of the Spanish at least – the exclusive province of the Spanish Crown. The Spaniard Vasco Núñez de Balboa reached the Pacific in 1513 by crossing the Isthmus of Panama, and duly claimed both the ocean and all lands on its shores for Madrid. García Ordóñez de Montalvo, a contemporary Sevillian novelist, had written of a mythical 'island called California, very close to a side of the Earthly Paradise' ruled by a Queen Calafia and 'populated by black women, without any man existing there, because they lived in the way of the Amazons'.

The invented name of California stuck to the coastal lands to the north of Mexico, even though it was not a Spaniard but the English privateer Sir Francis Drake who was the first to explore them. Drake reached Point Loma, near modern San Diego, in 1579 and named the land New Albion. He also explored further up the coast, almost certainly as far as San Francisco Bay and possibly up to modern-day Vancouver Island. He was the first European by some 200 years to sail the north-western coast of America, but neither Drake nor his countrymen made any attempt to follow up the claim.

It was only in the mid-eighteenth century that Bering's expeditions to the north Pacific and the Russian colonies in the area galvanized the Spanish authorities into making their theoretical claim to California a reality. In 1768 a team of Spanish colonists was dispatched to found a new port at San Blas in Mexico. Over the next twenty years a series of Spanish naval expeditions probed and mapped the Pacific coast as far as Kodiak. In 1788 the two empires finally made contact when Captain Gonzalo Lopez de Haro sailed into Three Hierarchs Bay and entertained Evstrat Delarov to wine and honey cakes on board his frigate the *San Carlos*. In 1789 a Spanish naval lieutenant's violent challenge to

British ships at Nootka Sound – discussed in detail in Chapter 4 – almost set off a world war. But by that time the Spanish had already established a chain of nineteen Catholic missions, protected by six *presidios,* or military garrisons, along the coast. The northernmost and newest outpost, consisting of a small *presidio*, a mission church and a farm, was established in March 1776. The friars named the settlement for their patron saint, San Francisco de Asís.

As the fog cleared on the morning of 28 March 1806,[8] the *Juno*'s officers had their first view of the Golden Gate and, beyond, into San Francisco Bay. On the right-hand shore they could see a small fort. Above, on the bluffs where the southern end of the Golden Gate Bridge stands today, was the tiny whitewashed *presidio*. Rezanov 'deemed it useless to send in and ask permission to enter, since in the event of a refusal we should necessarily perish at sea'.[9] Khvostov put the *Juno* straight into the bay with all sails set. 'A great commotion was observed among the soldiers' at the fort, who hailed the *Juno* through a speaking trumpet and ordered her to anchor. 'We merely replied, "Si señor, si señor" and simulated an active effort to comply with their demand, but in the meantime we had passed the fort and were running up the Bay, and at a cannon-shot complied [by anchoring].'[10] A party of horsemen galloped from the fort, and Rezanov ordered Lieutenant Davydov, in his full-dress naval uniform of blue frock coat and high boots, and Langsdorff ashore. Rezanov briefed them carefully on the lies he wanted them to tell. They were to 'inform [the Spanish] that I was the Russian officer of whose coming I hoped they had been notified by their government' and claim that the *Juno* was en route to Monterrey – the capital of Nueva California – but had been forced to stop for urgent repairs.

Twenty horsemen were waiting on the shore. One was a Franciscan monk with 'several officers and a well-looking young man wearing very singular dress . . . a mantle of striped woollen cloth like the coverlet of a bed, his head coming through a hole in the middle'. This was the *gala serape*, the decorated poncho worn by Spanish soldiers. The officers wore undress uniforms of black and scarlet, with soft deerskin boots and 'extravagantly large spurs'.[11] The two parties had no common language but Latin, which happily both Langsdorff and Padre José Antonio Uria spoke well.

'*Habitationes nostras in regione ad septentrionem tenemus, appelata Russia est*,' Langsdorff explained – 'Our abode is in a northern region called Russia.' The Spanish replied, to the Russians' surprise, that they were indeed expecting a Russian voyage of discovery to pass their way, but of two ships not one. The viceroy in Mexico had ordered all *presidios* to extend every hospitality to the visitors. Spanish diplomatic intelligence had reported to Madrid on the departure of the *Neva* and *Nadezhda* for the New World three years before, and the news was duly passed on to Mexico and thence to the most distant outposts of the empire. The Spanish had even diligently reported on the identity of the expedition's leader. Rezanov was, much to his own consternation, indeed expected.

Half-starving, his breath stinking from scurvy ('which spared no one, not even the officers'[12]), Rezanov was helped by his valet into his now baggy full-dress uniform. Sitting proudly in the *Juno*'s longboat in his green *kamerheer*'s livery, the keys of his chamberlain's office, his diamond Order of St Anne and his gold Order of the Crown of Wurttemberg shining on his breast, a high bicorne hat perched on a head crawling with lice, Rezanov was rowed ashore. San Francisco's *comandante*, Don José Dario Arguello, was absent in Monterrey leaving his eldest son Lieutenant Luis Arguello in command. After an exchange of bows and compliments, Arguello cordially invited Rezanov to dine. Rezanov, happy to be on dry land after a rough month at sea, chose to walk the one *verst* – roughly a kilometre – up the hill to the *presidio*.

Today the area around the old *presidio* is thickly wooded, but the magnificent trees were planted by the US Army in the 1890s. In April 1806 the bluffs would have been covered only in tall grass and brush, commanding an unbroken view of the Bay and its sea approaches. The *presidio* itself consisted of a white adobe barrack in a small settlement of neat houses around a swept parade ground. Langsdorff was delighted by the sight of the simple but regularly-built houses, which he thought resembled a German farmstead. 'My eyes were so hungry for some-thing peaceful and ordered and sunny and un-tragic.'

Vancouver, who visited the *presidio* in November 1792, thought it 'resembles a pound for cattle', with just two rooms and no glass in the windows. Langsdorff also considered 'the habitation of the Commander is small and mean', scantily furnished and with a beaten-earth floor covered in straw. But the *comandante*'s family was plainly close-knit and happy. 'Friendship and harmony reigned in the whole behaviour of these worthy, kind-hearted people,' wrote Langsdorff. The *comandante*'s wife, Dona María Ignacia Arguello, received the new arrivals 'in the most polite and friendly manner', and eleven of the Arguellos' thirteen children were produced to bow and curtsey to their distinguished visitor.

Dona María de Concepción Marcela Arguello – known to her family and later to history as Conchita – was, at fifteen, the eldest daughter of the family. Her brother Luis described her as the 'beauty of the two Californias'.* She was tall, shapely and had the clear pale skin of the pure Spanish ruling class. Her mother was the niece of the first *comandante* of San Francisco, and when Conchita was baptized on 26 February 1791 the *comandante* of the neighbouring *presidio* of San Diego stood godfather. The priest carefully recorded that Dona María de Concepción was the sixty-fifth white child born in the colony since its foundation. In this tiny community on the edge of the known world, Conchita Arguello was an aristocrat.

Langsdorff was immediately smitten. 'She was lively and animated and had sparkling and love-inspiring eyes, excellent and beautiful teeth, a smiling expression and beautiful features, a fine form and a thousand other charms including an artless and natural demeanour.'[13] Rezanov had barely seen any European women since Kamchatka. He was immediately taken with Conchita and found himself 'staring quite helplessly'.

The Arguellos treated their Russian guests to a simple dinner, impressing them with 'as handsome a service of [silver] plate as could be seen; this costly American metal is indeed to be found in the most remote Spanish possessions'.† The Russian visitors found the food – mutton, salad, vegetables, pulses, fruit, milk and white bread – more overwhelm-

---

* Upper and Lower California, today the US and Mexican states of California and Baja California.

† This silver was looted during a British raid on the Mexican port of Loreto in February 1822, where Don Arguello finally settled after a lifetime's service. The raid's commander, Sir Thomas Cochrane, went on to become admiral of the fleet and retired to Ipswich. Perhaps a family in East Anglia is still eating dinner off heavy provincial Spanish plate.

ing still. 'Our palettes had for so long been strangers to these things.'[14]

In the course of this agreeable luncheon Rezanov found it necessary to tell a few more half-truths. He informed his hosts that he had ordered the *Neva* and *Nadezhda* back to Russia and that he 'had been entrusted by the Emperor with command over all His American territories and had visited them the previous year . . . [now] I had finally decided to visit the *governador* of Nueva California to confer with him as the Chief of a neighbouring territory as to our mutual interests.' Lest this whopping piece of self-aggrandizement get back to St Petersburg, Rezanov was careful to explain in his report to the emperor later that summer: 'Be pleased, gracious Sire, not to consider that it was from empty pride, but merely to impress the Spaniards of the importance of our possessions in the North that I thus proclaimed myself *comandante*. The welfare, the interests of our country required it.'

While the officers lunched with the Arguellos, fresh food was sent aboard the *Juno*. After the privations of Russian America, the casual generosity of the *presidio* was extraordinary: four fat oxen, two sheep, onions, garlic, salad, cabbages, pulses, vegetables and even cherries. The effect this feast had on the starving crew was immediate: even as Rezanov's party returned to the *Juno* that evening the fitter sailors were scrubbing out the stinking forecastle. For the first time since his departure from Kodiak the previous summer Rezanov could sleep without fear of shipwreck or murderous Tlingit.

A courier was sent to Monterrey with a polite letter from Rezanov to the governor-general of Alta California, requesting permission to come and pay his respects in person – one chief to another, as it were. The following morning, a glorious breezy spring day, horses were brought by Don Luis, who led Landsdorff, Rezanov, Khvostov and Davydov on a short expedition to the Misión Dolores de San Francisco itself, a mile away from the *presidio* over 'naked country covered with low shrubs'.[15] The fathers received the Russians enthusiastically, despite the visitors' Orthodox religion. They were shown the mission's collection of 'ecclesiastical paraphernalia' in the treasury – probably as unimpressive then as it is now – and prayers were offered. Langsdorff hit it off immediately with 'our Cicerone, Father Uria, an intelligent and well-informed man', with whom the doctor shared an interest in natural history. Paradoxically, the fathers were more aware of the outside world than the officers of the *presidio* and the local gentry because the priests served only ten years in the New World before returning to Spain. Over 300 ecclesiastics came and went from the viceroyalty every year. As Franciscans they were forbidden from owning property, which made them – crucially for the Russians – unusually open-handed with the food and other products of their vast ranches.

On returning to the *presidio* for hot chocolate and honey cakes, Rezanov launched his charm offensive with a flurry of gifts brought up from the *Juno*. 'Fitting and valuable presents' were distributed to everyone, male and female, 'thus displaying every evidence of wealth and demonstrating our generosity'. Rezanov was acutely aware of the need to 'hide from the Spaniards our distress and needfulness, of which the Boston vessels had told them to our disadvantage'.[16] A single day ashore had demonstrated that California was a land of plenty beyond the wildest dreams of the Russians of Alaska, or indeed of almost any other part of Russia. Yet the 'Spanish government is extremely suspicious,' and had since the sixteenth century expressly forbidden its subjects in New Spain from any trade or barter with foreigners. American ships were not allowed to dock at all; the Russians were only allowed to do so because of the government order to extend them hospitality. But formally the ban on trade was absolute. This, Rezanov was determined to change.

Madrid's philosophy of government remained essentially medieval. The New World was run like a vast feudal estate. Land was held either directly by the Crown, or by the Church or aristocracy, who were accountable respectively to the cardinal and the viceroy in Mexico City. The third estate of professionals, freeholders and merchants, the class which had overthrown monarchs in England, France and America, was deeply distrusted by the Spanish authorities. The peasantry were landless and, in the case of natives, often semi-enslaved. It has been South America's tragedy that its greatest revolutionary, Simón Bolívar, shared the prejudices of his old masters. The nations he created from the ruins of Madrid's empire later in the nineteenth century were run by tiny oligarchies, and continued to be so well into the twentieth century. The American continent's other great liberating general, George Washington, presided over a very different society, in which property-owning merchants and small landowners insisted that they were collectively sovereign, and made their government and laws accordingly.

A reactionary government was not the only similarity between the Russian and Spanish empires. The men on the edges of both states were, as Rezanov quickly established as he chatted to the *misioneros*, just as ready to bend their monarch's laws in the right circumstances. Rezanov was also evidently in agreement with Vancouver that the Spanish Empire was weak and ripe for the plucking. Rezanov carried the French translation of Vancouver's *Voyage of Discovery* with him to the New World: the *presidios* were 'so wide from each other and so unprotected' that 'instead of strengthening the barrier to their valuable possessions in New Spain they have thrown irresistible temptations in the way of strangers to trespass over their boundary',[17] quoted Rezanov in a letter to the directors of the Company. Rezanov certainly considered himself one of the tempted.

A reply arrived by return courier from Monterrey. Rezanov was not to trouble himself with the journey; the governor was preparing to come to him instead. 'Thereupon I recognized the suspicious nature of the Spanish government, which at every point prevents visitors from gaining a knowledge of the interior of the country and from observing the weakness of their military defences,' grumbled Rezanov. In this case the Spaniards' suspicions were extremely well founded. During his first days Rezanov spied out the colony's armaments, garrison and defences, taking careful note of the 'five brass guns of twelve pounds' calibre' which now stand in front of the *presidio*, covering the car park. They are fine late-sixteenth-century naval long-guns, decorated with coats of arms and cast in Spain; they were already antiques when Rezanov saw them in 1806 but nonetheless still deadly.

The Russians spent their days shooting partridge and duck with Don Luis and taking chocolate at the *presidio* with his charming sister Conchita, under the watchful eye of their mother. 'Our past sufferings

were delightfully requited, for our time passed very joyously,'[18] Rezanov
wrote to Rumiantsev. 'Dona Concepción is the universally recognized
beauty of Nueva California. Pardon me, gracious Sire, that in such a
serious report I mingle something of the romantic but perhaps I must
be very sincere.'

Langsdorff was touched by 'the simple artless attachment that every
part of this family seemed to feel for each other'.[19] The Arguellos' simple
domesticity stood in sharp and obvious contrast to the brutality of
Russian America. Don Luis and Father Uribe's curiosity got the better
of them, and they accepted Rezanov's invitation to come aboard and
inspect the goods on the *Juno*. The Spanish were particularly impressed
by the 'coarse and fine linen, the Russian ticking, iron shears, axes,
saws, bottles, casks, glasses, plates and handkerchiefs'. Luis carried a
shopping list from the women of the house for cotton muslin, printed
cotton and pins. Rezanov gave Don Luis a fine English fowling rifle,
while Langsdorff loaded Father Uria with English cloth and a piece of
'gold stuff' for decorating his church.

New Archangel was more isolated from mainland Russia than San
Francisco was from Mexico – but not by much. The prevailing south-
bound California current flows strongly against vessels coming north
from San Blas, and the shipbuilding there was slow and shoddy, just
as it was at Okhotsk. Between 1770 and 1821 an average of between
two and three Spanish ships visited California every year; for thirteen
of those years there were no recorded ships at all. Overland from
Monterrey was a journey of at least thirty days by mule, and the road
was frequently closed by hostile Indians. A voyage to Madrid, via
Mexico, would take five months, almost as long as it took Russian
colonists to cross Siberia to Moscow. California certainly did not lack
for food, but the ban on trading with the Bostonians meant that the
colony suffered from a chronic shortage of manufactures. Within
days of Father Uribe's visit to the *Juno* word of the trade goods available had spread through the colony. Priests were coming from
missions as distant as San José, eager to place orders with the Russians
if and when the governor would allow it. Don Pedro de la Cueva of
the Misión de San José cheerfully informed the Russians that he

already had dozens of Indians busy grinding corn into flour ready to exchange for good Boston broadcloth. 'It was clear that this was *far* from the first time he had engaged in commerce.'[20]

The *Juno*'s crew found California every bit as agreeable as their officers. Rather too much so, in fact. Within three days of arrival five of D'Wolf's men – four Bostonians and a Prussian – who had signed up for Company service the previous autumn in New Archangel, requested permission to remain in San Francisco. Several Russians appeared keen to join them. Clearly, if Rezanov were to let them go he would soon have no crew left with which to return to Sitka.

Don Luis was not keen on Protestant Yankee sailors wandering his colony and offered a picket and mounted patrol to guard the *Juno* and prevent any desertions. A court martial was held on the *Juno*'s quarterdeck, which condemned the five for conspiracy to desert and ordered them confined to a small stockade on an uninhabited island in the Bay known to the Spanish as La Isla de los Alcatraces – the Island of the Pelicans. Thus the *Juno* Five became the first prisoners of Alcatraz. But despite these precautions two of the Company's 'most esteemed seamen' nonetheless managed to abscond while washing their clothes in a creek. They were never found. Rezanov asked Arguello for them to be deported to Russia via Vera Cruz, if ever caught, and followed up by asking Rumiantsev to ensure that if these miscreants ever showed up in their homeland they should be 'returned to [Russian] America for ever' – apparently the most horrible punishment he could think of.

On the afternoon of 7 April a salute of nine guns from the shore battery and another from a second, hidden battery – duly noted by the diligent amateur spy Rezanov – announced the arrival of the gubernatorial party from Monterrey. The following morning Father Pedro arrived with an invitation to dine with Don José Joaquin Arrillaga, Alta California's governor. Rezanov, obsessed as always with form and protocol, bridled at the lowly status of the messenger. 'Are the Holy padres not as worthy of respect as officers?' retorted the priest, brushing aside the snub. 'We live in America and I'll wager we know nothing but sincerity.'

Rezanov chose to set aside his irritation and mounted up. On the way up the hill Father Pedro confided that a considerable obstacle had arisen to Rezanov's trade mission. 'Previous to his leaving Monterrey the Gobernador received information from Mexico to the effect that if we are not now at war with Russia we soon shall be.' Rezanov laughed off the report as a 'blunder'. 'Would I have come here at such a time?' if war was in the offing, he bluffed.[21] Yet he sent a message back to the *Juno* – on the pretext of sending for a forgotten handkerchief – ordering no-one to leave the ship. Riding into the courtyard of the *presidio* Rezanov feared that he might be arrested. 'When crossing the Plaza I noticed the pleasant, smiling faces of the beautiful Spanish señoritas, and at once my suspicions vanished, as, if there had been any ground for suspicions the señoritas would no doubt have been secluded.'

Waiting for Rezanov on the steps of the *presidio* were Don Arrillaga and Don José Dario Arguello, Conchita's father. Elaborate compliments were exchanged in French, which Arrillaga spoke well. Rezanov was solicitous of Don Arrillaga's bandaged foot. 'Everything in California is subject to my commands, yet my right foot refuses obedience,' joked the governor, whom Langsdorff found 'a very polite and respectable elderly gentleman.'[22]

The Spanish apologized for the informality of the invitation; Rezanov airily claimed that 'I had not given the matter any serious consideration, I had made all conventionalities subordinate to my desire to secure the benefits which attracted me to Nueva California.' Strange as Rezanov's obsession with protocol seems today, in truth he had very little to offer his Spanish hosts except an impressive front. For both Russian and Spanish noblemen of the time the political culture of the court and its elaborate codes were more than simply ritual; they were crucial signifiers of status. Rezanov's seemingly boorish insistence on being accorded due deference at all times was, to his mind at least, part and parcel of his mission to impress the Spanish with the dignity, wealth and power of Russia, their new neighbour and rival.

The foundations of the *presidio* that Rezanov knew lie under the floorboards of a US Army officers' club built on the site a century later. It was a small room, perhaps fifteen feet by thirty, with adobe walls nearly six feet thick. It had no glass in the windows and was roofed with thatch. Yet with its rough-hewn furniture and impressive silver plate and lit by home-made candles, Rezanov found the place had 'a subdued, barbaric beauty'. At dinner Rezanov talked a big game, as might be expected from a man who was, by his own account, posing as head of a neighbouring state. Brushing aside rumours of war – 'Men like us who are inured to all kinds of dangers must not take notice of such rumours,' he told the Spanish – Rezanov's message was clear and wholly disingenuous. He assured his hosts that Russia had no designs on California. 'Dismiss from your minds this erroneous idea,' Rezanov told Arrillaga. 'The Southern parts of America are not necessary to us . . . Even if it were otherwise, you must acknowledge that so strong a power [as Russia] would not need to disguise its intentions and you could never prevent us from carrying it out.' At the same time he warned Arrillaga that once Napoleon was defeated the Spanish were doomed to lose California to the Americans unless they strengthened their empire by opening to trade – with the Russians, for instance.

Rezanov apparently believed that Arrillaga was reassured by these arguments. 'The gobernador listened with much pleasure,'[23] he reported, though the old man maintained that decisions about 'intercourse that might be established between Russian settlements and this Spanish province'[24] were above his station. Not even the viceroy in Mexico City could decide such weighty matters of state, mumbled Arrillaga, even 'though he perfectly concurred in considering it advantageous to both parties'.[25] This was surely a matter for the cabinet in Madrid to decide.

Yet, as he returned to the *Juno* that evening accompanied by an honour guard of Spanish dragoons, Rezanov was in high spirits. As anyone who has ever tried to get anything done in Russia knows, invoking ever higher and more distant authority is in reality a sign that purely local problems are about to be resolved, here and now, man to man. 'God is high and the Tsar is far,' the Russians say, and the further away and higher the obstacles to Rezanov's problems, the better the chance he would be able to persuade the old governor to bend the rules a little here in his own backyard.

18

Love and Ambition

He, from grave provincial magnates oft had turned to talk apart,
With the Comandante's daughter on questions of the heart,
Until points of gravest import yielded one by one,
And by love was consummated what diplomacy begun.

Francis Bret Harte, 'Conception de Arguello', 1872

A ball was arranged at the *presidio* for the distinguished visitors. The garrison's barrack – the largest roofed space in the compound – was cleared of furniture and bedding, and the women of the Arguello household busied themselves preparing the hall. They decorated it with a Spanish flag and a Russian standard borrowed from the *Juno*. A small orchestra was assembled from among the garrison's soldiers: drummers, guitar players and fiddlers. Indian servants were sent out on the hazardous mission of gathering wild honey and, less perilously, spring salad leaves.

Rezanov and the officers wore full-dress uniform. Langsdorff wore his black academic suit and waistcoat of cream lawn. The Arguello girls taught the Russians a dance called the *barrego*, in which two couples stood opposite each other, stamped their feet, clapped hands and turned around each other in a chain. Langsdorff, Khvostov and Davydov 'took pains to teach the ladies English country dances and they liked them so much that afterwards we often danced them'.[1] Rezanov and the doctor took turns at the violin, accompanied by the soldiers' guitars. At ten the company broke off dancing to eat *dulces* – small honey cakes – and drink sweet yellow wine.

Rezanov danced with Conchita. It seems he was immediately attracted to her; it is even likely that the feeling was mutual. Conchita was, at fifteen years and two months, already considered a famous beauty. Rezanov, though forty-two and gaunt from a hungry winter, was the most impressive man she or indeed anyone in California had ever seen. The doomed romance of Conchita and Rezanov has inspired epic poems, plays and novels in English and Russian, as well as the Soviet Union's first rock opera. But we have only two contemporary accounts of what happened in the five weeks the *Juno* was at San Francisco: Langsdorff's travelogue – which is coloured by unconcealed resentment of his chief – and Rezanov's own letters to the Company, which are necessarily dry and put the relationship in purely political terms.

What is clear is that their affair was at least partly political. 'Our constant friendly intercourse with the family of Arguello – the music, the singing, the sports and the dancing – awakened in the mind of Chamberlain von Rezanov some new and important speculations which gave rise to his forming a plan of a very different nature from the first for establishing a commercial intercourse between the Russian and Spanish settlements,' wrote Langsdorff. 'The bright eyes of Dona Concepción had made a deep impression on his heart and he conceived that a nuptial union with the daughter of the *comandante* at San Francisco would be a vast step gained towards the political objects he had so much at heart.'[2]

Rezanov undoubtedly went out of his way to be charming; it seems also that he was charmed in turn by the Arguello's harmonious family life and the chatter of the womenfolk. The Russian party became daily visitors to the *presidio* to take chocolate with Conchita and her mother. Rezanov worked hard at transforming his fluent French into basic Spanish. When Don José Dario and the governor arrived from Monterrey Rezanov was already on such good terms with the family that 'I was told the next day word for word all that had been said there after I left thanks to my close intimacy with the house of Arguello.'[3]

Conchita was clearly intelligent – Rezanov, who did not suffer fools, spent hours chatting to her. 'Associating daily and paying my addresses to the beautiful Spanish señorita I could not fail to perceive her active venturesome disposition and character,' he wrote to Rumiantsev. Moreover, Conchita was ambitious and hungry for a world beyond the confines of the *presidio*. Rezanov speaks of her 'unlimited and over-weening desire for rank and honours which, with her age of fifteen years, made her, alone of her family, dissatisfied with the land of her birth. She always referred to it jokingly; thus "a beautiful country, a warm climate, an abundance of grain and cattle – and nothing else".'[4] These are Conchita's only words recorded by Rezanov or Langsdorff.

But there is also a third source. María Manuela Francesca Salgado, born in 1838, joined the Dominican Convent of Monterrey in 1852 and was close to Conchita in the last years of her life. Salgado, known as Sister Vincentia or Old Vinnie, recounted her memories of Conchita to an Irish-American priest in the years before her death in 1940. A third-hand account, then, and one which is riddled with improbabilities – but Old Vinnie helps us to imagine the flesh-and-blood Conchita. She found Conchita

> beautiful of face and figure, a little below medium height. Her face was small – oval rather than round – and even then, when past sixty, her face was not wrinkled . . . Her eyes were rather large and through the years did not lose any of their luster. They were deep pools of dark blue, just like the Heavens, and looking into them one could sense the deep dark blue of the ocean. Her voice had a most soothing cadence. It was low and had its own special charm. Her Spanish was faultless. When in conversation with anyone – man or woman regardless – she looked at them straight in the eyes, not searchingly but with a perfect trust and the innocence of a little child.[5]

At fifteen Conchita seems to have been a mix of her father's peasant prag-matism and ambition and her mother's refinement. Don José Dario had risen from private in the Mexican dragoons to an ensign's commission in the newly founded *presidio* of Santa Barbara in 1781, and was given command of the San Francisco garrison in 1798.* Hubert Bancroft, an early historian of California, interviewed men who had known Arguello. They reported that he was tall and stout with a commanding bearing and very dark skin. Despite the handicap of a dark complexion, Arguello married into the highest nobility in the colony. Dona María Ignacia Moraga was of pure Spanish blood, the niece of the founder of the San Francisco *presidio* and kinswoman by blood or marriage of most of the colony's leading families. Dona María bore him fifteen children – single-handedly accounting for almost a quarter of white children born in the twenty years of San Francisco's existence. [6]

Dona María de Concepción was educated by the Franciscan priests of the Misión Dolores. The furthest she would have ever been from home would have been to the provincial capital of Monterrey, a two-day ride away. The white population of San Francisco numbered just seventy. The journey to Mexico City was unimaginably difficult and dangerous for a lady of her status. To travel to Spain was even more inconceivable. Conchita grew up in one of the remotest outposts of the civilized world. Small wonder her desire to be free of it was, as Rezanov says, 'unlimited'. Rezanov may have seen in Conchita a way to realize his political ambitions, and for Conchita, Rezanov represented the only chance she was ever likely to get to escape into a wider world.

Two powerful women had dominated Rezanov's career: Catherine the Great and Natalia Shelikhova. He knew the power women could wield, even in a man's world, and set about making the women of the *presidio* his friends, allies and spies. His target was Don Arrillaga, and his object was to persuade the dutiful old bureaucrat to bend the rules of his government to fill the *Juno*'s hold with breadstuffs. The gifts to the womenfolk had been nicely chosen: the linen and calico and mirrors and scissors were daily reminders in the Arguello household of the wealth and generosity of their Russian guest.

Women, then, were one pincer of Rezanov's diplomatic offensive. The priests would form the other. Langsdorff, wittingly or not, had

---

* In 1814, after the death of Don José Arrillaga, Arguello became governor of Alta California – as did his son, Don Luis, after him.

become his key liaison with the padres. Rezanov had forbidden the doctor from leaving the vicinity of the *presidio* until Arrillaga's arrival to avoid the impression that the Russians were sending out spies. But now that Rezanov's personal diplomacy was in full swing, Langsdorff was allowed to head off to spend most of his time inspecting the flora and fauna surrounding the mission.

The German doctor, though a Rhineland Protestant and man of science, quickly made firm friends with the Franciscan monks, the only educated men in this distant outpost. He found them simple and intelligent, refreshingly free of the ambition and single-mindedness that Langsdorff found so irritating in Rezanov. At the same time Langsdorff pumped his new ecclesiastical friends for every detail of the colony's politics and husbandry. In exchange he told them (in Latin) all the gossip he could think of that would interest them: the fate of the Church in Napoleonic France and the intrigues of the Jesuit Father Grueber at the court of Tsar Paul. They, in turn, made it clear that they were not only frustrated by Madrid's interdiction of trade with all foreigners but had flouted it in the past and were willing to do so again.

The order that Langsdorff found at the Misión Dolores ranch made an impressive contrast to the starving chaos of New Archangel. 'The monks conduct themselves in general with so much prudence, kindness and paternal care towards their converts that peace, happiness and obedience universally prevail . . . Two or three monks, in voluntary exile, [succeed in] civilizing a wild and uncultivated race of men, teach them husbandry and various useful arts, instruct and cherish them as if they were their own children.'[7] The native workers were essentially slaves and their womenfolk were prudently kept under lock and key – but their barracks were clean and well built. Beyond were rows of tanneries, grain stores and workshops producing tallow candles, soap and furniture. There may have been room for improvement for the missions's cabinet makers – every visitor from Vancouver to young Otto Kotzebue, who visited in command of his own round-the-world mission in 1816, commented on the poor quality of the *presidio*'s furniture – but overall Langsdorff found the colony a model of order and industry.

One reason for this happy harmony was, in Langsdorff's view, that the local Indians were simple-minded to the point of imbecility. They were 'wholly incapable of forming among themselves any plan for their eman- cipation' because of 'the extreme simplicity of these poor creatures – who of stature no less of mind are certainly of a very inferior race of human beings'. Langsdorff, as an enthusiastic amateur anthropologist, could claim to be something of a connoisseur of native peoples. He contrasted the Californians, 'small, ugly, ill proportioned in their persons and heavy and dull in their minds', with the Tlingit of New Archangel, who were 'strong, well-made, handsome and possessing such acuteness of mind that by their address they have often foiled both English and Russians'. [8]

Unlike the state of near-siege in Russian America, just four or five Spanish soldiers at each mission were sufficient to keep the Indians 'under proper restraint . . . without spirit of mutiny or insurrection'. On the rare occasions they ran away, they were always caught because they returned straight to their own villages, 'a circumstance which perhaps [the fugitive] scarcely thought of beforehand'. The escapees were beaten on the soles of the feet. But again unlike Russian America, labour was plentiful. Indeed the monks told Langsdorff that there were no windmills in this hilly and windy grain-producing country because they were 'afraid of making the natives idle'.[9]

Getting the priests on his side was a canny piece of diplomacy by Rezanov. In Russia Peter the Great had effectively made the Church a branch of the state bureaucracy, but in New Spain the roles were reversed: it was the Church that was the real power in the land. Indeed as Rezanov discovered from his long conversations with Father Uria, the founding ideology of the colony was a purely religious one, to evan- gelize the natives. The missions *were* California – the *presidios*, with their garrisons and governors, were there only to provide security and civil administration for the missions. Despite the agricultural plenty of the land, Madrid's insistence on a ban on trade of any sort made the colony an expensive undertaking. Half a million piastres a year were spent by the Spanish Crown to maintain the nineteen missions in the four *presidial* districts of California. In return, His Most Catholic Majesty expected no reward other than a heavenly one.

This high principle had been funded for two centuries by the gold and silver of the New World, but by the turn of the nineteenth century even the Spanish state was starting to realize that it must engage with the grubby world of commerce or face bankruptcy. In the 1780s King Charles III of Spain had taken shares in the merchant-adventuring Caracas Company, just as Alexander I would later buy into the Russian American Company.

What Rezanov was proposing – to open New Spain to trade – was nothing less than an invitation to join the modern world. 'The proximity of our settlements in the New World, the great mutual advantages which may result from trade have compelled me to come to New California,' Rezanov wrote to Don José Iturrigaria, viceroy of New Spain in Mexico City. Continuing his pose as the Tsar's appointed chief of Russian America, Rezanov stressed how essential trade is 'for regions located at a vast distance from their Mother countries'.[10] To Arguello and Arrillaga, during their frequent dinners and nightly informal dances at the *presidio*, Rezanov proposed a credit arrangement to disguise the fact that trading had taken place. It was a fairly feeble fudge: Rezanov would buy the missions' grain with a letter of credit, and the missions buy the *Juno*'s cargo, also on credit, with no money changing hands. Arrillaga was unimpressed. '"No, no," said he, "that is equivalent to trading. After living sixty years without reproach I cannot take that upon my conscience."'

Rezanov, a master of the straight face from his years at court, protested that 'it was not love of gain but merely a desire to benefit your countrymen that would urge you to infringe slightly in your regulations'. Arrillaga, not Madrid, was in a position to help the people in his charge, and in addition, Rezanov added, 'the Holy Padres will bend their knee in prayers for you.' But the old governor was no fool. 'Oh, I see clearly that the Holy Padres have already bent the knee for *you*,' he answered wryly.[11]

A deadlock then. How was a gambling man like Rezanov to break it but by raising the stakes, quickly and dramatically? Arrillaga had already warned him that he 'hourly expected a report of a total breach of concord between our governments' in the form of news from Europe of a new twist in the wars. The Bourbon King Charles IV of Spain had gone to war against revolutionary France in 1793 after the execution of his kinsman Louis XVI. He had lost badly, and as a result Spain had been in a forced alliance with France since 1796. Great Britain, France's perennial enemy, had led two coalitions against France between 1792 and 1801, both involving Russia. Neither had been successful. But as Arrillaga had rightly suspected, by April 1805 indefatigable British Prime Minister William Pitt had signed Russia up for the Third Coalition, along with Austria, Prussia and Portugal. In other words, by the time Rezanov landed in California, Russia had been at war with Spain's ally France for a year. Fortunately for Rezanov, relations between Madrid and Paris were strained – hence the warm welcome the Spanish authorities had ordered extended to the Russian circumnavigators. Nonetheless, it was only a kind of diplomatic suspension of disbelief that kept Spain and Russia – whose allies were each other's enemies – from being at war directly with each other.

This was the narrow diplomatic corridor that Rezanov had to navigate. Clearly, any twist in the volatile situation in Europe could have an immediate and disastrous effect on his mission. Unbeknown to Rezanov, the British had crushed a Franco-Spanish fleet at Trafalgar the previous October, seizing or destroying twenty-two ships of the line and losing none of their own. In retaliation Napoleon had defeated the Russian, Prussian and Austrian armies at Austerlitz in December 1805 – and with them had destroyed the Third Coalition. Exactly what this see-saw of defeat and victory meant for relations between Spain and Russia was by no means clear, certainly not in California – though it was obvious that the destruction of her fleet at Trafalgar further undermined Spain's ability to protect its sea lines of communication with her colonies. In any case, as Arrillaga told Rezanov, they were five and a half months behind the news.[12]

The last news the governor had heard was that Prussia had entered the Third Coalition the previous autumn, inevitably heralding another round of European war. So both the Spanish and Russians daily expected a dust cloud on the Monterrey road signalling the arrival of a courier with news of a breach between Russia and Spain. As a gesture of his bona fides, Rezanov ordered all the powder unloaded from the *Juno* and stored at the fort. The *presidio*'s long heavy guns may have been antiques, but they were still deadly and there would be no escape from them if the Spanish were ordered to seize his ship. A 'friend' of Rezanov's in the *presidio* – presumably Conchita herself – had told him that a company of soldiers had secretly been ordered up from Monterrey to the Mission Santa Clara de Asis, a day's march away, in readiness for exactly such an eventuality.

Even after three years at sea and in the wilds of the Pacific Rim Rezanov had lost none of his talent for showmanship or his appetite for risk-taking. Two weeks after his arrival in San Francisco Rezanov proposed marriage to Conchita Arguello.

'Seeing that our situation was not getting better, expecting every day that some serious unpleasantness would arise and having but little confidence in my men, I decided that I should assume a serious bearing where I had before been but formally polite and gracious,' was how he reported his démarche to Rumiantsev. 'I described Russia to her as a colder country, but still abounding in everything, and she was willing to live there, and at length I imperceptibly created in her an impatient desire to hear something more explicit from me. When I proffered my hand she accepted.'[13] The news came as a bombshell to Don José Dario and Dona María Ignacia. 'My proposal was a shock to her parents, whose religious upbringing was fanatical. The difference in religion, besides the prospective separation from their daughter, was, in contemplation, a dreadful blow to them,' wrote Rezanov.

Conchita was promptly bundled off to the mission to be confessed. But she refused to yield to her parents' or the priests' arguments against the match – 'her brave front finally quieted them all'. The practicalities, however, were less easily resolved. Rezanov refused out of hand to convert to Catholicism – though of course Paul I had mooted a union of the Russian and Roman Churches. His reasons were social and political rather than religious: converting to the Spaniards' religion would be seen as tantamount to going over to their side. And this was the difficulty that the fathers and Arguello family latched on to. The final decision on such a controversial mixed marriage would have to be left to the Pope. One imagines the regretful spread-handed gesture with which news of this obstacle was conveyed to Rezanov.

If the priests' intention was to stop the marriage plans in their tracks, it failed. To 'a philosophic head like the Chamberlain's,'[14] Langsdorff noted sarcastically, difference in religion was by no means an insurmountable problem. Rezanov immediately assured his future parents-in-law that as soon as he returned to St Petersburg he would ask his friend the Tsar to appoint him ambassador to Spain. There he would 'obviate every kind of misunderstanding between the two powers' and return to California via Mexico to claim his bride. Langsdorff clearly believed that his chief was bamboozling the provincial Arguellos. 'It will be seen from this detail that the chamberlain was no less spirited in forming his projects for the accomplishment of his wishes than ardent and active in carrying them into execution.' The doctor called the marriage negotiations a 'trade' whose object 'was the insuring a regular supply of corn and flour from New California'.[15]

But if it was a trade, Conchita was a willing participant. The manoeuvre also worked. 'Being not able to bring about the marriage, I had a written conditional agreement made and forced a betrothal,' reported Rezanov. The arrangement was to be kept secret – but of course in practice wasn't – until the Pope's final decision. Rezanov even presented the setback as an important and unique opportunity to get in some spying on his return trip to marry Conchita, which he seemed sincerely intent on doing. 'I shall be in a position to serve my country once again by a personal examination of the harbour of Vera Cruz, Mexico, and by a trip through the interior parts of America,' he told Rumiantsev. 'This could not be accomplished by, nor would permission be granted to, anyone else, the suspicious Spanish temperament forbidding such investigations.'[16] Moreover, such a progress from Madrid to New Mexico would give Rezanov a fresh diplomatic role to further the Tsar's interests by 'securing an entrance for Russian vessels to the Eastern ports (of the Pacific)'.[17] Thus would the embarrassment of Japan be eclipsed by a new and important phase of his career: bringing together the two great old monarchies on the edges of Europe in a community of interest at the extremities of their empires.

Probably slightly dazed and certainly confused by Rezanov's world-historical strategies involving their teenage daughter, the Arguellos invited Rezanov to live at the *presidio*. 'Thereafter my deportment in the house of Comandante Arguello was that of a near-relative, and I managed this Puerto of his Catholic Majesty as my interests called for,' boasted Rezanov, at his least likeable when bragging of his own success. 'The Gobernador was now very much perplexed . . . as he now found himself to be in fact my guest.' Rezanov lost no time in investigating the colony's secret business. 'Every official document received by Gobernador Arrillaga passed through the hands of Comandante Arguello and consequently through mine . . . his subordinate officers, seeing as I had become almost Hispaniolized, vied with each other to be apprised of any new occurrence, so that the information of the possible arrival of any courier was not dreaded.'[18]

It was an impressive coup of diplomacy – or espionage. In just over a fortnight Rezanov had gone from being an overdressed stranger with bad breath to a member of the colony's ruling family, privy to state secrets. And not before time. Tidings of both the Spanish defeat at Trafalgar and the French victory at Austerlitz and subsequent occupation of Vienna in November arrived by the same post shortly after Rezanov moved into the *presidio*. News of the inevitable collapse of the Third Coalition was clearly imminent, with its consequent reshuffling of Europe's alliances. But thanks to his betrothal to Conchita, Rezanov felt at least partially insured against such reversals of fortune.

Conchita, for her part, hoped and believed that her engagement was the beginning of a new life. In old age she told Sister Vincentia how 'Nikolai Rezanov came bounding into her life. How she loved him and how they planned for a life of love and happiness in far-off Russia.' The couple went walking on the beach and arranged 'a tryst' at the spring of San Polin, just below the *presidio* – though Rezanov himself makes no mention of this and it is difficult to imagine that such a meeting would have happened without a chaperone present. They took a trip to the island of 'La Bellisima', now known as Angel Island in San Francisco Bay, and there Conchita said she gave Rezanov a locket.

'Concha detailed how she cut strands of hair from Nicolai's head and wove them with strands of her own,' recalled Sister Vincentia. 'This accomplished, both of them placed their plaited hair in the little gold and enamel locket with a cross set with pearls on its front. Having placed the locket around his neck with a golden chain, he in turn gave her a cross of gold encrusted with diamonds and sapphires and, last but not least, he gave her a picture of himself as a remembrance. Concha spoke softly as she recalled the vows of lasting devotion and fidelity to each other.'[19]

How much of this is true and how much the romantic imagination of a woman dwelling for half a century on the only few weeks of romance that fate had allotted her? Conchita's account, as recalled by Vincentia, contains much that is improbable. She claims for instance that a Russian visitor came to the *presidio* years later and returned the locket she had given Rezanov. She might have meant Otto Kotzebue in 1816, but he would surely have recorded such a symbolically important and logistically complex feat as carrying Rezanov's locket around the world. But what does ring true is that Conchita sincerely felt that those 'six weeks of her life made her a woman and gave her the strength, the power and the endurance to live out the many years of loneliness that followed'.[20]

To Rezanov, his immediate problems appeared solved. Arrillaga allowed himself to be talked into a scheme whereby the *Juno*'s commissary signed for the purchase of grain, while the missions filed formal petitions asking for permission to sell grain to (rather than trade with) the visiting Russians. The sale of the *Juno*'s cargo in the other direction would be off the books. Arguello confided to Rezanov that the padres had been holding back from delivering grain not just because of legal scruples but because of rumours that the *Juno* might soon be confiscated.

Rezanov suggested that if the Monterrey garrison could be recalled from Santa Clara, such rumours would subside. 'The Gobernador was surprised to learn that his secret orders were known to me, and, turning it off as a joke, sent orders at once for the troops to return,'[21] reported Rezanov, apparently unconcerned that his only possible source in the *presidio* – Conchita – might get into trouble with her father for leaking such information. Within days such a quantity of grain began to arrive that the *Juno*'s crew could not load it fast enough.

Festivities were arranged. A bear was caught in the nearby hills and dragged on an ox skin down to the *presidio*. To Langsdorff's disappointment, the animal died before he could properly inspect it. To make up for this – and apparently misunderstanding the doctor's interest in natural history – Arguello ordered wild bulls caught instead and baited by dogs for the amusement of the local population. Langsdorff was surprised that the holy fathers 'never oppose these national amusements though they are cruel and barbarous. Perhaps they are no more affected by seeing the useless slaughter of animals than the Nukakhivans are by the eating of human flesh.'[22]

The Indians of San José dance for Langsdorff.

Langsdorff, with the help of the padres, set off with Davydov on an expedition to the Misión de San José, sixteen leagues down the coast. The original plan had been to take the *Juno*'s three longboats and pick up more grain, but the winds being contrary, the party set off in Aleut *baidarkas* into the open Pacific instead. The journey took two days. The fathers of San José welcomed the Russians warmly; even in this tiny mission founded only two years before they had 200 measures of surplus wheat stored in their barns.

'In a land with such a plenty of wood and water and excellent harbours persons of enterprising spirit could in a few years establish a flourishing colony,' Langsdorff wrote; in time the RAC should 'plant a colony of Russia's own'. His hosts, unaware that their guest was eyeing their mission with the greedy eye of empire, arranged for the natives to dance for them with 'dreadful gestures and contortions'. Langsdorff's pen-and-ink portraits of these Indians, now in the University library of Göttingen, are remarkably accomplished. The natives' party trick was to swallow hot coals plucked from the fire. 'This was no deception; I observed them very closely and it is utterly incomprehensible to me how they do it,' wrote the baffled Langsdorff.[23]

The *presidio* of San José.

The doctor was in for a rude shock when he returned to the *Juno*, which was being loaded with her new cargo. He found his painstakingly-prepared scientific specimens casually discarded. 'Skins of sea dogs and birds laid on deck to dry were I know not by what means thrown overboard,' complained Langsdorff. The blotting paper he needed for drying plants was packed deep in the hold and a collection of live birds he had bought had been released. He was told – presumably by Rezanov – 'that they had more important business to attend to and that our expedition was not undertaken for the promotion of natural history'. Langsdorff professed himself 'so entirely discouraged' by this philistinism that he 'relinquished the idea of further labours and surrendered myself to the wishes of Chamberlain von Rezanov as interpreter to the *misiones*'.

Rezanov was obsessively single-minded. Nothing, not Langsdorff's natural history, not the emotions of a young girl nor the scruples of religion, was going to get in the way of his dream. Russian America would be made prosperous and viable, and in time Russia would conquer the *presidio* of San Francisco just as Rezanov had conquered its fairest daughter.

19

I will never see you – I will never forget you

Patience and sincerity will change the manners of people. Even bears
can be trained to obey.

> Nikolai Rezanov, letter to the directors of the Russian American
> Company[1]

I sailed the seas like a duck, suffered from hunger and thirst and from
humiliation. But twice worse than this was my suffering from my heart's
wounds.

> Nikolai Rezanov to Mikhail Buldakov, 1807[2]

Bolts of fine cotton nankeen and English broadcloth, chests full of
Boston-made shoes and round felt hats, caskets of scissors and saws,
barrels of iron and brass nails, cases of cutlasses and tomahawks were
hauled up from the *Juno*'s hold. In its place nearly 200 tons of grain –
all packed in leather sacks, such was the abundance of cattle and the
dearth of sackcloth – was loaded in. Four and a half thousand pounds
of tallow, butter and salt followed, as well as dried beans and peas, fresh
beef and vegetables. Rezanov had succeeded in provisioning Russian
America to the tune of 24,000 Spanish dollars.

While the ship was being loaded Don José Dario invited his future
son-in-law and his companions to an open-air meal at his family's ranch
at El Pinar, some thirty miles south of San Francisco.[3] The ladies of the
presidio travelled cross-country on highly-sprung carriages; the men

rode. The Arguellos' ranch was a park-like expanse of fruit trees dominated by a large adobe house. Beef was grilled over hot coals on a large
suspended metal frame the Spanish called a *barbacoa*; its use continued
to be popular among later generations of Californians. The feast was
followed by spectacular displays of horsemanship by the Spanish
soldiers and natives. Rezanov was greatly impressed by these 'Californian
Cossacks'. He also pondered how lightly defended the Spanish territories were. 'If the RAC had a force comparable to its position it would
be very easy to seize from 34 degrees [Santa Barbara] North and keep
this territory for ever,' he wrote.[4]

Back at the *presidio* some uncomfortable news awaited the Russian
chief. A party of Boston men in the *Peacock*, under Captain Oliver
Kimball, had landed at San Diego to take on fresh food and water. The
Spanish, rightly suspecting them of being en route to poach sea otter in
Spanish waters, arrested four of the Bostonians and clapped them in
irons. Under questioning, the Americans claimed they were on their
way to Sitka to trade their cargo of arms and other goods to the
Russians. What was the meaning of this? Rezanov was politely asked.

One imagines Rezanov's brow furrowing with a look of indignation and concern. Whatever Rezanov's good points may have been,
it's also clear that he was an accomplished and convincing liar. 'I am
very glad that you reminded me of this proceeding,' Rezanov replied,
according to his own account to Rumiantsev. 'These Bostonians do
more harm to us than they do to you. They land people here [in
California] but they steal from us . . . This rascal of whom you speak
captured a party of our Americans and stole forty Kadiaks and their
families. In the following year Captain Barber, a man of the same
stamp, brought to us twenty-six of these stolen people saying he had
ransomed them from captivity and would only give them up upon
the payment of ten thousand rubles.'[5]

Even by the extravagant standards of Rezanov's untruths, this was
outstanding. 'Our Americans' had in truth not been kidnapped by
Kimball but were put aboard quite willingly by Baranov specifically to
loot sea otter off California, and the 'stolen people' had in fact been
rescued by Barber, at some risk to himself, from Tlingit servitude after

the destruction of Fort St Michael. 'We should take steps to drive off intruders of that character,' Rezanov gravely told Arguello, who seemed reassured that he had an ally in Rezanov against the depredations of the wicked Bostonians.

With the hold of the *Juno* filled, the time had come for Rezanov to leave while he still could. More embarrassing news of Baranov's Bostonian associates could emerge at any moment, and all his personal friendliness with the Arguellos would not outweigh a direct order from the viceroy to seize his ship. Rezanov announced the necessity of his departure to his hosts. He also promised Conchita that he would return. He probably even meant it.

A farewell ball was arranged at the *presidio*. All the colony's persons of quality – the *gente de razon* – arrived in their finery, trundling in carriages across the dusty countryside from Monterrey, Santa Barbara and even from Nuestra Señora la Reina de Los Ángeles, the tiny pueblo founded by Arguello a decade before. Musical instruments were lent by the garrison of Santa Barbara and dutifully chronicled by Langsdorff: '4 flutes, 3 clarinets, 2 trumpets, 2 bass viols, one bass drum, 2 kettle drums, 6 old fiddles, 4 new fiddles, one triangle and one Chinesco [xylophone]'. At the dance itself, held in the afternoon, the Spanish dignitaries wore sombreros and heavy spurs, while the women wore mantillas and lace. Rezanov was of course by far the most splendid man in his uniform and decorations. He danced with Conchita for the last time.

The following day, 10 May, a service of blessing for the Russians' safe passage was held at the mission; the officers of the *Juno* all attended in full uniform. There was a final dinner at the *presidio*. Later novelists and poets have written much on the last meeting between Rezanov and Conchita – the most famous piece is by the Russian poet Andrei Voznesensky, who speculated that the doomed couple believed that they would never see each other again. 'I will never see you – I will never forget you,' says Conchita in his poem 'Avos!' But in truth the only eyewitness account of the parting is Langsdorff's rather prosaic one: 'The Governor, with the whole family of Arguello, and several other friends and acquaintance, had collected themselves at the fort and wafted us an adieu with their hats and pocket-handerchiefs.' The *Juno* gave a six-gun salute (indeed she only had six guns; the rest were wooden dummies) and was answered by a nine-gun salute from the waterside fort.

Nearly half a century later Conchita confided to her young protégée Sister Vincentia that she had been filled with deep foreboding even as the ship sailed out of sight. 'Although Concha . . . never doubted as to [Nikolai's] deep loyalty and intense sincerity in her regard, she told me that from the evening he sailed away out through the Golden Gate she had somehow a deep, hidden, eerie feeling that stayed with her night and day.'[6]

The *Juno*'s return journey was no more than usually onerous. They spent ten days becalmed; there was an outbreak of 'rheumatic fever' on board and the ship's rigging rotted through and collapsed. But they were plentifully provisioned and the crew had 'healthy counte-nances . . . their colour and strength was so perfectly restored that nobody could have supposed them the same people who had left the settlement such miserable, pale, lean, emaciated figures'.

The *Juno* nosed into Sitka Sound on 7 June after twenty-seven days at sea. In rude good health after their California rest-cure, her company eagerly looked out for their mates ashore. But no one came to meet them, despite a signal gun. Finally, as they approached the dock a bedraggled pair of *baidarkas* emerged, 'their rowers looked like living skeletons they were so starved and thin'.[7] Baranov was moved to tears by the sight of the provisions. He had been preparing for the final anni-hilation of the colony at the hands of a thousand-strong Tlingit war party which had moved onto the northern shores of Baranov Island ostensibly in search of a vast shoal of herring but also drawn by rumours of Russian vulnerability. They had even sent their women into the Sitka stockade as whores in order to spy on the colonists' deteriorating strength. Rezanov had returned just in time.[8]

Not that the denizens of New Archangel had been living the quiet life while the *Juno* had been away. Jonathan Winship, the new captain of the Boston boat *O'Cain*, had called in early May and unwisely invited Baranov and his officers aboard for lunch and drinks. By dusk, he recorded in his diary, 'our visitors, the governor [Baranov] and other dignitaries, being mostly in a state of intoxication and creating such confusion and disorder that I concluded would be imprudent to put to sea. At five bells [of the third watch – 9 p.m.] our visitors had the good-ness to depart, doubtless not a sober man among them, I saluted with five guns and three cheers and heartily rejoiced at their departure.'[9] Winship took a hunting party of one hundred borrowed Aleut hunters and twelve native women with him, further cheering Baranov, who was pleased to be rid of the burden of feeding them. Winship's 1806 hunting season would bring 4,820 pelts, a record catch never surpassed in the history of Russian America.

The *O'Cain* had in fact also brought something more important than free alcohol: a message from King Kamehameha of Hawaii to Baranov, offering friendship and proposing to trade *taro* (a vegetable), breadfruit, pigs and rope for lumber for shipbuilding, linen cloth and iron. The powerful king also proposed a royal visit to New Archangel to see the settlement for himself and open trade between Russian America and Hawaii. Rezanov had dreamed and written of the cross-Pacific trade that was vital to the future of Russian America, and here it was echoed in a concrete business proposition by an important neigh-bouring monarch.

Rezanov settled down to compose dispatches to Rumiantsev, the directors of the Company and the Tsar. During his forty-two-day stay in California he had composed just one report to Rumiantsev, a short and formal dispatch reporting his presence in Spanish America, sent by the Spanish royal post from San Francisco to St Petersburg via Mexico. Afraid of compromising himself, he saved all the details of his affair with Conchita, negotiations with the friars and his designs on Spanish California until he was safely back on home turf.

The letter that reached Rumiantsev is a hundred and twenty closely-written pages long and is now in the Archive of the Russian Foreign Ministry in Moscow.[10] We know that Rezanov made an exact copy of this report, which he sent on different ships.[11] It is this version that is quoted in the standard histories of the Russian American Company. But there is also another, earlier version of the letter that has never been published. A close read of the text shows that it is almost certainly an earlier draft which Rezanov never sent and was found among his papers when he died in Krasnoyarsk. This version was lost for over 150 years and only included in the Rezanov papers in the State Historical Archive in St Petersburg in the 1940s. There are over a hundred differences between the draft and the final version, differences that give us important clues to Rezanov's true feelings for Conchita.

Almost all the changes Rezanov made were to distance himself from Conchita and make the relationship appear more political and calculated. In the draft version, for instance, Rezanov writes, 'Let me tell you our American habits – when we love someone sincerely, then the whole family makes a holiday of baking biscuits which the beloved guest is invited to prove that the whole house is occupied in favouring his tastes and so they will lead you to where you are awaited. I went into the very clean kitchen where Dona Ignacia sat by her children and female relations. Each of the Spaniards brought up the biscuits she had baked and so I had to dine one more time.' This charming episode was omitted from the formal report, presumably because Rezanov believed that this warm recollection of a Californian bake-off was evidence that he was too intimate with the Arguellos.

Of his relationship with Conchita, he originally wrote, 'The lovely Concepciön multiplied her courtesies to me daily, as well as many other small services and sincerities. For a long time I was indifferent to them, but they began, unnoticed, to fill a void in my heart. We became closer every day in our conversation, which ended in my offering her my hand.' This he changed to the much more callous 'Associating daily with and paying my addresses to the beautiful Spanish señorita I could not fail to perceive her active, venturesome disposition and character, her unlimited and overweening desire for rank and honours which, with her age of fifteen years, made her, alone of her family, dissatisfied with the land of her birth.' Of their betrothal itself Rezanov first wrote that 'the decisiveness of *both* parties at last calmed everyone'. This he changed to '*her* decisiveness at last convinced everyone'.

Rezanov clearly feared that his engagement to Conchita could become a liability and open him to suspicion of treason. He was therefore at pains to demonstrate to Rumiantsev that he had not 'gone native'. 'My romance [was] not begun in hot passion, which is not becoming at my age, but arising under the pressure of conditions – remoteness, duties, responsibilities – perhaps also under the influence of remnants of feelings that in the past were a source of happiness in my life,' he assured his patron in his final report. Rezanov was at pains to cast himself as a calculating diplomat, not a besotted middle-aged lover.

With the directors of the Company Rezanov had a different problem. Buldakov was married to the sister of Rezanov's late wife; his two children were the Buldakovs' wards. Coming less than four years after Anna's death, Rezanov was concerned that his shenanigans with a second teenage heiress might be *mal vu* by his Shelikhov in-laws – who also controlled the Company's board. He therefore hastened to assure Buldakov that the Conchita business was just that – business. 'Don't think me a weathervane because of my California report my friend,' he wrote to Buldakov. 'My true love is still with you [in St Petersburg], at the churchyard of Alexander Nevsky under a piece of marble. And here – all is the consequences of enthusiasm and ever-newer sacrifices for the Fatherland . . . Concepción is fair as an angel, wonderful, kind of heart, loves me and I love her and weep for the fact that there is no room for her in my heart. Here my friend, as a sinner in confession, I repent. But you are my pastor; keep my secret.'[12]

Yet for all the distancing from Conchita, Rezanov nonetheless insisted even in the official report that he would go back for her. Already in his letter to Rumiantsev he suggested how useful to Russia his return voyage, via Spain and Mexico, could be. 'I shall be in a position to serve my country once again, as by a personal examination of the harbour of Vera Cruz, Mexico, and by a trip through the interior parts of America. This could not be accomplished by anyone else, the suspicious Spanish temperament forbidding such investigations . . . Upon becoming acquainted with the viceroy of Nueva España I could make an attempt to secure an entrance for Russian vessels to the Eastern ports.'

Was this Rezanov's overactive imperial vision once again running away with him or the musings of a man seeking an official excuse to return to his young Californian bride? We have two contradictory versions of the relationship, both written by Rezanov himself. He was clearly an intensely sentimental man: he writes constantly of love – for his country, for his emperor, for Conchita. Yet in both versions of the affair his sincerity towards his fiancée is nonetheless calculated – or perhaps coloured would be a kinder word – by the giant political implications of founding a new Russo-Spanish dynasty.

Behind the politics, did Rezanov truly feel something for the 'fair angel' who waited for him so faithfully in San Francisco? After two years in the company of the man's diaries, reports and letters, following his travels in the wilder corners of Asia and America, I would venture that he did. 'I sailed the seas like a duck, suffered from hunger and thirst and from humiliation,' he wrote to Buldakov. 'But twice worse than this was my suffering from my heart's wounds.' Wounds of love – or wounds of guilt that he had 'no space in his heart' for Conchita? We will never know. But behind Rezanov's monumental ambition, his bullying and his dissembling, his obsession with appearance, and later with his posterity, was a passionate and lonely man, as intemperate in his affections as he was in his dreams.

Rezanov's time in California also seems to have changed his thinking about the nature of Russia's colonies in America. Rather than seeing the place as a convict colony, a kind of Russian Australia, Rezanov became a disciple of Adam Smith and the power of capitalism's invisible hand to transform the settlement's fortunes. During the summer he spent at New Archangel Rezanov penned extensive instructions on root-and-branch reform of the colony to the long-suffering Baranov, who had of course been on the receiving end of such orders since Shelikhov's day. However unlike Shelikhov's breezy and unrealistic *ukazes*, Rezanov's ideas are not only economically sound but remarkably modern. Recognizing that an economy of confiscation and obligation did nothing to incentivize its employees and encouraged theft, sloth and drunkenness, Rezanov argued that money in the form of cash must urgently be introduced to replace the current practice of paying colonists a lump sum on their return to Okhotsk after years in America.

'Money,' Rezanov wrote, 'will define the value of each person's labour; it will encourage arts and crafts. Gardening will become more attractive when the products raised bring returns . . . marketplaces will spring up. Fish, vegetables, berries, everything will be found in the market and each one will provide for his needs according to his wealth.' He even proposed that Aleuts be paid cash for their services to foreign ships. 'In a word, everything is dead now, but with the introduction of monetary circulation the whole region will be alive,' he enthused. Sending Russians home after five or ten years in the colonies was also wrong, Rezanov decided. 'All artisans and port workers should remain permanently in their places.' If colonists were allowed to earn and amass money,

> each one will become more determined to raise a family and establish a household and this will lead to a permanency of the population . . . They will form a citizenry, especially if they are granted lands for their permanent and hereditary ownership. After a certain number of tax-exempt years they will pay a land tax. First they will cultivate gardens of vegetables. In time they will build houses, they should be encouraged to do so by assistance from the Company. Having their own property and amassing it they will find so much pleasure in settled life that they will lose the desire to leave it.

This prescription for a free, property-owning, taxpaying society, where 'even the domestic servants will have an opportunity to improve their circumstances'[13] was of course exactly the formula by which the English colonies on the other side of America had thrived so prodigiously. In the end Rezanov's ideas were never implemented. If they had been, the history of Russian America – and perhaps Russia itself – would have turned out very differently.

Rezanov left Russian America believing that he had helped improve the lot of the miserable colonists and their native underlings, a thought which evidently gave him great satisfaction. 'I saw that my single happy life leads whole peoples to their happiness, and that I may spend myself on their welfare,' he wrote in his last letter to Baranov. 'I have seen how a single line written by me can lighten their lot and gives me such pleasure as I could never have imagined and all this tells me that I have not been idle in this world.'14

Baranov accepted his chief's 'secret instructions' with a show of grave deference and, ignoring them like other instructions before and after, continued with business as usual as Rezanov sailed away to Russia.

20

The Weeping Country

I do not believe that Your Majesty will consider it criminal when . . . I build ships and set out next year to destroy [Japanese] settlements on Matmai [Hokkaido], to push them from Sakhalin, and ravage their coasts.

Nikolai Rezanov informs the Tsar of his personal declaration of war against the Japanese, 1806[1]

The deceased – blessed he is not – Rezanov must be declared the biggest scoundrel whom the D[evil] ever put into the world!'

Georg Heinrich Langsdorff to Johann Caspar Horner, February 1808[2]

D'Wolf and Langsdorff were both impatient to continue immediately to Okhotsk, D'Wolf because he was eager to cash his letters of credit in St Petersburg and Langsdorff because he had become increasingly irritated by Rezanov's high-handedness since his precious specimens had been thrown overboard in San Francisco Bay.

'I, for my part, had been long enough in Sitka. Tired of living on fish, shell-fish and sea dogs, I had determined that I would depart with the first ship that should sail for Europe,' wrote Langsdorff in his published account. Privately he excoriated Rezanov. 'You can imagine that such an ignoramus, as Rezanov was, did not have the slightest feeling for science and also did not provide any support at all,' he wrote to Krusenstern. 'Everything we experienced in Brazil, the South Seas and in Kamchatka is nothing compared to the events and sad scenes I was forced to witness. Oh, how often I have remembered your well-intentioned advice [not to follow Rezanov]!'[3]

But the options for leaving New Archangel were limited. The Company brig *Maria* had been hauled up on shore the previous autumn and used as barracks. So shoddy was her construction that she had to be partly dismantled and reassembled before she could sail again. Another transport, the *Avos* – 'Unexpected Good Fortune' – was only half-built. Rezanov resolved to keep the *Juno* at New Archangel until the *Avos* was ready. The only available boat, therefore, was the Kodiak-built *Rostislav*, just forty-one feet long. D'Wolf's men had made it to Canton in the not much larger *Yermak*, so he suggested he repeat the feat in her even smaller and flimsier sister ship. Both D'Wolf and Langsdorff decided that the risk was preferable to remaining in Russian America. With D'Wolf skippering, the *Juno*'s second mate (and barber, tailor and blues-banishing fiddle player) Edward Parker promoted to first officer, Langsdorff as ship's doctor and three Koniags and one Russian as crew, the *Rostislav* set out to cross 2,000 miles of the north Pacific. 'I thank the heavens that on the first of July I was able to leave that deathtrap of Sitka and the arch-scoundrel Rezanov,' Langsdorff wrote. 'I have been among the living dead for the past year.'[4],[5]

One last piece of unfinished business remained, in Rezanov's judgment, before he could return to St Petersburg: punishing Japan for its insolence towards the Russian Empire as represented by her ambassador – in other words, himself. The diplomatic slight he had suffered in Nagasaki would have to be righted. Dreams of revenge for his humiliation had evidently been preying on Rezanov's mind the whole hard winter in Sitka. Already in February 1806 he had written to the emperor from Unalaska effectively informing the Tsar that he intended to declare a private war on Japan.

By strengthening our American establishments and building ships we may oblige the Japanese government to open the trade which their people most earnestly desire. I do not believe that Your Majesty will consider it criminal when, aided by such noble assistants as Khvostov and Davydov, I build ships and set out next year to destroy their settlements on Matmai [Hokkaido], to push them from Sakhalin, and ravage their coasts. By cutting off their supply of fish and depriving 200,000 people of their food we will force them to open up trade with us. I hear that they have even dared to establish a trading post on Urup. If it be Your Will, Most Gracious Sovereign, punish me as a criminal for taking action without your command; but my conscience will reproach me more if I let time pass in vain and do not make this sacrifice to Your Glory particularly when I see that I may help effectuate the fulfillment of your Imperial Majesty's High Intentions.'[6]

Rezanov enclosed carefully thought-out details of his coming campaign against the Japanese. A Russian colony would be founded on Sakhalin, he informed the Tsar, guarded by artillery and a garrison, while Company ships rounded up the light Japanese coastal craft. 'These raids, especially if repeated several times, would cause popular unrest in Japan which would compel the government to agree to a mutually profitable peaceful agreement.'[7] A month later, just before his departure for California, Rezanov followed this letter up with a personal missive to the Shogun, informing him that all lands to the north of Hokkaido were henceforth to be considered part of the Russian Empire and any settlements found upon them would be destroyed.[8]

Rezanov had made many winning gambles in his life. His unilateral declaration of war on Japan, it turned out, would not be one of them. Coastal raids would not force the Japanese to trade, and the Tsar's 'High Intentions' most certainly did not include authorizing Rezanov to start a war against Russia's Pacific – in every sense – neighbour. Nonetheless, far from St Petersburg and with the prospect of a return post many months distant, Rezanov busied himself with preparations for hostilities. He ordered Baranov to build stockades for the Japanese prisoners-of-war that he intended – his new-found enthusiasm for Adam Smith notwithstanding – to send to Russian America as slave labourers.

The war party, consisting of the *Juno* under Davydov and the *Avos* under Khvostov, was ready for sea by the end of July. However, as his long-planned punitive expedition became a reality Rezanov suddenly got cold feet. He would first return to St Petersburg to confer with the Tsar, he told Davydov on 21 July. A few days later Rezanov changed his mind again: no, he would lead the expedition personally, he told his captains, and both ships would immediately attack Sakhalin. Just before the ships finally set sail from Sitka on 27 July Rezanov changed the plan a third time: the *Avos* was to sail direct to Sakhalin while the *Juno* would deliver Rezanov to Okhotsk and join up with the *Avos* later in the year.

On board the *Juno* as she headed west, Rezanov penned a long and detailed instruction to Khvostov on the conduct of the coming operation. All Japanese commercial goods he found on Sakhalin were to be destroyed, Rezanov wrote; all Japanese taken prisoner, and the native 'hairy Ainu' tribesmen of Sakhalin and Hokkaido promised the protection of the Tsar. Khvostov was also to make sure to kidnap a Japanese priest and the 'heathen relics' from any temples they might find, for the future benefit of Japanese prisoners in Russian America. 'The Japanese in the free conduct of their faith might be more satisfied with their relocation and might eventually settle down, thus attracting their fellow countrymen.' In conclusion Khvostov was sworn to secrecy as to the purpose of the expedition.

So far, so clear – Khvostov was off to war, on written orders from the Tsar's representative. After a record run across the north Pacific the *Juno* anchored off Okhotsk in late August 1806. Rezanov, with his luggage, was rowed ashore. Yet even as he installed himself in the Company's offices he changed his mind one final time and distanced himself from the expedition he had planned for so long. 'The recent break in the foremast, contrary winds hindering your navigation and the lateness of the autumn season oblige you now to hasten to America,' Rezanov wrote from Okhotsk town to Khvostov, a few hundred yards away on board the *Juno* in Okhotsk Bay. 'The designated time for your meeting with [the *Avos*] has passed . . . and the fishing season has ended, so the hoped-for success can no longer be realized, so, everything considered, I find it better for you to abandon the previous orders and proceed to America.' But at the same time if Khvostov happened to pass Sakhalin, Rezanov wrote, he should 'attempt to win the natives' favour with gifts and medals.'[9]

Was the mission cancelled or not? Khvostov rushed ashore to clarify these confusing orders, but was told that Rezanov had left town in a hurry and was already over the hills and en route to St Petersburg. So Rezanov's ambiguous final order apparently left it up to Khvostov to decide whether to proceed or not. One can only conclude that Rezanov's backtracking was his way of covering his back in case the expedition failed while leaving open the possibility of gaining the credit if it succeeded.

Unfortunately for all concerned – but mostly for himself and his fellow captain Davydov – Khvostov interpreted Rezanov's last orders as meaning that he should proceed if not prevented by weather and the damaged mast. 'The ambiguity of this instruction placed Khvostov in no little difficulty,' wrote Vice Admiral Alexander Shishkov in his fore-word to Khvostov's diaries, published in 1810. 'However, considering that Rezanov could not cancel an expedition of which he had already informed the Emperor . . . [and believing that] Rezanov had appar-ently not cancelled the expedition entirely but merely postponed it, Khvostov decided to go to Sakhalin.'[10]

As Rezanov had anticipated, the firepower of the *Juno* was indeed devastating to the fragile Japanese fishing fleets and settlements. Over the next six months the *Juno* and *Avos* burned the settlements on Aniva Island, Urup and Kunashiv, torching warehouses and fishing nets and taking six Japanese prisoners and capturing supplies of millet, fish and salt. Well pleased with their haul, Khvostov and Davydov returned triumphantly to Okhotsk, only to be thrown in jail in irons for waging an illegal war. There they would have remained, at the mercy of the Okhotsk port commander Captain Ivan Bukharin, a personal enemy of Khvostov's if local sympathizers had not helped them escape. Khvostov and Davydov then made their way as starving fugitives with only the clothes they stood up in to Irkutsk, where they were able to appeal to the governor of Siberia and to the naval ministry in St Petersburg. 'None of us knew the level of empowerment of His Excellency the chamberlain and had no right to ask,' Khvostov wrote in his plaintive petition to Admiral Chichagov at the Navy Ministry. The two captains' names were finally cleared only in 1809.

But it was the commander of Russia's second round-the world expedition who was to feel the full consequences of Rezanov's war. On landing at Kunashiri on the Kurile Islands in 1811, Captain Vasily Golovnin was invited to tea in a Japanese fort. But when he and his officers tried to leave they were surrounded by soldiers, disarmed and taken prisoner. 'The governor [of Kunashiri], who had hitherto conversed in a soft and gentle voice now altered his tone and spoke loudly and with warmth,' wrote Golovnin in his memoirs. 'He frequently mentioned "Resanoto" [Rezanov] and "Nicola-Sandrejetsch" [Nikolai Alexandrovich Khvostov] and struck several times on his sabre.'[11] Golovnin was to spend two years in Japanese captivity before he was able to persuade the authorities that Khvostov and Davydov were not acting on government orders. 'Rezanov himself brought much harm to the RAC and himself ruined much of what he had created,' wrote Golovnin; understandably, he was not Rezanov's greatest fan.

So ended Russia's first attempt to open relations with Japan. There would not be another for a generation. Indeed Japan and Russia are technically at war still, for in the final days of World War II Joseph Stalin seized the South Kurile Islands – the same islands that Rezanov had first claimed for the Russian Empire in 1806 – and the Japanese have never signed a peace treaty with Moscow as a result.

Rezanov himself would never learn of the series of unfortunate events that his contradictory orders had set in train. As Khvostov was rowed ashore to Okhotsk in search of clarification, Rezanov was hightailing it up the trail to the Stanovoi Mountains. Once across the range, Rezanov kept up a punishing pace across the marshlands the Yakut called 'the weeping country'. 'I galloped over the chain of the Okhotsk Mountains day and night without leaving the saddle,' he wrote to his St Petersburg friend Count Ivan Maletsky. This was an exaggeration. Transporting a single grandee and his entourage post-haste across Siberia was a vast enterprise. Rezanov travelled with his valet, four Cossack bodyguards, Yakut guides, plus tents, bedding and provisions for six weeks. The train would have required at least sixty horses. Nonetheless Rezanov clearly drove his suite west as fast as the lumbering pack animals would allow.

'At this late time in the autumn I was forced to ford half-frozen rivers. I was warmed by fast riding during the day but by spending the night in the snow I became so ill with cold that I suddenly fell from my horse and remained unconscious for twenty-four hours. In this condition I was taken to a Yakut yurt on the Aldan River on 7 October. Here I regained my senses but was obliged to wait until the river froze,' Rezanov reported from Yakutsk . 'When it froze I galloped here on 23 October, where I suffered a severe relapse. I fought with death and this is only the second day since I left my bed. Now I am waiting for snow and when it comes I will ride without stopping on the way.'[12]

Despite his fever Rezanov was cheered by his new celebrity status as a member of the famous round-the-world expedition. 'Arriving in Yakutsk I saw the gratitude of my countrymen; all the town came out to greet me and invited us to their houses one after the other,' he wrote in evident satisfaction. Rezanov pressed on up the frozen Lena to Irkutsk, where the reception was even warmer.

'Here in Irkutsk I heard even more of their praises and allowed myself to be dragged all over town, simply out of my generosity of spirit, for I drew no pleasure from it. This same generosity prompted me to give a lunch and ball for the whole town in the House of Scholarship, followed by supper for three hundred. This cost me two thousand rubles.' The party Rezanov threw in his own honour dazzled society and entered into local legend for the lavishness of the entertainment. The Irkutsk merchant Ivan Kalashnikov recorded that the 'breakfast with dancing began at eleven and continued until the early hours of the next day'.[13]

However Rezanov's three-month sojourn in Irkutsk did not solely comprise gala lunches. News reached him that the *Nadezhda* and *Neva* had safely docked in St Petersburg and that their crews had been treated to a rousing welcome. The Empire, reeling from the disastrous defeat at Austerlitz the previous year, was badly in need of some good news, and of a few heroes.[14] Lisiansky, defying orders to wait for the *Nadezhda* to catch up in the Baltic, had actually pipped Krusenstern to the post and arrived at Kronstadt on 6 August 1806, a week before his chief, to become a national hero. The Tsar decorated all the voyagers lavishly. And if any ambiguity remained as to who had been in charge of the expedition it was put to rest by the Emperor's rescript conferring the Order of St Vladimir third class on Krusenstern, which began, 'By Our Will you were entrusted with leadership of the expedition ...' Calculated or not, this was a blow to Rezanov. He wrote self-pityingly to Buldakov, 'Thank God it is all over, all have been rewarded and only I wish for nothing. I think not of that, and feel nothing.'[15]

Each post seemed to bring more bad news. It is likely – though not confirmed by the Company's usually scrupulous letter books – that the fast-moving Rezanov finally received the letters Rumiantsev had sent from St Petersburg expressly and vociferously forbidding him to mount any military action against Japan. Doubtless this made for uncomfortable reading, and would have been more so if Rezanov had known that Khvostov had actually gone ahead with the planned raids.

He was also still ill. From the symptoms he reports it seems likely that he had pneumonia, with a fever that rose and fell sporadically for several months. Certainly by the end of January, still in Irkutsk, Rezanov suffered a relapse so severe that he believed that he was dying. 'The letter from Mother [Natalia Shelikhova] and the children received today by courier upset all of my wounds,' he wrote to his brother-in-law in late January 1807. 'They were expecting me by the New Year, but they do not know that perhaps I shall not see them again while I live.'[16]

Shelikhova was evidently staying with her surviving daughter Avdotia at the Buldakov house in St Petersburg. The old lady had not hesitated to inform her son-in-law that he had seriously damaged his reputation in the capital with his hysterical letter from Kamchatka and his private Japanese war. 'Mother writes that I am the reason that the Count [Rumiantsev] is displeased with me, but he promises to be as benevolent towards me as previously, and wishes me all manner of good. I am sorry that the old woman is aggrieved. I regret that the Count makes no allowances for my weakness. I was upset in the extreme and wrote in anger.'[17]

This last letter is full of spelling mistakes and was probably dictated to a secretary over four days between 24 and 27 January 1807. 'My strength is leaving me; I will see [Anna] before you,'[18] he wrote – or dictated – miserably. But at least Ivan Pil, the governor of Irkutsk, was a regular visitor, attending the celebrity invalid twice a day. Rezanov was most concerned for the fate of his children and was comforted that Rumiantsev had taken them under his protection. 'Mother writes that Count N. P. [Rumiantsev] is sending people to ask after my orphans. My tears are flowing, and gratitude has evoked them . . . My only remaining wish is that my labours are pleasing to my Monarch. Believe me that I need for nothing.'

A week later he was feeling well enough to take to the road again. By 1 March, after another three gruelling weeks on the road, he had reached the trading entrepôt of Krasnoyarsk, on the Yenisei River. Rezanov, usually a prolific correspondent, wrote no more letters on this last stage of his journey. By the time he reached the town on 8 March 1807, he was unconscious. His Cossack escorts carried him from his *kibitka* (a small closed travelling carriage) to the house of the merchant Rodyukov. Rezanov died the same day.

The fame that he had so long sought and enjoyed so much in Yakutsk pursued him, in death, to Krasnoyarsk. According to a local diarist, Rezanov's body lay in a chilly room for two weeks while artists 'were busy taking his likeness to send to St Petersburg'.[19] He was finally buried in the cemetery of the Cathedral of the Resurrection. In 1807 Gavriil Derzhavin wrote an ode to the fallen chamberlain, his former protégé. It feels heartfelt and is one of the old courtier-poet's finest works, all the more moving for being so sadly far from the truth.

> Rezanov! Who does not wish to be part of his immortal fame?
> And who can ever hope to rival his energy, his bravery, his fearless soul?
> Let the great icy cliffs advance, and the stony mountains smoke,
> And fierce Aeolus blow,
> But the Russia which you founded
> Will bestride the wide Ocean,
> And ornament the Throne of Alexander.[20]

Epilogues

Russian America

On a bluff overlooking the Pacific Ocean just off California Highway 1 stands a wooden stockade roughly two hundred yards square. At the corners are timber bastions with cannon pointing out of the gun-ports. A stumpy Russian church tower overlooks a large graveyard filled with nearly three hundred wooden Orthodox crosses. Inside the compound is a collection of buildings of distinctly north Russian design, a Russian-style well with a long pivoted pole to dip the bucket and a row of cannon. On summer days the smell of cooking borscht and woodsmoke drifts across the area; small figures carrying muskets and wearing mismatched tsarist uniforms troop up and down in the distance.

Fort Ross, seventy miles north of San Francisco, was the southern-most outpost of Russia's American empire from 1812 until 1842. In 1974 California's Parks Service rebuilt the fort as a State museum. The only remaining original building is the house of General Manager Alexander Rotchev, built circa 1836, but the armoury, chapel, store-house and artisans' quarters have been meticulously rebuilt and stocked with muskets and trade goods, furs and traps, authentic tools and furniture. Thousands of Californian schoolchildren come to summer camps at Fort Ross every year. They dress up as Russian colonists, the boys in fur hats and rabbit-skin waistcoats and the girls in aprons and headscarves. The boys march around the compound with muskets to the command of '*Levo! Levo!*' – 'Left! Left!' – and fire real half-pound gunpowder charges from the cannons. The girls cook Russian soups on open fires and sweep the floors with twig brooms. A Russian priest comes up from San Francisco to hold services in the chapel and summons the faithful by ringing a large bell cast in St Petersburg.

Rezanov's death had come at the worst possible moment for the execution of his grand design. Within a year of his demise at Krasnoyarsk the Spanish empire was decapitated as Napoleon occupied Madrid and deposed the Spanish King Charles IV. The convulsions of 1808 would have been Russia's moment to advance on the leaderless Spanish colonies. But by that time the Tsar's attention was too absorbed with brokering another peace with Napoleon to worry about the fate of Spain's suddenly orphaned overseas territories, and there was no Rezanov on hand to talk him into mounting a bold grab for the floundering empire's Californian colonies.

But Rezanov's vision of a Russian American empire did not entirely die with him. The Company did, as Rezanov had urged, eventually colonize not only California but Hawaii too. In 1812 Baranov's deputy Ivan Kuskov founded the Fort Ross settlement near Port Rumiantsev – now Bodega Bay – in Sonoma County, California. It was the ultimate – in every sense – Cossack *ostrog*, with its stockade and barracks for the Aleut hunters and Russian settlers. Kuskov and his successor, Naval Captain Leonty Hagemeister, were energetic general managers and successfully negotiated purchases of land from the local Indians along what is now the Russian River. But Fort Ross was not a well-chosen site. The nearest deep-water harbour was several miles to the south; sea-otter numbers along the whole coast were dwindling steadily, and attempts at growing grain to supply Alaska were foiled by plagues of gophers.

Fort Ross never became the thriving colony that Rezanov envisaged and was eventually sold to John Sutter, a Mexican citizen of Swiss origin, in 1842. The sale was poorly timed: seven years later the richest vein of gold ever recorded was found at another Sutter property, Sutter's Mill, inland of the Russian River, sparking the California Gold Rush of 1849 and the surge of wealth, immigration and development which followed.

The Russian colony on Hawaii proved even shorter-lived. It was the creation of one of the Company's most remarkable employees, Dr Georg Anton Schäffer, a native of Franconia in modern Bavaria. Schäffer joined the Russian navy as a surgeon in 1811. The following year, during Napoleon's invasion of Russia, he attempted to interest the Russian army in designs for military balloons.[1] When the scheme failed, Schäffer went back to the navy and sailed as ship's doctor on the *Suvorov* on Russia's third round-the-world voyage. He argued with the captain and was put ashore – or by his own account, resigned his post – at New Archangel.[2] Baranov, always short of officers, immediately hired the adventure-seeking German.

Baranov had been eyeing Hawaii as a potential victualling base for the company as early as 1808, but never had enough money, ships or men to make it a reality. His opportunity came in 1815, when a Company ship, the *Bering*, ran aground on the Hawaiian island of Kauai and was plundered by the island's chief, Kaumualii. Baranov dispatched Schäffer to Kauai with orders to demand compensation in the form of trade concessions. Schäffer, however, had grander ideas. He ordered the two Company ships sent out to support him in 1816 to the Big Island to force King Kamehameha, the high king of all Hawaii, into conceding land for a Russian settlement.

Kamehameha resisted Schäffer's bluster, but King Kaumualii of Kauai did not. On 21 May 1816 the flag of the Russian American Company was hoisted over the chief's longhouse on Kauai by Kaumualii himself, dressed in a Russian naval uniform lent to him by Lieutenant Yakov Podushkin of the Company ship *Otkritye*. Kaumualii also seconded a 300-strong workforce to Schäffer to construct Fort Elizabeth, a star-shaped fortress built of stone and adobe to a scientific European design sketched by the multi-talented doctor.

Schäffer was convinced that he had gained a Svengali-like hold over the chief and his wife, for the king also authorized a 500-strong native army to invade the neighbouring islands of Oahu, Lanai, Maui and Molokai for the Russian crown. 'The King provides Doctor Schäffer carte blanche for this expedition and all assistance in constructing the fortresses on all islands,' read one of the treaties that Schäffer talked

Kaumualii into signing. Believing himself to be the author of a great imperial coup, Schäffer sent victorious messages to Baranov and St Petersburg requesting a full-blown naval expedition to protect his 'fantastic achievements'. He began work on two more Russian settlements, Fort Alexander and Fort Barclay-de-Tolly, and toured Kauai giving German names to various landmarks. He named the Hanalei River valley the Schäfferthal, or Schäffer's Valley.

In truth it was Schäffer who had been bamboozled by the wily Kaumualii, who needed Russian ships and guns to back his own rebellion against Kamehameha. Schäffer's short-lived Russian colony came to an abrupt end the following summer when American merchants allied to Kamehameha attacked Kauai and tore down the Russian flag. Schäffer escaped to Macau on an American brig, leaving his colleagues at the Russian American Company to pick up the pieces of his disastrous experiment. Otto von Kotzebue, once midshipman on the *Nadezhda* and now a captain, had to apologize to Kamehameha and explain that Schäffer had exceeded his orders, just as Russian officers had had to grovel to the Japanese after Rezanov's personal war on Hokkaido. The Company, belatedly hearing of Schäffer's adventures late in 1817, fired him. The Tsar also forbade the Company from any further attempt to settle Hawaii.[3]

Dr Schäffer quickly recovered from his disgrace and ended up in Brazil, where he pursued a successful career as a courtier and administrator and certainly met the new Russian ambassador there, Dr Georg Langsdorff, of whose career we shall hear more below.[4]

St Petersburg might have looked with more indulgence on such misadventures had the Russian American Company been bringing in more money. But Rezanov had been entirely right when he warned Rumiantsev in 1806 that the fur trade was unsustainable and that the Company would only survive if it succeeded in diversifying into general trade. In real terms the Company's most profitable year was 1802; thereafter the fur catch steadily declined while the costs of the Company's growing navy and increasingly numerous settlements rose. The government took more and more control. By 1818 almost all the officers were navy men, and the Company's old freewheeling identity as a merchant-run operation was subsumed as the RAC became effectively an arm of the Russian state.

That same year Alexander Baranov finally succeeded in retiring. He had built himself a handsome dacha near Sitka in which to pass his old age, but he changed his mind and instead decided to return to St Petersburg, perhaps to be close to his creole son, who was studying at the Naval Academy. Chief Katlian came to say farewell to the old foe whose arrival in Tlingit country nineteen years before had transformed his tribe's fortunes so radically.[5] But Baranov never saw his homeland again. At Batavia, modern Java, he fell sick, and he died in the Straits of Sunda. His body was consigned to the waters of the Pacific, which he had tried so hard to make a Russian sea.

The end for the Company as an independent, adventurous entity came when a group of idealistic but indecisive young officers attempted a *coup d'état* against the new tsar, Nicholas I, on Senate Square on 26 December 1825. Most of the conspirators were young aristocrats who had been active in various secret political societies which had arisen in the wake of the Napoleonic Wars under the influence of Freemasonry. They hoped to install Nicholas's more liberal brother Constantine on the throne. Nearly a dozen of the Decembrists' leaders had been closely associated with the Russian American Company, especially the romantic poet Kondraty Ryleyev, the driving force behind the radical Northern Society and one of the Decembrists' ringleaders.[6] At the time of their arrest Ryleyev and two other conspirators lived and worked at the Company's St Petersburg headquarters on the Moika Canal. Ryleyev was the RAC's office manager and had arranged secret meetings of the plotters at the Company's office after hours – perhaps even under the stern gaze of Rezanov's portrait in the boardroom. During the inquisition following the abortive uprising the Tsar asked a suspect where he worked, and when the latter replied, 'At the Russian American Company,' Nicholas I snorted, 'And that's a fine company you have assembled there.'

The Decembrists' connection to the RAC was more than just coincidental. Many Russian reformers of the era had had their eyes opened to their country's shortcomings by travelling abroad.[7] A generation of

Russian officers had criss-crossed Europe during the Napoleonic Wars, and when they occupied Paris in 1814 had seen the contrast between post-republican France and feudal Russia at first hand.[*] In the same way, a generation of young naval officers had travelled around the world on RAC business. The Company headquarters also attracted bright and questing young men keen to travel and learn foreign languages. Many young officers returned from the colonies with heads full of radical ideas – like Rezanov, who had urged the Company to transform its colonies into communities of property-owning entrepreneurs in his 1806 manifesto. In thinking how the affairs of Russian America might be improved, men like Ryleyev also turned their thoughts to reform of their homeland.

The Decembrist rebellion not only tainted the RAC with treason by association but was also the cause of an epochal reverse for the Company and for Russia. In 1821, after years of civil war, Mexico finally gained its independence from Spain. In 1827 the new nation began making diplomatic overtures to Russia, offering to allow the RAC's claim to parts of Alta California in exchange for the Tsar's recognition of the Mexican Republic. RAC General Manager Baron Ferdinand von Wrangel strongly supported the idea. But the Company had fallen out of royal favour, and Nicholas I, who styled himself Europe's arch-reactionary, refused to countenance recognizing the Mexican anti-monarchist rebels. Russia's chance to gain a slice of California – probably including the area where gold was struck in 1849 – from the disintegrating Spanish empire was lost for ever. One wonders if Rezanov, had he lived, might have talked the Tsar into a different decision.

From Rezanov's death onward, it seemed, Russia never missed an opportunity to miss an opportunity in the New World. Company revenues declined, and corruption and the dead hand of state control took their toll. By the time of the outbreak of the Crimean War in 1853 it was clear that the Russian navy was not powerful enough to defend Russia's own Pacific coast, let alone its further-flung possessions in

---

[*] The occupiers' impatience with Parisian waiters gave rise to the term bistro, from the Russian '*Bistro!*' – 'Fast!'

Alaska. A British squadron bombarded Petropavlovsk on Kamchatka, though the force failed to take the fortress, and Britain established two crown Colonies on Alaska's doorstep – Vancouver Island (1849) and British Colombia (1858). Royal Navy ships cruised the Inside Passage to New Archangel and beyond with impunity. Tsar Alexander II decided that Russian America would inevitably be lost in the event of a future war with Britain and in 1859 instructed his ambassador in London to offer to sell the territory to the British. Lord Palmerston, newly-elected for a second term of office, decided that the fledgling provinces of Canada already had plenty of uncharted wilderness to deal with and declined the offer.

Alexander simultaneously approached the Americans, but the United States was sliding into its own civil war and had no interest in acquiring even more land. Only in March 1867 did Alexander's energetic emissary to the United States, Eduard de Stoeckl, * manage to reopen negotiations with Secretary of State William Seward. The two men haggled all night over cigars – a contemporary painting depicts Stoeckl standing in front of a giant globe, gesticulating – and an agreement was finally signed at 4 a.m. on 30 March 1867, with the purchase price set at $7.2 million, or about two cents per acre.[8] It took Congress more than a year to approve the funds – it was busy attempting to impeach President Andrew Jackson – but Stoeckl, assisted by hefty bribes to recalcitrant representatives, eventually got his way. The cheque for the full sum, drawn on Riggs Bank of Washington, DC, was finally issued on 1 August 1868.

The handover ceremony took place on the hill of Sitka, site of the original Tlingit village, on 18 October 1867. The last moments of Russian rule proceeded in much the same spirit of incompetence and misadventure as the previous eighty years of Russian administration. 'Now they started to pull the [Russian double-headed] eagle down, but – whatever had gone into its head – it only came down a little bit, and then entangled its claws around the spar so that it could not be pulled down any further,' wrote Toomas Ahllund, a Finnish blacksmith who witnessed the ceremony.

---

* The Constantinople-born son of an Austrian diplomat and a Levantine Italian.

A Russian soldier was therefore ordered to climb up the spar and disentangle it, but it seems that the eagle cast a spell on his hands, too – for he was not able to arrive at where the flag was, but instead slipped down without it. The next one to try was not able to do any better; only the third soldier was able to bring the unwilling eagle down to the ground. While the flag was brought down, music was played and cannons were fired off from the shore; and then while the other flag was hoisted the Americans fired off their cannons from the ships equally many times.[9]

The ceremony is repeated every year on the anniversary of the handover, which is now Alaska Day. It's a touching event, part small-town American pageant and part slightly confused tribute to the territory's Russian past. Sikta's fire trucks, Forest Ranger jeeps and National Guard Humvees trundle past St Michael's Orthodox cathedral, followed by high school and military bands playing patriotic American music. The crowd files up to the top of the Castle Hill, site of Baranov's leaky hut and later fortified with ramparts and cannon bearing the Russian double-headed eagle, which are still there. Local historical re-enactors in the dark blue uniforms of the Union army represent the new American authorities. A more motley group in striped naval shirts and rabbit-fur hats stands in for the Russians, led by a huge bearded fellow in a scarlet frock coat who plays the Russian commissioner, Captain Aleksei Peshchurov. Drums roll. The flag of the Russian American Company is lowered and the American one raised. The National Guard fires salutes from rifles. The dean of St Michael's, an Orthodox priest born of Russian émigré parents in Venezuela, says some prayers in English. Alaska's former governor, Sarah Palin, dressed in a bright North Face anorak against the driving rain, grins and waves. The National Guard band strikes up the 'Star-Spangled Banner' and almost everyone in the crowd stands to attention, hands on hearts.

Again, it turned out, Russia sold up at the wrong moment. In 1897 a record gold strike was made on the Yukon River, which runs from modern Canada into Alaska. But it was Alaska's new Yankee masters, not Russia, which profited from the Klondike gold rush. Rezanov had been proved right – both about the fantastic promise of the lands of California and the Pacific north-west, and about Russia's failure to rise to the challenge of the New World.

Friends and Enemies

For most of the gentlemen of the *Nadezhda* and the *Neva,* the round-the-world voyage marked the beginning of a glittering career. 'We already have a horror of the smeared vapour smoke that, after our return, will appear in print,' wrote Löwenstern, referring to the number of scribblers on board.[10] He was right: Langsdorff, Lisiansky, Krusenstern and Tilesius all wrote bestselling accounts of the voyage, published in London and St Petersburg, which established their fame as naturalists and ethnographers across Europe.[11]

Langsdorff returned to Brazil as Russian ambassador in 1813 and spent the rest of his life there leading expeditions and cataloguing the country's flora and fauna. Löwenstern had predicted that 'Rezanov will not be deficient, through written lies, of confusing everything even more than he spoiled irreparably by his behavior and certainly will not refrain from decorating himself with others' words and others' achievements. There will be so much written, smeared, invented, and lied in this way that Krusenstern's description of the voyage will be doubted if he tells the truth.'[12] But in this he was mistaken: Rezanov's lengthy diary of the voyage and his detailed account of the Japanese debacle – both in fact rather sober and free of invective against his shipmates – remained unpublished until the 1980s.[13]

Oddly it was Fyodor Tolstoy who became the most famous of the circumnavigators in their own lifetime. Despite – or perhaps because of – his boasting, his duelling, his gambling and his outrageous Gypsy wife, Tolstoy became a social lion.[14] Society dubbed him Tolstoy *Amerikanets* – Tolstoy the American, though the closest he ever got to America was Hawaii – and he dined out on tall stories of his adventures in the South Seas for the rest of his life.[15] This violent and charismatic man also served as the model for several fictional anti-heroes. Alexander Pushkin immortalized him as the duellist Zaretsky, friend of Evgeny Onegin:

'Zaretsky, sometime king of brawls,
And hetman of the gaming halls.
Arch-rake, pothouse tribuna persona . . .'[16]

It is the fictional Zaretsky who eggs Vladimir Lensky on to challenge his friend Onegin to a pointless duel in which Lensky is killed. Tolstoy was also the model for the evildoer Repetilov in the diplomat and playwright Alexander Griboyedov's 1825 play *Woe from Wit*: 'Nocturnal Bandit and duellist . . . some kind of demon;/ With bloodshot eyes and burning face . . .'

Tolstoy's famous nephew Lev, born in 1828, knew his crazy uncle as a child and in later life immortalized him as the hero of his 1856 short story 'Two Hussars'. 'A gambler, duellist and libertine – but a real Hussar!' There is another, less flattering, portrait in *War and Peace*: the cruel and bloodthirsty duellist Dolokhov, who fights Pierre Bezukhov. Dolokhov shares the *Amerikanets's* name and patronymic – Fyodor Ivanovich – as well as his 'handsome, insolent eyes'.

Many of the other members of the expedition also prospered, if less spectacularly than Tolstoy. By 1820 no fewer than eight of the twenty-two men who had sat down at the *Nadezhda*'s company table had become generals, senators or admirals. A string of geographical features scattered around the world are named for them. Lisiansky holds the record: no fewer than eight islands, bays, rivers, peninsulas from Okhotsk to Alaska bear his name. Krusenstern (Cape Krusenstern in Alaska) became an admiral, as did Makar Ratmanov (Cape Ratmanov in the Kerguelen Islands, off South Africa). Fabian Gottlieb von Bellinghausen (the Bellinghausen Sea off Antarctica) discovered and mapped the Antarctic and also became an admiral. Moritz von Kotzebue was appointed to the Russian Senate as representative for Warsaw. His brother Otto (Kotzebue Sound, the city of Kotzebue, Alaska) stayed in the navy and led two round-the-world expeditions of his own. Hermann Karl von Friderici, cartographer and astronomer to Rezanov's embassy, rose to be a general of infantry.

Second Lieutenant Pyotr Golovachev's fate was a less happy one. After Rezanov's departure for Kodiak, Golovachev became the target of the Great Cabin's collective bullying. During his protracted feud with the captain Rezanov had on at least two occasions offered command of the *Neva* to Golovachev – and Golovachev, fatally for his reputation among his shipmates, had accepted.[17] His attempted lese-majesty was not forgiven. Golovachev was cold-shouldered, taunted and ostracized by turns until he lost his mind.

'Several times he said to the sailors, "All but one of us will arrive home well,"'[18] noted Löwenstern as Golovachev became more depressed and fatalistic. At Canton, in a pathetic bid to regain popularity, he bought all his messmates expensive presents – tortoiseshell boxes and decorated gourds – and had their names engraved or embossed on them. But his mental state deteriorated steadily and, like Rezanov before him, he spent much of his time in his cabin writing denunciations of his shipmates. 'Recognize! Captain, Espenberg, Horner, Tilesius and Romberg – that beginning in Kamchatka you have wished my death and promised me death in the Straits of Sunda.'[19] On several occasions Golovachev announced that he was going to kill himself, dramatically forgiving his fellow officers for their transgressions and retiring to his cabin with loaded pistols. While the *Nadezhda* was docked at the island of St Helena in the mid-Atlantic he finally did it, shooting himself in the head while most of his fellow officers were on shore.

He left a sheaf of mad letters. To Krusenstern he wrote, 'I will continue, still groaning, to bear your revenge and evil until the unfortunate moment when all is clear. Yours, Golovachev.' To Ratmanov, 'Tyrant of humanity! You owe me 29 rubles. Keep them . . . Farewell, you monster.' To Tilesius, 'You wrote against me and tried to blacken my character . . . You are at fault for my death.'[20] Golovachev asked that a small portrait bust he had had made of himself in Canton be given to Rezanov – who, unbeknown to him, was already dead. He addressed a final, sealed, packet of letters to the Tsar with a request that he order them read aloud in front of the ship's company. The dutiful Krusenstern – who had wept when he read the suicide's denunciation of him – did so, though the Tsar wisely burned the letters unread and ordered all controversies with Rezanov to be forgotten.[21]

Fyodor Brinkin, who had been Krusenstern's family doctor in their native Estonia, also killed himself – by poisoning in St Petersburg soon after his return from the voyage. It is not known what drove him to it.[22] The artist Stepan Kurliantsev failed to interest the world in his genius, and died destitute in 1822; the Academy of Arts refused to buy his sketches from the voyage of discovery and they have been lost.[23]

Perhaps the strangest fate of any of Rezanov's associates befell Khvostov and Davydov. The government exonerated them both after the debacle of the Hokkaido raids and their subsequent imprisonment in Okhotsk. Nonetheless, and perhaps understandably, neither returned to the Company's service or to Russian America. In 1809 they bumped into John D'Wolf by chance on the street in St Petersburg. D'Wolf, now a successful Rhode Island shipowner, was in town to offload a cargo of American cloth. The delighted American immediately dragged his old shipmates to Langsdorff's rooms for a convivial dinner. The four men drank heavily late into the night and parted with warm embraces and tears.[24] They would never meet again, for on their way home Khvostov and Davydov fell in the Neva while trying to cross an open bridge and both drowned. Eyewitnesses reported that they had attempted to jump onto a passing barge from the Trinity Bridge, which then, as now, opened at night to allow shipping to pass. Their bodies were never recovered from the fast-flowing water.[25]

Derzhavin, who seems to have penned an ode for every twist of Rezanov's strange story, wrote a poem 'In Memory of Davydov and Khvostov'. It is perhaps a too-grand epitaph for men with such chequered careers, and certainly makes no mention of Khvostov's drunken threats to bombard Sitka. But Derzhavin's elegy is a measure of the reverence in which St Petersburg society held its mariners after the triumph of the expedition.

> They, like the eagles' chicks sent by Zeus to fly around the Earth
> To know her dimensions, surprised the world . . .
> You did not mount the chariot of happiness,
> But Russians will not forget your travels' great fame,
> As the Cooks and Nelsons are not forgotten
> And the mind of Newton, and the Age of Alexander.[26]

Rezanov left a more ambiguous legacy. The Tsar had clearly been offended by the hysterical tone of Rezanov's angry letter from Kamchatka, and snubbed him by never writing again. Alexander also lavished praise for the success of the round-the-world voyage on Krusenstern when the *Nadezhda* returned to St Petersburg in August 1806. News of the Khvostov–Davydov raids on Hokkaido ordered by Rezanov further tarnished his memory. Derzhavin, ever loyal, stuck up for him: 'Rezanov died from all the unpleasantness caused by his jealous subordinates,' he wrote.

After news of Rezanov's demise reached St Petersburg the Tsar magnanimously confirmed his son Pyotr as a royal page. Sadly, young Pyotr's glittering start in life availed him little: he died of fever at the age of twelve. His younger sister Olga did better, marrying St Petersburg's chief of police[27] and inheriting the Okunev estates in Pskov, as well as a handsome chunk of the Russian American Company. But she died in childbirth, just as her mother Anna had died bearing her, at the age of twenty-six.[28]

With characteristic inefficiency, it was not until the 1830s that the Company got around to putting up a monument to Rezanov in Krasnoyarsk. But when they did, it was, at a staggering 100,000 rubles, the most lavish gravestone the city had ever seen. Pre-Revolutionary photographs show it to have been a pompous, neoclassical affair, an urn on a large pedestal surrounded by stone wreaths and carved texts. The tomb, as well as the cathedral where it stood, was demolished in 1932 to make way for a new cultural centre for the city's aircraft engineers. The city repented its philistinism in 2007 and erected a replica of the original monument, though Rezanov's actual remains have been lost. Krasnoyarsk is a boom town today, one of the centres of Siberia's giant oil and gas industry, and oil money paid for a large new plaza named for Rezanov as well as a handsome bronze statue on a porphyry plinth depicting him in full chamberlain's uniform and sword. Rezanov visited the minor Company entrepôt of Krasnoyarsk only three times in his life, each time en route to somewhere else. Nonetheless it is here that Rezanov has his greatest physical monument, gazing masterfully over a vast sea of Siberian forest.

Conchita

It was Conchita Arguello who was the real victim of Rezanov's untimely death, and of his ambition. She waited in full faith that he would return until 1808, when Russian otter hunters brought disturbing rumours that Rezanov had died on the road to St Petersburg. 'When Don Luis Antonio eventually told [his sister] what he had heard, Concha laughed it off regardless of how she felt within, and no one suspected how this rumour affected her life,' recalled Sister Vincentia. 'She made herself believe that such a rumour would not and could not discourage her. She doubled and redoubled her prayers and hopes . . . knowing that in the final analysis the Great Comforter alone would take care of all of them – of Nikolai and of her.'[29]

But as the years passed, the realization that death had separated them must have grown into a grim certainly. Conchita followed her father from San Francisco to the much larger settlement of Santa Barbara when he was promoted to *comandante* there in 1807, and later to Monterrey when he became governor of Alta California after the death of Don José Arrillaga in July 1814. The next year, still with his unmarried daughter in tow, Don José Dario became governor of Baja California. By 1818 Conchita was at Loreto, Mexico, and she wrote to her brother Don Luis Antonio that she was being wooed by an American, one James Wilcox Smith, also known as Don Santiago, who had even agreed to convert to Catholicism. She refused him, despite, as she says, the knowledge that 'I might have saved his soul' by converting him.[30]

She told Sister Vincentia that 'busybodies far and wide strongly urged her to marry, and the constant pressure was almost unbearable'. It was certainly highly unusual for a gentlewoman of her status and beauty to remain unmarried, yet Conchita chose to remain loyal to the memory of her dead fiancé. She confided to Vincentia that she 'could have married several times. Without exception, the men who sought my hand were worthy and honourable. After much delibera-tion and prayer I concluded that I could not and would not be joined in marriage to one whom I did not love . . . I felt that a certain lasting loyalty was demanded of me by a Higher Power – a loyalty to Nikolai and myself!'

Don José Dario finally retired from government service in 1822, the same year his son Don Luis – who had entertained the Rezanov party when they first arrived – became Alta California's first native-born governor. Conchita's father took her with him into retirement in Guadalajara, where he died in 1828. After the death of her mother the following year, Concha returned to California and, donning the dark nun's habit of the Third Lay Order of St Francis, busied herself caring for the sick, teaching scripture to the natives and performing other good works.[31]

The English traveller and merchant Sir George Simpson, governor-general of the Hudson's Bay Company, met Conchita in 1842.[32]

> Not withstanding the ungracefulness of her conventual costume and the ravages of an interval of time which had tripled her years we could still discover in her face and figure, in her manners and conversation the remains of those charms which had won for the youthful beauty Rezanov's love and Langsdorff's equally enthusiastic admiration . . . Though Dona María de Concepción apparently loved to dwell on the story of her blighted affections, yet, strange to say, she did not know now until we mentioned it to her the immediate cause of the Chancellor's sudden death.[33]

Conchita asked Simpson to copy out the parts of Langsdorff's book that pertained to her story.

When a Dominican convent was founded at Monterrey in 1851 Conchita joined as a novice, and on 13 April 1852 she took her perpetual vow as Sor María Dominga, becoming California's first nun. The thirteen-year-old novice Vincentia Salgado became her pupil and protégée. Sister Vincentia recalled that Conchita was 'far from being a moping, whining malcontent bemoaning her fate or indulging in self-pity. True, Concha carried about her an air of wistfulness, which was but the outward reflection of a heart that was wearied with life's burdens and a soul that was well acquainted with grief.' But at the same time Conchita was at all times pleasant, joyous and exceptionally happy in her Convent life . . . Once, in my childlike innocence, I cautiously asked: 'Sister, I heard that you could have been a great lady at the Russian Court!' Concha was silent for a moment and then slowly and deliberately, in a very low, well-modulated voice, said: 'Yes, Vinnie, today I am in a very beautiful Court making my way towards Heaven. I am a real Princess with Jesus as my Spouse and King. Nothing in this whole wide world could make me more content or more happy.[34]

The order moved to Benicia, on the northern shore of San Francisco Bay, in 1854, and Conchita died there on 23 December of that year.[35] Her gravestone – as María Dominga Arguello – survives in the nuns' graveyard. A rose bush grows next to it.

Conchita had been born a subject of His Most Catholic Majesty at a time when the non-native population of Alta California was less than 5,000. She died a citizen of the United States of America, after the state of California had been admitted to the Union in 1850, its population swollen to 300,000 and her home town of San Francisco transformed from a backwater of a dying empire into a boom town of a boisterous new republic.

The Legend of Rezanov and Conchita

Rezanov's unlikely journey to literary immortality began with Francis Bret Harte, a writer of Western adventure stories and poems, who was the first to fictionalize the tragic love story of Rezanov and Conchita.[36] Harte penned the poem 'Conception de Arguello' for the *Atlantic Monthly* in March 1872.[37] Harte took the story – and the erroneous identification of Rezanov as a count – from George Simpson's *Narrative of a Voyage Around the world 1841–2* published in London and Philadelphia in 1847.

Till beside the brazen cannon the betrothed bade adieu,
And from sallyport and gateway north the Russian eagles flew.
Long beside the deep embrasures, where the brazen cannon are,

Did they wait the promised bridegroom and the answer of the Czar;
Day by day on wall and bastion beat the hollow, empty breeze,–
Day by day the sunlight glittered on the vacant, smiling seas:
Week by week the near hills whitened in their dusty leather cloaks,–
Week by week the far hills darkened from the fringing plain of oaks;
Till the rains came, and far breaking, on the fierce southwester toss'd,
Dashed the whole long coast with color, and then vanished, and were lost.
So each year the seasons shifted – wet and warm, and drear and dry,
Half a year of clouds and flowers, half a year of dust and sky.
Still it brought no ship nor message – brought no tidings, ill or meet,
For the statesmanlike Commander, for the daughter fair and sweet.
Yet she heard the varying message, voiceless to all ears beside:
'He will come,' the flowers whispered; 'Come no more,' the dry hills sighed.
Still she found him with the waters lifted by the morning breeze,–
Still she lost him with the folding of the great white-tented seas;
Until hollows chased the dimples from her cheeks of olive brown,
And at times a swift, shy moisture dragged the long sweet lashes down;
Or the small mouth curved and quivered as for some denied caress,
And the fair young brow was knitted in an infantine distress.

The poem ends with Simpson, visiting San Francisco, mentioning the death of Rezanov forty years before and asking after his Spanish fiancée – who is, unbeknown to him, in the banqueting hall.

'Lives she yet?' A deathlike silence fell on banquet, guests, and hall,
And a trembling figure rising fixed the awestruck gaze of all.
Two black eyes in darkened orbits gleamed beneath the nun's white
    hood;
Black serge hid the wasted figure, bowed and stricken where it stood.
'Lives she yet?' Sir George repeated. All were hushed as Concha drew
Closer yet her nun's attire. 'Señor, pardon, she died, too!'

Such an epic love story could not escape the prolific pen of Gertrude Atherton, the grande dame of Californian writers. Atherton was born in San Francisco in 1857 and produced over sixty romantic novels before her death in 1948, mostly on American historical themes. She developed a special interest in the picturesque and romantic life of the Spanish colonial period. One of her best-known books was *Before the Gringo Came*, later reissued as *The Splendid Idle Forties: Stories of Old California*. Photographs of her in middle age show a formidable woman with towering hair, a monumentally corseted bust and a faraway look in her eyes.

Atherton met Oscar Wilde on a visit to London and disliked him thoroughly. She wrote that he symbolized 'the decadence, the loss of virility that must follow over-civilization'. In Rezanov she imagined she had found Wilde's opposite: as she wrote in her novel *Rezanov* (1906), he 'was by far the finest specimen of a man the Californians had ever beheld . . . with an air of highest breeding and repose, he looked both a man of the great world and an intolerant leader of men'. Conchita was, as one might anticipate, drawn as the symbolic flower of innocent Spanish beauty. 'Concha's cheeks were as pink as the Castilian roses that grew before the kitchen door and were quivering at the moment under the impassioned caroling of a choir of larks. Her black eyes were full of dancing lights, like the imprisoned flecks of sun under the rose bush.' Atherton decorously made her heroine sixteen, rather than the fifteen years and two months Conchita actually was when she became engaged to Rezanov.

The novel can only be described as fascinatingly bad. The epic first sentence is irresistible, a stylistic and informational tour de force which gallops on for an entire paragraph.

As the little ship that had three times raced with death sailed past the majestic headlands and into the straits of San Francisco on that brilliant April morning of 1806, Rezanov forgot the bitter humiliations, the mental and physical torments the deprivations and dangers of the last three years; forgot those harrowing months in the harbour of Nagasaki when the Russian bear had caged his tail in the presence of eyes aslant; his dismay at Kamchatka when he had been forced to send home another to vindicate his failure, and to remain in the Tsar's incontiguous and barbarous northeastern possessions as representative of His Imperial Majesty, and plenipotentiary of the company his own genius had created; forgot the year of loneliness and hardship – and peril in whose jaws the bravest are impotent; forgot even his pitiable crew, diseased when he left Sitka, who had filled the Juno with their groans and laments; and the bells of youth, long still, rang in his soul once more.[38]

It was in Russia that Rezanov got his most serious literary treatment. Andrei Voznesensky was a protégé of Boris Pasternak and one of the young poets whose edgy work tested the limits of Khruschev's post-Stalin thaw.[39] In 1970[40] he penned an epic poem on the Rezanov story, whimsically entitled 'Avos! A description, in sentimental documents, verse and prayers of the glorious misfortunes of Kamerheer Nikolai Rezanov'.* 'Avos!' is an odd period piece, sentimental and postmodern at the same time. Voznesensky mixes quotes from Rezanov's and Baranov's actual dispatches with metaphysics and musings on everlasting love. 'When we at last give up the ghost,/ And become at last stars, or manure,/ Poets will write their lyrics about our story . . .'

In the poem Rezanov makes passionate love to Conchita – 'two body-crosses entwined in the night' – and the poor girl ends up pregnant. But, historical liberties aside, 'Avos!' is a rather moving work, a poignant paean from a late Soviet generation which was tightly penned in, physically and intellectually, to a Russian ancestor, who was free to travel and conquer foreign worlds. 'Forgive us, we were born too soon,' Voznesensky's Rezanov says. 'Wishing for the impossible,/ The best of us quit halfway,/ We are the children of half travelled roads,/ Our name is "Halfway"/ Forgive us.'[41] The poet puts the words in the mouth of a nineteenth-century aristocrat, but the sentiment is the authentic lament of 1970s Soviet dissidents for being born too soon to see change in their homeland.

In 1978 rock composer Alexei Rybnikov and theatrical producer Mark Zakharov teamed up to adapt 'Avos!' into a rock opera inspired by *Jesus Christ Superstar*. Everything about *Junona i Avos* was politically daring, from the glorification of a tsarist aristocrat on an imperialist mission to Rybnikov's use of Church liturgy. Vladimir Vasiliyev, later

---

* It took its title from the *Avos*, the single-masted sloop that Baranov was building in Sitka in the winter of 1805–6 and which Davydov later sailed on his ill-fated raid on Japan.

director of the Bolshoi Ballet and the premier dancer of his generation, arranged the choreography.[42]

The show premiered in July 1981. Moscow audiences had never seen anything like it – 'decadent' Western hard rock mixed with Russian Orthodox chants, Russia's imperial flag raised on stage, a chorus of 'Hallelujah' and a message of cross-cultural love and harmony. 'O you inhabitants of the twentieth century, your century is drawing to its close, is it not time to answer why peoples cannot live in agreement?' asks a guitar-strumming narrator. 'Agreement' – *soglasiye* in Russian – had the added frisson of being a buzzword often used by Western leaders urging détente with Russia. 'The Russian Empire is a prison,' sings a chorus of the *Juno*'s sailors, prophetically. 'Abroad is foreign to us, but we are bored with home,/ Our generation has been unformed, we slouch towards truth alone.'

It is hard to overstate just how extraordinary an impression the rock opera made on me when I first saw it in 1986. Everything else in late-Soviet Moscow operated in a weird dimension of frozen time, from the dip-pens and blotters in the post offices to men's square-cut 1950s suits and womens' flowery housecoats. And then there was *Junona I Avos*. I hated it, actually, since as a bookish and bespectacled young chap I didn't like pop music much and found the production loud and shocking. But it was undoubtedly radically modern. The perspex stage sloped, the costumes randomly mixed 1806 with 1986, and members of the backstage crew joined the actors on stage to sing the final chorus.

But the rest of the audience exploded with enthusiasm. Soviet audiences were always more emotional than their Western counterparts, but this was beyond anything I had ever seen. The standing ovation continued for fifteen minutes, and half the auditorium appeared to have brought flowers for the stars Nikolai Karachensov, who played Rezanov, and Elena Shagina as Conchita.[43] Small wonder that when the record finally came out on the state Melodiya label the album sold ten million copies.*

---

* Amazingly the original Zakharov production is still going, making it the second-longest-running stage show in history. *The Fantasticks*, an off-Broadway romantic comedy, holds the record with a 42-year run between 1960 and 2002, but *Junona I Avos* is set to take the crown in 2023.

Thanks to Voznesensky and Rybnikov, Nikolai Rezanov and Conchita Arguello are famous in Russia: they have entered the pantheon of the great tragic couples of its modern literature. Rezanov has become, to his millions of admirers, a romantic hero torn between love and duty. Conchita is the woman who sacrificed her life to the love of a man, waiting for him long after all others would have given up.*

Silent suffering, enforced separation, impossible dreams, love torn apart by the currents of the world – these are themes which resonate deep in the Russian psyche. Whatever the personal shortcomings of Rezanov the man, however ephemeral his imperial legacy, he has at least bequeathed this to his homeland: an ideal of epic failure, a glorious dream of love and empire which was wrecked on the shores of cruel circumstance.

---

* 'Wait', as the great Second World War poet Konstantin Simonov put it, 'when yesterdays are past and others are forgot …/ Wait, when those with whom you wait doubt if I'm alive;/ Wait, when from that far-off place, letters don't arrive./ Wait until the end!'

Notes

Prologue

1   M. V. Lomonosov, tr. by the author, *Pyotr Veliky* in *M. V. Lomonosov, Izbranniye Proizvedeniya*, Biblioteka Poeta, Leningrad 1986, p. 280.

2   Norbert R. Adami, *Eine schwierige Nachbarschaft: Die Geschichte der russisch-japanischen Beziehungen* (*A Difficult Neighbourhood: the history of Russo-Japanese Relations*), vol. 1, Munich 1990, pp. 83–91, quoted in Victoria Moessner, 'The First Russian Ambassador to Japan Nikolai Petrovich Rezanov (1764–1807) as portrayed in contemporary German language sources', unpublished article, 2007.

3   Georg Heinrich von Langsdorff, *Voyages and Travels in Various Parts of the World during the years 1803–1807*, Henry Colburn, London 1813 (facsimile edition Da Capo Press, New York 1968), vol. 2, p. 158.

4   Ibid., p. 163.

5   Ibid., p. 176.

6   Ibid., p. 175.

7   Only one portrait of Rezanov survives, painted in the summer of 1803 between him receiving the Order of St Anne first class from Emperor Alexander I and his departure on the round-the-world voyage. For much of the nineteenth century the portrait hung in pride of place in the boardroom of the Russian American Company on the Moika Canal in St Petersburg. It is in now in the collection of the State Historical Museum in Moscow. Rezanov's death mask and some sketches made of him after his death in Krasnoyarsk would give us a better idea of what Rezanov really looked like, but alas they are lost.

8   Langsdorff to Krusenstern, Tobolsk, 20 December 1807, Archive of the Academy of Sciences, St Petersburg, Fond 31, 1, 11.

9   Langsdorff to Horner, Tobolsk, 7 February 1808, Zentralbibliothek Zürich, Horner-Nachlass, Ms.M.5,60. Quoted in Moessner, 'The First Russian Ambassador to Japan'.

10   Ralph H. Vigil, 'The Hispanic Heritage and the Borderlands', *Journal of San Diego History*, vol. 19, no. 3 (summer 1973).

11   Langsdorff, *Voyages,* p. 180.

12   Ibid., p. 160.

13   Ibid., p. 161.

Introduction

1   Andrei Voznesensky, 'Avos!', *Selected Poems of Andrei Voznesensky*, Random House, New York 2000.

2   Gwenn A. Miller, *Kodiak Kreol: Communities of Empire in Early Russian America*, Cornell University Press, Ithaca 2010, p. 89.

3   Like the British Captain George Vancouver, who had surveyed the Pacific coast of America a few years before.

4   Nikolai Rezanov, *The Rezanov Voyage to Nueva California in 1806,* Thomas Russell, San Francisco 1926, p. 39.

5   Ibid., p. 46.

6   Ibid., p. 45.

1. Man and Nature

1   Simon Dixon, *Catherine the Great*, Profile Books, London 2009, p. 42.

2   Ibid., p. 14.

3   Ibid., p. 42.

4   Letter to Frau Bielke, Ibid., p. 211.

5   Ibid., p. 43.

6   Ibid., p. 258.

7   'Transport du piédestal de la statue de Pierre le Grand', *La Nature Magazine*, second semester 1882.

8   See Engraving by A. K. Melnikov of the 1782 drawing by A. P. Davydov *Opening of the Monument to Peter the Great on Senate Square, St Petersburg*, State Hermitage St Petersburg.

9   Dixon, *Catherine the Great*, p.225.

10   Anna Reid, *The Shaman's Coat: A Native History of Siberia*, Walker Books, New York 2002, p.16.

11   Leonid Sverdlov, 'Nikolai Petrovich Rezanov (1764–1807): Khudozhestvenny Obraz I Istorichaskaya Lichnost', *Moskovsky Zhurnal*, no. 8 (257), Moscow 2012.

12   George Vernadsky, *The Mongols and Russia*, Yale University Press, 1953, pp. 385–90.

13   Douglas D. C. Chambers, 'Evelyn, John (1620–1706)', *Oxford Dictionary of National Biography*, Oxford University Press, 2004.

14 Hugh Chisholm (ed.) 'Münnich, Burkhard Christoph', *Encyclopædia Britannica*, Cambridge University Press, 1911.

15 Franz A. J. Szabo, *The Seven Years' War in Europe 1756–1763*, Longman, 2007, p. 2.

16 Igor Nikiforovich Yermolaev, 'Pskovsky Chinovnik Nikolai Rezanov i ego "Yunona i Avos"', *Pskovsaya Provintsiya*, Pskov April 2004.

2. The Final Frontier

1 Konstantin Mochulsky, *Dostoevsky: His Life and Work*, Princeton University Press, 1971, p. 646.

2 Prince A. Lobanov-Rostovsky, *Russia and Asia*, Macmillan, New York 1933, pp. 33–8.

3 Reid, *Shaman's Coat*, p. 26.

4 Ibid., p. 16.

5 G. Patrick March, *Eastern Destiny: Russia in Asia and the North Pacific*, Praeger, New York 1996, p. 20.

6 Lobanov-Rostovsky, *Russia and Asia*, pp. 33–8.

7 Raymond H. Fisher, *The Russian Fur trade 1550 –1700,* University of California Press, Berkeley 1943, pp. 29 –33.

8 Quoted in Samuel Purchas, *Hakluytus Posthumus or Purchas his Pilgrimes, contayning a History of the World in Sea Voyages and Lande Travells, by Englishmen and others*, London 1625, reprinted J. MacLehose and sons 1905–7, vol. 4, p. 215.

9 Vernadsky, *Mongols and Russia* pp. 385–90.

10 James Forsyth, *A History of the Peoples of Siberia: Russia's North Asian Colony 1581–1910*, Cambridge University Press, 1998, p. 42.

11 Reid, *Shaman's Coat,* p. 64.

12 Mikhail Khodarkovsky, 'Russia's Orient – Ignoble Savages and Unfaithful Subjects', *The Russian Orient: Imperial Strategies and Oriental Encounters*, Indiana University Press, Bloomington 1997, p. 11.

13 Basil Dmitryshkin, E. A. P. Crownhart-Vaughan and Thomas Vaughan, *Russia's Conquest of Siberia 1558–1700*, Oregon Historical Society, Portland 1985, vol. 1, p. 198.

14 Miller, *Kodiak Kreol*, p. 13.

15 Ibid., p. 19.

16 March, *Eastern Destiny*, p. 27.

17 Fisher, *Russian Fur Trade*, p. 3.

18 Lydia T. Black, *Russians in Alaska, 1732–1867*, University of Alaska Press, Fairbanks 2004, p. 20.

19 Admittedly mostly a plaintive plea for back wages – 'I beat my head upon the floor, most merciful sovereign . . . I have starved and frozen for your Majesty's greater glory' – rather than news of ground-breaking exploration.

20 Reid, *Shaman's Coat*, p. 28.

21 Or at any rate in the pocket of the Pacific partially protected by the Kamchatka peninsula, the Kurile Islands and Japan now known as the Sea of Okhotsk.

22 Black, *Russians in Alaska*, p. 30.

23 Stepan Krasheninnikov, tr. James Grieve, *The History of Kamtschatka and the Karilski Islands with the Countries Adjacent*, Gloucester 1764 (facsimile edition Quadrangle Books, Chicago 1962), p. 247.

24 Elton Engstrom and Allan Engstrom, *Alexander Baranov – A Pacific Empire*, Juneau 2004, p. 4.

25 See Allan Engstrom, *Yakobi Island, the lost village of Apostolovo and the fate of the Chirikov expedition,* Allan Engstrom, Juneau 2007.

26 A 1991 Russian–Danish expedition which exhumed Bering's remains analysed teeth and bones and concluded that he did not die from scurvy. Based on analyses made in Moscow and on Steller's original report, heart failure was the likely cause of Bering's death.

27 Orcutt William Frost (ed.), *Bering: The Russian Discovery of America*, Yale University Press, New Haven 2003.

28 Their docile nature and high nutritional value proved their undoing – Steller's sea cows had been hunted to extinction by the 1780s.

29 Black, *Russians in Alaska*, p. 182.

30 Ibid., p. 187.

31 Reid, *Shaman's Coat*, p. 13.

32 Colin Thubron, *In Siberia*, Harper Perennial, London 2000, p. 114.

33 Ibid., p. 168.

34 Reid, *Shaman's Coat*, p. 41.

35 Thubron, *In Siberia*, p. 161.

3. The Court

1 For those who were not serfs, who were essentially slaves who remained the personal property of their masters. America's founding fathers also saw no paradox between their Enlightenment enthusiasms and the ownership of slaves: President Thomas Jefferson had seven children with his slave Sally Hemmings, who was also his wife's half-sister.

2 Sverdlov, 'Rezanov: Obraz I Lichnost'.

3 See www.imha.ru.

4 Quoted in Dixon, *Catherine the Great*, p. 87.

5 Yermolaev, 'Pskovsky Chinovnik Rezanov'.

6 Ibid.

7 Ibid.

8 Sverdlov, 'Rezanov: Obraz I Lichnost'.

9 Again the Pushkin thread surfaces: Chernyshev's niece Natalya Petrovna Galitzine, better known at the Russian court as Princesse Moustache, was romanticized by Pushkin under the name of the Queen of Spades in his eponymous story from 1834.

10   Robert K. Massie, *Catherine the Great: Portrait of a Woman*, Random House, New York 2011, p. 276.

11   Geoffrey Hosking, *Russia: People and Empire*, Harvard, 1997, p. 98.

12   Dixon, *Catherine the Great*, p. 169.

13   As Pushkin put it, 'Russian revolts are cruel and pointless.'

14   Massie, *Catherine the Great*, p. 430.

15   Dixon, *Catherine the Great*, p. 194.

16   Massie, *Catherine the Great*, p. 527.

17   Leonid Parfenov, *The Russian Empire*, NTV Television, 2003, episode 4.

18   Potemkin brought his military and organizational genius to bear on the affairs of the empire. His great design was to retake Constantinople for Christendom and the creation of a new Orthodox empire on the Black Sea, a dream he dubbed his Greek Project. Potemkin conquered and annexed swathes of southern Russia for the crown, and founded the great cities of Kherson and Sevastopol. In the summer of 1787 he arranged a triumphant tour of the new territories for Catherine, who was accompanied for part of her progress by the Austrian Emperor Joseph II, traveling incognito. Potemkin constructed new roads and ordered livestock moved from outlying areas so that these signs of prosperity could be visible from the Empress's carriage – the origin of the slander of 'Potemkin's villages'. An all-female regiment of sharpshooting Amazons was assembled as part of the entertainments, as well as firework displays featuring 20,000 rockets and a hillside display of 50,000 burning pots spelling the royal initials.

19   Simon Sebag Montefiore, *Potemkin: Catherine the Great's Imperial Partner*, Vintage, London 2005, p. 349.

20   20 August 1795, quoted in Ibid., p. 414.

21   Catherine to Vyazemsky, January 1764. He served until 1792. Quoted in Dixon, *Catherine the Great*, p. 134.

22   Orlando Figes, *Natasha's Dance*, Picador 2003, p. 3.

23   Sebag Montefiore, *Potemkin*, p. 425.

24   Dixon, *Catherine the Great*, p. 132.

25   Kazimierz Waliszewski, *Paul the First of Russia, the Son of Catherine the Great*, William Heineman, New York 1913, p. 143.

26   Adami, *Eine schwierige Nachbarschaft*, pp. 83–91, quoted in Moessner, 'The First Russian Ambassador to Japan'.

27   Nikolai Rezanov to Mikhail M. Buldakov, Kamchatka, 6 June 1805, quoted in Alexei Alexandrovich Istomin, 'Dva Varianta Pisma N. P. Rezanova Grafu N P Rumiantsevu ot 17/29 iyulya 1806 g. – Sravnitelno-tekhnologichesky analyz I legenda o velikoi lyubvi', *Russkoe Otkritiye Ameriki*, M, Moscow 2002.

28   John D'Wolf, *A Voyage to the North Pacific and a Journey Through Siberia More than Half a Century Ago*, Boston 1861 (facsimile edition Ye Galleon Press, Fairfield 1968), p. 30.

29   Rezanov's final instructions to Baranov quoted in Viktor Lopatnikov, 'Nikolai Rezanov', *Zolotoi Lev*, no. 127–8, RFS, Moscow 2007.

4. King of Siberia

1 30 November 1793, quoted in Wilhelm Lagus, *Eric Laxman, his Life, Voyages, Discoveries and Correspondence*, St Petersburg 1890, p. 269.

2 This remarkable Irkutsk merchantwoman was the first Russian to transcribe the folk tale *Kolobok*, about a ball of dough which rolls away from its grandparents to freedom and is eaten by a fox. Ekaterina Avdeeva-Polevaya and Alexei Polevoi, *Zapiski*, quoted in Black, *Russians in Alaska*, p. 111.

3 Natalia Shelikhova, ed. and tr. by Dawn Lea Black, Alexander Petrov and Marvin W. Falk, *Natalia Shelikhova, Russian Oligarch of Alaska Commerce*, University of Alaska Press, Fairbanks 2010, p. xvii.

4 Or possibly Trapeznikova, daughter of a wealthy merchant and Old Believer from the northern Dvina. M. I. Tsiporukha in his essay 'Odna iz Stroitelei Imperii na Tikhookeanskom Severe', *Istoriya Nauki I Tekhniki*, no. 8, Moscow 2004, pp. 34–41, and Soviet historian L. A. Sitnikov make a slightly stronger case for Kozhevin, however. See Dawn Lea Black's introduction to *Shelikhova*.

5 Under Captains Pyotr Krenitsyn and Mikhail Levashev.

6 Stephen W. Haycox, *Alaska: An American Colony*, University of Washington Press, Seattle 2002, pp. 53–8.

7 Engstrom, *Baranov*, p. 22.

8 Black, *Russians in Alaska*, p. 92.

9 See John Robson (ed.) *The Captain Cook Encyclopædia*, Chatham, London 2004, p. 62.

10 Also instead of a layer of blubber like seals they have a double coat – under layer deep and soft, upper layer coarse and waterproof. According to William Sturgis, an officer on Cook's third voyage, their pelt 'is 5 feet long 24–30 inches wide, rich jet black with a glossy surface and exhibits a silver colour when blown open'. See Lieutenant William Sturgis, ed. by S.W. Jackman, *The Journal of William Sturgis*, Sono Nis Press, Victoria 1978.

11 Black, *Russians in Alaska*, p. 93.

12 Shelikhova, *Natalia Shelikhova*, p. 34.

13 Andrei Grinev, 'Osnovatel Russkoi Ameriki (neskol'ko shtrikhov k portretu G. I. Shelikhova)', *Istoriya Peterburga*, no. 2, St Petersburg 2005.

14 Black, *Russians in Alaska*, p. 104.

15 Ibid., p. 105.

16 Mikhail I. Tsiporukha, 'Odna iz Stroitelei Imperii na Tikhookeanskom Severe', *Istoriya Nauki I Tekhniki*, no. 8, Moscow 2004, pp. 34–41.

17 Ibid., p. 34.

18 Grinev, 'Osnovatel Russkoi Ameriki'.

19 Izmailov testimony quoted in Miller, *Kodiak Kreol*, p. 38.

20 Grinev, 'Osnovatel Russkoi Ameriki'.

21 Miller, *Kodiak Kreol*, p. 19.

22 Captain Nathaniel Porlock, *A Voyage Round the World, but more particularly to the North West Coast of America*, John Stockdale, London 1798, p. 60.

23 Tsiporukha, 'Odna iz Stroitelei', p. 38.

24 Shelikhova, *Natalia Shelikhova*, p. xxxi.

25 Tsiporukha, 'Odna iz Stroitelei', p. 36.

26 Shelikhov continued to take an interest in the Kodiak children: he wrote to
Delarov, 'Do your best to teach more boys reading, writing, singing and arithmetic. Train them to be good navigators and seamen; and teach them crafts, especially
carpentry. The boys who were brought here are studying music in Irkutsk, and we
are paying the bandmaster fifty rubles for each of them per year. We are going to
send a fine band to America to you.' Quoted by Pavel A. Tikhmenev as 'Letter,
Shelikhov to Delarov, from Okhotsk, 30 August 1789,' in vol. 2 (*Documents*) of
his *History of the Russian American Company*, p. 21, citing no precise archival location because the 'letters . . . most were probably lost in the destruction of
company files after the sale of the Russian-American colonies' (Grigory Shelikhov,
tr. Marina Ramsay, Preface by Richard A. Pierce, *A Voyage to America, 1783–1786*,
Limestone Press, Kingston 1981, Preface, p. iv).

27 Shelikhova, *Natalia Shelikhova*, p. xxxv.

28 Black, *Russians in Alaska*, p. 108.

29 Ibid., p. 140.

30 Miller, *Kodiak Kreol*, p. 31.

31 30 November 1793. Lagus, *Laxman*, p. 269.

32 *Polnoye sobranye Zakonov Rossiskoi Imperii* (Complete Law Code of the Russian
Empire), St Petersburg 1830, vol. 20, no. 14,275, clauses 82–6.

33 A. V. Khrapovitskii, *Dnevnik (Diary) 18 January 1782 to 17 September 1793*,
Universitetskaya Tipografiya, Moscow 1901, p. 45.

34 Black, *Russians in Alaska*, p. 119.

35 In July 1788 Catherine signed an ukaz dispatching two navy ships to the Aleutians.
Along with instructions to map as much of Russia's new territories as possible,
Billings was also charged with investigating Biryukov's accusations of abuses by
Russian colonists. Probably unbeknown to the Admiralty board that dispatched
the expedition, Billings also happened to be a close friend of Shelikhov and his
final report was, unsurprisingly, favourable. This was not the last time that the
American Company's St Petersburg diplomacy would be scuppered by scurrilous
reports from the field.

36 The tactic of creating a web of front companies is popular among Russian busi-
nessmen competing for state tenders today.

37 Samuel and Jeremy Bentham were well-to-do brothers from Houndsditch in east
London. Samuel, a naval architect who had been apprenticed at Woolwich dock-
yard at the age of fourteen, came to Russia in 1780 to make his fortune. His break
came two years later when he was presented to Prince Potemkin, a fervent
Anglophile. The twenty-five-year-old Bentham was immediately hired and put in
charge of the construction of Potemkin's brand-new Black Sea fleet. He also
experimented with an articulated river barge, used by Catherine during her
triumphant progress through the Crimea in 1789, and with the invention that

was to be Bentham Major's greatest contribution to science, the use of watertight compartments to make safer ship hulls.

In 1785 Samuel recruited his brilliant younger brother Jeremy to Potemkin's service. Together with their father they hired Englishmen and -women to populate a modern village with factories that Potemkin planned to create in Byelorussia. 'Any clever people capable of introducing improvements in the Prince's Government might meet with good encouragement' was one of the advertisements the Benthams placed in English newspapers. 'The Prince wants to introduce the use of beer,' announced another. Milkmaids were recruited to service Potemkin's 'elegant dairy' with 'the best of butter and as many kinds of cheese as possible.' Thanks to the good offices of the banker Sutherland, Potemkin's credit was virtually limitless and the Benthams had no shortage of volunteers.

The former prime minister William Petty-FitzMaurice, first Marquess of Lansdowne, had his doubts both about Potemkin's trustworthiness and the Bentham boys' business acumen. 'Both your sons are too liberal in their temper to adopt a mercantile spirit,' Landsdowne wrote to their father, his friend Jeremiah Bentham. 'And your Sam's mind will be more occupied with fresh inventions than with calculating compound interest which the dullest man in Russia can perhaps do as well.'

Unfortunately many of the English recruits turned out to be a 'Newcastle mob, hirelings from that rabble town'. Despite Jeremy's brilliant idea of making the factories circular so that managers could supervise the workforce from one central observation point, the Byelorussian experiment failed. The milkmaids and gardener that Jeremy had taken on turned out to be woefully underqualified – the latter was a 'shameless imposter who had not even planted a single blade of grass' while 'Mamzel has not made a single cheese.'

Jeremy returned to England to turn his brilliant brain to less mundane tasks, such as designing a circular prison known as the panopticon, which was actually constructed at Millbank on the site of the modern-day Tate Britain, and formulating his 'felicific calculus' with its classification of twelve pains and fourteen pleasures by which the 'happiness factor' or 'utility' of any action might be tested. But Sam remained in Russia. He dabbled in trading English cloth across Russia's rivers from Riga on the Baltic to Kherson on the Black Sea. Naturally enough his interest turned to Russia's other waterways, the great rivers of Siberia. In 1788 Potemkin sent Samuel Bentham to Siberia with a broad-ranging commission which included commanding two battalions of troops, creating a new military engineering school in Irkutsk, discovering new lands, pursuing diplomacy with the Mongols and even 'opening trading links with Japan and Alaska'.

It is possible that Shelikhov and Bentham already knew each other from St Petersburg; they certainly spent much time together in Irkutsk. The two young men shared an imaginative enthusiasm for the potential of Siberia and the creation of a Russian maritime empire on the Pacific. The Englishman took the opportunity to travel from Irkutsk to the Chinese border-trading entrepôt of

Maimichin and beyond, to the river port of Nerchinsk, where he studied the design of Chinese junks. Shelikhov attempted to recruit Bentham to his own business, which badly needed expert naval architects and professional commanders. But he could not hope to compete with Potemkin's vast wealth and network of patronage, and Bentham was soon recalled to the Black Sea to fight the Empress's new Turkish war.

After his return to Britain Brigadier General Sir Samuel Bentham became the inspector general of works for the Royal Navy, and was responsible for the fleet that won Trafalgar.

38 In May 1797 the *North Eastern Eagle* set a company speed record, logging 600 miles in seven days en route from Okhotsk to Yakutat.

39 Shelikhova's report to 'His Radiance' Count Zubov of 18 November 1795. Shelikhova, *Natalia Shelikhova*, p. 51.

40 Black, *Russians in Alaska*, p. 114.

41 Ibid., p. 122.

42 Ibid., p. 95.

43 20 May 1795, quoted in Pavel A. Tikhmenev, tr. Dmitry Krenov, *Supplement of Some Historical Documents to the Historical Review of the Formation of the Russian American Company*, St Petersburg 1863 (reprinted by Limestone Press, Kingston 1979) vol. 2, p. 128.

5. A Nabob in St Petersburg

1 Fitzgerald Molloy, *The Russian Court in the Eighteenth Century*, Hutchinson, London 1905, p. 202.

2 Dixon, *Catherine the Great*, p. 307.

3 John T. Alexander, *Catherine the Great: Life and Legend*, Folio Society, London 1999, p. 308.

4 www.ceremonija.lv/pages/zubov.ru.php.

5 Ekaterina Romanovna Dashkova, tr. Kyril FitzLyon, *The Memoirs of Princess Dashkova*, Duke University Press, Durham 1995.

6 V. K. Napper *Odessa v Perviye Epokhi ee Sushestvovaniye*, Optiumum, Odessa 2007, p. 191.

7 Natalia Shelikhova confirmed Zubov's crucial role in a letter to Archpastor Juvenaly on 10 November 1795, after her husband's death: 'I wrote about this to His Radiance Count Platon Aleksandrovich Zubov, who has protected my company, and because of his protection, ploughmen and craftsmen were selected for the company in order for them to settle in America, along with the sending, by Your Beatitude, of the Russian Orthodox spiritual mission. I hope that His Radiance will report on that subject to Her Majesty.'

8 Engstrom, *Baranov*, p. 62.

9 Only one would ever return. Their expedition proved disastrous not only for Shelikhov but for the divines themselves. Iosaf would be appointed bishop of

Kodiak in 1799, but drowned alongside James Shields in the wreck of the *Phoenix* later that year. Hieromonk Yuvenaly, a former artillery officer, became an enthusiast of forced baptism and would be murdered by natives in 1795. Hieromonk Afanasii, a former serf, went mad and never saw his homeland again. Hieromonk Makarii, after eight years in the colonies, would make a secret dash to vent a list of bitter complaints against the company personally to the Emperor Paul. But unlike his mother Catherine, who always turned a sympathetic ear to such whistle-blowers, Tsar Paul punished Makarii for leaving his post without his superiors' authority. Archdeacons Stefan and Nektarii got into such a desperate feud with Baranov over the colonists' drinking and whoring that they locked the church at Easter, and only opened it when Baranov threatened to hang Nektarii from the bell tower. Only Novices Asaf and Herman escaped the monumental catastrophe that providence had prepared for the party. Asaf's fate is unrecorded. But Herman left the vice-ridden Kodiak in 1808 to become a hermit on nearby Spruce Island, lived until the age of seventy-seven and was later canonized as St Herman of Alaska.

10   Sverdlov, 'Rezanov: Obraz I Lichnost'.

11   Miller, *Kodiak Kreol*, p. 83.

12   Shelikhov/Pierce, *Voyage*, p. 132.

13   Miller, *Kodiak Kreol*, p. 23.

14   Rezanov, letter to the directors of the RAC from Novoarkhangelsk, 18 November 1806, Dimitryshkin, *The Russian American Colonies 1768–1867*, Oregon Historical Society, Portland 1989, p. 62.

15   Black, *Russians in Alaska*, p .111.

16   De Haro quoted in Miller, *Kodiak Kreol*, p. 49.

17   Iosaf's complaint quoted in Hieromonk Gideon, tr. with an introduction and notes by Lydia Black, *The Round the World Voyage of Hieromonk Gideon 1803–1809*, Limestone Press, Fairbanks 1989, p. 86.

18   Engstrom, *Baranov*, p. 66.

6. To China

1   Quoted in Reid, *Shaman's Coat*, p. 78.

2   Shelikhova, *Natalia Shelikhova,* p. 39.

3   ww.ru.rodovid.org (see Zapis' 625661).

4   Donald F. Lach and Edwin J. Van Kley, Asia in the Making of Europe, University of Chicago Press, Chicago 1994, vol. III, *A Century of Advance*, vol. IV, *East Asia*, pp. 1756–7.

5   Lo-Shu Fu (ed.), A documentary chronicle of Sino-Western relations, vol. 1, *1644–1820*, University of Arizona Press, Tucson 1966, p. 24.

6   Ibid., p. 332.

7   Charles William Vane, Marquis of Londonderry, *Recollections of a Tour in the North of Europe in 1836–1837*, Richard Bentley, London 1838, vol. 2, pp. 214–15.

Even at the end of the nineteenth century travellers found the sharp contrast between the two trading towns a shock. 'One moment you are in a Russian provincial village with its characteristic shops, log houses, golden domed churches, droshkies, soldiers and familiar peasant faces,' wrote the young American diplomat George Kennan in 1891. 'The next moment you pass behind the high screen that conceals the entrance to the Mongolian town and you find yourself apparently in the middle of the Chinese empire, you can hardly believe that you have not suddenly been transported on the magical carpet of the Arabian nights over a distance of a thousand miles.' George Kennan, *Siberia and the exile system*, Century, New York 1891, p. 108.

8 George Alexander Lensen, 'Early Russo-Japanese Relations', *Far Eastern Quarterly*, vol. 10, no. 1, November 1950, pp. 17–22.

9 Rezanov letter to Buldakov, quoted in Istomin, 'Dva Varianta Pisma'.

10 S. S. Shashkov, 'Istoriia Russkoi Zhenshchiny', *Sobranie sochenenii S. S. Shashkova*, Tipografiia I. N. Skorokhodova, St Petersburg 1898, p. 762.

7. Empire Builder

1 Tsiporukha, 'Odna iz Stroitelei', p. 36.

2 Ibid., p. 38.

3 Irkutsk, 11 June 1794, Shelikhova, *Natalia Shelikhova*, p. 44.

4 31 January 16 1796, Ibid., p. 34.

5 Tsiporukha, 'Odna iz Stroitelei', p. 41.

6 The same building also has a façade on ul Pestela 27. The house was bought by the Greek Prince Alexander Murusi, who rebuilt in eclectic style in 1874–7.

7 Letter to Buldakov quoted in Istomin, 'Dva Varianta Pisma'.

8 Alexei Polevoi, *Zapiski*, quoted in introduction to Shelikhov/Pierce, *Voyage*, p. 30.

9 Shelikhova, *Natalia Shelikhova*, p. 44.

10 Ibid., p51.

11 Rezanov, *Voyage to Nueva California*, p. 46.

12 Nikita Nikitich Demidov to Natalia A. Shelikhova – sent from St Petersburg on 10 December 1795, received in Irkutsk on 26 January 1796, answered on 7 February 1796. Shelikhova, *Natalia Shelikhova*, p. 67.

13 Molloy, *Russian Court*, p. 268.

8. Tsar Paul

1 Parfenov, *Russian Empire*, episode 6.

2 Ibid.

3 Captain George Vancouver, *A Voyage of Discovery to the North Pacific Ocean and Round the World in the Years 1790, 1791, 1792, 1793, 1794 and 1795*. G. G. and J. Robinson and J. Edwards, London 1798, vol. 2, pp. 502–3.

4 Ibid., pp. 500–1.

5   Rezanov, *Voyage to Nueva California*, p. 41.
6   Black, *Russians in Alaska*, p. 113.
7   Engstrom, *Baranov*, p. 63.
8   Tsiporukha, 'Odna iz Stroitelei', p. 40.
9   Yermolaev, 'Pskovsky Chinovnik Rezanov'.
10 Molloy, *Russian Court*, p. 298.
11 Ibid., p. 312.
12 St Petersburg, 18 March 1800. See Alex Zotov, 'The Failed Franco-Russian Expedition to India: Diplomatic Correspondence' on www.history-gatchina.ru and Prince S. Vorontsov's Archive, Moscow 1870–95, vol. XXIX, p. 390.
13 Waliszewski, *Paul*, p. 363.
14 Ibid., p. 379.
15 Zotov, 'Expedition to India'.

9. Russia's East India Company

1   Quoted in Konstantin Mochulsky, *Dostoevsyky, His Life and Work*, Princeton University Press, Princeton 1971, p. 646.
2   Sverdlov, 'Rezanov: Obraz I Lichnost'.
3   Clarence Manning, *Russian Influence on Early America*, NY Library Publishers, New York 1953, pp. 27–38.
4   Anthony Wild, *The East India Company, Trade and Conquest from 1600*, HarperCollins, London 2000.
5   Semen B. Okun, tr. Carl Ginsburg, Preface by Robert L. Kerner, *The Russian American Company*, Harvard University Press, Cambridge Mass. 1955, p. 50.
6   Black, *Russians in Alaska*, p. 95.
7   Gideon, *Voyage*, p. 101.
8   Black, *Russians in Alaska*, p. 155.
9   Gideon, *Voyage*, p. 99.
10 Lopatnikov, 'Nikolai Rezanov'.
11 Hermann Ludwig von Löwenstern, tr. Victoria Moessner, *The First Russian Voyage Around the World*, University of Alaska Press, Fairbanks, 2003, p. 3.
12 K. Voensky, *Posolstvo N.P. Rezanova v Yaponiyu* Russkaya Starina, Moscow 1995 No. 9-10.
13 Rezanov letter to Buldakov quoted in Gideon, *Voyage*, p. 87.
14 Ibid., p. 85.
15 Miller, *Kodiak Kreol*, p. 59.
16 Gideon, *Voyage*, p. 95.
17 S. P. Mel'gunov, *Otechestvennaya Voina I Russkoe Oshestvo* in *Rossia Pered 1812*, vol. 2, ch. 1.
18 Löwenstern, *First Russian Voyage*, p. 3.
19 Also packed in the groaning hold were two copies of *The Peoples of Russia*, printed in St Petersburg with illustrations, as well as four large maps of the Russian empire

and an entire library for Kodiak consisting of 'metaphysical books, travelogues of Siberia history, economy and veterinary science' donated by St Petersburg's beau monde.

10. From Newgate to Brazil

1 Gavriil Derzhavin in *Almazna Sypletsya Gora* Sovietskaya Rossiya, Moscow 1972.
2 Gideon, *Voyage*, p. 83.
3 Book of Proverbs 30:19.
4 Nikolai Tolstoy, *The Tolstoys: 24 Generations of Russian History 1353–1983*, Hamilton, London 1983, p. 124.
5 S. L. Tolstoy, *Fyodor Tolstoy Amerikanets*, AIN, Moscow 1926.
6 Löwenstern, *First Russian Voyage*, p. 2.
7 Ibid., p. 4.
8 Gideon, *Voyage*, p. 87.
9 Langsdorff, *Voyages and Travels*, p. 2.
10 Löwenstern, *First Russian Voyage*, p. 14.
11 Langsdorff, *Voyages and Travels*, p. 2.
12 Löwenstern, *First Russian Voyage*, p. 17.
13 Langsdorff, *Voyages and Travels*, p. 5.
14 Löwenstern, *First Russian Voyage*, p. 20.
15 Tolstoy, *The Tolstoys*, p. 126 .
16 Löwenstern, *First Russian Voyage*, p. 38.
17 Langsdorff, *Voyages and Travels*, p. 11.
18 Löwenstern, *First Russian Voyage*, p. 22.
19 Ibid., p. 25.
20 Ibid., p. 28.
21 Ibid., p. 27.
22 Ibid., p. 20.
23 Ibid., p. 29.
24 Langsdorff, *Voyages and Travels*, p. 27.
25 Löwenstern, *First Russian Voyage*, p. 32.
26 Ibid., p. 36.
27 Ibid., p. 37.
28 Ibid., p. 46.
29 Tikhmenev, *Russian American Company*, vol. 2, p. 144.
30 Löwenstern, *First Russian Voyage*, p. 37.
31 Ibid., p. 46.
32 Langsdorff, *Voyages and Travels*, p. 35 .
33 Ibid.
34 Ibid., p. 56.
35 Löwenstern, *First Russian Voyage*, p. 56.
36 Ibid., p. 64.

11. Cape Horn to the Court of the Hawaiian King

1 This draft of a letter witten by Tilesius to a member of the Academy of Sciences in St Petersburg was written on 24 September/6 October 1805 before the *Nadezhda*'s departure from Kamchatka for Macao. (Stadtarchiv Múhlhausen, Tilesius-Bibliothek N. 82/661).

2 Löwenstern, *First Russian Voyage*, p. 69.

3 Ibid., p. 73.

4 Ibid.

5 Langsdorff, *Voyages and Travels*, p. 84.

6 Löwenstern, *First Russian Voyage*, p. 73.

7 Ibid., p. 87.

8 Ibid.

9 Langsdorff, *Voyages and Travels*, p. 87.

10 Löwenstern, *First Russian Voyage*, notes, p. 450.

11 Langsdorff, *Voyages and Travels*, p. 93.

12 Löwenstern, *First Russian Voyage*, p. 92.

13 Langsdorff, *Voyages and Travels*, p. 93.

14 Löwenstern, *First Russian Voyage*, p. 93.

15 Ibid., p. 94.

16 Langsdorff, *Voyages and Travels*, p. 94.

17 In two places in Löwenstern's description of the voyage around the world scissors have been taken to the text – 28 August 1803 and 26-27 January 1804. In addition an anecdote about missionaries in Nukakhiva has been erased (25/27 April 1804) as well as part of the passage about an argument between Rezanov and Shemelin. (16/28 December 1804). Perhaps these passages were considered too risqué for women readers, though scatological Russian words that Löwenstern does not translate are not erased. The diaries contain numerous illustrations, mainly in the form of watercolours and ink drawings. See Moessner, 'The First Russian Ambassador to Japan'.

18 Langsdorff, *Voyages and Travels*, p. 94.

19 Löwenstern, *First Russian Voyage*, p. 96.

20 Langsdorff, *Voyages and Travels*, p. 118.

21 Tolstoy, *The Tolstoys*, p. 128.

22 Löwenstern, *First Russian Voyage*, p. 105.

23 Langsdorff, *Voyages and Travels*, p. 180.

24 Löwenstern, *First Russian Voyage*, p. 99.

25 Langsdorff, *Voyages and Travels*, p. 196.

26 Ibid., p. 189.

27 Löwenstern, *First Russian Voyage*, p. 119.

28 Langsdorff, *Voyages and Travels*, p. 198.

29 Ibid.

30 Löwenstern, *First Russian Voyage*, p. 120.

31 Ibid., p. 133.

32 Ibid.

33 Ibid.

34 See Krusenstern's uncensored diary in Tartu's Eesti Ajalooarhiiv F1414 N3 S7, also Moessner's introduction to Löwenstern's *First Russian Voyage*.

35 3/15 August 1804, quoted in Moessner, 'The First Russian Ambassador to Japan'.

36 Though this did not stop Krusenstern writing a letter of bitter complaint about Rezanov's behaviour: 'The papers relating to this unhappy transaction, transmitted by me to the Minister of Commerce, will convince Your Majesty that the Recommencement of disturbances was entirely owing to Him [Rezonav]. He dares ways to construe my words with High Treason; he threatens me with the most ignominious punishments . . . it is impossible to remain in the service of the American Company as long as Mr Rezanov remains her Representative. The Instructions I have received from the American Company, he has declared void. Since those he has from Your Majesty are not of the same Tenor. I have left Russia not knowing that I and all my officers were to be at his disposal, he did not proclaim it on coming on board, but he kept it a Secret till our Arrival upon Tenerife. I declare solemnly that till then I was entirely ignorant of it, and how could it be otherwise. Since the Instructions given me by the American Company and by Count Roumanzeff are in direct contradiction to it, and since it is impossible for him to conduct an Expedition like this.'

The Krusenstern Fond of the Russian Maritime Archives in St Petersburg (F.14, 1, T 292/20) contains Krusenstern's three-page letter written in English to the Emperor. It deals with Rezanov's behaviour after the stay in Nukakhiva and must have been written before the end of August 1804.

37 Rezanov to the Emperor, Petropavlovsk, 16 August 1804, in Tikhmenev, *Russian American Company*, vol. 2, p. 145.

38 12/24 August 1805, Löwenstern, *First Russian Voyage*, p. 146.

39 19 June/1 July 1805, Ibid., p. 115. Krusenstern responded by sending an opposing view to the president of the St Petersburg Academy of Sciences, Nikolai Nikolaevich Novosiltsev, on 25 July/8 August 1805, which is referred to by Löwenstern: 'Since Rezanov, before our voyage to Japan, wrote a report to the emperor that is to Krusenstern's disadvantage and, even though he reconciled with us, nevertheless [he] still sent letters of complaint and now once again paints Krusenstern black. Krusenstern, in a letter to Novosilzoff requested a court martial after our return. The emperor's love of justice will not and cannot deny this petition.' (Ibid., p. 118).

40 A. Sgibnev, 'Rezanov I Krusenstern', *Drevnaya i Novaya Rossiya*, vol. 1, no. 4, St Petersburg 1877, p. 389.

41 Löwenstern, *First Russian Voyage*, note 1, p. 452.

42 Tolstoy, *The Tolstoys*, p. 139.

12. Nangasac

1 Langsdorff, *Voyages and Travels*, p. 220.
2 Löwenstern, *First Russian Voyage*, p. 151.
3 Langsdorff, *Voyages and Travels*, p. 222.
4 Löwenstern, *First Russian Voyage*, p. 153.
5 Ibid., p. 154.
6 Ibid., notes p. 452.
7 Langsdorff, *Voyages and Travels*, p. 226.
8 Löwenstern, *First Russian Voyage*, p. 154.
9 Rumiantsev's instructions to Rezanov quoted in Lopatnikov, 'Nikolai Rezanov'.
10 Rumiantsev ordered Rezanov to describe Russia as 'the greatest by her extent of all the powers of Europe . . . in this State we have different climates because she occupies half the globe, that Russia in her might holds in awe and harmony half of Europe, China, the Turkish Empire and Persia and that she has forces in infantry and cavalry of over 700,000; that this land is ruled by an autocratic tsar and since Japan is also autocratic, describe our government in all her honour. You may say that many Tsars of Asia including Kalmyk Georgian Siberian are subdued to His power and are now counted merely among his illustrious subjects, that the Tsar emperor taking his ancestral throne and seeing the extent of his borders won by glorious victories of his ancestors has resolved to rule in peace and harmony with the whole world; and that his State is a shelter for sciences laws and arts.' See discussion in Lopatnikov, 'Nikolai Rezanov'.
11 Black, *Russians in Alaska*, p. 170.
12 Löwenstern, *First Russian Voyage*, p. 170.
13 William McOmie, 'With All Due Respect: Reconsidering the Rezanov Mission to Japan', *Proceedings of the Japan Society*, no. 148, London 2011, p. 204.
14 Löwenstern, *First Russian Voyage*, p. 174.
15 Langsdorff, *Voyages and Travels*, p. 246.
16 See McOmie, 'Reconsidering the Rezanov Mission,' endnotes.
17 It is not clear how much Japanese Rezanov, despite his efforts actually spoke. Löwenstern recorded, 'R very conceitedly thinks he understands some Japanese, speaks Japanese with the common Japanese wherever he can get hold of them, especially with the boys who daily stand in flocks behind the bamboo.' The boys probably spoke the local dialect and certainly not the language of the court. (Löwenstern, *First Russian Voyage*, p. 225).
18 *The Chinese Repository*, vol. IX, May 1840, no. 1, Canton 1840, p. 278.
19 McOmie, 'Reconsidering the Rezanov Mission', p. 207.
20 Ibid., p. 209.
21 Even then Doeff and his men were not even on the mainland of Japan proper. Rather they occupied Deisima, a tiny man-made island 182 by 75 metres joined to the mainland by a stone bridge.

22 McOmie, 'Reconsidering the Rezanov Mission', p. 212.
23 Rezanov, *Diary* quoted in Y. P. Avdyukov, N. S. Olkhova, A. I. Surnik (eds), *Komandor: Stranitsy Zhizni I Deyatelnosti Dvora ego Imperatorskogo Velichestva Deistvitelnogo Kamergera Nikolaya Petrovicha Rezanova*, TKISO, Krasnoyarsk 1995, p. 169.
24 Löwenstern, *First Russian Voyage*, p. 177.
25 Langsdorff, *Voyages and Travels*, p. 231.
26 Rezanov, *Diary*, p. 171.
27 Löwenstern, *First Russian Voyage*, p. 179.
28 Langsdorff, *Voyages and Travels*, p. 275.
29 Or rather the interpreters told Rezanov part of the name of the current shogun, Tokugawa Ienari, but they left out the second syllable, and added an honorific title at the end, which was recorded in Russian in Rezanov's diary as 'Ieri-ko.' See McOmie, 'Reconsidering the Rezanov Mission,' p. 209.
30 Löwenstern, *First Russian Voyage*, p. 182.
31 William McOmie, 'From Russia With All Due Respect: Revisiting the Rezanov Embassy to Japan', *Jinbun Kenkyu (Studies in Humanities)*, no. 163, December 2007, Kanagawa Daigaku Jinbun Gakkai (Society of Humanities at Kanagawa University), Yokohama 2007, p. 147.
32 Löwenstern, *First Russian Voyage*, p. 455.
33 Ibid., p. 183.
34 Ibid., p. 187.
35 Langsdorff, *Voyages and Travels*, p. 269.
36 Ibid., p. 271.
37 Löwenstern, *First Russian Voyage*, p. 189.

13. Humiliation

1 Iemitsu did not proclaim *sakoku* per se – the term was not invented until 1804 by Shizuki Tadao, a Nagasaki interpreter of Dutch in response to Russian incursions from the north.
2 McOmie, 'Reconsidering the Rezanov Mission', p. 219.
3 McOmie, 'Revisiting the Rezanov Embassy', p. 131.
4 Perhaps that is why he reacted first with aggression and arrogance, and finally deep depression.
5 Langsdorff, *Voyages and Travels*, p. 202.
6 Löwenstern, *First Russian Voyage*, p. 203.
7 Langsdorff, *Voyages and Travels*, p. 288.
8 Ibid., p. 322.
9 Löwenstern, *First Russian Voyage*, p. 207.
10 Löwenstern sketch of Shmelin fight.
11 McOmie, 'Revisiting the Rezanov Embassy', p. 137.
12 Löwenstern, *First Russian Voyage*, p. 230.

13 Langsdorff, *Voyages and Travels*, p. 309.
14 Löwenstern, *First Russian Voyage*, p. 254.
15 Ibid., p. 257.
16 Ibid., p. 261.
17 Langsdorff, *Voyages and Travels*, p. 332.
18 Löwenstern, *First Russian Voyage*, p. 269.
19 Langsdorff, *Voyages and Travels*, p. 310.
20 Ibid., p. 312.
21 Löwenstern, *First Russian Voyage*, p. 278.
22 Ibid., p. 279.
23 Ibid., p. 283.
24 Ibid., p. 289.

14. The Voyage of the *Maria*

1 Rezanov, *Voyage to Nueva California*, p. 61.
2 Rezanov, *Voyage to Nueva California*, p. 45.
3 Löwenstern, *First Russian Voyage*, p. 311, 25 May 1805.
4 Technically a revolt of officers is a barratry rather than a mutiny.
5 Löwenstern, *First Russian Voyage*, p. 316.
6 The draft of a letter witten by Tilesius to a member of the Academy of Sciences in St Petersburg, written on 24 September/6 October 1805 before the departure from Kamchatka for Macao (Stadtarchiv Múhlhausen, Tilesius-Bibliothek N. 82/661).
7 Rezanov, *Voyage to Nueva California*, p. 44.
8 Langsdorff, *Voyages and Travels*, vol. 2, p. 17.
9 Löwenstern, *First Russian Voyage*, p. 317.
10 Rezanov had already left for Russian America by the time his accommodation was demolished by the drunken soldiery.
11 Löwenstern, *First Russian Voyage*, p. 326.
12 Ibid., p. 329.
13 Letter of Rezanov to the RAC from New Archangel 6 November 1805, Tikhmenev, *Russian American Company*, vol. 2, p. 153.
14 Langsdorff, *Voyages and Travels*, vol. 2, p. 67.
15 Ibid., vol. 2, p11.
16 Ibid.
17 Ibid., vol. 2, p. 12.
18 Ibid., vol. 2, p. 13.
19 Ibid., vol. 2, p. 58.
20 Ibid., vol. 2, p. 67.
21 Rezanov, *Voyage to Nueva California*, p. 50.
22 Black, *Russians in Alaska*, p. 102.
23 Rezanov, *Voyage to Nueva California*, p. 52.

24 Langsdorff, *Voyages and Travels*, vol. 2, p. 73.

25 Ibid., vol. 2, p. 17.

26 Rezanov to the Emperor from Unalaska, 18 July 1805, Tikhmenev, *Russian American Company*, vol. 2, p. 149.

27 Langsdorff, *Voyages and Travels*, vol. 2, p. 21.

28 Ibid., vol. 2, p. 25.

29 Ibid., vol. 2, p. 22.

30 Ibid., vol. 2, p. 29.

31 Sea otters are unusual among sea mammals because they can live for long periods of time at sea, even sleep at sea. (James Bodkin, 'Sea Otters', *Alaska Geographic*, 27 (2000), pp. 78–80.

32 Langsdorff, *Voyages and Travels*, vol. 2, p. 41.

33 The Aleut language has given English the words parka and kayak.

34 16 June, Unalaska.

35 Black, *Russians in Alaska*, p. 133.

36 Rez report to RAC, Tikhmenev, *Russian American Company*, vol. 2, p. 156.

37 Löwenstern, *First Russian Voyage*, p. 357.

38 Langsdorff, *Voyages and Travels*, vol. 2, p. 58.

39 Ibid., vol. 2, p. 69.

40 Hieromonk Gideon, *Voyage*, p. 107.

41 Vancouver was surprised how Russians 'appear to be perfectly content to live after the manner of the native Indians of the country partaking with equal relish and appetite of their food, adopting the same materials for their apparel'. (Vancouver, *A Voyage of Discovery*, London 1801, vol 2, p. 207).

42 Langsdorff, *Voyages and Travels*, vol. 2, p. 32.

43 Ibid., vol. 2, p. 31.

44 Though James Cook in Unalaska found the Aleuts gentle: 'To all appearances the most peaceable inoffensive people I ever met with and as to honesty they might serve as a pattern to the most civilized nation on earth.' James Cook, *Third Voyage*, vol.2, p. 508.

45 Ibid., vol. 2, p. 53.

46 Ibid., vol. 2, p. 64.

47 'There is hardly a family here not affected by venereal disease,' wrote Hieromonk Iosaf, quoted in Miller, *Kodiak Kreol*, p. 83.

48 Quoted Ibid., p. 8.

49 Langsdorff, *Voyages and Travels*, vol. 2, p. 37.

50 Ibid., vol. 2, p. 35.

51 Ibid., vol. 2, p. 53.

52 Ibid.

53 Black, *Russians in Alaska*, p. 128.

54 Gideon, *Voyage* pp. 84–5.

55 Langsdorff, *Voyages and Travels*, vol. 2, p. 59.

56 Ibid., 24 September 1805.

57 Rezanov's letter to RAC directors 6 November 1805, quoted in Gideon, *Voyage*, p. 86.

58 See Archives of the Holy Synod in TsGIA Rossii, Russian America Fond, p. 385.

59 Rezanov to Gideon from Sitka, 11 September 1805, quoted in Gideon, *Voyage*, p. 87.

60 See Tikhmenev, *Russian American Company*, vol. 2, pp. 153–73.

61 Rezanov's letter to RAC directors, 6 November 1805, quoted in Gideon, *Voyage*, p. 92.

62 Gideon's letter to Rezanov, in Gideon, *Voyage*, p. 93.

63 Langsdorff, *Voyages and Travels*, vol. 2, p. 78.

15. Baranov

1 Rezanov, *Voyage to Nueva California*, p. 65.

2 K. T. Khlebnikov, tr. Colin Bearne, ed. by Richard A. Pierce, *Baranov: Chief Manager of the Russian Colonies in America* (St Peterburg 1835), Limestone Press, Kingston 1973, p. xiv.

3 Khlebnikov, *Baranov*, p. 22.

4 Engstrom, *Baranov*, p. 19.

5 Miller, *Kodiak Kreol*, p. 88.

6 Ibid., p. 89.

7 Engstrom, *Baranov*, p. 20.

8 Miller, *Kodiak Kreol*, p. 107.

9 Tsiporukha, 'Odna iz Stroitelei', p. 41.

10 Russians in Tlingit America.

11 William Dane Phelps' remarks on the 'solid men of Boston' quoted in Engstrom, *Baranov*, p. 130.

12 Their hunting range from Kodiak was up to 1,400 miles from Yakutat to Unga. 'Natives make this journey both ways, 200 versts a day in a narrow *baidarka* without sails only paddles. They have to endure hunger and often perish in stormy seas . . . constant threat of attack by bloodthirsty people who inhabit these regions.' Baranov to Shelikhov, Tikhmenev, *Russian American Company*, vol. 2, p. 127.

13 'Depositions made at the Kodiak office of the American Company by the hunter Abrosim Plotnikov and others who were witnesses to the massacre of the New Archangel fort and who escaped from the Kolosh in 1802,' Tikhmenev, *Russian American Company*, vol. 2, p. 136.

14 Ibid., p. 138.

15 Though sadly there is no mention of the artefacts' violent provenance.

16 Baranov's letter to Kuliakov quoted in Tikhmenev, *Russian American Company*, vol. 2, p. 265.

17 Lisiansky quoted in Engstrom, *Baranov*, p. 121.

18 Captain Urey Lisianski (Yury Lisiansky), *A Voyage Around the World*, John Murray, London 1814 (facsimile edition Da Capo Press, New York 1968), p. 203.

19 Ibid., p. 243.

20 Ibid., p. 245.

21 Ibid., p. 224.

22 See Andrei Grinev, 'Amerikanskaya Epopeya Aleksandra Baranova', *Voprosy Istorii*, no. 8, Moscow 2000.

16. Hunger, Disease, Shipwreck and Death

1 Rezanov's second secret letter to RAC, 15 February 1806, in Tikhmenev, *Russian American Company*, p. 190.

2 Langsdorff, *Voyages and Travels*, vol. 2, p. 70.

3 D'Wolf, *Voyage to the North Pacific*, p. 26.

4 Langsdorff, *Voyages and Travels*, vol. 2, p. 87.

5 Rezanov to Gideon from Sitka, 11 September 1805, Gideon, *Voyage*, p. 90.

6 Tikhmenev, *Russian American Company*, vol. 2, p. 157.

7 D'Wolf, *Voyage to the North Pacific*, p. 28.

8 When the pound went on the gold standard in 1823 the exchange rate was £1 = $4.86. In 1803 the pound was worth somewhat less than this because of the Napoleonic Wars.

9 Tikhmenev, *Russian American Company*, vol. 2, p. 160.

10 Langsdorff, *Voyages and Travels*, vol. 2, p. 89.

11 D'Wolf, *Voyage to the North Pacific*, p. 29.

12 Letter to Professor Blumenbach of Göttingen, February 1806 in Langsdorff, *Voyages and Travels*, vol. 2, p. 102.

13 Ibid., p. 99.

14 Langsdorff, *Voyages and Travels*, vol. 2, p. 69.

15 Rezanov's second secret letter to the RAC, 15 February 1806, in Tikhmenev, *Russian American Company*, p. 190.

16 Ibid., p. 193.

17 Rezanov, *Voyage to Nueva California*, p. 43.

18 Ibid., p. 45.

19 Tikhmenev, *Russian American Company*, vol. 2, p. 165.

20 Langsdorff, *Voyages and Travels*, vol. 2, p. 70.

21 Ibid., vol. 2, p. 73.

22 Ibid., vol. 2, p. 85.

23 Ibid., vol. 2, letter to Professor Blumenbach of Göttingen, February 1806, p. 110.

24 Ibid., vol. 2, p. 103.

25 Tikhmenev, *Russian American Company*, vol. 2, p. 157.

26 Ibid., p. 196.

27 D'Wolf, *Voyage to the North Pacific*, p. 42.

28 Langsdorff, *Voyages and Travels*, vol. 2, letter to Professor Blumenbach of Göttingen, February 1806, p. 99.

29 Ibid., vol. 2, p. 92.

30 Ibid., vol. 2, p. 93.

31 Ibid.

32 Ibid.

33 Ibid., vol. 2, p. 96.

34 Rezanov, *Voyage to Nueva California*, p. 7.

35 Langsdorff, *Voyages and Travels*, vol. 2, p. 98.

17. Conchita

1 Jeremy Atiyah, *The Great Land: How Western America Nearly Became a Russian Possession*, Parker press, Portland 2008, p. vii.

2 Langsdorff, *Voyages and Travels*, vol. 2, p. 98.

3 Ibid., vol. 2, p. 140.

4 Stephen A. Ambrose, *Undaunted Courage: Meriwether Lewis, Thomas Jefferson, and the Opening of the West*, Simon & Schuster, New York 1996, p. 322.

5 Elin Woodger and Brandon Toropov, *Encyclopedia of the Lewis and Clark Expedition*, Infobase Publishing, 2004, p. 150.

6 Langsdorff, *Voyages and Travels*, vol. 2, p. 145.

7 Ibid., vol. 2, p. 183.

8 8 April in the Western calendar.

9 Rezanov, *Voyage to Nueva California*, p. 11.

10 Ibid.

11 Langsdorff, *Voyages and Travels*, p. 150.

12 Rezanov, *Voyage to Nueva California*, p. 7.

13 Langsdorff, *Voyages and Travels*, p. 153.

14 Ibid., p. 152.

15 The mission, its roof supported on squat adobe pillars, still stands, and gives its name to the surrounding district, which is still predominantly Spanish-speaking.

16 Rezanov, *Voyage to Nueva California*, p. 15.

17 Vancouver, *A Voyage of Discovery*, vol. 2, pp. 502–3.

18 Rezanov, *Voyage to Nueva California*, p. 18.

19 Langsdorff, *Voyages and Travels*, vol. 2, p. 154.

20 Ibid., p. 180.

21 Rezanov, *Voyage to Nueva California*, p. 14.

22 Langsdorff, *Voyages and Travels*, vol. 2, p. 163.

23 Rezanov, *Voyage to Nueva California*, p. 28.

24 Langsdorff, *Voyages and Travels*, p. 178.

25 Ibid., p. 178.

18. Love and Ambition

1   Langsdorff, *Voyages and Travels*, p. 181.

2   Ibid., p. 180.

3   Rezanov, *Voyage to Nueva California*, p. 37.

4   Ibid., p. 64.

5   Eve Iverson, ed. by Richard A. Pierce, *The Romance of Nikolai Rezanov and Concepción Arguello: A Literary Legend and its Effect on Californian History*, University of Alaska Press, Fairbanks 1998, p. 85.

6   Thomas Russell, *Notes to The Rezanov Voyage to Nueva California in 1806*, Thomas Russell, San Francisco 1926, p. 83.

7   Rezanov, *Voyage to Nueva California*, p. 62.

8   Langsdorff, *Voyages and Travels*, vol. 2, p. 181.

9   Ibid., p. 179.

10 Rezanov letter to Iturrigaria, Dmitryshkin, *Russian American Colonies*, p. 109.

11 Langsdorff, *Voyages and Travels*, p. 177.

12 Indeed when Rezanov arrived in April the governor had only just heard the previous autumn's European sensation – that Prussia had entered the Third Coalition, heralding another round of European war.

13 Rezanov, *Voyage to Nueva California*, p. 37.

14 Langsdorff, *Voyages and Travels*, vol. 2, p. 180.

15 Ibid., p. 183.

16 Rezanov, *Voyage to Nueva California*, p. 64.

17 Ibid., p. 64.

18 Ibid., p. 38.

19 Iverson, *Romance*, p. 100.

20 Ibid., p. 101.

21 Rezanov, *Voyage to Nueva California*, p. 39.

22 Ibid., p. 181.

23 Langsdorff, *Voyages and Travels*, vol. 2, p. 185.

19. I will never see you – I will never forget you

1   Rezanov's second secret letter to the RAC, 15 February 1806, in Tikhmenev, *Russian American Company*, p. 190.

2   Surnik, *Poslednee pismo Rezanova*.

3   In 1795 Governor Diego de Borica issued Arguello a Spanish land grant for the Rancho de las Pulgas – the Ranch of the Fleas. This was the largest grant on the San Francisco Peninsula and consisted of 35,260 acres (142.7 square kilometres) in present-day San Mateo County. It encompasses the present-day towns of San Mateo, Belmont, San Carlos, Redwood City, Atherton and Menlo Park. See Moessner, 'The First Russian Ambassador to Japan'.

4   Rezanov, *Voyage to Nueva California*, p. 21.

5   Ibid., p. 47.

6   Sunday, 11 January 1931, Iverson, *Romance*, p. 135.

7   Rezanov, *Voyage to Nueva California*, p. 52.

8   Engstrom, Baranov, p. 166.

9   Ibid., p. 162.

10   Istomin, 'Dva Varianta Pisma'.

11   The second copy is now lost.

12   24 Jan 1807, Istomin, 'Dva Varianta Pisma'.

13   Secret instruction left by Rezanov to Baranov, 20 July 1806, Yudin Collection, Library of Congress, box 1, folder 11.

14   Lopatnikov, 'Nikolai Rezanov'.

20. The Weeping Country

1   Tikhmenev, *Russian American Company*, vol. 2, p. 101.

2   Zentralbibliothek Zürich, Horner-Nachlass, Ms.M.5,60.

3   Quoted in Moessner, 'The First Russian Ambassador to Japan'.

4   Langsdorff continued, 'The deceased, as one is wont to say, now may be answering before God's judgement chair for all of his cruelties and heinous deeds. As with everyone, Rezanov cheated the Spaniards here [in California]. He claimed our ship was on a voyage of discovery and purchased with contraband goods – to Russia's shame – grain and flour to stave off the threat of starvation in Sitka.'

5   Langsdorff to Krusenstern, Tobolsk, 20 December 1807, Archive of the Academy of Sciences, St Petersburg, Fond 31, 1, 11.

6   Tikhmenev, *Russian American Company* p. 101.

7   Ibid., p. 102.

8   Sitka, 23 March 1806, quoted in Sverdlov, 'Rezanov: Obraz I Lichnost'.

9   See Leonid Sverdlov, A. V. Postnikov (ed), *Krusenstern i Rezanov* Argo, Moscow, 2006.

10   See Vice Admiral Shishkov's Preface to Gavriil Davydov, tr. by Colin Bearne, ed. by Richard A. Pierce, *Two Voyages to Russian America 1802–1807*, St Petersburg 1810, reprinted by Limestone Press, Kingston, Ontario 1977, p. 4.

11   Captain Vasily Golovnin, *Memoirs of a captivity in Japan during the years 1811, 12 and 13 with observations of the country and people*, Henry Colburn and Co., London 1824, vol. 1, pp. 67–75.

12   Draft of letter to Count Maletsky-Yakutsky, 5 November 1806, Yudin Collection, box 2, folder 9 pp. 213–14.

13   Ivan Kalashnikov *Zapiski irkutskogo zhitelya*, 10 January 1807. Quoted in Black, *Russians in America*, p. 177.

14   Lopatnikov, 'Nikolai Rezanov'.

15   Ibid.

16   Anna Surnik, *Poslednee Pismo Kemergera: Rashifrovka* in *Russkaya Amerika*, Vologda no. 1, Vologda 1994, pp. 29–31.

17 Ibid.

18 Rezanov to Buldakov, 25 January 1807 from Irkutsk, received at RAC 6 March 1807, ibid.

19 See memoirs of Krasnoyarsk merchant I. F. Parfentyev 1891, quoted in Avdyukov et al., *Komandor*.

20 Yermolaev, 'Pskovsky Chinovnik Rezanov'.

Epilogues

1 Lee B. Croft *George Anton Schaeffer: Killing Napoleon From the Air*, Sphynx Publications, 2012, pp. 14, 53.

2 Nikolay Bolkhovitinov, 'Adventures of Doctor Schäffer in Hawaii, 1815–1819', *Hawaiian Journal of History*, 1973, vol. 7, pp. 55–78.

3 Though the Tsar later relented a little and allowed trading operations.

4 Peter R. Mills, *Hawaii's Russian adventure: a new look at old history*, University of Hawaii Press, 2002.

5 For the worse, it must be said.

6 See James R. Gibson, *The Decembrists*, Fort Ross, 2009.

7 Marc Raeff, *The Decembrist Movement*, Prentice-Hall, Englewood Cliffs, New Jersey 1966, pp. 19-21.

8 Frederick W. Seward. *Seward at Washington as Senator and Secretary of State*, vol. 3, 1891, p. 348.

9 T. Ahllund, tr. by Panu Hallamaa, ed. by Richard Pierce, 'From the Memoirs of a Finnish Workman', *Alaska History*, 21, Anchorage Fall 2006, 1–25, originally published in Finnish in *Suomen Kuvalehti*, no. 15/1873 – no. 19/1873.

10 19 April/1 May 1805, Löwenstern, *First Russian Voyage*.

11 On 22 April 1807 the astronomer on the voyage, Johann Caspar Horner (1774–1834), wrote to Krusenstern about Tilesius' unfulfilled plans to publish his own work about the voyage, which Count Nikolai Petrovich Rumjantsev would pay for, and mentioned Löwenstern's voluminous journal:

   'Such vermiform professors indeed remain deplorable, unreliable spirits. I am sure that if something comes [of the descriptions of the voyage], the Count will have more sea birds and dung worms than historical views. If he really intends to contribute something historical [about the voyage] or even to anticipate the publication of your voyage, then I will produce a work with woodcuts for which Lwn [Löwenstern] can give me the data, which my untroubled memory has forgotten. There is no danger in doing that since such spirits as T[ilesius] and R[ezanov] do not like each other. In addition, T produces so much all at once that nothing can come of it and he does not have endless numbers of views and pictures.' (Ernst F. Sondermann, 'Johann Caspar Horner über Japan', *Tohoku Gakuin Daigaku Kyoyogabu Konshu*, Nr. 149, 2008, 1–26).

   Löwenstern did not wish this to be published, as he makes clear in his scoffing remarks about the quill drivers on board the *Nadezhda* shortly before the departure from Nagasaki. (19 April 19 / 1 May 1805): 'The one, with quite a lot of talent, the least ability, and the greatest pretensions is Tilesius. Langsdorff will not be deficient in keeping himself undamaged through the voyage in every way, even if at the cost of others. Espenberg also seems inclined through the voyage to want to be brilliant in the literary world. Horner has to prove and make known to the world his observations and research in astronomy and the physical world in order to give our work validity. Romberg, who works on translations, also will not be deficient (through Karamsin) in giving the world his two bits. There are as many journals as people onboard (all the better).'

The allusion is to the famous writers of travelogues Johann Georg Forster (1759–94) and Count Marc Antoine Louis Claret de Fleurieu de Latrouette (1729–93), who described the exploration of the south Pacific.

12 Moessner, 'The First Russian Ambassador to Japan'.

13 Instead RAC historians chose to publish Rezanov's scheming and unbalanced letters to St Petersburg in their 1867 offical history of the company.

14 There were a few hitches on the way. Tolstoy was arrested at the gates of St Petersburg in 1805 on the orders of the Tsar and sent to serve in a distant fortress for three years before he was finally allowed back to reap the social glory in the capital. See Filipp Vigel, *Zapiski*, Moscow 1892.

15 Aleksei Polikovskii, *Graf Bezbrezhnyi: dve zhizni grafa Fedora Ivanovicha Tolstogo-Amerikantsa*, Minuvshee, Moscow, 2006.

16 Alexander Sergevich Pushkin, *Eugene Onegin*, tr. by Charles H. Johnston, Penguin Books Ltd, London 1977, book 6, verse 4.

17 Istomin, 'Dva Varianta Pisma'.

18 Löwenstern, *First Russian Voyage*, p. 416.

19 Ibid.

20 Ibid., p. 417.

21 Moessner, 'The First Russian Ambassador to Japan'.

22 Löwenstern, *First Russian Voyage*, note 1, p. 452.

23 Ibid., note 20, p. 444.

24 Davydov, *Two Voyages*, p. 19.

25 D'Wolf, *Voyage to the North Pacific*, p. 124.

26 Gavriil Derzhavin, *Sochineniya Derzhavina s obyasnitelnymi primechaniyami Ya. Grota*, Russian Academy of Sciences, St Petersburg 1866, part 3, pp. 30–36.

27 Sergei Alexandovich Kokoshkin.

28 www.ru.rodovid.org/wk/Запись:625661.

29 Iverson, *Romance*, p. 136.

30 Russell, *Notes*, p. 93.

31 According to Thomas Russell she lived with the family of Don José Antonio de la Guerra y Noriega, the 'first family of California' .

32 Russell, *Notes*, p. 95.

33 Sir George Simpson, *An Overland Journey Around the World 1841–2*, Lea and Blanchard, Philadelphia 1847, p. 207.

34 Iverson, *Romance*, p. 89.

35 Henry Lebbeus Oak, *Annals of the Spanish Northwest: California*, San Francisco, 1886 (facsimile edition Kessinger Publishing, 2010), vol. 4, p. 9.

36 Like many bright New Yorkers of his generation, Harte had gone to seek his fortune in California in 1853 at the age of seventeen. He tried his hand at mining, teaching (unhindered by having left school at thirteen himself), messenger boy and finally journalist and writer. While working as assistant editor for the *Northern Californian* Harte began writing stories of the American frontier such as 'The Luck of Roaring Camp' (1868), a tale of roistering miners tamed by the responsibility of raising an orphan infant. The legend of the Wild West had been a thriving genre since James Fenimore Cooper's *Last of the Mohicans* was published in 1826, but Harte quickly became a master of the Western short story.

37 Gary Scharnhorst, *Bret Harte: opening the American literary West*, Oklahoma University Press, Norman, Oklahoma 2000, p. 87.

38 Thanks to the popularity of Harte and Atherton, the story of Conchita and Rezanov became a part of Californian lore. 'When we think of the love stories that have survived the ages, Alexander and Thais, Pericles and Aspasia, Antony and Cleopatra, and all the rest of them – some of them a narrative unfit to handle with tongs – shall we let this local story die?' thundered one John F. Davis, a former judge who in retirement was the grand president of a club which grandly called itself the Native Sons of the Golden West. The occasion was a dinner on 24 November 1913 marking the placing of a commemorative bronze tablet upon the oldest adobe building in San Francisco, the former *presidio*, now the US Army Officers' Club. 'Shall not America furnish a newer and purer standard? If to such a standard Massachusetts is to contribute the Courtship of Miles Standish, may not California contribute the Courtship of Rezanov? You men of this army post have a peculiar right to unsheathe a flaming sword. For this memory of the *comandante*'s daughter is yours – yours to cherish, yours to protect. In the barracks and on parade, at the dance and in the field, this "one sweet human fancy" belongs to this *presidio*; and no court martial nor departmental order can ever take it from you.'

39 Like his contemporaries Bella Akhmadulina and Evgeny Yevtushenko, he was allowed to travel to the West, where he so impressed W. H. Auden that the latter translated several of Voznesensky's poems into English.

40 During a visit to Vancouver in 1970 Voznesensky read about the Rezanov–Conchita tale in *Russia's Eastward Expansion* (1964) by American scholar George Lensen.

41 'The Deathbed Sstory of Rezanov', a companion poem to 'Avos!'

42 Before the dress rehearsal, which would be attended by state censors, Rybnikov and Voznesensky took a taxi to Moscow's Patriarchal Cathedral and lit a candle in front of the icon of the Holy Virgin of Kazan – which is mentioned in Voznesensky's libretto. She seems to have worked the necessary miracle: the state censor, who had rejected Rybnikov's attempts at rock operas eleven times, approved *Junona I Avos* entire and uncut.

43   In 1983 the show, with its original cast, was broadcast on Soviet TV and was widely seen as a landmark in the post-Brezhnev thaw. After a special plea by the French designer Pierre Cardin, the show toured to Paris, Germany and the Netherlands and then New York, where *Hair!* producer Joseph Papp began work on an English production. It became a kind of traveling showcase of Mikhail Gorbachev's glasnost, a defiantly non-Soviet work of art for a new age.

Select Bibliography

Archival Sources

Archive of the Academy of Sciences, St Petersburg, Fond 31, letters from Langsdorff to Krusenstern

Arkhiv Rossiskogo Voenno-Morskogo Flota (Russian Maritime Archives) St Petersburg, *Fond Kruzenshterna* (Fond 14, 1, T 292)

Library of Congress, Washington DC, Golder Collection and Yudin Collection (Alaska History Research Project, *Documents Relative to the History of Alaska*, tr. by T. I. Lavrischeff, 15 vols, 1936–8)

Materialy dlia istorii russkikh zaselenii po beregam Vostochnogo Okeana. Appendix to *Morskoi Sbornik*, 1–4, St Petersburg 1861

National Archives, Washington DC, *Records of the Russian American Company*

Pervoye puteshestviye Russiyan okolo sveta, opisannoe N Rezanovym, chrezvechainym poslannikom ko dvoru yaponskomu, Otechestveniye Zapiski, vols 10–15, St Petersburg 1822

St Petersburg Public Library, *Doklad Kamergera N P Rezanova o Posolstvo v Yaponiyu v 1805 g.*

Stadtarchiv Múhlhausen, *Tilesius-Bibliothek N. 82*, Tilesius' correspondence and illustrations

Tartu Eesti Ajalooarhiiv (Estonian State Archives, Tartu), *Krusenstern Archive* F1414 (includes Löwenstern's diary)

Published Primary Sources

T. Ahllund, tr. by Panu Hallamaa, ed. by Richard Pierce, 'From the Memoirs of a Finnish Workman', *Alaska History*, 21, Anchorage Fall 2006, 1–25

(originally published in Finnish in *Suomen Kuvalehti*, no. 15/1873 – no. 19/1873)

Y. P. Avdyukov, N. S. Olkhova, A. I. Surnik (eds), *Komandor: Stranitsy Zhizni I Deyatelnosti Dvora ego Imperatorskogo Velichestva Deistvitelnogo Kamergera Nikolaya Petrovicha Rezanova*, TKISO, Krasnoyarsk 1995

Nina N. Bakshina, David F. Trask (eds), *The United States and Russia: The beginning of relations 1765–1815*, US Government Printing Office, Washington 1980

Glynn Barratt (ed.) *The Russian Discovery of Hawaii – the Journals of Eight Russian Explorers*, Editions Limited, Honolulu 1987

Captain James Cook, *A Voyage to the Pacific Ocean . . . in the Years 1776, 1777, 1778, 1779, and 1780*, 3 vols, G. Nichol and T. Cadell, London 1785

Reverend William Coxe, *Account of the Russian Discoveries between Asia and America. To which are added, the Conquest of Siberia, and, the History of the Transactions and Commerce between Russia and China*, T. Cadell, London 1780

Ekaterina Romanovna Dashkova, tr. by Kyril FitzLyon, *The memoirs of Princess Dashkova*, Duke University Press, Durham 1995

Lieutenant Gavrila Davydov, tr. by Colin Bearne, ed. by Richard A. Pierce, *Two Voyages to Russian America 1802–1807*, St Petersburg 1810, reprinted by Limestone Press, Kingston, Ontario 1977

Gavrila Derzhavin, ed. by Ya. Grot, *Sochineniya Derzhavina s obyasnitelnymi primechaniyami Ya. Grota*, Imperial Academy of Sciences, St Petersburg 1866

A. D. Dridzo and R. V. Kinzhalov (eds.), *Russkaia Amerika: po lichnym vpechatleniiam missionerov , zemleprokhodtsev, moriakov, issledovatelei i drugikh ochevidtsev*, Mysl' Publications, Moscow 1994

Captain John D'Wolf, *A Voyage to the North Pacific and a Journey Through Siberia More than Half a Century Ago*, Boston 1861 (facsimile edition Ye Galleon Press, Fairfield 1968)

Hieromonk Gideon, tr. with an introduction and notes by Lydia Black. *The Round the World Voyage of Hieromonk Gideon 1803–1809*, Limestone Press, Fairbanks 1989

A. V. Khrapovitskii, *Dnevnik* (Diary), 18 January 1782 to 17 September 1793, Universitetskaya Tipografiya, Moscow 1901

Stepan Krasheninnikov, tr. by James Grieve, *The History of Kamtschatka and the Karilski Islands with the Countries Adjacent*, Gloucester 1764 (facsimile edition by Quadrangle Books, Chicago 1962)

Captain Adam Johann von Krusenstern, *Voyage Round the World in the years 1803, 1804, 1805 & 1806, by order of His Imperial Majesty Alexander the First, on board the ships Nadeshda and Neva*, Printed by C. Roworth for John Murray, London 1813

Wilhelm Lagus, *Eric Laxman, his Life, Voyages, Discoveries and Correspondence*, St Petersburg, 1890

Georg Heinrich von Langsdorff, *Voyages and Travels in Various Parts of the World during the years 1803–1807*, Henry Colburn, London 1813 (facsimile edition Da Capo Press, New York 1968)

Captain Urey Lisianski (Yury Lisansky), *A Voyage Around the World*, John Murray, London 1814 (facsimile edition Da Capo Press, New York, 1968)

Mikhail Lomonosov, *M.V. Lomonosov Izbranniye Proizvedeniya*, Biblioteka Poeta, Leningrad 1986

Lieutenant Hermann Ludwig von Löwenstern, tr. by Victoria Joan Moessner, *The First Russian Voyage Around the World*, University of Alaska Press, Fairbanks 2003

Captain Nathaniel Porlock, *A Voyage Round the World, but more particularly to the North West Coast of America*, John Stockdale, London 1798

Nikolai Rezanov, *The Rezanov Voyage to Nueva California in 1806*, Thomas Russell, San Francisco 1926

Edward Robarts, ed. by Greg Dening, *The Marquesan Journal of Edward Robarts*, Australian National University Press, Canberra 1974

Dr Martin Sauer, *An Account of a Geographical and Astronomical Expedition to the Northern Parts of Russia . . . performed by Commodore Joseph Billings in the years 1785–1794*, T. Cadell, Jun. and W. Davies, London 1802

Frederick W. Seward, *Seward at Washington as Senator and Secretary of State*, vol. 3, Derby and Miller, New York 1891

Natalia Shelikhova, ed. and tr. Dawn Lea Black, Alexander Petrov and Marvin W. Falk, *Natalia Shelikhova Russian Oligarch of Alaska Commerce*, University of Alaska Press, Fairbanks 2010

Fyodor Shmelin, *Zhurnal Pervogo Puteshestviye Rossiiskoi Vokrug Zemnogo Shara.* St Petersburg 1816

Grigory Shelikhov, tr. by Marina Ramsay, introduction by Richard A. Pierce, *A Voyage to America, 1783–1786*, St Petersburg 1793, Limestone Press, Kingston 1981

Lieutenant William Sturgis, ed. by S. W. Jackman, *The Journal of William Sturgis*, Sono Nis Press, Victoria 1978

Captain George Vancouver, *A Voyage of Discovery to the North Pacific Ocean and Round the World in the Years 1790, 1791, 1792, 1793 1794, and 1795.* 3 vols, G. G. and J. Robinson and J. Edwards, London 1798

Charles William Vane, Marquis of Londonderry, *Recollections of a Tour in the North of Europe in 1836–1837*, Richard Bentley, London 1838

Secondary Sources

John T. Alexander, *Catherine the Great: Life and Legend*, Folio Society, London 1999

Stephen A. Ambrose, *Undaunted Courage: Meriwether Lewis, Thomas Jefferson, and the Opening of the West*, Simon & Schuster, New York 1996

A. I. Andreyev (ed.), tr. by Carl Ginsburg, *Russian Discoveries in the Pacific and North America in the 18th and 19th Centuries*, American Council of Learned Societies, Washington DC 1952

Jeremy Atiyah, *The Great Land: How Western America Nearly Became a Russian Possession*, Parker press, Portlan, 2008

Hubert Howe Bancroft, The Works of Hubert Howe Bancroft, vol. 33, *History of Alaska 1730–1885*, A. L. Bancroft and Co., San Francisco 1886

Yury Berezin and Sergei Korsun, *Halls of Kunstkamera: North America Exhibition Guide*, Aztec, Saint Petersburg 2008

Lydia T. Black, *Russians in Alaska, 1732–1867*, University of Alaska Press, Fairbanks 2004

Benson Bobrick, *East of the Sun: The Epic Conquest and Tragic History of Siberia*, Poseidon Press, New York, 1992

Nikolai Bolkhovitinov, *Istoria Russkoi Ameriki, 1732–1867*, three vols, Russian Academy of Sciences, Institute of General History, Moscow, 1997

——, *Rossiia otkryvaet Ameriku, 1732–1799*, Progress, Moskva 1991

——, 'Adventures of Doctor Schäffer in Hawaii, 1815–1819', *Hawaiian Journal of History*, vol. 7, Honolulu 1973

Stephen R. Bown, *Madness, Betrayal and the Lash: The epic voyage of Captain George Vancouver*, Douglas and McIntyre, Vancouver 2008

Walter Buehr, *The Spanish Conquistadors in North America*, Putnam, New York 1962

James Burney, *A Chronological History of North-Eastern Voyages of Discovery, and the Early Eastern Navigations of the Russians*, Payme and Foss, London 1819

Warren L. Cook, *The Flood Tide of Empire: Spain and the Pacific Northwest, 1543–1819*, Yale University Press, New Haven 1973

Aron Crowell and William W. Fitzhugh, *Crossroads of Continents: Cultures of Siberia and Alaska*, Smithsonian Institution Press, Washington DC 1988.

Nora Marks Dauenhauer, Richard Dauenhauer and Lydia T. Black (eds.), *Anooshi Lingit Aani ka: Russians in Tlingit America, the Battles of Sitka 1802 and 1804*, University of Washington Press, Seattle 2008

George Davidson, *The Tracks and Landfalls of Bering and Chirikof on the Northwest Coast of America*, Ye Galleon Press, Fairfield 1994

Simon Dixon, *Catherine the Great*, Profile Books, London 2009

E. O. Essig, Adele Ogden and Clarence John Du Four, *Fort Ross, California: Outpost of Russian Alaska 1812–1841*, Limestone Press, Fairbanks 1991.

Basil Dmitryshkin, E. A. P Crownhart-Vaughan and Thomas Vaughan, *Russia's Conquest of Siberia 1558–1700*, Oregon Historical Society Press, Portland 1985

——, *Russian Penetration of the North Pacific Ocean, A Documentary Record 1700–1797*, Oregon Historical Society Press, Portland 1988

——, *The Russian American Colonies 1768–1867*, Oregon Historical Society, Portland 1989

Allan Engstrom, *Yakobi Island, the lost village of Apostolovo and the fate of the Chirikov expedition,* Allan Engstrom, Juneau 2007

Elton Engstrom and Allan Engstrom, *Alexander Baranov – A Pacific Empire*, Elton and Allan Engstrom, Juneau 2004

Svetlana Fedorova, *Rossiya I Amerika – 200 let. Dokumentalniye Materialy*, State Historical Museum, Moscow 1999

——, *Russiaya Amerika: ot pervykh poselenii do prodazhi Alyaski*, Lomonosov, Moscow 2011

——, tr. by Alton S. Donnelly, ed, by Richard A. Pierce, *The Russian Population in Alaska and California Late 18th Century–1867*, Limestone Press, Kingston 1973

Raymond H. Fisher, *The Russian Fur trade 1550–1700*, University of California Press, Berkeley 1943

James Forsyth, *A History of the Peoples of Siberia: Russia's North Asian Colony 1581–1910*, Cambridge University Press, Cambridge 1998

Orcutt William Frost (ed.), *Bering: The Russian Discovery of America*, Yale University Press, New Haven 2003

James R. Gibson, *Imperial Russia in Frontier America*, Oxford University Press, New York 1976

——, *Otter Skins, Boston Ships and China Goods: The Maritime Fur Trade of the Northwest Coast 1785–1841*, University of Washington Press, Seattle 1992

Frank A. Golder, *Russian Expansion on the Pacific, 1641–1950*, Paragon Book Reprint Corp., New York 1971

——, *Bering's Voyages: An Account of the Russians to Determine the Relationship of Asia and America*, two vols, American Geographic Society, New York 1922

Andrei Grinev, *The Tlingit Indians in Russian America, 1741–1867*, University of Nebraska Press, Omaha, 2005

——, 'O "kolonialnom politarizme" v Ispanskoi i Russkoi Amerike, revolutsiakh I sudbakh Rossii', *Etnograficheskoye Obozreniye*, no.3, Moscow 1996

——, 'Russkaya Amerika I SSSR: Udivitel'niye Paralleli', *Klio*, no. 1 (7), Riga 1999

——, 'Vneshnyaya Ugroza Russkoi Amerike: Mify ili Realnost', *Novaya I Noveishaya Istoriya*, no.3, Moscow 2012

——, 'Tuzemtsy Alyaski, Russkiye Promyshleniki I Rossisko-Amerikanskaya Kompaniya: Sistema Ekonomicheskikh Otnoshenii v Russkoi Ameriki (konets XVIII v – 1867 g.)', *Etnograficheskoe Obozreniye*, no. 3, Moscow 2000

——, 'Osnovatel Russkoi Ameriki (neskol'ko shtrikhov k portretu G.I. Shelikhova)', *Istoriya Peterburga*, no. 2, St Petersburg 2005

——, 'Amerikanskaya Epopeya Aleksandra Baranova', *Voprosy Istorii*, no. 8, Moscow 2000

——, 'Problemy Menedzhmenta Rossiskoi-Amerikanskoi Kompanii (1799–1867)', *Klio*, no. 8, Riga 2011

——, ed. by Nikolai Bolokhovitinov, *Kto est' kto v Istorii Russkoi Ameriki*, Academia, Moscow 2009

——, 'The Plans for Russian Expansion in the New World and the North Pacific in the Eighteenth and Nineteenth Centuries', *European Journal of American Studies Special Issue: The North-West Pacific in the 18th and 19th Centuries*, 2010

Stephen W. Haycox, *Alaska: An American Colony*, University of Washington Press, Seattle 2002

M. A. Ilyina (ed.) and O. E. Miniuk (tr.), *Russia and America: 300 years in Books, Maps and Documents*, St Petersburg Academy of Sciences Library, St Petersburg 2003

Alexei Alexandrovich Istomin, 'Dva Varianta Pisma N P Rezanova Grafu N P Rumiantsevu ot 17/29 iyulya 1806 g. – Sravnitelno-tekhnologichesky analyz i legenda o velikoi lyubvi in Russkoe Otkritiye Ameriki', *M*, Moscow 2002

——, J. Gibson and V. A. Tishkov, *Rossiya v Kalifornii*, Nauka, Moscow 2005

Eve Iverson, ed. by Richard A. Pierce, *The Romance of Nikolai Rezanov and Concepión Arguello: A Literary Legend and its Effect on Californian History*, University of Alaska Press, Fairbanks, 1998

Fred T. Jane, *The Imperial Russian Navy*, Conway Maritime Press, London, 1904

K. T. Khlebnikov, ed. by Richard A. Pierce, tr. by Colin Bearne, *Baranov: Chief Manager of the Russian Colonies in America* (St Peterburg 1835), Limestone Press, Kingston, 1973

——, ed. by Svetlana G. Fedorova and Richard A. Pierce, tr. by Serge LeComte, *Notes on Russian America part 1 – Novo-Arkhangelsk*, Limestone Press, Fairbanks 1994

Mikhail Khodarkovsky, *Russia's Orient – Ignoble Savages and Unfaithful Subjects in the Russian Orient: Imperial Strategies and Oriental Encounters*, Indiana University Press, Bloomington 1997, pp8–32.

Vladislav Khodasevich, tr. by Angela Brintlinger, *Derzhavin: A Biography*, University of Wisconsin Press, Madison 2007

Stephen Kotkin and David Wolff (eds), *Rediscovering Russia in Asia: Siberia and the Russian Far East*, M. E. Sharpe, Armonk 1995

Donald F. Lach and Edwin J. Van Kley, *Asia in the Making of Europe, vol. III A Century of Advance, vol. IV East Asia*, University of Chicago Press, Chicago 1994

D. M. Lang, *The First Russian Radical: Alexander Radischev*, Greenwood Publishing Group, Westport 1977

George V. Lantzeff and Richard Pierce, *Eastward to Empire; Exploration and Conquest on the Russian Open Frontier to 1750*, McGill-Queen's University Press, Montreal 1973

George Alexander Lensen, *The Russian Push Towards Japan: Russo-Japanese Relations 1697–1875*, Princeton University Press, Princeton 1959

——, (ed.), *Russia's Eastward Expansion*, Prentice Hall, Englewood Cliffs 1964

——, 'Early Russo-Japanese Relations', *Far Eastern Quarterly*, vol. 10, no.1, November 1950, pp2–37

W. Bruce Lincoln, *The Conquest of a Continent: Siberia and the Russians*, Random House, New York 1994

Prince A. Lobanov Rostovsky, *Russia and Asia*, Macmillan, New York 1933

Senator Viktor Lopatnikov, 'Nikolai Rezanov', *Zolotoi Lev*, no. 127-8, RFS, Moscow 2007

Lo-Shu Fu (ed.), *A documentary chronicle of Sino-Western relations, vol. 1 1644–1820*, University of Arizona Press, Tucson 1966

Raisa V. Makarova, ed. and tr. by Richard A. Pierce and Alton S. Donnelly, *Russians on the Pacific, 1743–1799*, Limestone Press, Kingston 1975

Mary Malloy, *Boston Men on the Northwest Coast: The American Fur Trade 1788–1844*, Limestone Press, Fairbanks 1998

G. Patrick March, *Eastern Destiny: Russia in Asia and the North Pacific*, Praeger, New York 1996

Robert K. Massie, *Catherine the Great: Portrait of a Woman*, Random House, New York 2011

William McOmie, 'With All Due Respect: Reconsidering the Rezanov Mission to Japan', *Proceedings of the Japan Society*, no. 148, London 2011

——, 'From Russia With All Due Respect: Revisiting the Rezanov Embassy to Japan', *Jinbun Kenkyu (Studies in Humanities)*, no. 163, December 2007, Kanagawa Daigaku Jinbun Gakkai (Society of Humanities at Kanagawa University), Yokohama 2007

Gwenn A. Miller, *Kodiak Kreol: Communities of Empire in Early Russian America*, Cornell University Press, Ithaca 2010

N. A. Minenko (ed.), *Kazaki Urala i Sibiri v XVII-XX vv.*, Russian Academy of Sciences, Urals Division, Ekaterinburg, 1993

Mairin Mitchell, *The Maritime History of Russia*, Sidgwick and Jackson, London 1949

Victoria Moessner, 'The First Russian Ambassador to Japan Nikolai Petrovich Rezanov (1764–1807) as portrayed in contemporary German language sources', unpublished article, 2007

Fitzgerald Molloy, *The Russian Court in the Eighteenth Century*, Hutchinson, London 1905

Gerhard Muller, *Nachrichten von Seereisen – Bering's Voyages*, University of Alaska Press, Fairbanks 1986

V. V. Nevskiy, *Pervoye Puteshestviye Rossiyan Vokrug Sveta*, Gosudarstvennoe Izdatelstvo Geograficheskoi Literatury, Moscow 1951

Semen B. Okun, tr. by Carl Ginsburg, Preface by Robert L. Kerner, *The Russian American Company*, Harvard University Press, Cambridge mass. 1955

Wallace M. Olson, *The Spanish Exploration of Alaska 1774–1792*, Heritage Research, Auke Bay 2004

——, *With Vancouver in Alaska*, Heritage Research, Auke Bay 2004

Kenneth Owens and Alton S. Donnelly, *The Wreck of the Sv. Nikolai*, The Press of the Oregon Historical Society, Portland 1985.

Alexander Petrov, *Obrazovanie Rossiisko-amerikanskoi kompanii*, Nauka, Moscow 2000

——, *Natalia Shelikhova u istokov Russkoi Ameriki*, Ves Mir, Moscow, 2012

Richard A. Pierce, *Russian America, A Biographical Dictionary*, Limestone Press, Kingston 1990

——, (ed.) *Russia in North America: Proceedings of the Second International Conference on Russian America*, Limestone Press, Kingston 1990

——, (ed.) and Marina Ramsay (tr.), *Documents on the History of the Russian-American Company*, Limestone Press, Kingston 1976

Aleksei Polikovskii, *Graf Bezbrezhnyi: dve zhizni grafa Fedora Ivanovicha Tolstogo-Amerikantsa*, Minuvshee, Moscow 2006

Anna Reid, *The Shaman's Coat: A Native History of Siberia*, Walker Books, New York 2002

John Robson, (ed.) *The Captain Cook Encyclopædia*, Chatham, London 2004

Gary Scharnhorst, *Bret Harte: opening the American literary West* Oklahoma University Press, Norman, Oklahoma 2000

Simon Sebag Montefiore, *Potemkin: Catherine the Great's Imperial Partner*, Vintage, London 2005

Iurii N. Semenov, *The Conquest of Siberia*, G. Routledge & Sons, London 1944

S. A. Sgibnev, 'Rezanov i Krusenstern', *Drevnaya i Novaya Rossiya*, vol. 1, no. 4, St Petersburg 1877. Shashkov, 'Istoriia Russkoi Zhenshchiny', *Sobranie sochenenii S. S. Shashkova*, Tipografiya I. N. Skorokhodova, St Petersburg 1898

R. G. Skrynnikov, *Sibirskaia ekspeditsiia Ermaka*, Nauka, Novosibirsk 1982.

Yuri Slezkine, *Arctic Mirrors: Russia and the Small Peoples of the North*, Cornell University Press, Ithaca 1994

Anna Surnik, 'Poslednee Pismo Kemergera: Rashifrovka', *Russkaya Amerika*, *Vologda*, no. 1, pp29–31, Vologda 1994

Leonid Sverdlov, 'Nikolai Petrovich Rezanov (1764–1807): Khudozhestvenny Obraz I Istorichaskaya Lichnost', *Moskovsky Zhurnal*, no, 8 (257), Moscow 2012

——, ed. by A.V. Postnikov, *Krusenstern i Rezanov*, Argo, Moscow 2006

Barbara Sweetland Smith and Redmond Barnett (eds) *Russian America: The Forgotten Frontier*, Washington State Historical Society, Tacoma 1990

Pavel A. Tikhmenev, tr. by Dmitry Krenov, *A History of the Russian American Company* (St Petersburg 1863), Limestone Press, Kingston 1979

——, (ed.), tr. by Dmitry Krenov, *Supplement of Some Historical Documents to the Historical Review of the Formation of the Russian American Company* (St Petersburg 1863), Limestone Press, Kingston 1979

Colin Thubron, *In Siberia*, Harper Perennial, London 2000

Nikolai Tolstoy, *The Tolstoys: 24 Generations of Russian History 1353–1983*, Hamilton, London 1983

S. L. Tolstoy, *Fyodor Tolstoy Amerikanets*, AIN, Moscow 1926

Mikhail I. Tsiporukha, 'Odna iz Stroitelei Imperii na Tikhookeanskom Severe', *Istoriya Nauki I Tekhniki*, no. 8, Moscow 2004

George Vernadsky, *The Mongols and Russia*, Yale University Press, 1953

Ralph H. Vigil, 'The Hispanic Heritage and the Borderlands', *Journal of San Diego History*, vol. 19, no. 3, summer 1973

Ilya Vinkovetsky, *Russian America: An Overseas Colony of a Continental Empire 1804–1867*, Oxford University Press, New York 2011

Irina Viter and Aleksandr Smyshlyaev, *Gorod nad Avachinskoi Buhtoi* (*A History of Petropavlosk-Kamchatksty*), Novaya Kniga, Petropavlovsk-Kamchatsky 2011

K. Voensky, *Posolstvo N. P. Rezanova v Yaponiyu*, Russkaya Starina, Moscow 1995 no. 9-10

Kazimierz Waliszewski, *Paul the First of Russia, the Son of Catherine the Great*, William Heineman, New York 1913

Antony Wild, *The East India Company, Trade and Conquest from 1600*, HarperCollins, London 2000

Igor Nikiforovich Yermolaev, *Pskovsky Chinovnik Nikolai Rezanov i ego 'Yunona i Avos'*, Pskovsaya Provintsiya, Pskov, April 2004

Fiction

Gertrude Atherton, *Rezanov*, Authors and Newspapers Association, New York 1906

Hector Chevigny, *Lord of Alaska. Baranov and the Russian Adventure*, Viking Press, New York 1944.

———, *Lost Empire. The Life and Adventures of Nikolai Petrovich Rezanov*, MacMillan, New York 1943.

———, *Russian America: The Great American Venture, 1741–1867*, Viking Press, New York 1965

Andrei Voznesensky, *Selected Poems of Andrei Voznesensky*, Random House, New York 2000

Acknowledgements

Researching a book which touches on many worlds, as Rezanov's story does, has been a humbling experience. It could not have been done without the help of dozens of people from St Petersburg to San Francisco who shared their expertise, scholarship, hospitality and friendship.

I would like to thank the following people in particular. In Sitka, the Tlingit woodcarver (and Blue Peter Badge-holder) Tommy Joseph keeps his people's traditions alive – and quietly boycotted the commemoration of the handover of Alaska from one group of white colonists to another as 'their party, not ours'. Thad Poulson of the Sitka Sentinel was generous with contacts, while Dusty Kidd of the National Parks Service and Bob Medinger of the Sitka Historical Society were kind enough to organize a lunch of local historians in my honour. David Nordlander of the Library of Congress in Washington was invaluable in tracking down the Russian American Company's scattered archives and has been instrumental in putting much of the most important material online in the brilliant Meeting of Continents website.

In Juneau, I would like to thank bookshop owner and scholar Dee Longenbaugh for searching out hard-to-find monographs on Rezanov – and for keeping in touch over several years with latest titbits which have come her way. Jim Simard at the Alaska State Archive and Steve Hendrickson at the Alaska State Museum helped me sift the often chaotic archives the Russians left behind them when they abandoned their American colony. Alan Engstrom – the biographer of Alexander Baranov and discoverer of the true fate of Chirikov's crewmen in Jakobi Bay – drove me around Juneau and introduced me to key Russian America scholars in both Alaska and Moscow.

In Kodiak, I explored the storm-lashed Artillery Point with Marnie Leist of the Alutiiq Museum. Father Ioann of the Holy Resurrection Cathedral in Kodiak keeps the Orthodox tradition alive in the church originally paid for by Alexander Baranov, and generously allowed me to examine the relics of Saint Hermann of Alaska kept in his church. Deacon Innocent (Phil Hayes) arranged for me to visit Spruce Island – no easy feat, since communication was largely by text message picked up once every few days by the monks on the one remote point on the island with faint reception. The Fathers of St Michael's Skete (who modestly insisted that they not be named to avoid worldly vanity) rode five-foot high swells to transport me across the straits to their island home and graciously guided me around the habitations of St Hermann and his followers.

In San Francisco, Alla Sokoloff was kind enough to drive me to Benicia to pay our respects at Conchita Arguello's grave. Natalie Sabelnik of the Congress of Russian Americans introduced me to local historians and let me browse her archive – a fascinating collection of flotsam washed up after the disappearance of the Russian empire and the scattering of many of its brightest and best to California, in Rezanov's footsteps.

At Fort Ross, Sarah Sweedler and Marion MacDonald were incredibly generous with their time and Hank Birnbaum keeps the Russian language alive at the Fort by marching platoons of musket-bearing schoolchildren around the compound to the command of 'Levo! Levo!'

In Moscow, Vladimir Kolychev is the energetic head of the Russian American Society and indefatigable organizer of events, from simultaneous bell-ringing in churches in Moscow and Kodiak to outings to productions of *Junona I Avos*. Kolychev is a great admirer of Rezanov and asked me 'not to be too hard on his memory': I hope he judges that I have been fair, at least. Dr Alexander Petrov has continued the late Professor Nikolai Bolkhovitinov's rigorous scholarship of Russian

America. I greatly enjoyed open-air debates under the plane trees in a museum garden with Leonid Sverdlov, another of the greatest living experts on Rezanov.

In St Petersburg, Andrei Grinev has been kind enough to answer streams of questions on the finer points of Company history, and the Kunstkammer's Sergei Korsun gave me an in-depth tour of the unique Tlingit articles collected by Lisiansky in 1804. In Kamchatka, Irina Vitter of the regional public library loaded me with advice and monographs, while I stayed at the home of Martha Madsen, a proud Kamchatkan by adoption.

I am particularly grateful to two scholars who took the time to read all or part of the manuscript and saved me from many embarrassing mistakes. Professor William McOmie of Kanagawa University in Yokohama worked through the Japanese sections several times over. Victoria Moessner, translator of Löwenstern's diaries, spent many days correcting and commentating my account of Rezanov's voyages. My dear friends and colleagues Andrew Meier and Mark Franchetti both made invaluable suggestions on structure and style.

Michael Fishwick at Bloomsbury is the world's finest editor – not least because he knows what your book should really be about even if you don't. He is ably assisted by Anna Simpson and Oliver Holden-Rea. My agent Natasha Fairweather is an old and dear friend and mentor, who is also a fine deal-maker. If I am any historian at all it is thanks to my tutors at Christ Church, the late Patrick Wormald, William Thomas and Katya Andreyev.

Finally I would like to thank my wife Ksenia, who spent hours speed-reading tedious Russian archival sources as I took notes and who tolerated my long absences on the road in pursuit of my elusive hero.

Index

A Note on the Type

The text of this book is set Adobe Garamond. It is one of several versions of Garamond based on the designs of Claude Garamond. It is thought that Garamond based his font on Bembo, cut in 1495 by Francesco Griffo in collaboration with the Italian printer Aldus Manutius. Garamond types were first used in books printed in Paris around 1532. Many of the present-day versions of this type are based on the *Typi Academiae* of Jean Jannon cut in Sedan in 1615.

Claude Garamond was born in Paris in 1480. He learned how to cut type from his father and by the age of fifteen he was able to fashion steel punches the size of a pica with great precision. At the age of sixty he was commissioned by King Francis I to design a Greek alphabet, for this he was given the honourable title of royal type founder. He died in 1561.